Ontology Learning and Population from Text
Algorithms, Evaluation and Applications

Ontology Learning and Population from Text
Algorithms, Evaluation and Applications

by

Philipp Cimiano
University of Karlsruhe
Germany

 Springer

Philipp Cimiano
Univ. Karlsruhe
Inst. AIFB
Englerstr. 11
76131 KARLSRUHE
GERMANY
cimiano@aifb.uni-karlsruhe.de

Ontology Learning and Population from Text:
Algorithms, Evaluation and Applications

by Philipp Cimiano

e-ISBN-10: 0-387-39252-1

ISBN-13: 978-1-4419-4032-2   e-ISBN-13: 978-0-387-39252-3

Printed on acid-free paper.

Dissertation, genehmigt von der Fakultät für Wirtschaftswissenschaften der
Universität Fridericiana zu Karlsruhe, 2006. Referent: Prof. Dr. R.Studer,
Koreferenten: Prof. Dr. A. Geyer-Schulz und Prof. Dr. S. Staab

9 8 7 6 5 4 3 2 1

springer.com

To the memory of Frida.

Contents

List of Figures

List of Tables

Foreword

In the broad area of data and knowledge engineering — and including disciplines like databases, semantic web, knowledge representation as well as overlapping areas such as computational linguistics, artificial intelligence or information management — one may recognize some grand challenges that puzzle many researchers and practitioners alike:

1. Combining statistics and logics;
2. Scaling towards large complex systems;
3. Turning what still often remains an art into a science and/or an engineering discipline.

This book responds to these challenges by moving ontology learning and population forward a very large step.

From Statistics to Semantics.

Access to information on the Web or in large enterprise information repositories is mostly restricted to *statistics*-based keyword search. Even though keyword search is often successful on the Web for general purpose queries, it often remains unsatisfying for the professional user who searches more than an address, more than a document and less than one million answers.

Statistics will certainly remain the major ingredient for finding information. Nevertheless, statistics need to be augmented by *semantics* such as described in conceptual models, e.g. in ontologies. The volume of information generally accessible makes it highly improbable that ontologies would be constructed for very many domains, if it were not for the statistics themselves to jump in and facilitate and partially automate the construction of the very same ontologies. Thus, the statistics about information lead to *semantic* descriptions of textual as well as other information resources in a way that makes searching more powerful (e.g., because it integrates unstructured, semi-structured and fully structured information sources) and more rewarding (e.g., because it offers a semantically guided dialog between the search engine and its users).

This book proposes new paradigms to derive semantics from statistics. In doing so, it also gives a comprehensive account of which statistical methods complemented by means of computational linguistics and knowledge representation serve the purposes of ontology learning and population.

From Small Scale to Large Scale.

If previous work has focused on the bridge between statistical and conceptual knowledge (e.g. machine learning), it has restricted itself to small scale with what regards the conceptual knowledge, i.e. at most a couple of concepts which were to be distinguished.

This book tackles scaling into large conceptual spaces. Working with hundreds of target concepts it scales the richness of textual information not only towards Gigabytes of ASCII text, but also towards real-world sized ontologies instead of toy domains.

From Art to Science and Engineering.

Finally, ontology learning and — to lesser extent — population has remained an art rather than a discipline within science and/or engineering. The basis for making ontology learning a scientific discipline lies in measuring appropriateness of learned concept definitions.

This book gives a precise and comprehensive evaluation of ontology learning and population measures. It gives evaluation procedures for closed world settings by gold standards and appropriate measures. It also gives evaluations that consider the open world nature of ontologies, i.e. that consider the fact that it is hard, if not even impossible, to draw an exact line around which concepts should and which should not be included in a particular ontology. Hence, never before has a book in this area given such precise and comprehensive evaluations that moreover are accessible to the general public.[1]

Koblenz, June 2006   *Steffen Staab*

---

[1] cf. http://www.cimiano.de/olp/

Preface

In recent years, there has been a surge in research on knowledge acquisition from text and other sources, which is to a great extent due to a renewed interest in knowledge-based techniques in the context of the Semantic Web endeavor. A crucial question, however, still remains: where is the necessary knowledge supposed to come from? How will we feed machines with the relevant knowledge, that is, how will we deal with the so called *knowledge acquisition bottleneck*? The formalisms for knowledge representation are now in place. The Semantic Web community has developed, actually building on decades of research in knowledge representation, standard ontology languages such as RDFS or OWL to represent knowledge in a way which is understandable by machines. But again, how will we acquire all the knowledge available in people's head to feed our machines with?

Natural language is THE means of communication for humans, and consequently texts are nowadays massively available on the Web: terabytes and terabytes of texts containing opinions, ideas, facts and information of all sorts waiting to be extracted or mined to find interesting patterns and relationships or used to annotate the corresponding documents to facilitate their retrieval. Let me thus dare to say that a semantic web which ignores the massive amount of information encoded in texts, might actually be a semantic, but not a really very useful web. Knowledge acquisition from text has to be in fact regarded as a crucial step within the vision of a semantic web.

Looking at the history of knowledge acquisition from text, let me highlight three, possibly arbitrary, snapshots. First of all, there has been extensive research in the 80s and early 90s on extracting knowledge from machine readable dictionaries. This research showed that it is in fact possible to extract knowledge from text with a more or less regular structure. Such approaches will probably become fashionable again in the context of currently emerging large online dictionaries such as WikiPedia[2]. Second, the seminal work of Grefenstette which found its way into his book *Explorations in Automatic*

---

[2] http://en.wikipedia.org/wiki/Main_Page

Thesaurus Construction, showed that we can move from regular to free text and use syntactic or distributional similarity as a guiding principle for knowledge acquisition from text. Third, the recent work of Mädche and Staab in Karlsruhe, which ultimately lead to the book *Ontology Learning for the Semantic Web*, brought knowledge acquisition from texts into renewed interest by connecting it with research on the Semantic Web. Mädche's work addressed in particular methodological aspects related to the creation of a usable ontology learning framework which eases the application of ontology learning techniques for ontology engineers.

The present book can be seen as a follow-up to Alexander Mädche's work, taking up his basic framework, but focusing on algorithms and their evaluation. In fact, the book is largely influenced by hands-on experience with diverse datasets and algorithms. Originally, the aim was to investigate in much more depth the relation between natural language, lexica and ontologies, but this aim had to stand back in favor of the necessity to develop practical algorithms in the context of the projects that I have been involved in. Thus, I have to confess that I have neither found a satisfactory definition of what a concept is supposed to be nor what the relation between language, the mind and ontology actually is. Thus, there is little I have to say about the relation between lexical semantics and ontologies because, if there is an answer, it is definitely out of the scope of the work presented in this book.

The work described in the present book is thus of a pragmatic nature and driven by practical needs for supporting the ontology learning process. I have attempted to provide a reasonable trade-off between breadth and depth, providing in-depth empirical analysis of certain techniques, but also covering a wide range of ontology learning aspects. Here and there, the methods used might seem a bit adhoc, for example the named entity recognition, anaphora resolution or morphology components used. Ontology learning builds on a lot of natural language processing and machine learning techniques, and, in the case such techniques are not available off-the-shelf, they need to be implemented in a way which is good enough to allow for the proof-of-concept of some method. It is obviously out of the scope of a book on ontology learning to implement the state-of-the-art in other fields.

I have devoted a considerable amount of work to the evaluation of the algorithms and methods presented. Evaluation is a very problematic endeavor because, on the one hand, it is very time intensive and involves twiddling around with tiny details, and, on the other hand, bullet-proof evaluations hardly exist. Nevertheless I am convinced that evaluation is an absolutely necessary part of research in computer science. The amount of publications is constantly increasing and the time for reviewing is decreasing at the same pace. Sometimes, a good evaluation is at least a guarantee that the method has been actually implemented and thus a good indicator of feasibility. I support formal theories and novel ideas, but algorithms and approaches need to be evaluated on real datasets to demonstrate their benefits. Only then can meaningful comparisons between approaches be drawn, allowing the 'fittest' approaches to survive. In this sense I adhere to what we could call the *principle of natural selection* in computer science.

Finally, let me say a bit about the book in general. I have attempted to create a book useful for novices and for experts in the field, with introductory material and a lot of related work on the one hand, but also detailed descriptions of algorithms, evaluation procedures etc. on the other. I have also attempted to give a broad and systematic overview of ontology learning in general. The aim has also been to make each section of this book as self-contained as possible to allow for selective reading. Let me conclude saying that, though many researchers might disagree with the views put forth in this book, as well as with the algorithms and evaluation procedures described, at least I hope they will find the overview provided in this book of value.

The views on ontologies contained in this book have been largely shaped by the Knowledge Management group at the University of Karlsruhe. The views on ontology learning have been influenced by comments and fruitful discussion with other researchers. I am in fact indebted to a lot of people which have either contributed to this work directly or helped to shape many of the ideas expressed herein. However, I am the only one to blame for errors and inaccuracies which have made it into the book as you find it here in front of you. I am always happy to receive comments, feedback, criticism on this material, so don't hesitate to contact me. Eventually, your comment might be considered for a revised version of this book at some stage. Finally, as a lot of people drop me emails asking for datasets and algorithms, I have decided to create a website in which a lot of the material presented in this book can be downloaded for a hands-on experience[3]. This material is of a highly experimental nature, but hopefully useful for research purposes.

I hope you enjoy the book.

Karlsruhe, June 2006   *Philipp Cimiano*

---

[3] See http://www.cimiano.de/olp

Acknowledgements

There are many people who I am indebted to for support in the context of this endeavor.

First of all, I would like to thank my supervisors Prof. Rudi Studer and Prof. Steffen Staab. I am grateful to Prof. Studer for providing a very stimulating environment at the department of Knowledge Management at the institute for Applied Computer Science and Formal Description Methods (AIFB) at the University of Karlsruhe. I thank Prof. Studer especially for giving me the freedom to pursue the things which I was interested in, having always an open ear to discuss about problems related to research or other issues.

I am very indebted to Steffen Staab for important contributions and in particular for the good comments and feedback on my work. I thank Steffen especially for his critical view and conceptual clarity in thinking as well as for his intuition for significant scientific contributions. Thanks especially for drawing in many occasions my attention to issues which needed to be done to make my research round.

Thanks also to my co-advisor Prof. Geyer-Schulz for very valuable comments on the 'almost' final version of the manuscript.

I would also like to thank all my colleagues for providing a very stimulating and friendly environment in the group. I would like to thank especially (in alphabetical order) Stephan Bloehdorn, Marc Ehrig, Peter Haase, Markus Krötzsch, Julien Tane and Johanna Völker for giving feedback on chapters of this book. Special thanks go to my room mate Johanna for the fruitful joint work on several topics related to ontology learning.

I would also like to thank the former colleagues Andreas Hotho (now at University of Kassel) and Lars Schmidt-Thieme (now at University of Freiburg) for the good cooperation and many useful comments on chapters of this book. Thanks to Gerd Stumme (now at University of Kassel) for feedback and advice concerning Formal Concept Analysis. I would also like to thank Aleksander Pivk from Jozef Stefan Institute in Ljubljana for the good cooperation during his stay in Karlsruhe. Thanks also to Paul Buitelaar for the nice joint work in the context of the SmartWeb Project on our edited collection on ontology learning, appeared at IOS Press, on the tutorials held at ECML/PKDD 2005 as well as EACL 2006 as well as the workshop organized at COLING/ACL 2006. Special credit goes to Fabio Ciravegna (University of Sheffield) for coordinating the Dot.Kom project as well as Victoria Uren and Enrico Motta from KMi at the Open University for the good cooperation in the context of Dot.Kom. Thanks to my former supervisor Uwe Reyle for the joint work on topics which, though not directly related to the material presented in this book, have shaped my overall understanding of natural language processing. Thanks also to Uwe for encouraging me to work on the topics of ontology learning and ontologies.

I also thank my students Laurent Cicurel, Matthias Hartung, Simon Sparn, Katrin Tomanek and Johanna Wenderoth for joint work on topics which, either directly or indirectly, have contributed to the material presented in this book. Thanks also to Günther Ladwig, Matthias Mantel, and Honggang Zhou for taking much of the programming workload in projects from me, thus leaving me more time for research. Special thanks go to Laura Goebes, who assisted in many of the evaluations presented in this book and designed the web pages for our ontology learning tutorials at ECML/PKDD and EACL.

Thanks also to all the reviewers which have provided very useful comments in the last years on material on which this book is based on. These comments have ultimately lead to improvements on the material as you find it in the book in front of you.

Thanks also to the people from Springer: Susan Lagerstrom-Fife and Sharon Palleschi for their friendly support in preparing this book. It was very nice working with them. Thanks also to the secretaries at our institute Gisela Schillinger, Susanne Winter and Rita Schmidt for making our life easier by taking care of a lot of administrative stuff.

Last not least, I would like to thank my family and all my friends for being there. Very special thanks go to my parents, Lieselotte Cimiano and Benito Cimiano for their life-long support and love. I would especially like to thank Lieselotte Cimiano for carefully reading all this book, providing useful comments on the style. Most important, I would like to thank my wife Ursula for her moral support and love during the last years. I can only guess that it is not easy to spend life with someone whose mind is often absent, far away from daily life. I thank Ursula in particular for being so vitally drawn from life and reminding me every day that there are more important and rewarding things in life other than research. Thanks also to Ursula for doing a great job in designing the cover as well as improving many of the figures contained in the book.

Oh yes, and there's the money, without which, nothing would have been possible. I herewith acknowledge financial support from the BMBF project

SmartWeb[4] as well as the EU funded projects Dot.Kom[5], SEKT[6], KnowledgeWeb[7] and X-Media[8].

---

[4] http://www.smartweb-project.de/
[5] http://nlp.shef.ac.uk/dot.kom/
[6] http://www.sekt-project.com/
[7] http://knowledgeweb.semanticweb.org/
[8] http://nlp.shef.ac.uk/X-Media/

Abbreviations

AI Artificial Intelligence
DAML DARPA Agent Markup Language
GL Generative Lexicon
HAC Hierarchical Agglomerative Clustering
HTML HyperText Markup Language
IE Information Extraction
ILP Inductive Logic Programming
IR Information Retrieval
JS Jensen-Shannon divergence
KB Knowledge Base
KM Knowledge Management
KR Knowledge Representation
LSI Latent Semantic Indexing
LSA Latent Semantic Analysis (=LSI)
MRD Machine Readable Dictionary
MT Machine Translation
MUC Message Understanding Conferences
NER Named Entity Recognition
NLP Natural Language Processing
NP Noun Phrase
OIL Ontology Inference Layer
OWL Web Ontology Language
PLSI Probabilistic Latent Semantic Indexing
PMI Pointwise Mutual Information
POS Part Of Speech
PP Prepositional Phrase
RDF(S) Resource Description Framework (Schema)
SVMs Support Vector Machines
VP Verb Phrase
QA Question Answering
UML Unified Modelling Language

XML eXtensible Markup Language
XML-DTD XML-Document Type Definition
WSD Word Sense Disambiguation

Mathematical Notation

$A \cup B$ (set union)

$A \cap B$ (set intersection)

$A \backslash B$ (set difference)

$\emptyset$ (the empty set)

$|A|$ (cardinality of a set)

$2^A := \mathfrak{P}(A)$ (powerset of A)

$A^+ := \bigcup_i A^i$ for $i \in \mathbb{N}$

$\mathbb{R}$ (the set of real numbers)

$\mathbb{N}$ (the set of natural numbers)

$[\![x]\!]$ (ontological extension of x)

$\text{lcs}(a, b)$ (least common subsumer of concepts a and b)

$f : A \to B$ (A function from values of A to values of B)

$\max f$ (the maximum value of f)

$\min f$ (the minimum value of f)

$\text{argmax}_x\ f(x)$ (the value for x maximizing f)

$\text{argmin}_x\ f(x)$ (the value for x minimizing f)

$E(X)$ (expectation of a random variable X)

$\text{Var}(X)$ (variance of a random variable X)

μ (mean)

σ (standard deviation)

$P(A|B)$ (conditional probability of A given B)

$H(X)$ (entropy of the random variable X)

$I(X;Y)$ (mutual information)

$I(x, y)$ (pointwise mutual information)

$D(p||q)$ (Kullback-Leibler divergence)

$<\mathbf{x}> := \sum_i x_i$ (vector length)

$|\mathbf{x}| := \sqrt{\sum_i x_i^2}$ (Euclidean vector length)

$\mathbf{x} \cdot \mathbf{y} := \sum_{i=1}^n x_i y_i$ where $\mathbf{x}, \mathbf{y} \in \mathbb{R}^n$ (dot product)

$\oplus$ (the string concatenating operator)

$\pi(w)$ the plural of word w

df_i (document frequency of i)
tf_i (term frequency of i)
$tf_{i,j}$ (term frequency of i in document j)

Part I

Preliminaries

1

Introduction

A crucial characteristic of human intelligence is its adaptive behavior. In fact, humans can easily adapt to new situations by drawing on their earlier experiences and previous knowledge. Assume a child learns that *Yoyo* is a cat, that cats are animals and that animals are not to be hurt. The child will certainly be able to apply this knowledge to infer that in particular Yoyo should not be hurt. Since the late 1950s, Artificial Intelligence (AI) has devoted enormous efforts to developing computer systems able to mimic human intelligence. The first definition of artificial intelligence in fact goes back to Alan Turing. Turing defined a test, widely known as the *Turing-test*, according to which a machine would merit to be called intelligent if a human interacting with it as well as with a human counterpart would not be able to keep both apart [Turing, 1950, Shieber, 2004].

Much research in artificial intelligence (AI) has in fact been devoted to building systems incorporating knowledge about a certain domain in order to reason on the basis of this knowledge and solve problems which were not encountered before. Such *knowledge-based systems* have been applied to a variety of problems requiring some sort of intelligent behavior like planning, supporting humans in decision making or natural language processing. An early planning system was for example STRIPS [Fikes et al., 1972] in which goals as well as the preconditions and effects of actions were specified in a declarative fashion using a logical formalism. A prominent example of an expert system applied to support humans in decision making is *Mycin* [Shortliffe, 1976]. Mycin was an expert system developed at Stanford in the 1970s. Its goal was to support doctors in the diagnosis and recommendation of treatment for certain blood infections. An early natural language system making use of a logical representation of the domain in question was the JANUS system [Weischedel, 1989]. Further details about the history, methods and applications of AI can be found in the early handbook of Cohen and Feigenbaum [Cohen and Feigenbaum, 1981] and in the more recent introductory book of Russel and Norvig [Russel and Norvig, 2003].

Common to all the above mentioned systems is an explicit and symbolic representation of knowledge about a certain domain. Such a symbolic representation of knowledge has the advantage that it can be separated from procedural aspects related to its application and can in principle be reused across systems. Computers are essentially symbol-manipulating machines, and they need clear instructions about how to manipulate these symbols in a meaningful way. For this reason, knowledge is represented using some logic with model-theoretic semantics as well as with a syntactic procedure for verifying semantic validity which is executable by a computer. When representing knowledge symbolically in such a way that a computer can process it, the question arises which symbols to use and what they stand for. Thus, an ontology as model of the domain in question is needed. Such an ontology would state which things are important to the domain in question as well as define their relationships. In the context of knowledge-based systems, an underlying ontology would essentially tell us which symbols are needed and how they are supposed to be interpreted. At the logical level, the interpretation can then be constrained according to the ontology by appropriately axiomatizing the symbols.

Knowledge representation and ontologies have actually gained importance in the last decade. Nowadays, ontologies are applied for agent communication [Finin et al., 1994], information integration [Wiederhold, 1994, Alexiev et al., 2005], web service discovery [Paolucci et al., 2002] as well as composition [Sirin et al., 2002], description of content to facilitate its retrieval [Guarino et al., 1999, Welty and Ide, 1999], and natural language processing [Nirenburg and Raskin, 2004]. This surge of interest in ontologies has even been carried over to industry, where providers of semantic technologies such as ontoprise GmbH[1] are cooperating with large companies such as Audi[2] or Deutsche Telekom[3].

Though ontologies can provide potential benefits for a lot of applications, it is well known that their construction is costly [Ratsch et al., 2003, Pinto and Martins, 2004]. This problem is typically referred to as the *knowledge acquisition bottleneck* and is witnessed by the large amount of publications on methodologies for ontology engineering (compare [Uschold, 1996, Fernandez et al., 1997, Holsapple and Joshi, 2002, Sure, 2003, Pinto et al., 2004]). The modeling of a non-trivial domain is in fact a difficult and time-consuming task. The main difficulty lies in the fact that the ontology is supposed to have a significant coverage of the domain and to foster the conciseness of the model by determining meaningful and consistent generalizations at the same time. The trade-off between modeling a large amount of knowledge and providing as many abstractions as possible to keep the model concise makes ontology engineering indeed a challenging

---

[1] http://www.ontoprise.de/content/index.html

[2] http://www.ontoprise.de/content/e212/e52/e320/index_ger.html

[3] http://www.ontoprise.de/content/e212/e52/e304/index_ger.html

enterprise. Further, as ontologies are typically shared by a group of people or a community, their construction is additionally complicated due to the fact that different parties have to agree on certain design choices.

An ideal solution to this problem would be an approach to automatically learn ontologies from data. Such an approach would indeed dramatically reduce the costs for building an ontology. As text documents are and will always be massively available, many researchers have attempted to learn ontologies from textual resources. Given a certain critical amount of texts, we would expect such methods to provide a reasonable coverage of the domain. The bottleneck of such methods lies in the fact that correctness and consistency of the model can not be guaranteed, thus making human postprocessing definitely necessary. Assuming that the documents in the text collections stem from different authors, the resulting ontologies can to some extent even be regarded as shared, thus overcoming problems inherent in the agreement process between different parties.

The aim of this book is to investigate methods for automatically learning ontologies from domain-specific text collections. The main contributions are:

- the *formal definition* of the ontologies to be learned as well as *of the tasks addressed* in order to foster consensus within the ontology learning community,
- the *development of novel algorithms* with the aim of learning ontologies from textual data,
- the *comparison of different methods* in order to provide guidelines for ontology engineers,
- the *description of measures and methodologies for the evaluation* of the learned ontologies, providing a basis to compare different approaches,
- an *analysis of the impact of ontology learning for certain applications.*

The challenge in ontology learning from text is certainly to derive meaningful concepts on the basis of the usage of certain symbols, i.e. words or terms appearing in the text. It is in particular challenging to learn what the crucial characteristics of these concepts are and in how far they differ from each other in line with Aristotle's notion of *differentiae*. Such a characterization of concepts is typically referred to as their *intension*. However, concepts can also be defined *extensionally* by enumerating all the entities which share the concept's characteristics. To foster economy of representation in a knowledge base, it is also important to have an underlying hierarchical organization of concepts, semantically interpreted as subsumption of extension. Such a concept hierarchy fosters economy of representation in the sense that it allows to represent relations, rules, etc. at the appropriate level of generalization for which they hold, thus eliminating the necessity of representing each case explicitly. Besides deriving a concept hierarchy, we are also interested in discovering relations among concepts. Such relations will in fact provide a basis to constrain the interpretation of concepts by explicitly stating their relation to other concepts in form of logical axioms.

The challenge in ontology learning is thus one of bridging the gap between the world of symbols, e.g. words used in natural language, and the world of concepts, which in essence can be seen as abstractions of human thought. It should already become clear that ontology learning from text is a highly error-prone endeavor. The automatically learned ontologies will thus need to be inspected, validated and modified by humans before they can be applied for applications relying on crisp logical reasoning. However, there are a number of applications in text mining and information retrieval for which the automatically derived ontologies can be applied as such. In fact, while the benefit of explicit knowledge representation in form of ontologies for text mining applications still remains unclear today, the assumption of this book is that the real benefit will only be unveiled once the knowledge-acquisition-bottleneck has been overcome, i.e. once we have algorithms and tools to automatically derive knowledge from domain-specific text collections. This would allow to perform large-scale experiments on different domains and datasets and thus to draw definite conclusions. The research presented in this book can be understood as a step in this direction.

The structure of the book is as follows:

- The first part of the book continues in Chapter 2 with a formal and math-ematical definition of an ontology which will provide the basis for the formalization of ontology learning tasks as well as of the evaluation mea-sures used throughout the book. From the description of this chapter it will also be clear which are the ontological structures we aim to learn.
- In Chapter 3 we present in more detail the field of ontology learning from textual data, in particular describing its history as well as the main learn-ing paradigms exploited. In this chapter, we will also come back to the issues which make ontology learning especially challenging.
- Chapter 4 then introduces the basics necessary to understand the remain-ing chapters of the book. In particular, it introduces fundamental tech-niques of natural language processing as well as inductive learning.
- In Chapter 5 we describe the datasets used in the diverse experiments presented in this book.
- In the main part of the book, i.e. *Methods and Applications*, we present the algorithms and approaches developed. In Chapter 6 we present algorithms to learn concept hierarchies, which can be seen as the backbone of an ontology, fostering economy of representation as described above.
- In Chapter 7 we turn to the issue of learning relations between concepts and present three approaches addressing different aspects of the task of learning ontological relations.
- In Chapter 8 we address the important issue of populating an ontology with instances, i.e. learning the extension of concepts. The latter three chapters represent the main contribution of the book to the field of on-

tology learning from textual data. Besides presenting the algorithms and evaluation methods developed, each chapter describes related work, summarizes the main contributions and discusses open issues. The aim here has been to make each section as self-contained as possible in order to allow for selective reading.

- Chapter 9 discusses applications for ontology learning methods and presents some results on document clustering and classification as well as on an information retrieval task.
- Finally, in the last part *Conclusion*, Chapter 10 summarizes the main contributions of the book and discusses open issues and further work. Chapter 11 concludes the book with a few remarks.

2

Ontologies

In this chapter, we introduce our formal ontology model. The model presented will provide a basis for the formalization of ontology learning tasks in Chapter 3 as well as for the evaluation measures used throughout the remainder of the book.

The term *ontology* comes from the Greek *ontologia* and means "talking" (-logia) about "being" (ôn / onto-). Ontology is a philosophical discipline which can be described as the *science of existence* or the *study of being*. Platon (427 - 347 BC) was one of the first philosophers to explicitly mention the *world of ideas or forms* in contrast to the real or observed objects, which according to his view are only imperfect realizations (or *shadows*) of the ideas (compare [Annas, 1981]). In fact, Platon raised ideas, forms or abstractions to entities which one can talk about, thus laying the foundations for ontology. Later his student Aristotle (384 - 322 BC) shaped the logical background of ontologies and introduced notions such as *category*, *subsumption* as well as the superconcept/subconcept distinction which he actually referred to as *genus* and *subspecies*. With *differentiae* he referred to characteristics which distinguish different objects of one genus and allow to formally classify them into different categories, thus leading to subspecies. This is the principle on which the modern notions of ontological concept and inheritance are based upon. In fact, Aristotle can be regarded as the founder of *taxonomy*, i.e. the science of classifying things. Aristotle's ideas represent the foundation for object-oriented systems as used today. Furthermore, he introduced a number of inference rules, called *syllogisms*, such as those used in modern logic-based reasoning systems [Sowa, 2000a].

In modern computer science parlance, one does not talk anymore about 'ontology' as the science of existence, but of 'ontologies' as formal specifications of a conceptualization in the sense of Gruber [Gruber, 1993]. So, whereas 'ontology' was originally a science, 'ontologies' have received the status of resources representing the conceptual model underlying a certain domain, describing it in a declarative fashion and thus cleanly separating it from procedural aspects.

Whereas the number of applications for ontologies in computer science is steadily growing, the necessity for a clear and formal definition of an ontology arises at the same time. In the past, there have been many proposals for an ontology language with a well-defined syntax and formal semantics, especially in the context of the Semantic Web, such as OIL [Horrocks et al., 2000], RDFS [Brickley and Guha, 2002] or OWL [Bechhofer et al., 2004]. In the context of this book, we will however stick to a more mathematical definition of ontologies in line with Stumme et al. [Stumme et al., 2003]. Our definitions are to a great extent borrowed from there. However, we take the freedom to modify the definitions for our purposes. Furthermore, we illustrate the definition with a running example.

Definition 1 (Ontology) *An* ontology *is a structure*

$$\mathcal{O} := (C, \leq_C, R, \sigma_R, \leq_R, \mathcal{A}, \sigma_A, \mathcal{T})$$

consisting of

- *four disjoint sets C, R, $\mathcal{A}$ and $\mathcal{T}$ whose elements are called* concept identifiers, relation identifiers, attribute identifiers *and* data types, *respectively,*
- *a semi-upper lattice $\leq_C$ on C with top element $root_C$, called* concept hierarchy *or* taxonomy,
- *a function $\sigma_R \colon R \to C^+$ called* relation signature,
- *a partial order $\leq_R$ on R, called* relation hierarchy, *where $r_1 \leq_R r_2$ implies $|\sigma_R(r_1)| = |\sigma_R(r_2)|$ and $\pi_i(\sigma_R(r_1)) \leq_C \pi_i(\sigma_R(r_2))$, for each $1 \leq i \leq |\sigma_R(r_1)|$, and*
- *a function $\sigma_A \colon \mathcal{A} \to C \times \mathcal{T}$, called* attribute signature,
- *a set $\mathcal{T}$ of datatypes such as strings, integers, etc.*

Hereby, $\pi_i(t)$ is the i-th component of tuple t. In some cases, when it is clear from the context whether we are referring to a relation or an attribute, we will simply use σ.

Further, a semi-upper lattice $\leq$ fulfills the following conditions:

$$\forall x \; x \leq x \; \textit{(reflexive)} \tag{2.1}$$

$$\forall x \, \forall y \; (x \leq y \land y \leq x \to x = y) \; \textit{(anti-symmetric)} \tag{2.2}$$

$$\forall x \, \forall y \, \forall z \; (x \leq y \land y \leq z \to x \leq z) \; \textit{(transitive)} \tag{2.3}$$

$$\forall x \; x \leq top \; \textit{(top element)} \tag{2.4}$$

$$\forall x \, \forall y \, \exists z \; (z \geq x \land z \geq y \land \forall w \; (w \geq x \land w \geq y \to w \geq z)) \tag{2.5}$$

(supremum)

So every two elements have a unique most specific supremum. In the context of ontologies, we will refer to this element as the *least common subsumer.* It is obviously defined as follows:

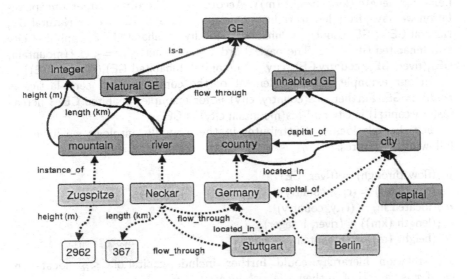

Fig. 2.1. Example ontology

$$lcs(a,b) := z \text{ such that } z \geq a \wedge z \geq b \text{ and } \forall w \ (w \geq a \wedge w \geq b \rightarrow w \geq z) \quad (2.6)$$

Often we will call concept identifiers and relation identifiers just *concepts* and *relations*, respectively, for the sake of simplicity. For binary relations, we define their *domain* and their *range* as follows:

Definition 2 (Domain and Range) *For a relation* $r \in R$ *with* $|\sigma(r)| = 2$*, we define its* domain *and* range *by* $\mathrm{dom}(r) := \pi_1(\sigma(r))$ *and* $\mathrm{range}(r) := \pi_2(\sigma(r))$.

If $c_1 <_C c_2$, for $c_1, c_2 \in C$, then c_1 is a *subconcept* of c_2, and c_2 is a *superconcept* of c_1. If $r_1 <_R r_2$, for $r_1, r_2 \in R$, then r_1 is a *subrelation* of r_2, and r_2 is a *superrelation* of r_1.

If $c_1 <_C c_2$ and there is no $c_3 \in C$ with $c_1 <_C c_3 <_C c_2$, then c_1 is a *direct subconcept* of c_2, and c_2 is a *direct superconcept* of c_1. We note this by $c_1 \prec c_2$. *Direct superrelations* and *direct subrelations* are defined analogously.

Let us illustrate all the above definitions on the basis of a simple example ontology graphically depicted in Figure 2.1. The set C of concepts is $C := \{$GE, Natural GE, Inhabited GE, mountain, river, country, city, capital$\}$, where GE stands for *geographical entity*. The set R of relations is: $R := \{$located_in, flow_through, capital_of$\}$. Further, we have two attributes, i.e. $A := \{$length (km), height (m)$\}$. According to the direct superconcept relation we have, from left to right: mountain $\prec$ Natural GE, river $\prec$ Natural GE, Natural GE $\prec$ GE, country $\prec$ Inhabited GE, city $\prec$ Inhabited GE, capital $\prec$ city and Inhabited GE $\prec$ GE. The partial order $\leq_C$ is then $\leq_C := \prec \cup \{$(mountain, GE),(river, GE),(country,GE),(city, GE),(capital, Inhabited GE),(capital, GE)$\}$.

In our example, the top element of the concept upper semi-lattice is $root_C :=$ GE. Further, lcs(country, city) is for example Inhabited GE, whereas lcs(city,capital) is city and lcs(mountain,city) is GE.

For the relations and attributes in the example ontology we have the following signatures:

σ_R(flow_through) $=$ (river, GE)
σ_R(capital_of) $=$ (city, country)
σ_R(located_in) $=$ (city, country)
σ_A(length (km)) $=$ (river, integer)
σ_A(height (m)) $=$ (mountain, integer)

The relation hierarchy could further include capital_of $\leq_R$ located_in, i.e. if x is capital of y, then x is also located in y.

Having defined the basic elements of a core ontology, we now define an axiom system for it. Though we are not directly concerned with learning axioms, we introduce an axiom system for the sake of completeness.

Definition 3 ($\mathcal{L}$-Axiom System) *Let $\mathcal{L}$ be a logical language. A $\mathcal{L}$-axiom system for an ontology $\mathcal{O} := (C, \leq_C, R, \sigma_R, \leq_R, A, \sigma_A, \mathcal{T})$ is a triple*

$$S := (AS, \alpha, \mathcal{L})$$

where

- *AS is a set whose elements are called axiom schemata and*
- *$\alpha \colon AS \to AS_{\mathcal{L}}$ is a mapping from AS to axiom schemata defined over $\mathcal{L}$.*

An ontology with an $\mathcal{L}$-axiom system is a pair

$$(\mathcal{O}, S)$$

where $\mathcal{O}$ is an ontology and S is an $\mathcal{L}$-axiom system for $\mathcal{O}$.

We will formalize these axiom schemata using the untyped lambda calculus (compare [Barendregt, 1984]) originally introduced by Church [Church, 1936]. The lambda calculus essentially provides a means to describe arbitrary unnamed functions. A lambda expression consists of a variable which we abstract over - the argument of the function - and which is bound by the λ operator. A function $f(x) = x^2$ can thus be written in the lambda calculus notation as $\lambda x.x^2$, where the dot (.) separates the lambda operator from the actual body of the function. In what follows, we will regard the standard lambda calculus notation as equivalent to the *uncurried* notation in which lists of λ-bound variables are used. Thus, $\lambda x.\ (\lambda y.\ (x+y))$ will be written in the more handy form: '$\lambda x, y.\ x+y$, omitting the parenthesis by assuming that the λ-operator binds the variables in the list until the end of the whole expression.

For example, one axiom schema could be $\lambda P, Q.\ disjoint(P, Q)$ which is mapped by α to a first-order logic schema as

$$\lambda P, Q.\ \forall x\ (P(x) \rightarrow \neg Q(x)).$$

$\alpha(disjoint)(river)(mountain)$ would thus yield:

$$\forall x\ (river(x) \rightarrow \neg mountain(x)).$$

The obvious benefit of such an $\mathcal{L}$-axiom system is that by being independent of some concrete knowledge representation formalism, the axioms formulated can be translated into a variety of different languages. This is important for ontology learning as the statements learned from textual data have in fact an intuitive interpretation independent of any knowledge representation formalism. The learned statements can then get assigned a specific interpretation with respect to a concrete KR formalism via the α mapping. Axiom schemata capture frequently occurring patterns used in ontology engineering (compare [Staab et al., 2001]). In addition to instantiations of these axiom schemata, other general axioms have to be added to the logical theory. The difference between axiom schemata and general axioms is thus only a pragmatic one, i.e. it depends on the fact whether a type of general axiom occurs often enough to deserve the status of an axiom schema. For example, we will assume the following two axioms as being part of our logical theory:

$$\forall x\ (country(x) \rightarrow \exists y\ capital\_of(y, x) \wedge \forall z(capital\_of(z, x) \rightarrow z = y))$$
$$\forall x\ (capital(x) \leftrightarrow \exists y\ capital\_of(x, y) \wedge country(y))$$

The first axiom states that every country has a unique capital, while the second defines the concept capital as equivalent to saying that there is a country which stands in a capital_of relation with the corresponding city. Depending on the view adopted and if axioms as the above occur frequently, one could introduce the following axiom schema:

$$\lambda C_1, C_2, R.\ C_1 = \exists R.C_2$$

which would be mapped to the following first-order axiom schema:

$$\lambda C_1, C_2, R.\ \forall x\ (C_1(x) \leftrightarrow \exists y\ \wedge R(x, y) \wedge C_2(y))$$

The instantiation $\lambda C_1, C_2, R.\ C_1 = \exists R.C_2(\text{capital})(\text{country})(\text{capital\_of})$ would then be mapped to the following first-order formula:

$$\forall x \ (capital(x) \leftrightarrow \exists y \ \wedge \ capital\_of(x,y) \wedge country(y))$$

The crucial question here certainly is whether the corresponding axiom occurs frequently enough to be lifted to the status of an axiom schema.

In what follows, we also define what a lexicon for an ontology is:

Definition 4 (Lexicon) *A lexicon for an ontology*

$$\mathcal{O} := (C, \leq_C, R, \sigma_R, \leq_R, \mathcal{A}, \sigma_A, \mathcal{T})$$

is a structure

$$Lex := (S_C, S_R, S_A, Ref_C, Ref_R, Ref_A)$$

consisting of

- *three sets S_C, S_R and S_A whose elements are called* signs for concepts, relations *and* attributes, *respectively,*
- *a relation $Ref_C \subseteq S_C \times C$ called* lexical reference for concepts,
- *a relation $Ref_R \subseteq S_R \times R$ called* lexical reference for relations, *and*
- *a relation $Ref_A \subseteq S_A \times \mathcal{A}$ called* lexical reference for attributes.

Based on Ref_C, we define, for $s \in S_C$,

$$Ref_C(s) := \{c \in C \mid (s,c) \in Ref_C\}$$

and, for $c \in C$,

$$Ref_C^{-1}(c) := \{s \in S_C \mid (s,c) \in Ref_C\}.$$

Ref_R and Ref_R^{-1} as well as Ref_A and Ref_A^{-1} are defined analogously.

An ontology with lexicon is a pair

$$(\mathcal{O}, Lex),$$

where $\mathcal{O}$ is an ontology and Lex is a lexicon for $\mathcal{O}$.

For our example ontology, we could for instance specify that both *nation* and *country* refer to the concept country, i.e. $Ref_C^{-1}(\text{country}) = \{nation, country\}$.

It is important to mention that the above definition accommodates a great variety of lexical structures to which concepts and relations can refer, depending how the sets S_C, S_R and S_A are defined. In fact, they could merely contain labels, i.e. plain strings for the concepts and relations as typically assumed, but also highly structured objects (compare [Buitelaar et al., 2006]).

Whereas ontologies formally specify the conceptualization of a domain, the extensional part is provided by a knowledge base which contains assertions about instances of the concepts and relations.

Definition 5 (Knowledge Base (KB)) *A knowledge base for an ontology*
$\mathcal{O} := (C, \leq_C, R, \sigma_R, \leq_R, \mathcal{A}, \sigma_A, \mathcal{T})$ *is a structure*

$$KB := (I, \iota_C, \iota_R, \iota_A)$$

consisting of

- *a set I whose elements are called* instance identifiers *(or instances or objects for short)*,
- *a function $\iota_C \colon C \to 2^I$ called* concept instantiation,
- *a function $\iota_R \colon R \to 2^{I^+}$ with $\iota_R(r) \subseteq \prod_{1 \leq i \leq |\sigma(r)|} \iota_C(\pi_i(\sigma(r)))$, for all $r \in R$. The function ι_R is called* relation instantiation, *and*
- *a function $\iota_A \colon \mathcal{A} \to I \times \bigcup_{t \in \mathcal{T}} [\![t]\!]$ with $\iota_A(a) \subseteq \iota_C(\pi_1(\sigma(a))) \times [\![\pi_2(\sigma(a))]\!]$, where $[\![t]\!]$ are the values of datatype $t \in \mathcal{T}$. The function ι_A is called* attribute instantiation.

In our example ontology, we have for instance: $I :=$ {Zugspitze, Neckar, Germany, Stuttgart, Berlin}. Further, we have the following instantiation relations:

$\iota_C(\text{mountain}) := \{\text{Zugspitze}\}$
$\iota_C(\text{river}) := \{\text{Neckar}\}$
$\iota_C(\text{country}) := \{\text{Germany}\}$
$\iota_C(\text{city}) := \{\text{Stuttgart, Berlin}\}$
$\iota_R(\text{flow\_through}) := \{(\text{Neckar, Germany}), (\text{Neckar, Stuttgart})\}$
$\iota_R(\text{located\_in}) := \{(\text{Stuttgart, Germany})\}$
$\iota_R(\text{capital\_of}) := \{(\text{Berlin, Germany})\}$
$\iota_A(\text{length (km)}) := \{(\text{Neckar, 367})\}$
$\iota_A(\text{height (m)}) := \{(\text{Zugspitze, 2962})\}$

As for concepts and relations, we also provide names for instances.

Definition 6 (Instance Lexicon) *An* instance lexicon *for a knowledge base $KB := (I, \iota_C, \iota_R, \iota_A)$ is a pair*

$$IL := (S_I, R_I)$$

consisting of

- *a set S_I whose elements are called* signs for instances,
- *a relation $R_I \subseteq S_I \times I$ called* lexical reference for instances.

A knowledge base with lexicon is a pair

$$(KB, IL)$$

where KB is a knowledge base and IL is an instance lexicon for KB.

When a knowledge base is given, we can derive the extensions of the concepts and relations of the ontology based on the concept instantiation and the relation instantiation.

Definition 7 (Extension) *Let* $KB := (I, \iota_C, \iota_R, \iota_A)$ *be a knowledge base for an ontology* $\mathcal{O} := (C, \leq_C, R, \sigma_R, \leq_R, \mathcal{A}, \sigma_A, \mathcal{T})$. *The* extension $[\![c]\!]_{KB} \subseteq I$ *of a concept* $c \in C$ *is recursively defined by the following rules:*

- $[\![c]\!]_{KB} \leftarrow \iota_C(c)$
- $[\![c]\!]_{KB} \leftarrow [\![c]\!]_{KB} \cup [\![c']\!]_{KB}$, *for* $c' <_C c$.
- *instantiations of axiom schemata in* S *(if* $\mathcal{O}$ *is an ontology with* $\mathcal{L}$-*axioms),*
- *other general axioms contained in the logical theory.*

The extension $[\![r]\!]_{KB} \subseteq I^+$ *of a relation* $r \in R$ *is recursively defined by the following rules:*

- $[\![r]\!]_{KB} \leftarrow \iota_R(r)$
- $[\![r]\!]_{KB} \leftarrow [\![r]\!]_{KB} \cup [\![r']\!]_{KB}$, *for* $r' <_R r$.
- *instantiations of axiom schemata in* S *(if* $\mathcal{O}$ *is an ontology with* $\mathcal{L}$-*axioms),*
- *other general axioms contained in the logical theory.*

The extension $[\![a]\!]_{KB} \subseteq I \times [\![\mathcal{T}]\!]$ *of an attribute* $a \in \mathcal{A}$ *is defined as:*

- $[\![a]\!]_{KB} \leftarrow \iota_A(a)$
- *general axioms contained in the logical theory.*

If the reference to the knowledge base is clear from the context, we also write $[\![c]\!]$, $[\![r]\!]$ and $[\![a]\!]$ instead of $[\![c]\!]_{KB}$, $[\![r]\!]_{KB}$ and $[\![a]\!]_{KB}$. Given our example, we get in particular (taking into account the relation hierarchy and our general axioms defining capitals and their relation to countries):

$[\![\text{mountain}]\!] := \{\text{Zugspitze}\}$
$[\![\text{river}]\!] := \{\text{Neckar}\}$
$[\![\text{country}]\!] := \{\text{Germany}\}$
$[\![\text{city}]\!] := \{\text{Stuttgart, Berlin}\}$
$[\![\text{capital}]\!] := \{\text{Berlin}\}$
$[\![\text{Natural GE}]\!] := \{\text{Zugspitze, Neckar}\}$
$[\![\text{Inhabited GE}]\!] := \{\text{Germany, Berlin, Stuttgart}\}$
$[\![\text{GE}]\!] := \{\text{Germany, Berlin, Stuttgart, Zugspitze, Neckar}\}$
$[\![\text{flow\_through}]\!] := \{(\text{Neckar, Germany}), (\text{Neckar, Stuttgart})\}$
$[\![\text{located\_in}]\!] := \{(\text{Stuttgart, Germany}), (\text{Berlin, Germany})\}$
$[\![\text{capital\_of}]\!] := \{(\text{Berlin, Germany})\}$

Finally, what is missing is a definition of the intension of a certain concept or relation. We extend the definitions of Stumme et al. [Stumme et al., 2003] to also accommodate the intension of concepts and relations as follows:

Definition 8 (Intension) *A structure*

$$\mathfrak{I} := (\mathcal{L}_I, i_C, i_R, i_A)$$

is called the intension *of an ontology* $\mathcal{O} := (C, \leq_C, R, \sigma_R, \leq_R, \mathcal{A}, \sigma_A, \mathcal{T})$ *and consists of:*

- *a language $\mathcal{L}_I$ capturing intensions of concepts, relations and attributes, respectively,*
- *three mappings i_C, i_R and i_A with $i_C : C \to \mathcal{L}_I$, $i_R : R \to \mathcal{L}_I$ and $i_A : A \to \mathcal{L}_I$, mapping concepts, relations and attributes to their corresponding intensions.*

We interpret the *intension* as a non-extensional definition of a certain concept or relation. The above definition also accommodates different languages for expressing the intension of concepts and relations. The *intension*, for example, could be represented through *differentiae* in the sense of Aristotle explaining why a certain concept is different from others and thus merits a status on its own. In this line, the language could consist of sets of attributes describing a concept in line with the theory of Formal Concept Analysis (see Section 4.2). However, the language could consist of strings describing the intuitive meaning of a concept in natural language such as done with the *glosses* of the WordNet lexical resource [Fellbaum, 1998] (compare Section 4.1.8). In this line, in our example the intension for capital could be $i_C(\text{capital}) :=$ *'town or city that is the center of government of a country, state or province'*. Having outlined our formal ontology model, the next chapter introduces the core topic of the book, i.e. ontology learning from text.

3

Ontology Learning from Text

In this section, we introduce *ontology learning* and in particular *ontology learning from text*. Further, we systematically organize the different ontology learning tasks in several layers and formally define them with respect to the ontology model presented in Chapter 2. After giving a short overview of the state-of-the-art with respect to the different tasks, we describe the structure and scope of this book.

Whereas ontologies formally specify a domain model, the extensional part is provided by a knowledge base that contains assertions about instances of concepts and relations as defined by the ontology (compare Section 2). The (semi-) automatic support in constructing an ontology is typically referred to as *ontology learning*.

The term *ontology learning* was originally coined by Alexander Mädche and Steffen Staab [Mädche and Staab, 2001] and can be described as the acquisition of a domain model from data. It is historically connected to the Semantic Web, which builds on ontology models or logic formalism restricted to decidable fragments of first-order logic, in particular description logics [Staab and Studer, 2004]. Thus, the domain models to be learned are also restricted in their complexity and expressivity.

Obviously, ontology learning needs input data from which to learn the concepts relevant for a given domain, their definitions as well as the relations holding between them. One crucial requirement is thus that the input data is representative for the domain one aims to learn an ontology for. Input data can be schemata such as XML-DTDs, UML diagrams or database schemata. We call this sort of ontology learning *lifting* [Volz et al., 2003] as it mainly consists of 'lifting' or mapping definitions from the schema to corresponding ontological definitions. Ontology learning can also be performed on the basis of semi-structured sources such as XML or HTML documents or tabular structures (compare [Pivk et al., 2005]). In case ontology learning is performed on the basis of unstructured textual resources, we will speak of *ontology learning from text*.

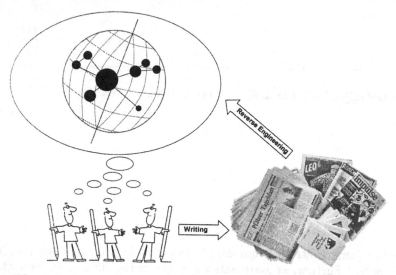

Fig. 3.1. Ontology learning from text as a reverse engineering task

Ontology learning can be regarded to some extent as a process of reverse engineering (compare Figure 3.1). The author of a certain text or document has a world or domain model in mind which he shares to some extent with other authors writing texts about the same domain. This implicit domain model, among many other factors such as the intended message, shapes the content of the resulting text. The task of reconstructing the world model of the author or even of the model shared by different authors can thus be seen as one of reverse engineering. The task is inherently complex and challenging mainly due to two reasons. First of all, there is typically only a small part of the authors' domain knowledge involved in the creation process, such that the process of reverse engineering can, at best, only partially reconstruct the authors' model. Second, and much more important, world knowledge – unless we are considering a text book or dictionary – is rarely mentioned explicitly. Brewster et al. [Brewster et al., 2003], for example, have argued that text writing and reading is in fact a process of background knowledge maintenance in the sense that basic domain knowledge is assumed, and only the relevant part of knowledge which is the issue of the text or article is mentioned in a more or less explicit way. In fact, world knowledge is typically contained only implicitly in texts in the way certain words or linguistic structures are used by the writers.

This is very related to the principle underlying the so called *meaning triangle*, which illustrates that in every language (formal or natural) there are symbols which need to be interpreted as evoking some concept as well as referring to some concrete individual in the world. The meaning triangle in Figure 3.2 is derived from Sowa [Sowa, 2000b] and illustrates this principle

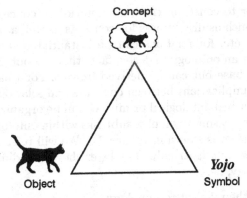

Fig. 3.2. Meaning triangle taken from Sowa [Sowa, 2000b]

with the string *Yojo*. For persons with the appropriate contextual information, this string evokes the concept of a cat and furthermore denotes a specific cat in the world. This corresponds to the *sense (Sinn)* and *reference (Bedeutung)* distinction introduced by Frege [Frege, 1892]. Ontology learning from text thus deals with uninterpreted symbols or signs for which the appropriate sense needs to be identified as some sort of reverse engineering, i.e. contrary to the direction by which these symbols are produced.

The process of learning the extensions for concepts and relations is commonly referred to as *ontology population*. Further, we will speak of *knowledge markup* or *annotation* if the population is done by selecting text fragments from a document and assigning them to ontological concepts such as in the OntoMat Annotizer framework [Handschuh et al., 2001].

A large collection of methods for ontology learning from text have been developed over recent years. Unfortunately, there is not much consensus within the ontology learning community on the concrete tasks, which makes a comparison of approaches difficult. It is therefore one goal of this book to contribute to a better understanding of the ontology learning tasks and help to develop metrics and benchmarks to compare research in this field.

In order to discuss the state-of-the-art in ontology learning, we first need to establish the subtasks that together constitute the complex task of ontology development (either manual or with any level of automatic support). Ontology development is primarily concerned with axiomatizing the definition of concepts as well as the relationships between them. For some applications of ontologies in text mining or natural language processing as well as for the purpose of human readability, it is also important to connect concepts and relations to the symbols that are used to refer to them. In our case this implies the acquisition of linguistic knowledge about the terms that are used to refer to a specific concept and potential synonyms of these terms. An ontology further consists of a concept hierarchy as well as other, non-hierarchical relations. In order to constrain the interpretation of concepts and relations, axiom schemata such as disjointness for concepts as well as symmetry, reflexivity, transitivity, etc. for relations can be instantiated. Finally, one is also interested in using an ontology to derive facts that are not explicitly modeled in the knowledge base but can be derived from it. For this purpose, logical axioms modeling implications between concepts and relations can be defined. All the above described ontological primitives can be organized in a layer cake according to the increasingly complex subtasks within ontology learning to acquire them. This layer is shown in Figure 3.3. We will refer to this layer cake as the *ontology learning layer cake*. The layer shows the different subtasks of learning an ontology, i.e.

- acquisition of the relevant terminology,
- identification of synonym terms / linguistic variants (possibly across languages),
- formation of concepts,
- hierarchical organization of the concepts (concept hierarchy),
- learning relations, properties or attributes, together with the appropriate domain and range,
- hierarchical organization of the relations (relation hierarchy),
- instantiation of axiom schemata,
- definition of arbitrary axioms.

In most cases, the layers conceptually build one upon another in the sense that the processes within higher layers rely on the output of processes situated at lower layers, i.e. concepts can only be ordered hierarchically if appropriate concepts have already been formed. However, from a processing point of view, the tasks within different layers can be grouped together and performed by one and the same algorithm. As we will see in later chapters of the book, there are algorithms such as Formal Concept Analysis which discover concepts and order them hierarchically at the same time.

For illustration purposes, Figure 3.3 includes some concrete examples from the domain of geography on the left of each layer. Within the terminology acquisition step, we would find relevant terms such as *river, country, nation, city, capital*. At the synonym discovery step, we might group together *nation* and *country* as in certain contexts they are synonyms. This group of synonyms might then provide the lexicon Ref_C for the concept country $:=< i(\text{country}), [\![\text{country}]\!], Ref_C(\text{country}) >$ with an intension $i(\text{country})$ and its extension $[\![\text{country}]\!]$. The intension might for example be specified as *'area of land that forms a politically independent unit'*. Further, we could learn a concept hierarchy between the concepts acquired. For the geographical domain, we might learn that capital $\leq_C$ city, city $\leq_C$ Inhabited GE, etc. In addition, we might learn relations together with their domain and range such as the flow_through relation between a river and a GE. As defined in our ontology model, relations can also be ordered hierarchically. We might for example learn that the capital_of relation is a specialization of the located_in relation. At the

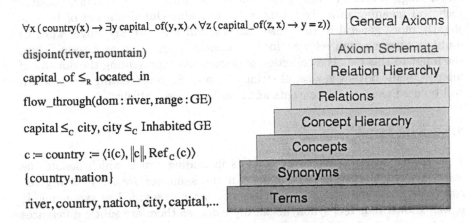

$\forall x\,(\,\text{country}(x) \rightarrow \exists y\,\text{capital\_of}(y,x) \wedge \forall z\,(\,\text{capital\_of}(z,x) \rightarrow y=z))$ — General Axioms

disjoint(river, mountain) — Axiom Schemata

capital_of $\leq_R$ located_in — Relation Hierarchy

flow_through(dom : river, range : GE) — Relations

capital $\leq_C$ city, city $\leq_C$ Inhabited GE — Concept Hierarchy

$c := \text{country} := \langle i(c), \|c\|, \text{Ref}_C(c)\rangle$ — Concepts

{country, nation} — Synonyms

river, country, nation, city, capital,... — Terms

Fig. 3.3. Ontology learning layer cake

axiom schema instantiation level, we might derive that river and mountain are disjoint concepts. Finally, we also might derive more complex relationships between concepts and relations in the form of axioms. The rule in Figure 3.3, for example, says that every country has a unique capital.

As mentioned at the beginning, one aim of this chapter is to provide a systematic organization and formalization of ontology learning subtasks with respect to our ontology model. In what follows, we provide such a formalization which will serve as the basis for the definition of ontology learning evaluation measures in the rest of the book.

3.1 Ontology Learning Tasks

In this section, we describe the different ontology learning subtasks along the lines of the ontology learning layer cake.

3.1.1 Terms

Term extraction is a prerequisite for all aspects of ontology learning from text. Terms are linguistic realizations of domain-specific concepts and are therefore central to further, more complex tasks. The task here is to find a set of relevant terms or signs for concepts and relations, i.e. S_C and S_R which are characteristic for the domain as represented in the underlying text collection and which will provide the basis in order to define a lexicon for an ontology as described in Section 2. From a linguistic point of view, terms are either single words or multi-word compounds with a very specific, possibly technical meaning in a given context or domain. Our definition of term is slightly more general in the sense that we will refer to any single word or multi-word compound relevant for the domain in question as a term. Thus, the input to this task is a collection of documents representing the domain of interest, while output is a set of strings S_C and S_R representing terms which will be used as signs for concepts and relations, respectively.

3.1.2 Synonyms

The task of synonym discovery consists in finding words which denote the same concept and which thus appear in the same set $Ref_C(c)$ for a given concept c. To some extent, these elements can be regarded as synonyms. It is well known that real synonyms hardly exist, as there are subtle differences even between words which are commonly considered as such. Thus, our definition of synonymy is less strict. We will regard two words as synonyms if they share a common meaning which can be used as a basis to form a concept relevant for the domain in question. This definition corresponds to the *synsets* in WordNet [Fellbaum, 1998]. Note that there is thus a significant overlap between our definition of synonymy and the lexical relation of cohyponymy. Cohyponymy is typically defined as the relation between hyponyms of a common hypernym, i.e. the descendants of a word in a thesaurus. It is important to mention that synonymy, cohyponymy, hypernymy as well as hyponymy are lexical relations which can not be seen as equivalent to the notions of equality, sibling, superconcept and subconcept relations between concepts, which are defined extensionally. Lexical relations are defined on the level of words. For a more detailed definition of these lexical relations consult Section 4.1.8.

3.1.3 Concepts

In our view, *concept formation* should ideally provide (i) an intensional definition of concepts, (ii) their extension and (iii) the lexical signs which are used to refer to them [Buitelaar et al., 2006]. Thus, for the purpose of ontology learning we define a concept as a triple $< i(c), [\![c]\!], Ref_C(c) >$ where $i(c)$ is the intension of the concept, $[\![c]\!]$ its extension and Ref_C describes its lexical realization in a corpus. The lexicon can also contain more complex structures enriched with statistical information as described by Buitelaar [Buitelaar, 2000] or even parse trees, subcategorization frames, etc. Though there is no explicit definition of an intension within the model described in Section 2, we will assume an intension to be a natural language description of the intuitive meaning of a concept in line with the glosses in WordNet [Fellbaum, 1998] or a collection of attributes in line with the theory of Formal Concept Analysis (see Section 4.2).

3.1.4 Concept Hierarchies

In what follows, we present tasks related to inducing, extending and refining the ontology's backbone, i.e. its concept hierarchy.

Definition 9 (Concept Hierarchy Induction) *We define concept hierarchy induction as the task of, given a set of concepts* C*, typically together with their lexical realization* Ref_C*, learning pairs* (c_i, c_j) *where* $c_i, c_j \in C$ *such that* $\leq_C = \bigcup_{i,j} \{(c_i, c_j)\}$ *forms a semi-upper lattice. The task here is thus to induce a concept hierarchy from scratch.*

Starting from a set of concepts $C := \{$city, mountain, river, country, capital, ...$\}$, the task here would be to derive a relation $\leq_C$ mirroring, for example, the concept hierarchy depicted in Figure 2.1.

Definition 10 (Refinement) *We define concept hierarchy refinement as the task of, given a set of concepts* C *as well as a semi-upper lattice* $\leq_C$ *on* C*, learning pairs* (c_i, c) *such that* $c \in C$*. The refined hierarchy* $C' := C \bigcup_i c_i$ *and* $\leq_{C'} = \leq_C \cup \bigcup_i \{(c_i, c)\}$ *should still form a semi-upper lattice* $(C', \leq_{C'})$*. The task here is to extend the existing concept hierarchy with additional subconcepts of already existing concepts, thus refining the hierarchy. Note that refinement is defined monotonically here.*

As a result of a refinement, we could, for example, add the tuple (valley, Natural GE) to the concept hierarchy $\leq_C$ depicted in Figure 2.1.

Definition 11 (Lexical Extension) *We define lexical extension or lexical refinement of a concept hierarchy as the task of, given a concept* c *together with its lexical reference function* $Ref_C(c)$*, finding new lexical realizations* s_i *of the concept* c*, thus extending* $Ref_C(c)$*, i.e.,* $Ref'_C(c) := Ref_C(c) \bigcup_i \{s_i\}$*.*

As a result of lexical extension, we would, for example, add the term 'creek' to the set Ref_C(river).

3.1.5 Relations

In the context of the work described in this book, we will restrict ourselves to binary relations and define *relation learning* as the task of learning relation identifiers or labels r as well as their appropriate domain dom(r) and range range(r). In fact, the following three tasks can be distinguished here:

- finding concepts in C standing in some non-taxonomic ontological relation,
- specifying R, i.e. finding appropriate labels and relation identifiers on the basis of the given corpus,
- given a certain relation $r \in R$, determining the right level of abstraction with respect to the concept hierarchy for the domain and range of the relation,
- learning a hierarchical order $\leq_R$ between the relations in R.

3.1.6 Axiom Schemata Instantiations

Concerning the axiomatic definition of concepts and relations, the aim of ontology learning is not to learn the axiom schemata itself. We assume the existence of some $\mathcal{L}$-axiom system, defining axiom schemata which are often used in ontology engineering and therefore deserve a special status. For concepts we have, for example, *disjointness* or *equivalence* axioms, while for relations we have axioms describing the properties of the relation, i.e. *transitivity, symmetry*, etc. The task here is thus to learn which concepts, relations or pairs of concepts the axioms in our system apply to, i.e. we may want to learn which pairs of concepts are disjoint, which relations are symmetric, the minimal and maximal cardinality of a relation, etc. However, we will not be concerned with this problem in the context of the book.

3.1.7 General Axioms

The situation is different for the task of learning general axioms, in which the axioms themselves have to be learned and not merely instantiated. Here the type of axioms strongly depends on the logical formalism used in the background. General axioms can be thought of as logical implications constraining the interpretation of concepts and relations. They differ from axiom schemata in that they do not occur as frequently and therefore deserve no special status. The task of learning axioms can thus be understood as consisting in deriving more complex relationships and connections between concepts and relations. These axioms can then be represented, for example, using the Horn-fragment of first-order logic. As we are not concerned with the automatic acquisition of general axioms, we will not specify the form of such rules any further as it heavily depends on the underlying knowledge representation formalism used.

3.2 Ontology Population Tasks

Ontology population consists in learning the extensional aspects of a domain. In particular, the aim is to learn instances of concepts as well as relations. Hereby, an *instance-of* relation is the set-membership relation between an instance $i \in I$ and the set $\iota_C(c)$ of some concept c, i.e. instance-of$(i,c) \leftrightarrow i \in \iota_C(c)$. A similar definition holds for relation instantiation: instance-of$_R((i_1, i_2), r) \leftrightarrow (i_1, i_2) \in \iota_R(r)$. The tasks within *ontology population* are thus to learn *instance-of* and *instance-of$_R$* relations. More specifically, if an ontology is populated by (i) keeping a link to the text in which the instances were found as well as by (ii) contextualizing the assignment to a concept or relation with respect to the context specified by the document or text in question, we will speak about *knowledge markup* or *annotation*.

3.3 The State-of-the-Art

Given the ontology learning layer cake as discussed above, we can take a closer look at the state-of-the-art in this field. We first examine it layer by layer and finally draw some general conclusions.

3.3.1 Terms

The literature provides many examples of term extraction methods that could be used as a first step in ontology learning from text. Most of these are based on information retrieval methods for term indexing [Salton and Buckley, 1988], but many are inspired by terminology and NLP research (see [Frantzi and Ananiadou, 1999], [Borigault et al., 2001], [Pantel and Lin, 2001]).

Term extraction implies more or less advanced levels of linguistic processing, i.e. phrase analysis to identify complex noun phrases that may express terms and dependency structure analysis to identify their internal structure. As such parsers are not always available, much of the research on this layer in ontology learning has remained rather restricted. The state-of-the-art is mostly to run a part-of-speech tagger over the domain corpus used for the ontology learning task and then to identify possible terms by manually constructing ad-hoc patterns. In order to identify only relevant term candidates, a statistical processing step may be included that compares the distribution of candidates between corpora using for example a χ^2 test or similar (compare Section 4.1.6).

3.3.2 Synonyms

Most research has tackled acquisition of synonyms by clustering and related techniques, in particular exploiting Harris' hypothesis that words are semantically similar to the extent to which they share linguistic contexts [Harris, 1968]. Examples for such an approach can be found in the work of Grefenstette [Grefenstette, 1994]. In very specific domains, some researchers have exploited integrated approaches to word sense disambiguation and synonym discovery (compare [Turcato et al., 2000], [Buitelaar and Sacaleanu, 2002] and [Navigli and Velardi, 2004]).

An important technique for synonym discovery is certainly LSI (Latent Semantic Indexing) [Landauer and Dumais, 1997], PLSI (Probabilistic Latent Semantic Indexing) [Hofmann, 1999] or other variants, which essentially reduce the dimension of standard text representation models such as the bag-of-words-model, thus leading to the discovery of strongly correlated groups of terms.

Currently, there seems to be a trend to use statistical information measures defined over the web in order to detect synonyms (compare [Turney, 2001] and [Baroni and Bisi, 2004]). In general, the research on synonym discovery is relatively mature and has been shown to achieve a human comparable performance on the TOEFL synonyms selection tasks (compare [Landauer and Dumais, 1997] and [Turney, 2001]).

3.3.3 Concepts

The extraction of concepts from text is not only a very difficult problem, but also a very controversial one as it is not clear what concept extraction is supposed to be. Some researchers have addressed the question from a clustering perspective and considered clusters of related terms as concepts (see [Hindle, 1990], [Lin and Pantel, 2001c], [Lin and Pantel, 2002] or [Reinberger and Spyns, 2005]). Again, very promising in this context seem approaches applying dimension reduction techniques such as described by Schütze [Schütze, 1993] or Landauer and Dumais [Landauer and Dumais, 1997] and which reveal inherent connections between words, thus leading to group formation. In fact, LSI-based techniques are especially interesting as they run into fewer data sparseness problems than approaches relying on raw data. Actually, there is a great overlap between techniques used for synonym and concept detection which is due to the fact that both tasks typically aim at discovering semantically similar words which share some meaning. In the case of synonym discovery, the semantically similar words are regarded as potential candidates for synonyms. In the case of concept formation, they provide the basis for creating concepts.

Other researchers have addressed concept formation from an extensional point of view. Evans [Evans, 2003], for example, derives hierarchies of named entities from text, thus also discovering concepts from an extensional point of view. The Know-It-All system [Etzioni et al., 2004a] also aims at learning the extension of given concepts, such as, for example, all the actors appearing on the Web. In the approach of Evans [Evans, 2003], the concepts as well as their extensions are thus derived automatically, while Etzioni et al. [Etzioni et al., 2004a] essentially learn the extension of existing concepts. Finally, other systems learn concepts intensionally. The OntoLearn system [Velardi et al., 2005], for example, derives WordNet-like glosses for domain-specific concepts on the basis of a compositional interpretation of the meaning of compounds.

3.3.4 Concept Hierarchies

There are currently three main paradigms exploited to induce concept hierarchies from textual data. The first one is the application of lexico-syntactic patterns indicating the relation of interest in line with the seminal work of Hearst [Hearst, 1992]. However, it is well known that these patterns occur rarely in corpora. Thus, though approaches relying on lexico-syntactic patterns have a reasonable precision, their recall is very low. Other approaches exploit the internal structure of noun phrases to derive taxonomic relations [Buitelaar et al., 2004].

The second paradigm is based on Harris' distributional hypothesis. In this line, researchers have mainly exploited hierarchical clustering algorithms to automatically derive concept hierarchies from text (see [Faure and Nedellec, 1998], [Bisson et al., 2000] and [Cimiano et al., 2004c]). In general, clustering approaches typically accomplish two tasks in one: concept formation and concept hierarchy induction. This is due to the fact that, on the one hand, they create clusters or groups of similar words, which can be regarded as representing concepts to some extent, and further order these clusters hierarchically.

The third paradigm relies on the analysis of co-occurrence of terms in the same sentence, paragraph or document. Sanderson and Croft [Sanderson and Croft, 1999], for instance, have presented a document-based notion of subsumption according to which a term t_1 is more specific than a term t_2 if t_2 appears in all document in which t_1 occurs.

Sections 6.1 and 6.5 contain a much more detailed description of related work and the state-of-the-art in the field of automatic concept hierarchy induction from text. We conclude this section by noting that, while a lot of research has been devoted to develop approaches exploiting the different learning paradigms, little effort has been spent on systematically comparing and evaluating different approaches based on one paradigm, as well as on combining techniques from different paradigms.

3.3.5 Relations

There have only been a few approaches addressing the issue of learning ontological relations from text. One of the first was the work of Mädche and Staab [Mädche and Staab, 2000], in which a variant of the association rules extraction algorithm based on sentence-based term co-occurrence is presented (see Section 7.5 for more details).

The use of syntactic dependencies has been, for example, proposed by Gamallo et al. [Gamallo et al., 2002]. To our knowledge, the only approaches to generalize the relations based on syntactic dependencies with respect to an underlying concept hierarchy are the ones of Mädche and Staab [Mädche and Staab, 2000] and more recently also of Ciaramita et al. [Ciaramita et al., 2005]. The problem is very related to the task of acquiring selectional restrictions for verbs at the right level of abstraction (compare [Resnik, 1993, Ribas, 1995, Clark and Weir, 2002]). In general, it seems that the current approaches to relation extraction, e.g. [Mädche and Staab, 2000], [Gamallo et al., 2002], [Ciaramita et al., 2005] or [Schutz and Buitelaar, 2005] have only scratched at the surface of the problem. Sections 7.1 and 7.5 discuss the state-of-the-art in learning relations in much more detail.

3.3.6 Axiom Schemata Instantiation and General Axioms

Initial blueprints for the task of learning instantiations of axiom schemata can be found in the work of Haase and Völker [Haase and Völker, 2005]. They present an approach to learn instantiations of the disjointness axiom schema. The approach is based on the assumption that, if terms appear coordinated in an expression such as *'men and women'*, they are likely to be disjoint.

The extraction of general axioms is probably the least researched area in the context of ontology learning. Shamsfard and Barforoush [Shamsfard and Barforoush, 2004] have suggested deriving axioms from quantified conditional expressions such as *'Every man loves a woman'*. With respect to learning implications between relations, which can be used as a basis to define general axioms, Lin and Pantel [Lin and Pantel, 2001a] have shown that one can also find similar dependency tree paths. Some of the extracted similarities correspond to inverse relations such as *author_of* and *written_by*, which could be used to axiomatize the meaning of some relation.

The recent PASCAL textual entailment challenge[1] represents a very related problem. In fact, this challenge has strongly increased the awareness of the problem of deriving lexical entailment rules and led many researchers to address the problem, so that a plethora of approaches to tackle the problem of learning ontological rules from text corpora can be expected in the near future. Provided there would be enough explicitly given training data, one could also apply techniques from inductive logic programming (ILP) [Lavrac and Dzeroski, 1994] to the task of deriving Horn-like rules from a dataset.

3.3.7 Population

The task of populating an ontology is very related to the named entity recognition (NER) and information extraction (IE) tasks.

Information extraction (IE) consists of filling a predefined set of *target knowledge structures* – commonly referred to as templates – by applying natural language processing techniques. Historically, the information extraction task has been linked to the Message Understanding Conferences (MUC) which provided datasets based on which different systems can be compared. The task in MUC-7 was to spot *management succession* events in newswire articles, for example. Recently, the information extraction community has emphasized the adaptivity of systems and focused on the automatic induction of extraction rules in a supervised manner (compare [Freitag and Kushmerick, 2000, Muslea et al., 2001, Ciravegna, 2001, Sigletos et al., 2003]). In general, this has led to a simplification of the extraction tasks such as in the so called *seminar announcements* task, in which the location, speaker, topic, date, start and end time of a seminar have to be extracted. In general, many researchers have

---

[1] http://www.pascal-network.org/Challenges/RTE/

considered what is now referred to as *single-slot* information extraction, i.e. filling certain attributes of one instance of a given template. These systems are neither capable of extracting more than one template type nor several instances of the type in question, i.e. they rely on what could be called the *one-template-type-and-occurrence-per-document* assumption. Recently, there has been work addressing the learning from relational data, thus leading to the possibility of identifying multiple instances of a given relation (compare [Iria, 2005]).

Named entity recognition consists in finding instances of a certain concept in texts, where the set of relevant concepts is typically restricted to person, location and organization. However, recently more classes have been added in the context of the ACE framework[2]. Some researchers have further considered named entity recognition from a more general perspective. Evans [Evans, 2003], for example, considers a totally unsupervised approach in which the classes or concepts themselves are derived from the underlying text collection.

In general, research in information extraction and named entity recognition has been so far limited on a few classes of named entities as well as templates consisting of only a few slots. When moving to larger numbers of classes or slots to extract as specified by an ontology, current techniques face a serious scalability problem. Supervised approaches are especially affected by this problem as it is unfeasible to assume training data in the magnitude of hundreds of tagged examples.

3.4 Contribution and Scope of the Book

After having discussed the current state-of-the-art in ontology learning, we will now describe the contribution and scope of the book. But first of all, let us take stock and reflect on the current state-of-the-art. We have seen that there has already been a lot of work with respect to concept formation and concept hierarchy induction. However, on the one hand, we observe that there has not been much comparative work systematically analyzing different techniques and algorithms. Such a systematic analysis is however indispensable for ontology engineers needing guidelines about what learning techniques to apply for which purpose. On the other hand, there is almost no work aiming at combining different learning paradigms. However, as ontology learning from text is a highly error-prone process, it seems clear that the success of ontology learning from text lies exactly in the combination of different techniques to compensate for each other's erroneous predictions, thus increasing the overall accuracy. We summarize the main contributions and the scope of the book in the following.

---

[2] http://www.itl.nist.gov/iad/894.01/tests/ace/

Comparison and Combination of Techniques

We address both of the above issues in Chapter 6. Section 6.2 addresses the lack of comparative work in the field of concept hierarchy induction by defining an evaluation methodology and systematically comparing different clustering approaches with respect to the defined methodology. Furthermore, the book also presents innovative approaches to combine different learning paradigms examining, on the one hand, an approach in which an agglomerative clustering algorithm is guided by taxonomic relations extracted by other means, for example by applying lexico-syntactic patterns as defined by Hearst [Hearst, 1992]. This approach is elaborated in detail in Section 6.3. On the other hand, we also exploit a machine-learning approach to weight the evidences contributed by different paradigms. This approach is discussed in detail in Section 6.4.

Learning Relations

Our discussion of the state-of-the-art has also shown that there has not been much work on the acquisition of relations. In this book, we advance the state-of-the-art in three respects by developing novel approaches to learn attributes, determining the appropriate domain and range for relations with respect to a given concept hierarchy and deriving specific relations frequently occurring in any ontology. These approaches are described in Chapter 7. In particular, we describe an approach to learn attributes on the basis of the analysis of the adjectival modification of nouns (see Chapter 7.2). In Section 7.3, we examine different statistical measures for the task of finding the right level of abstraction when specifying the domain and range of a relation with respect to a given concept hierarchy. In Section 7.4, an approach to automatically learning so called *qualia structures* from the Web is described. This approach can be seen as a basis for learning a specific set of relations related to the purpose, origin as well as components of a given object.

Population of Ontologies

Concerning the population of ontologies, it has become clear from our discussion of the state-of-the-art that current methods do not scale to large numbers of concepts as specified within an ontology. The main aim of this book is to tackle this issue and present methods which are able to classify named entities appearing in texts with respect to hundreds of ontological categories. We discuss these approaches in Chapter 8. Two different approaches addressing this task are presented. Section 8.2 presents an unsupervised corpus-based approach in which instances are assigned to the concept sharing the most similar context, thus relying on some sort of memory-based learning [Daelemans et al., 1999b]. In particular, the focus is to explore the influence of different parameters and further extensions of such a similarity-based approach. Section 8.3 presents a learning paradigm called *Learning by*

Googling as well as a concrete instantiation of this paradigm called PANKOW (Pattern-based Annotation through Knowledge on the Web). The core idea of PANKOW is to match lexico-syntactic patterns on the WWW using a standard search engine. The results of these patterns are then aggregated to find an appropriate concept for a given instance. In this way, semantic annotations are approximated by analyzing the occurrences on the Web of certain syntactic structures indicating a semantic relation of interest.

Each of the above described main chapters 6, 7 and 8 are structured in the same way, giving first an overview of the common approaches applied to the task in question. Then, each chapter presents the methods developed. After describing other related approaches, each of these chapters concludes with a summary of the contributions and a brief discussion of open issues.

Applications

As already mentioned in the introduction, there is also a lack of task-based evaluation of ontologies. This lack is even clearer with respect to the evaluation of the benefit of ontology learning techniques for certain applications. In fact, it is our belief that the full benefit of ontologies for certain applications will only unleash if we have a set of techniques for automatically learning ontologies available, allowing to experiment with different parameters and to tune the learned ontologies for the application of interest. In this line, we address the task-based evaluation of ontologies and discuss applications for automatically learned ontologies within document clustering and classification tasks in Chapter 9, Section 9.1. We also discuss the application of methods for automatically populating an ontology in the context of information retrieval tasks (compare Section 9.2).

Formalization of Tasks

Last but not least, describing the different approaches and corresponding evaluation measures requires a formalization of the ontology model and the different ontology learning tasks. The formalization of the ontology model in Chapter 2 and of the ontology learning tasks presented in this chapter also represent an important contribution to the field. We hope in this line that our formalization might foster agreement within the ontology learning community.

Scope

In general, the book is mainly concerned with algorithmic and methodical aspects of ontology learning as well as with their evaluation and application. It completely neglects methodological issues related to the application of ontology learning techniques within knowledge acquisition or knowledge engineering processes. For this reason, it does not address very important conceptual, technical and legal issues involved in the acquisition of relevant documents for a certain domain. It also glosses over methodological aspects concerned with the integration of ontology learning into a concrete knowledge engineering methodology such as the ones presented in [Uschold, 1996], [Holsapple and Joshi, 2002], [Sure, 2003] and [Pinto et al., 2004]. Work addressing methodological issues can be found, for example, in [Aussenac-Gilles et al., 2000], [Mädche, 2002] or [Park, 2004].

The book is not concerned with philosophical, psychological or cognitive aspects related to knowledge representation, ontologies or ontology learning. It is neither concerned with the philosophical, psychological or cognitive issues related to the representation, definition or acquisition of concepts or knowledge in general. The interested reader is referred to Fodor [Fodor, 1998]. It does neither deal with philosophico-linguistic aspects of ontology learning from text nor with the inherent relation between language and ontology. We refer the interested reader to the work of Bateman [Bateman, 1995] as a starting point for further research.

4

Basics

In this chapter, we review basic formalisms and techniques which are necessary for the understanding of the remaining chapters of the book. First, we give an overview of the natural language processing techniques applied in the context of the experiments reported. In particular, we show how such techniques can be applied to extract features on the basis of which to describe and cluster words. Second, we introduce the theory of Formal Concept Analysis (FCA), which will be applied for different purposes in the remainder of the book. Finally, we also give a short description of the machine learning techniques used.

4.1 Natural Language Processing

Natural language is the primary medium by which humans communicate with each other, asking questions, expressing beliefs, desires, attitudes and commands as well as reporting events, actions and states. In general, different syntactic categories are used to refer to different types of ontological entities. Proper nouns are, for example, typically used to refer to individuals. Verbs in general express beliefs, attitudes, events, actions, states or commands, whereas nouns can be regarded as referring to classes. Determiners are typically used to pick out a set of members of a certain class, which does not always need to be concrete. Given a certain noun, say *'man'*, *'every man'* would, for example, refer to all the members of the class man, *'a man'* would refer to one non-specified element, *'some men'* would refer to some non-specified subset of the class, while *'the man'* would refer to one contextually unique man. Adjectives typically modify nouns and in general can be regarded as specifying the value of some attribute of the corresponding class. *'Green car'*, for example, states that the value of the attribute color of the car in question is *'green'*. Finally, adverbs modify verbs and describe the manner in which a certain event, action or state takes place, while prepositions followed by a noun phrase typically add some spatio-temporal conditions describing the modified entity represented by the noun or verb phrase.

Roughly speaking, we can distinguish between the following syntactic categories in natural language together with the type of entities they typically refer to:

verbs	events, states, actions, beliefs, attitudes, etc.
proper nouns	individuals
nouns	classes
adjectives	class attribute values
adverbs	description of manner
prepositional phrases	spatio-temporal conditions

It is important to mention that the above classification has to be regarded as a very rough one. Indeed, there are many exceptions to all of the above prototypical cases. Nouns can, for example, also denote events as in *the killing of John F. Kennedy*. Adjectives can also be non-attributive such as in *the alleged criminal*. However, as a rough approximation the classification can be seen as adequate for the purposes of the present work.

We have mentioned before that nouns can to some extent be seen as referring to classes of individuals. Therefore, adjectives and prepositional phrases modifying them, as well as verbs relating them should tell us something about the nature of these classes. Attributive adjectives, for example, tell us about which attributes the members of the class represented by the modified noun typically have. The expression *'green car'*, for instance, tells us that the members of a class of entities denoted by *'car'* have a color. Verbs also tell us a lot about the actions which can be performed with certain classes of entities. The sentence *'A man eats a cake'*, for example, tells us that the action denoted by *'eat'* can be performed on members of the class denoted by *'cake'* by members of the class denoted by *'man'*. This observation corresponds to what computational linguistics have called *selectional restrictions* [Ribas, 1995, Resnik, 1997, Clark and Weir, 2002]. Selectional restrictions can be seen as conditions specifying the type of classes to which certain verbs or adjectives are applicable.

We can conclude that certain natural language expressions provide us a lot of information about the nature of classes denoted by nouns. In the work presented here, we heavily exploit this observation with respect to the task of learning and populating ontologies on the basis of textual data. For this purpose, we need techniques to automatically process natural language. In the work described in this book we mainly make use of shallow text processing as well as statistical natural language processing techniques. The techniques applied are described in the following sections. For further details, the interested reader is referred to the introductions to natural language processing of Allen [Allen, 1995], Jurafsky and Martin [Jurafsky and Martin, 2000] and Carstensen et al. [Carstensen et al., 2004] (in German), as well as to

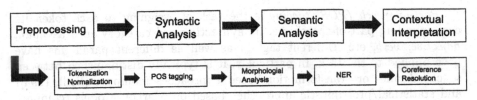

Fig. 4.1. Standard NLP pipeline

the book on statistical natural language processing by Manning and Schütze [Manning and Schütze, 1999].

4.1.1 Preprocessing

Natural language processing typically consists of the sequential application of different analysis components in a pipeline architecture as depicted in Figure 4.1. After the so-called *preprocessing* step, natural language processing systems typically produce a syntactic analysis of the input and perform a semantic analysis on the basis of the syntactic structure yielding a *logical form* (LF) of the input (compare [Allen, 1995]). The *contextual interpretation* component then interprets the logical form with respect to the context in question and taking into account pragmatic factors, that is, factors related to the intended meaning of the input. We will understand the preprocessing step rather loosely and regard it as consisting of the following substeps (not necessarily applied in this order):

- tokenization and normalization
- part-of-speech (POS) tagging
- lemmatization / stemming / morphological analysis
- named entity recognition (NER)
- coreference resolution

The purpose of the *tokenization* step is to detect sentence as well as word boundaries. Problems here are, for example, punctuation signs such as periods, which can either denote the end of a sentence, the end of an abbreviation such as '*Ltd.*', or can be used in the specification of dates, times, telephone numbers, ordinal numbers, etc. A further problem is that blanks do not always indicate word boundaries as it is the case for many named entities such as *New York*. Thus it would sometimes be useful to apply named entity recognition (see below) before actually performing tokenization.

The *normalization* step typically consists of finding dates, times, etc. and transforming them into a standard format. Sometimes, normalization also comprises the expansion of abbreviations, for which a corresponding abbreviation lexicon is needed. For more details about tokenization and normalization the reader is referred to the book of Manning and Schütze [Manning and Schütze, 1999].

Part-of-speech (POS) tagging is the task of assigning to each token its corresponding part-of-speech, i.e. its syntactic word category such as *noun, adjective, verb*, etc. Different tagsets as well as different paradigms have been applied to the task. In particular, it is typically distinguished between so called rule- or transformation-based approaches (compare [Brill, 1994]) and statistical/probabilistic approaches based on Markov Models (compare [Jelinek, 1985], [Church, 1988] and [Charniak et al., 1993]).

In the work presented in this book, we apply two part-of-speech taggers. We use TreeTagger [Schmid, 1994], which is based on decision trees (see Section 4.3) as well as the Qtag tagger [Tufis and Mason, 1998]. It is interesting to note that state-of-the-art taggers such as TreeTagger achieve a tagging accuracy between 95% and 97%, i.e. on average between 95 and 97 words out of 100 get assigned the correct syntactic category.

We also apply a lexicon-based *lemmatization* approach, i.e. we look up the lemma for nouns and verbs in the lexicon provided with the LoPar parser (see below). Lemmatization is typically applied as a normalization step, mapping morphological variants to their corresponding baseform. In our experiments, we neither apply stemming, which totally removes suffixes, nor a deeper morphological analysis unveiling the internal structure of words.

Named entity recognition (NER) consists of recognizing so called named entities, i.e. names referring to unique objects in the world, such as *Germany, George W. Bush, Mount Everest, Microsoft.* Named entity recognition has been so far restricted to small numbers of classes, considering in particular the classes person, organization, location, date, etc. Named entity recognition systems first attempt to recognize and classify named entities appearing in a text by a look-up in so called *gazetteer lists.* These gazetteer lists contain names as well as their corresponding type, class or tag. For new named entities which do not appear in such gazetteer lists, obviously more sophisticated approaches are needed. For this purpose, mainly supervised systems trained on the above mentioned classes have been used in the context of the information extraction contests organized under the auspices of the Message Understanding Conferences (MUC). We discuss the named entity recognition task as well as its relation to ontology population in more detail in Section 8.2.

Coreference resolution is often also seen as a preprocessing step. However, here we are referring to a very simple sort of coreference, i.e. the coreference relation between named entities. State-of-the-art systems are for example able to recognize that *John Adams, J. Adams* and *Mr. Adams* refer to one and the same real-world entity. Other sorts of coreference relations discovered by anaphora resolution algorithms or complex discourse inferences such as described in [Cimiano, 2003, Cimiano et al., 2005d] are typically not regarded as a preprocessing task. We do not apply techniques to detect coreferring named entities. However, we apply pronoun resolution techniques to increase the contextual information about named entities or nouns (compare Section 8.2).

4.1.2 Syntactic Analysis: Chunking

Chunking, also called *shallow* or *partial parsing*, applies shallow processing techniques (typically regular expressions and finite automata) to group together words to larger syntactic and meaning-bearing constituents, typically with a head which is modified by other words in the unit. A head is the main meaning-bearing unit within a syntactic constituent. The verb is the main meaning-bearing unit of a verb phrase and therefore its head. The main meaning-bearing word within an English noun phrase is typically the rightmost noun. In *'the exciting modern art museum'*, *'museum'* is certainly the main meaning-bearing word of the constituent, while the other words are essentially modifiers with a meaning-restricting function.

Syntactic units are generally called *chunks*. Chunks are non-overlapping, non-recursive, and non-exhaustive. Non-recursive means that chunks are not embedded within other chunks and non-exhaustive means that there may be words in a sentence which do not belong to a chunk. Chunkers or shallow parsers thus discover islands of words which build a syntactic unit. Typically, chunkers apply finite state technologies in so called cascades, where the output of one level forms the input to the next, thus being able to reuse groups of words detected in earlier phases. Chunkers typically proceed by first detecting the straightforward units and then proceeding to more complex ones. In general, chunkers do not discover grammatical relations such as subject, object, complementation or modification. Furthermore, they adopt a conservative strategy and tend to avoid producing errors, so most of the chunkers available do not attempt to resolve semantic or syntactic ambiguities. Syntactic ambiguities arise in case there is more than one possible syntactic structure for a given sentence. So called *PP-attachment ambiguities* arise from the fact that a prepositional phrase (PP) can either modify the preceding noun phrase or verb phrase as in *'I saw the man on the hill with the telescope'*, in which *'the telescope'* could either be *'on the hill'* or used as instrument for seeing. The obvious benefits of chunkers are in fact their robustness as well as efficiency. For this purpose, they are predestined for ontology learning tasks as we need to process large amounts of texts, and full parses are not as critical as in other applications, e.g. Information Extraction (IE), Machine Translation (MT) or Question Answering (QA) due to the statistical nature of the techniques applied.

In the work presented here, we either use self-created very simple chunkers (comprising a set of regular expressions) or use Steven Abney's chunker CASS [Abney, 1996]. The results of CASS on the input sentence *'The man caught the butterfly with the net'* is shown in Figure 4.2.

It is interesting to see that, while CASS has recognized the noun phrases *'The man'*, *'the butterfly'* as well as the prepositional phrase *'with the net'*, it has not attempted to resolve the PP-attachment ambiguity by either attaching the PP to the noun phrase *'the butterfly'* or the verb phrase.

```
<s>
  [c
    [c0
      [nx
        [dt The]
        [nn man]]
      [vx
        [vbd caught]]]
    [nx
      [dt the]
      [nn butterfly]]
    [pp
      [in with]
      [nx
        [dt the]
        [nn net]]]]
  [per .]
</s>
```

Fig. 4.2. Chunking produced by CASS for *The man caught the butterfly with the net.*

4.1.3 Syntactic Analysis: Parsing

Parsing, in contrast to chunking, aims at unveiling the full syntactic structure of a given input sentence. Syntactic structure is hereby represented using two main different paradigms: dependency grammars or phrase structure grammars. While syntactic dependencies are represented differently in both paradigms, they both aim at discovering larger coherent syntactic units of words, i.e. phrases, and make their dependency relations explicit. Figure 4.3 shows a typical parse tree as produced by a phrase structure grammar for the sentence *'The man caught the butterfly with the net.'* Notice that here the prepositional phrase *'with the net'* is correctly attached to the verb phrase (VP).

The search space for parsers is typically so large that there is no parser which can avoid exploring different alternatives at some stage. Furthermore, the larger grammars get, the more ambiguities a parser has to deal with, typically leading to an overwhelming number of parses per sentence. This is exactly the sort of complexity which is avoided when using chunk parsing. Most of the parsers used in the NLP community use a context-free backbone. An extension of context-free-grammars are so called unification grammars, which allow to model subcategorization as well as gender and number agreement in an elegant way, without leading to the proliferation of grammar rules (compare [Kamp and Reyle, 1993]). Another extension are lexicalized grammars, which assume a richly structured lexicon, thus being able to reduce the number of grammar rules by modeling certain phenomena in the lexicon. Examples for unification-based and lexicalized grammars are Lexical Func-

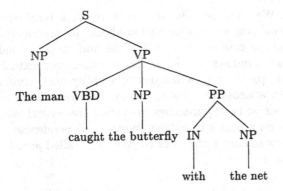

Fig. 4.3. Parse tree for *The man caught the butterfly with the net.*

tional Grammar (LFG) [Bresnan, 1994] as well as Head-driven Phrase Structure Grammar (HPSG) [Pollard and Sag, 1994] or Lexicalized Tree-Adjoining Grammars [Joshi and Schabes, 1997]. We have used LoPar[1], a statistical left-corner parser [Graham et al., 1980] developed at the Institute for Computational Linguistics of the University of Stuttgart [Schmid, 2000]. LoPar is a parser for probabilistic context-free grammars (PCFGs) a well as head-lexicalized probabilistic context-free grammars (HPCFGs). In particular, it produces a syntax tree corresponding to the most probable parse tree with respect to the probabilities specified in the probabilistic context-free grammar. For details about the algorithm the interested reader is referred to Schmid [Schmid, 2000].

4.1.4 Contextual Features

For many applications in NLP, it is crucial to represent the context of a certain word. This is important for word sense disambiguation, i.e. the task of finding the correct meaning of a word given its context (see [Ide and Veronis, 1998] for a detailed introduction to word sense disambiguation (WSD)). There are for example ambiguous words such as *'bank'*, which has two meanings: one in the sense of financial institute and one in the sense of a river bank. The correct meaning of such an ambiguous word can only be determined with respect to a certain context. Therefore, it is crucial for word sense disambiguation systems to represent the context of a word in some way (compare [Widdows, 2003a]).

A lot of work has considered word window models, in which n words to the left and right of the target word are considered as features to describe the context of a term. Though this is a valid approach, it is unclear in how far all these words within a window indeed tell us something about the nature

---

[1] http://www.ims.uni-stuttgart.de/projekte/gramotron/SOFTWARE/
LoPar-en.html

of the target word. We have seen above that there are several constructs in natural language conveying more information about the arguments or words they modify. This is the case of verbs, adjectives and prepositional phrases. Instead of using word windows as a basis for extracting contextual features, we rely on linguistic processing techniques to identify such constructs and transform them into appropriate contextual features describing a term. In what follows, we describe two approaches to extract contextual features. The first approach relies on a parser to extract syntactic dependencies, while the second applies shallow parsing techniques to extract so called *pseudo-syntactic* or *surface dependencies*.

4.1.4.1 Syntactic Dependencies

One possibility for extracting contextual features describing a term is to parse the text collection and extract syntactic dependencies between a verb and its subject, object and PP-complement from the corresponding parse trees by using tgrep[2]. In essence, tgrep provides support for searching certain paths in trees. The verbs can also be lemmatized. As mentioned above, lemmatization maps a word to its base form and may be used to normalize the text. Consider for instance the following two sentences:

The museum houses an impressive collection of medieval and modern art. The building combines geometric abstraction with classical references that allude to the Roman influence on the region.

After parsing these sentences, we would extract the following syntactic dependencies:

```
houses_subj(museum)
houses_obj(collection)
combines_subj(building)
combines_obj(abstraction)
combines_with(references)
allude_to(influence)
```

By the lemmatization step, *'references'* is mapped to its base form *'reference'* and *'combines'* and *'houses'* to *'combine'* and *'house'*, respectively, resulting in:

```
house_subj(museum)
house_obj(collection)
combine_subj(building)
combine_obj(abstraction)
combine_with(reference)
allude_to(influence)
```

---

[2] see http://mccawley.cogsci.uiuc.edu/corpora/treebank3.html

4.1.4.2 Pseudo-syntactic Dependencies

Another approach to extract contextual features is to apply a shallow parsing strategy and match certain regular expressions in the text to extract the syntactic dependencies. These dependencies are not really syntactical as they are not obtained from parse trees, but with a very shallow and heuristic method consisting of matching certain regular expressions over part-of-speech tags. The motivation for doing this is the observation of Grefenstette [Grefenstette, 1994] that the quality of using word windows or syntactic dependencies for distributional analysis depends on the rank or frequency of the word in question. Our intention is to make a compromise between using word windows and syntactic dependencies extracted from parse trees. Our pseudo-syntactic dependencies are surface dependencies extracted by matching regular expressions. In what follows, we list the syntactic expressions we use and give examples of object–attribute pairs extracted in predicate notation $a(o)$, where a is the attribute and o the object:

- adjective modifiers, i.e. *a nice city* → nice(city)
- prepositional phrase modifiers, i.e. *a city near the river* → near_river(city) and city_near(river), respectively
- possessive modifiers, i.e. *the city's center* → has_center(city)
- noun phrases in subject or object position. i.e. *the city offers an exciting nightlife* → offer_subj (city) and offer_obj(nightlife)
- prepositional phrases following a verb, i.e. *the river flows through the city* → flows_through(city)
- copula constructs[3] i.e. *a flamingo is a bird* → is_bird(flamingo)
- verb phrases with the verb *to have*, i.e. *every country has a capital* → has_capital(country)

Considering the above example sentences, we would extract the following dependencies:

```
house_subj(museum)
house_obj(collection)
impressive(collection)
combine_subj(building)
combine_obj(abstraction)
geometric(abstraction)
combine_with(reference)
classical(reference)
allude_to(influence)
roman(influence)
influence_on(region)
on_region(influence)
```

---

[3] A copula is a verb which links a subject to an object, an adjective or a constituent denoting a property of the subject.

Our approach based on syntactic dependencies relies on very simple attachment heuristics and attaches a prepositional phrase to the verb or noun phrase immediately preceding it.

4.1.5 Similarity and the Vector Space Model

Very important for ontology learning is the fact that context may be used as a basis on which to assess the similarity of words. This is formulated by the so called *distributional hypothesis* claiming that words are similar to the extent that they share similar context [Harris, 1968]. This hypothesis is also in line with Firth's well known statement that *'you shall know a word by the company it keeps'* [Firth, 1957]. In fact, empirical investigations corroborate the validity of the above hypothesis. Miller and Charles [Miller and Charles, 1991], for example, found in several experiments that humans determine the semantic similarity of words on the basis of the similarity of the contexts they are used in. Grefenstette [Grefenstette, 1994] further shows that similarity in vector space correlates well with semantic relatedness of words. The fact that semantic similarity of words can be approximated by their contextual similarity is a key assumption for most of the work in ontology learning. A crucial question in this respect is how to represent the context of a certain word.

Context is often represented as vector in high dimensional space $\mathbb{R}^n$, the dimensions corresponding to words found in the context of the word in question. This vector-based context representation constitutes the core of the so called *vector space model* used in information retrieval [Salton and McGill, 1983, Baeza-Yates and Ribeiro-Neto, 1999]. For further details on the vector-space model, the interested reader is referred to the enjoyable and instructive book of Widdows [Widdows, 2004], which contains information about the mathematical and historical background of the vector-space model as well as about interesting applications for natural language processing and information retrieval.

In general, what exactly is considered as the context of a word is a debatable question and can either be the whole document, such as described by Lesk or Salton [Lesk, 1969, Salton, 1971], words to the left and right of the word within a given window size (compare [Hearst and Schütze, 1993, Yarowsky, 1995, Schütze and Pedersen, 1997, Widdows, 2003b]), or specific grammatical constructs such as appositions, copulas, verb–object, verb–subject, adjective modifiers, nominal modifiers, etc. as in the work of Hindle [Hindle, 1990], Grefenstette [Grefenstette, 1994] or Caraballo [Caraballo, 1999].

While using words occurring in the same document yields very large vectors which are time-intensive to process, using only words with a grammatical relation to the target word yields much sparser context vectors which are easier and more efficient to process. Some people have also applied dimension reduction techniques like latent semantic indexing (LSI) [Landauer and Dumais, 1997], thus yielding smaller vectors which can be processed more efficiently [Schütze, 1993, Hearst and Schütze, 1993, Widdows, 2003b].

Context vectors as described above allow for comparing the contexts of different words and thus provide a basis for the assessment of the similarity or relatedness of two words. Thus, a lot of research in NLP has been devoted to the definition and analysis of different similarity measures (compare [Lee, 1999]). In the following section, we introduce some of the most common similarity measures used in NLP research. We distinguish between measures based on binary vectors, geometric measures as well as measures comparing probability distributions.

In what follows, we define what similarity and distance measures are and discuss some of their properties:

Definition 12 (Similarity Measure) *A similarity measure sim is a function* $sim : \mathbb{R}^n \times \mathbb{R}^n \to [0,1]$ *with the following properties:*

$$\forall v_1, v_2 \in \mathbb{R}^n \, sim(v_1, v_2) = 0 \text{ iff } v_1 \cdot v_2 = 0 \qquad (4.1)$$

$$\forall v_1, v_2 \in \mathbb{R}^n \, sim(v_1, v_2) > 0 \text{ iff } v_1 \cdot v_2 > 0 \qquad (4.2)$$

$$\forall v \, sim(v, v) = 1 \qquad (4.3)$$

Translated to a feature-based model, the first condition means that the similarity between two vectors is zero in case there is no dimension in which both have a non-zero value, i.e. they have no features in common. Conversely, the similarity will be greater than zero in case the vectors have at least one common feature, i.e. a dimension for which both vectors have non-zero values. In addition, a vector is maximally similar to itself.

It is important to emphasize that not every similarity measure needs to be symmetric (c.f. [France, 1994]). We will speak of a symmetric similarity measure in case the following condition holds:

$$\forall v_1, v_2 \, sim(v_1, v_2) = sim(v_2, v_1) \qquad (4.4)$$

In what follows, we also consider distance measures.

Definition 13 (Distance Measure) *A distance measure is a function* $dist : \mathbb{R}^n \times \mathbb{R}^n \to \mathbb{R}_0^+$ *with the following property:*
$\forall v \, dist(v, v) = 0$ *i.e. the distance of a vector to itself is 0.*

Definition 14 (Metric) *A distance measure is a metric if the following conditions hold:*
$\forall v_1, v_2 \in \mathbb{R}^n \, dist(v_1, v_2) = 0 \to v_1 = v_2$
$\forall v_1, v_2 \in \mathbb{R}^n \, dist(v_1, v_2) = dist(v_2, v_1)$ *(Symmetry)*
$\forall v_1, v_2, v_3 \in \mathbb{R}^n \, dist(v_1, v_2) + dist(v_2, v_3) \geq dist(v_1, v_3)$ *(Triangle Inequality)*

A distance measure *dist* can be transformed to a similarity measure *sim* by a bijective and monotonic decreasing function $f(dist)$. Examples for such functions are:

$$sim(x,y) = \frac{1}{1 + dist(x,y)} \qquad (4.5)$$

$$sim(x,y) = \begin{cases} -ln(dist(x,y)) & \text{if } dist(x,y) > 0 \\ 1 & \text{if } dist(x,y) = 0 \end{cases} \qquad (4.6)$$

$$sim(x,y) = e^{-dist(x,y)} \qquad (4.7)$$

In particular, the transformation function from a distance to a similarity measure needs to fulfill the following conditions:

$$dist(x,y) = +\infty \leftrightarrow sim(x,y) = 0 \qquad (4.8)$$

$$dist(x,y) = 0 \leftrightarrow sim(x,y) = 1 \qquad (4.9)$$

The above definition presupposes the introduction of a special symbol $+\infty$. Alternatively, we can also rely on the maximal distance *maxdist* and use the following transformation function:

$$sim(x,y) = 1 - \frac{dist(x,y)}{maxdist} \qquad (4.10)$$

Moreover, we can also use the following simple transformation function:

$$f(dist(x,y)) = k - dist(x,y) \qquad (4.11)$$

where k is an appropriate constant. Strictly speaking, the outcome is not a similarity measure as it is not bound to the interval [0,1]. However, it often suffices for the relative comparison of different similarity values. This simple transformation will be used in the experiments described in Chapter 6.2.

4.1.5.1 Binary Similarity Measures

One of the most well-known measures for assessing the similarity between binary vectors, i.e. containing only the values 0 and 1, are the *Dice* and *Jaccard* coefficient. The DICE coefficient is defined as:

$$Dice(\mathbf{x},\mathbf{y}) = \frac{2\, \mathbf{x} \cdot \mathbf{y}}{<\mathbf{x}> + <\mathbf{y}>} = \frac{2\sum_{i=1}^{n} x_i y_i}{\sum_{i=1}^{n} x_i + \sum_{i=1}^{n} y_i} \qquad (4.12)$$

or more easily formulated for sets X,Y containing the non-zero dimensions of the vectors $\mathbf{x}$ and $\mathbf{y}$, respectively:

$$Dice(X,Y) = \frac{2\,|X \cap Y|}{|X| + |Y|} \qquad (4.13)$$

The Jaccard or Tanimoto coefficient is defined as follows:

$$Jaccard(\mathbf{x}, \mathbf{y}) = \frac{\mathbf{x} \cdot \mathbf{y}}{<\mathbf{x}> + <\mathbf{y}> - \mathbf{x} \cdot \mathbf{y}} = \frac{\sum_{i=1}^{n} x_i y_i}{\sum_{i=1}^{n} x_i + \sum_{i=1}^{n} y_i - \sum_{i=1}^{n} x_i y_i} \quad (4.14)$$

again more easily formulated for sets X,Y containing the non-zero dimensions of the vectors $\mathbf{x}$ and $\mathbf{y}$ as follows:

$$Jaccard(X, Y) = \frac{|X \cap Y|}{|X \cup Y|} \quad (4.15)$$

4.1.5.2 Geometric Similarity Measures

The most well-known geometric similarity measure is definitely the *cosine* of the angle between two vectors. It ranges from 1 for vectors pointing in the same direction, over 0 for orthogonal vectors to −1 for vectors pointing in opposite directions. In text mining applications, where the dimensions of the vectors correspond to word frequency counts, the vectors never point in opposite directions. The cosine is defined as follows:

$$cos(\mathbf{x}, \mathbf{y}) = \frac{\mathbf{x} \cdot \mathbf{y}}{|\mathbf{x}||\mathbf{y}|} = \frac{\sum_{i=1}^{n} x_i y_i}{\sqrt{\sum_{i=1}^{n} x_i^2} \sqrt{\sum_{i=1}^{n} y_i^2}} \quad (4.16)$$

Furthermore, one can also assess the similarity between vectors as the distance between their end points as done by the L_q- or *Minkowski-measure*:

$$L_q(\mathbf{x}, \mathbf{y}) = \sqrt[q]{\sum_{i=1}^{n} |x_i - y_i|^q} \quad (4.17)$$

In particular, for $q = 1$ this formula yields the L_1-norm, *Manhattan* or *Taxicab* metric:

$$L_1(\mathbf{x}, \mathbf{y}) = \sum_{i=1}^{n} |x_i - y_i| \quad (4.18)$$

For $q = 2$ we get the L_2-norm or *Euclidean distance*, i.e.

$$L_2(\mathbf{x}, \mathbf{y}) = |\mathbf{x} - \mathbf{y}| = \sqrt{\sum_{i=1}^{n} |x_i - y_i|^2} \quad (4.19)$$

4.1.5.3 Measures based on Probability Distributions

In this section, we introduce measures based on probability distributions, i.e. *relative entropy, mutual information, pointwise mutual information* as well as the *Jensen-Shannon* (JS) and *Skew* divergences (SD). But before, we introduce basic notions of probability theory.

Probability theory deals with events as well as the probability that they occur. The set of possible events is typically represented as Ω. This set is typically also called *event space*. The probability that a subset of events of Ω actually takes place is captured by a *probability function* $P : 2^{\Omega} \to [0,1]$.

Probability functions obey the following basic rules:

$$P(A \in \Omega) \geq 0 \tag{4.20}$$
$$P(A \in \Omega) \leq 1 \tag{4.21}$$
$$P(\Omega) = 1 \tag{4.22}$$
$$P(\bigcup_i A_i \in \Omega) = \sum_i P(A_i) \text{ in case the } A_i's \text{ are disjoint} \tag{4.23}$$

Let us consider the rolling of a dice as an example. In particular, we have the following event space: $\Omega = \{1,2,3,4,5,6\}$. For each event in this event space we have a probability of $p = \frac{1}{6}$. Further, the probability of getting an odd number is $P(\{1,3,5\}) := P(1) + P(3) + P(5) = \frac{3}{6} = \frac{1}{2}$.

Sometimes we have partial knowledge about the probability of some event given that some other event occurs. This is captured by the notion of conditional probability. The conditional probability of an event A given that an event B has occurred is:

$$P(A|B) = \frac{P(A \cap B)}{P(B)} \tag{4.24}$$

An important theorem in this context is *Bayes' theorem* which allows to swap the order of dependence between events as follows:

$$P(B|A) = \frac{P(B \cap A)}{P(A)} = \frac{P(A|B)\ P(B)}{P(A)} \tag{4.25}$$

Instead of using concrete event spaces, often so called *random variables* are used. A *random variable* is essentially a function $X : \Omega \to \mathbb{R}$ and allows to talk about probabilities of numerical values related to the event space. A *discrete random variable* is a function $x : \Omega \to S$, where S is a countable subset of $\mathbb{R}$. For our dice example we have: X(1)=1, X(2)=2,... X(6)=6.

The *expectation* of a random variable distributed according to p is its mean, i.e.

$$E(X) = \sum_x x\ p(x) \tag{4.26}$$

For our dice example, we get an expectation of $E(X) = \sum_{i=1}^{6} \frac{1}{6} i = 3.5$.

The *variance* measures how much in average the variable's mean diverges from the expectation:

$$Var(X) = E((X - E(X))^2) \tag{4.27}$$

The commonly used *standard deviation* σ is the square root of the variance. For our dice example, the variance is calculated as follows:

$$\sigma^2 = \sum_x p(x)(x - E(X))^2$$
$$= \frac{1}{6} \left(2\,(2.5)^2 + 2\,(1.5)^2 + 2\,(0.5)^2\right)$$
$$= 2.92$$

The standard deviation thus is $\sigma = 1.71$.

Having defined what a random variable is, we can now define a number of measures.

First of all, *entropy*, or self-information, of a discrete random variable X distributed as the probability function $p(X)$ is its average uncertainty, i.e.

$$H(X) = - \sum_{x \in X} p(x)\,log_2\,p(x) \tag{4.28}$$

Entropy can be thought of as the average length of the message needed to transmit the outcome of that variable. For our dice example, we get in particular $H(X) = - \sum_{i=1}^{6} \frac{1}{6} log_2 \frac{1}{6} = log_2(6) = 2.58$. So we need on average 2.58 bits to encode and transmit the result of rolling a dice.

Relative Entropy or *Kullback-Leibler divergence* is a measure of how different two probability distributions (over the same event space) are:

$$D(p||q) = \sum_{x \in X} p(x)\,log_2 \frac{p(x)}{q(x)} \tag{4.29}$$

Relative Entropy measures the average number of bits wasted by encoding events from a distribution p with a code based on the distribution q. Relative Entropy can thus be seen as a distance measure between p and q.

The *Jensen-Shannon* and *Skew* divergences are defined on the basis of relative entropy:

$$JS(p,q) = \frac{1}{2}[D(p\,||\,\frac{p+q}{2}) + D(q\,||\,\frac{p+q}{2})] \tag{4.30}$$

$$SD(p,q) = D(p\,||\,\alpha \cdot p + (1-\alpha) \cdot q) \tag{4.31}$$

The latter is thus an example of an asymmetric distance measure and was introduced by Lee [Lee, 1999].

Mutual information is the reduction in uncertainty of one random variable due to knowing about another, i.e. the amount of information one random variable contains about another and is defined in terms of entropy as follows:

$$
\begin{aligned}
I(X;Y) &= H(X) - H(X|Y) \\
&= H(X) + H(Y) - H(X,Y) \\
&= \sum_{x,y} p(x,y) \; log \; \frac{p(x,y)}{p(x)\,p(y)}
\end{aligned}
\tag{4.32}
$$

For a detailed deduction of the above formula, the interested reader is referred to Manning and Schütze [Manning and Schütze, 1999].

Finally, the *pointwise mutual information* is calculated between two particular points in those distributions:

$$
PMI(x,y) = I(x,y) = log \; \frac{p(x,y)}{p(x)\,p(y)}
\tag{4.33}
$$

Mutual information and pointwise information can thus be seen as similarity measures between two random variables or two particular points, respectively.

4.1.6 Hypothesis Testing

Corpus-based co-occurrence counts are often sensitive to the frequency of the involved words. Thus, an interesting question in corpus statistics is whether two words occur more often together than chance would predict. Typically, statistical *hypothesis testing* is applied to the problem. Hypothesis testing involves formulating two hypotheses: H_0, the so called *null hypothesis*, and H_1, the *alternative hypothesis*. The null hypothesis typically states that the observed effect (typically difference in mean between two samples) is the result of chance. The alternative hypothesis conversely claims that the observations show a real effect. A statistical test is then performed to either reject H_0 or not to reject H_0. The statistical test then returns a p-value corresponding to the probability of wrongly rejecting the null hypothesis if it is in fact true. The smaller the p-value, the stronger is the evidence against the null hypothesis. The p-value is then compared to an acceptable significance threshold α (sometimes called an α-value). If $p \leq \alpha$, the observed effect is statistically significant, the null hypothesis is ruled out, and the alternative hypothesis is valid. When assessing the degree of association between words, the H_0 hypothesis assumes that the probability of the two words is independent of each other, i.e.

$$
P(w_1, w_2) = P(w_1)\,P(w_2)
\tag{4.34}
$$

Table 4.1. Example χ^2 2-by-2 table from [Manning and Schütze, 1999]

	A=new	$\neg A = \neg$ new
B=companies	$f(A, B) = 8$	$f(\neg A, B)) = 4667$
$\neg B = \neg$ companies	$f(A, \neg B) = 15820$	$f(\neg A, \neg B) = 14287173$

The independence hypothesis is rejected in case the observed probability is found to significantly differ from $P(w_1, w_2)$ as defined above. In what follows, we briefly describe the two most commonly applied statistical tests applied within NLP research, the Student's t-test and the χ^2-test.

4.1.6.1 The t-test

The t-test considers the mean and variance of a sample compared to a distribution with mean μ representing the null hypothesis. The test then looks at the difference between the observed and expected means, scaled by the variance of the data, and tells how likely one is to get a sample of that mean and variance assuming that the sample is drawn from a normal distribution with mean μ. In particular, the t-test calculates the following value:

$$t = \frac{\overline{x} - \mu}{\sqrt{\frac{s^2}{N}}} \tag{4.35}$$

where $\overline{x}$ is the sample mean, s^2 is the sample variance, N is the sample size and μ is the expected mean. It is important to note that the t-test assumes normally distributed data.

4.1.6.2 The χ^2-test

An alternative to the t-test, which does not assume normal probability distributions is Pearson's χ^2-test. The core of the test is the comparison of the observed frequencies in an event table as depicted in Table 4.1. The χ^2 value is now calculated as follows:

$$\chi^2 = \sum_{i,j} \frac{(O_{i,j} - E_{i,j})^2}{E_{i,j}} \tag{4.36}$$

where i ranges over the rows of the table and j over the columns; $O_{i,j}$ is the observed value in the cell (i, j) and $E_{i,j}$ is the expected value. From table 4.1, for example, we get:

$O_{1,1} = f(A, B)$=8
$O_{1,2} = f(\neg A, B))$=4667
$O_{2,1} = f(A, \neg B)$=15820

$O_{2,2} = f(\neg A, \neg B) = 14287173$

$E_{1,1} = \frac{O_{1,1}+O_{2,1}}{N} \cdot \frac{O_{1,1}+O_{1,2}}{N} = P(A) \cdot P(B)$

$E_{1,2} = \frac{O_{1,2}+O_{2,2}}{N} \cdot \frac{O_{1,1}+O_{1,2}}{N} = P(\neg A) \cdot P(B)$

$E_{2,1} = \frac{O_{1,1}+O_{2,1}}{N} \cdot \frac{O_{2,1}+O_{2,2}}{N} = P(A) \cdot P(\neg B)$

$E_{2,2} = \frac{O_{1,2}+O_{2,2}}{N} \cdot \frac{O_{2,1}+O_{2,2}}{N} = P(\neg A) \cdot P(\neg B)$

For the 2-by-2 case, the χ^2 value can be reduced to (compare [Manning and Schütze, 1999]):

$$\chi^2 = \frac{N(O_{1,1}O_{2,2} - O_{1,2}O_{2,1})^2}{(O_{1,1} + O_{1,2})(O_{1,1} + O_{2,1})(O_{1,2} + O_{2,2})(O_{2,1} + O_{2,2})} \quad (4.37)$$

where N is the number of observed events.

For our example in Table 4.1 we get for instance: $\chi^2 = 1.55$ which is not above the critical value of 3.841 at a probability level of $\alpha = 0.05$; that means, the fact that A and B occur jointly in some cases is due to chance with a high probability (compare [Manning and Schütze, 1999]). Though the χ^2 test does not assume normally distributed data, it also underlies some assumptions:

- The deviation between observed and expected values needs to be normally distributed.
- The sample should have been generated by a random process and be large enough (more than 20 or 50 samples).
- A minimum count in each cell is assumed, typically a minimum of 5.
- The observations need to be independent and finite; this means that an observation can only fall into one of a finite set of categories.
- Observations must have the same underlying distribution.

Finally, it is important to mention that χ^2 can be understood as a negative test on the unrelatedness of the variables in question. If the outcome of the test is above the critical value, then the hypothesis that the variables are unrelated has to be rejected. However, χ^2 is an undirected test, i.e. say we are considering a binary case with two variables A and B, we can neither conclude that A causes B nor that B causes A in case the test value is above the critical value.

4.1.7 Term Relevance

There are a lot of models from information retrieval to weight the relevance of a term in a corpus. The simplest way of measuring term relevance is by the absolute term frequency tf_i of a term i, i.e. the number of times a term occurs in a document collection. One refinement is to consider the relative frequency instead of the absolute one, i.e.

$$\text{rtf}_i := \frac{\text{tf}_i}{\sum_j \text{tf}_j} \tag{4.38}$$

Further, we can also look at how many times a term i occurs in a certain document j:

$$\text{tf}_{i,j} := \{n \mid i \ occurs\ n\ times\ in\ document\ j\} \tag{4.39}$$

In information retrieval, one typically also considers the number of documents df_i that term i occurs in. More formally, given a collection of documents D, df_i is defined as follows:

$$\text{df}_i := |\{d \in D \mid d \ contains\ i\}| \tag{4.40}$$

The latter is referred to as the so called *document frequency* on which the so called *inverse document frequency* builds on:

$$\text{idf}_i := log_2 \frac{|D|}{\text{df}_i} \tag{4.41}$$

where $|D|$ is the number of documents in the collection. The inverse document frequency thus penalizes terms which occur in a lot of documents. Term frequency and inverse document frequency are often combined by a family of measures known as *tf.idf*. One instance of the *tf.idf* family is the following measure:

$$\text{tf.idf}_{i,j} := \text{tf}_{i,j} \cdot \text{idf}_i \tag{4.42}$$

More elaborated and linguistically inspired approaches to discovering terms are, for example, the ones of Borrigault [Borrigault, 1992], Dagan and Church [Dagan and Church, 1995], Frantzi and Ananiadou [Frantzi and Ananiadou, 1999], Pantel and Lin [Pantel and Lin, 2001] as well as Ryu and Choi [Ryu and Choi, 2005].

Frantzi et al. [Frantzi and Ananiadou, 1999], for instance, present a method for the automatic extraction of multi-term words relying on the so called *C-value/NC-value* method. The method consists of two parts. The first part, the *C-value* method, relies on standard statistical techniques taking into particular account the frequencies of nested terms. The C-value method produces a list of terms ranked according to their 'termhood' as input for the second part, the NC-value method, which essentially reranks the terms by incorporating context information. In particular, the method aims at finding strong indicators for termhood in the context of the terms extracted with the C-value method.

Pantel and Lin [Pantel and Lin, 2001] have proposed a hybrid approach to term extraction relying on a combination of the mutual information and log-likelihood measures. In particular, they first detect two-word term candidates and then extend them with additional terms provided that their measure allows this.

Ryu and Choi [Ryu and Choi, 2005] present an information-theoretic approach to measure the relative specificity of terms by considering *inside* and *outside* information. Inside information relies on the mutual information of the term components and is used to calculate the relative specificity of two terms, of which one is nested in the other, while the outside information takes into account words occurring in the context of a term as in the NC-value method. A hybrid approach combining both types of information is also presented.

4.1.8 WordNet

WordNet [Fellbaum, 1998] is a lexical database for the English language developed by the Cognitive Science Laboratory in Princeton since 1985. In contrast to standard thesauri, WordNet distinguishes between a word form and its meaning by introducing so called *synsets* consisting of words sharing a common meaning in some context. WordNet provides information for four part-of-speeches: nouns, adjectives, verbs and adverbs. In the work described in this book, we only consider the WordNet information for nouns and adjectives. WordNet specifies a number of lexical relations between words and synsets. It distinguishes in particular the following relations:

- *Synonyms* are words which in a certain context have the same meaning. They provide the basis for WordNet's meaning unit, i.e. the synset.
- The *hypernymy* relation is defined on synsets. In particular, a synset s_1 is a hypernym of s_2 if the meaning of s_1 subsumes the one of s_2. The inverse relation is called *hyponymy*.
- The *meronymy* relation holds between a synset s_1 and a synset s_2, i.e. s_1 is a meronym of s_2 if s_1 denotes a part or member of s_2. The inverse relation is called *holonymy*.
- *Antonymy* is the relation between synsets which have opposite meaning.

Further, it distinguishes the following relations between adjectives:

- *Similar to* relates adjectives to similar adjectives, e.g. *big* to *great*.
- *Attribute* relates adjectives to the quality or attribute they describe, e.g *big* to *size*.
- By *antonymy*, adjectives are also related to adjectives with opposite meaning, e.g. *big* to *small*.
- *Derivationally related* gives words from other parts of speech to which the adjective is derivationally related, e.g. *big* to *bigness*.

Table 4.2 gives some examples for relations between nouns as contained in WordNet, and Figure 4.4 depicts graphically the structure of WordNet on the basis of an example.

Let us further introduce the following properties of relations:

Table 4.2. Examples for lexical relations in WordNet

Type	Paraphrase	Example
Synonym	means the same as	"illness means the same as disease" ⇒ *synonym(disease,illness)*
Hypernym	is the general term for	"furniture is the general term for chair" ⇒ *hypernym(furniture, chair)*
Hyponym	is a kind of	"a chair is a kind of furniture" ⇒ *hyponym(chair, furniture)*
Meronym	is part	"a branch is a part of a tree" ⇒ *meronym(branch, tree)*
	substance/	"wood is the substance of a tree" ⇒ *meronym(wood, tree)*
	member of	"a person is member of a group" ⇒ *meronym(person, group)*
Holonym	has part/	"a bicycle has a wheel as part" ⇒ *holonym(bicycle,wheel)*
	substance/	"a tree has wood as substance" ⇒ *holonym(tree, wood)*
	member	"a group has a person as member" ⇒ *holonym(group, person)*
Antonym	is the contrary of	"ascent is the contrary of descent" ⇒ *antonym(ascent, descent)*

- Two relations are *reciprocal* iff there is an inverse relation between them such as for the meronymy and holonymy relations, i.e. meronym(s_1, s_2) ↔ holonym(s_2, s_1).
- A relation r is *symmetric* iff $\forall x, y \; r(x,y) \leftrightarrow r(y,x)$. This applies to the *antonymy* relation, for instance, i.e. antonym(s_1, s_2) ↔ antonym(s_2, s_1).
- A relation r is *transitive* iff $\forall x, y, z \; r(x,y) \wedge r(y,z) \rightarrow r(x,z))$. This is, for example, the case of the hyponymy and hypernymy relations.

WordNet does not only contain synsets and lexical relations defined on these, but also a description of the meaning of each synset which is called *gloss*. The *glosses* can in fact be seen as the intensional description of a concept and have been used for several purposes within NLP (compare for example [Agirre and Rigau, 1996], [Resnik, 1997], [Peters, 2002], [Banerjee and Pedersen, 2003], [Navigli and Velardi, 2004]).

For the purposes of the experiments described in this book, we have used WordNet version 1.71. This version contains 107930 nouns and 74488 synsets. The average *polysemy* in WordNet is around 1.22, i.e. a word has on average 1.22 different meanings.

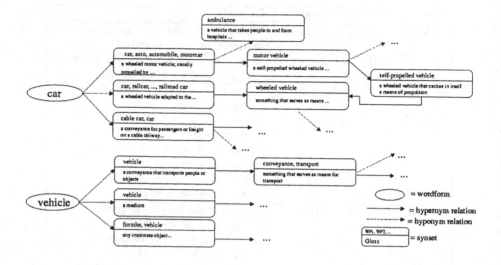

Fig. 4.4. The structure of WordNet

4.2 Formal Concept Analysis

In Section 2, we already briefly discussed Aristotle's notion of *differentiae*, i.e. characteristics which allow to either group objects or distinguish them from each other. In fact, Aristotle already noticed the inverse connection between objects and their characteristics, namely that the more characteristics we require, the less objects will fulfill these, and the more objects we consider, the less common characteristics they will share. This intuitive duality has been formalized as a so called *Galois connection* and represents the core of Formal Concept Analysis (FCA) (compare [Wille, 1982]). Galois connections can in fact be seen as a formalization of Aristotle's notion of differentiae. In the theory of Formal Concept Analysis, objects are represented by so called *formal objects*, and their characteristics are represented by *formal attributes*. The information about which attributes hold for each object is then represented via a binary relation called the *incidence relation*. The formal objects and attributes as well as the incidence relation then constitute a so called *formal context*.

Table 4.4 shows an example formal context. Let us suppose that the various attributes have been automatically extracted from a corpus using the syntactic dependency extraction process outlined in Section 4.1.4.1. Let us further assume that only verb–object pairs have been considered and that the verbs and objects in Table 4.3 have been extracted.

Table 4.3. Example for verbs and objects extracted from a text corpus

verb	objects
book	hotel, apartment, car, bike, excursion, trip
rent	apartment, car, bike
drive	car, bike
ride	bike
join	excursion, trip

Table 4.4. Tourism domain knowledge as formal context

	bookable	rentable	driveable	rideable	joinable
hotel	x				
apartment	x	x			
car	x	x	x		
bike	x	x	x	x	
excursion	x				x
trip	x				x

In the formal context shown in Table 4.4 we have further added the suffix 'able' to each verb thus emphasizing that the corresponding attribute applies to objects on which the action denoted by the verb can be carried out. Now we can try to find *closed sets* of objects and attributes. Intuitively speaking, a set of objects O and a set of attributes A are closed with respect to each other if the attributes in A are exactly those that are common to all objects in O and, conversely, the objects in O are exactly those that have all attributes in A. Let us consider the objects *excursion* and *trip* as an example. Both share the attributes *bookable* and *joinable*, and the only objects which have both these attributes in common are actually *excursion* and *trip*. Therefore, the set of objects {*excursion, trip*} forms a closed set with respect to the attributes {*bookable, joinable*}. Having described the important notion of a closed set with an example, we now turn to a more general description of Formal Concept Analysis. Formal Concept Analysis is a method mainly used for the analysis of data. In particular, FCA finds closed sets on the basis of a formal context, thus leading to creation of coherent groups or *formal concepts* as they are called in FCA. The data as given by the formal context are hereby structured into units which are formal abstractions of concepts of human thought, allowing meaningful comprehensible interpretation (compare [Ganter and Wille, 1999]). Thus, FCA can be seen as a conceptual clustering technique as it also provides intensional descriptions for the abstract concepts or data units it produces.

Central to FCA is the notion of a *formal context*:

Definition 15 (Formal Context) *A triple (G,M,I) is called a formal context if G and M are sets and $I \subseteq G \times M$ is a binary relation between G and*

M. *The elements of G are called objects, those of M attributes and I is the incidence relation of the context.*

For $O \subseteq G$, we define: $O' := \{m \in M \mid \forall g \in O : (g,m) \in I\}$

and dually for $A \subseteq M$: $A' := \{g \in G \mid \forall m \in A : (g,m) \in I\}$

Intuitively speaking, O' is the set of all attributes common to the objects of O, whereas A' is the set of all objects that have all attributes in A. Furthermore, we define what a *formal concept* is:

Definition 16 (Formal Concept) *A pair (O,A) is a formal concept of (G,M,I) if and only if $O \subseteq G$, $A \subseteq M$, $O' = A$ and $O = A'$.*

In other words, (O,A) is a *formal concept* if the set of all attributes shared by the objects of O is identical with A, and, on the other hand, O is also the set of all objects that have all attributes in A. O is then called the *extent* and A the *intent* of the formal concept (O,A). We can now define an order between formal concepts as follows:

$$(O_1, A_1) \leq (O_2, A_2) \Leftrightarrow O_1 \subseteq O_2 (\Leftrightarrow A_2 \subseteq A_1) \tag{4.43}$$

Thus, formal concepts are partially ordered with regard to inclusion of their extents or – which is equivalent – to inverse inclusion of their intent. In fact, it can be easily shown (c.f. [Ganter and Wille, 1999]) that the subconcept-superconcept relation forms a complete lattice which will be denoted by $(\mathfrak{B}(G, M, I), \leq)$.

In our example, $(\{excursion, trip\}, \{bookable, joinable\})$ thus represents a formal concept. Other concepts are, for example, $(\{bike\}, \{rideable, driveable, rentable, bookable\})$ and $(\{car, bike\}, \{driveable, rentable, bookable\})$. Further, the formal concept $(\{bike\}, \{rideable, driveable, rentable, bookable\})$ is a subconcept of $(\{car, bike\}, \{driveable, rentable, bookable\})$.

The concept lattice for our example formal context is depicted in Figure 4.5. Each node in the lattice diagram represents a formal concept. All the white boxes below a node together represent the extent of the concept represented by that node, while the intent consists of all the gray boxes above the node. The diagram compactly visualizes the fact that attributes are inherited by the intents of all nodes downwards and that objects are also contained in the extent of all formal concepts upwards. The lattice in Figure 4.5 is visualized using *reduced labeling*. Reduced labeling as defined by Ganter and Wille [Ganter and Wille, 1999] means that objects are in the extension of the most specific concept and attributes conversely in the intension of the most general one. This reduced labeling is achieved by introducing functions γ and μ. The name of an object g is attached to the lower half of the corresponding *object concept*, i.e. $\gamma(g) := (\{g\}'', \{g\}')$, while the name of attribute m is located at the upper half of the *attribute concept*, i.e. $\mu(m) := (\{m\}', \{m\}'')$.

For the sake of completeness, in what follows we present two algorithms for computing the formal concepts of a given finite formal context. In particular,

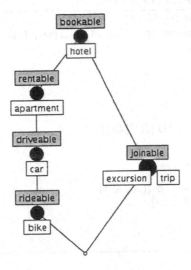

Fig. 4.5. The lattice of formal concepts for the tourism formal context

we will discuss a naive algorithm as well as the widely used algorithm of Ganter ([Ganter, 1984, Ganter and Reuter, 1991]). But before, we need to introduce a number of properties:

Theorem 1. *Let (G, M, I) be a formal context and $O_1, O_2 \subseteq G, A \subseteq M$, then the following properties hold (compare [Ganter and Wille, 1999]):*

1. $O_1 \subseteq O_2 \Rightarrow O'_2 \subseteq O'_1$
2. $O_1 \subseteq O''_1$
3. $O'_1 = O'''_1$
4. $O_1 \subseteq A' \Leftrightarrow A \subseteq O'_1$

The same relations hold for sets of formal attributes.

On the basis of this theorem, we can now formulate the naive procedure for finding all the formal concepts of a given formal context in Algorithm 1. The correctness of the algorithm follows from the definition of a formal concept and Theorem 1. In particular, a pair $(A, B) = (O'', O')$ is a formal concept as $A' = (O'')' = O' = B$ and $B' = O'' = A$. Obviously, as the algorithm needs to consider all possible subsets of objects or attributes, the above algorithm is always exponential in n, where $n = min(|M|, |G|)$. So its time complexity is $O(2^n)$. A widely used algorithm with a better complexity is Ganter's algorithm with a time complexity of $O(|G|^2 \times |M| \times |\mathfrak{B}(G, M, I)|)$. This means that Ganter's algorithm is bound by the actual number of formal concepts, which can be exponential in the worst case though. The difference is that Ganter's algorithm does not require iterating through all the subsets

---

Algorithm 1 Naive FCA Algorithm

Input: a formal context (G, M, I)
Output: a set of formal concepts $\{(O_1, A_1), ..., (O_q, A_q)\}$

$C := \emptyset$

if $(|G| < |M|)$
{
   for each $O \subseteq G$: $C := C \cup \{(O'', O')\}$
}
else
{
   for each $A \subseteq M$: $C := C \cup \{(A', A'')\}$
}

return C

---

of G or M, but is bound by the actual number of formal concepts. Ganter defines a lectic order $\prec$ on sets which is based on a total order for the sets G and M, i.e. $G = \{g_1, ..., g_u\}$ with $g_1 < ... < g_u$ and $M = \{m_1, ..., m_v\}$ with $m_1 < ... < m_v$.

The lectic order between sets is now defined as follows:

Definition 17 (Lectic Order) *Given two sets $O_1, O_2 \subseteq G$, we say that O_1 is lectically smaller than O_2 ($O_1 \prec O_2$) if the smallest element in which O_1 and O_2 differ is contained in O_2, or more formally*

$$O_1 \prec O_2 \Leftrightarrow \exists g_i \in O_2 \backslash O_1 \text{ such that}$$
$$O_1 \cap \{g_1, ..., g_{i-1}\} = O_2 \cap \{g_1, ..., g_{i-1}\}$$
$$O_1 \prec_i O_2 \Leftrightarrow g_i \in O_2 \backslash O_1 \text{ such that}$$
$$O_1 \cap \{g_1, ..., g_{i-1}\} = O_2 \cap \{g_1, ..., g_{i-1}\}$$

The definition holds analogously for attribute sets $A_1, A_2 \subseteq M$.
Now, the lectic order can be extended to formal concepts:

Definition 18 *Given two formal concepts $c_1 = (O_1, A_1)$ and $c_2 = (O_2, A_2)$, we say that c_1 is lectically smaller than c_2, i.e., $c_1 \prec c_2$, iff $O_1 \prec O_2$.*

Finally, the following two theorems build the core of Ganter's algorithm:

Theorem 2. *Let $c_1 = (O_1, A_1)$ and $c_2 = (O_2, A_2)$ be two formal concepts. Then it holds that $c_1 < c_2 \Leftrightarrow c_1 \prec_i c_2$ for some $g_i \in G$.*

This means in particular that, if c_1 is lectically smaller than c_2, then c_1 is also a subconcept of c_2. The proof can be found in the book of Ganter and Wille [Ganter and Wille, 1999]. The other crucial theorem is the following:

Theorem 3. *Given a set of objects $O_1 \subseteq G$, the smallest concept extent which is lectically greater than O_1 is $O_1 \oplus g_i$, where $O_1 \oplus g_i = ((O_1 \bigcap \{g_1, ...g_{i-1}\}) \cup \{g_i\})''$ and g_i is the greatest element in G such that $O_1 \prec_i O_1 \oplus g_i$.*

Thus, starting from a given formal concept $c_1 = (O_1, A_1)$, in order to find the next formal concept, we have to iterate over the set of objects in inverse order and identify the largest element $g_i \in G$ such that $O_1 \prec_i O_1 \oplus g_i$ holds. $O_1 \oplus g_i$ is then the extension of the lectically next formal concept. This means that the time complexity for finding the next formal concept is $O(|G|^2 \times |M|)$ as the operation $''$ has a time complexity of $O(|G| \times |M|)$, which has to be carried out at most $|G|$ times. Ganter's algorithm obviously starts with the lectically smallest formal concept, i.e. $(\emptyset'', \emptyset')$. The sketch of the procedure, which is often referred to as the *Next Closure* algorithm, is given by the pseudocode in Algorithm 2. The implementation of FCA we have used is the *concepts* tool by Christian Lindig[4], which basically implements Ganter's Next Closure algorithm with the extension of Aloui for computing the covering relation described by Godin et al. [Godin et al., 1995]. We apply this algorithm for the concept hierarchy induction task as described in Section 6.2.

Algorithm 2 Ganter's FCA Algorithm

Input: a formal context (G, M, I)
Output: a set of formal concepts $\{(O_1, A_1), ..., (O_q, A_q)\}$

$O = \emptyset''$
$C := \{(O, O')\}$
do
{
    changed:=**false**
    for g_i in G (in decreasing order $<$)
    {
        if $O \prec_i O \oplus g_i$ **AND NOT** changed
        {
            $C := C \cup \{(O \oplus g_i, (O \oplus g_i)')\}$
            $O := O \oplus g_i$
            changed = **true**
        }
    }
} **until NOT** changed
return C

---

[4] http://www.st.cs.uni-sb.de/~lindig/src/concepts.html

4.3 Machine Learning

Machine learning is concerned with the automatic recognition and detection of certain patterns and regularities within example data. Such patterns can be used to understand and describe the data or to make predictions. Machine learning is based on induction, i.e. on the idea of making inferences or generalizations from example data. Therefore, it is crucial for machine learning algorithms that examples are represented appropriately. Generally, examples are represented by a set of feature–value pairs often formalized in the form of a n-dimensional vector in real-valued space. Hereby, each dimension corresponds to one feature. Thus, given a set of examples E, each example $e \in E$ is represented by a vector $\mathbf{e} \in \mathbb{R}^n$.

In what follows, we will distinguish two types of inductive learning: *supervised* and *unsupervised*. They differ in the tasks they are applied to, but also in the learning paradigms applied.

Supervised learning is typically used for predicting the appropriate category for an example from a set of categories represented by a set of labels L. Provided that we are working on real-valued vector space, we can assume a function $l : \mathbb{R}^n \rightarrow L$ assigning each element a corresponding label. Supervised learning algorithms learn from labeled training examples. In addition to appropriate features describing the examples, supervised learning thus requires a mapping function l' from the set of training examples to a set of labels L, i.e. $l' : E \rightarrow L$. The goal of supervised learning algorithms is now to learn a mathematical function on the basis of l' approximating the function l. The crucial issue here lies in not approximating l' itself too closely to allow the function to predict the label for new examples. The trade-off between approximating the 'training' function l' too closely and thus loosing predictive power represents one of the main problems supervised machine learning algorithms have to cope with.

In unsupervised learning, however, there is no such supervision in terms of labeled examples. Thus, such algorithms search for common and frequent structures within the data. Therefore, unsupervised techniques are typically applied for data exploration.

In what follows, we survey each of these learning approaches.

4.3.1 Supervised Learning

The main application of supervised learning is prediction; that means, once a mapping is learned, new and unknown examples can be labeled. There are two types of prediction: *classification* and *regression*. We talk about classification when the labels of the training example are different categories or classes. The goal is to assign the proper category to a new example. *Binary classification* is the special case in which there are only two different classes. When the labels are continuous values, we talk about regression and the task consists in a numeric prediction.

We will use the following terminology when talking about supervised learning or machine learning, respectively. The set of *training examples* provided to the learning algorithm for learning is called *training set*. A training example is characterized by a *feature vector* and is labeled with a *target value* for the *target variable*, which is an additional feature representing the label of the example as described above.

Table 4.5 shows three training examples taken from an often cited training set (see [Witten and Frank, 1999]). The feature vectors contain the feature values for the three features: *outlook, windy*, and *temperature*. The binary target variable indicates whether the person in question would like to *play outside* given the weather conditions specified in the example.

Table 4.5. Training examples for the target variable *play outside*

example	features			target variable
	outlook	windy	temperature	play outside ?
1	sunny	false	warm	yes
2	rainy	true	cold	no
3	overcast	false	warm	yes

A learning algorithm builds a *model* for the training set, i.e. a mapping function between the feature vectors and the target values. Generally, in machine learning literature the feature vectors are called *input data*, the corresponding target values are known as *output*.

Classification is a supervised task in the sense that labeled training data is given and the task is to approximate the function which assigns an example to its correct target class. The result of learning this function from labeled training data is a classifier which can assign new examples to their class on the basis of the model derived from the training data. In order to quantify the accuracy of a model, typically a loss function is specified which quantifies the cost of misclassifying one example from one class as another. This loss function is specified as: $f : L \times L \to \mathbb{R}^+$. where L is the set of different categories. The aim of a classifier is thus to minimze the empirical risk of misclassification given by:

$$R_n(l') = \frac{1}{n} \sum_{i=1}^{n} f(l'(x_i), l(x_i))$$

where the x_i's are examples, l models the correct classification and l' is the induced classification function.

Two well-known problems encountered when training classifiers are *overfitting* and *skewed datasets*. Overfitting occurs when the learning algorithm approximates too closely the function inherent in the training data, thus loosing any generalizing power. For this reason, classifiers are never evaluated on the training dataset itself, but on held-out or test data. Another possibility is to perform a so called n-fold cross validation in which the data are split into n uniform parts and the classifier is trained n times on different subsets consisting of $n-1$ parts and evaluated on the remaining part. Cross validation is a particular type of *jackknife*, which essentially consists of sampling without replacement and is typically used to verify the statistical robustness of some model.

The second problem occurs when certain target classes are much more frequent than others. In that case, the classifier would naturally learn to always predict the majority class. For example, a system for credit card fraud detection [Stolfo et al., 1997] might apply a classifier to detect fraudulent transactions. The classifier will be learned from a training set that mainly consists of legitimate transactions and only few fraudulent transactions. Thus, a simple classifier always predicting 'legitimate' would yield an accuracy of, say, 99.9%. However, when applying such a system, a false alarm is rather acceptable, whereas an actual fraud that is not detected by the system has to be avoided.

4.3.1.1 Classifiers

There are a number of different classification paradigms, i.e. *Bayesian Classifiers, Decision Trees, Instance-Based Learning, Support Vector Machines, Artificial Neural Networks*, etc. We describe these learning paradigms briefly in the following.

Bayesian Classifiers

Statistical modeling is often also called Bayesian learning because it is based on Bayes' Theorem. Bayesian learners are probabilistic models making the simplifying assumption that all features are independent and have the same relevance. Because of this assumption, these algorithms are often called *naive* Bayesian learners. But despite their simple design, Bayesian learners outperform many more complex approaches when applied to real-world problems. Naive Bayesian learners are used for classification.

The classification with a naive Bayesian model is performed as following: Assume X denotes an unlabeled example. Let it have only the feature *color* with the value *red*. Now we want to classify this example into the categories *apple* or *banana*. H is the hypothesis that this example belongs to a certain category C, for example that it is an *apple*. The conditional probability $P(H|X)$ is the probability that our example is an apple given that it is red. With Bayes' Theorem we can calculate this probability if we know the probability that any example is an apple $P(H)$, that an example has the color red $P(X)$, and that an example has the color red if it is an apple $P(X|H)$.

$$P(H|X) = \frac{P(X|H) \cdot P(H)}{P(X)} \tag{4.44}$$

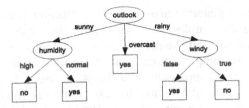

Fig. 4.6. Example for a decision tree

A Bayesian learner builds a model by estimating the probabilities $P(X)$, $P(H)$, and $P(X|H)$ from the training data. A new example is then classified by calculating the conditional probabilities $P(H|X)$ for the different categories and choosing the category with the highest probability. The interested reader is referred to [Mitchell, 1997] and [John and Langley, 1995] for further details. In our experiments, we have used the Naive Bayes implementation of WEKA [Witten and Frank, 1999].

Decision Trees

Decision trees are also models for classification. A decision tree compactly encodes a sequence of tests on the values of certain features. Each inner node of such a tree corresponds to a feature, the edges represent decisions for one of the feature's possible values. A leaf represents the predicted value of the target variable. Figure 4.6 shows a decision tree for the target variable *play outside*. The models underlying decision trees can essentially be seen as a set of Horn-like rules with the target variable as head and conditions on the features in the body.

A decision tree is constructed in an iterative way. In each step, the learning algorithm chooses one feature and creates a new branch for each of the possible feature values. At each branch, one of the remaining features is chosen. Thus, the hypothesis space is subsequently divided. The key issue in decision tree learning is which feature to chose for the next ramification. The features are generally selected by means of statistical tests. The goal is to build a tree where the features with higher discriminative power are closer to the root. There are many different algorithms for decision tree learning which employ different statistical tests and optimizations. We use the widely applied algorithm C4.5 [Quinlan, 1986] implemented in WEKA [Witten and Frank, 1999] in our experiments.

Instance-Based Learning

Instance-based learning techniques work essentially by memorizing typical examples. To categorize an unlabeled example, the classifier checks which of the stored training examples is most similar. Since instance-based learners only store some examples, learning is very efficient in contrast to other learning methods that extract general patterns and descriptions from the training set. Classification of new examples, however, is slow since the unlabeled example has to be compared with all the memorized ones. Hereby, a distance function is used to find the training examples that are most similar.

There are different approaches for instance-based learning, the most widely-used is the k-Nearest Neighbor learning method [Aha et al., 1991]. The target value is predicted corresponding to the target values of the k nearest neighbors.

Support Vector Machines

Support Vector Machines (SVMs) are used for binary classification. They are typically based on linear function models. The learning algorithm aims at creating the maximum-margin hyperplane that splits the training examples into the two classes. This hyperplane is the best discrimination between both classes and has the maximal possible distance to the training examples. The training examples that are closest to the hyperplane are called support vectors – only these are needed to finally define the hyperplane. Finding these support vectors and determining the parameters of the hyperplane is what is done by the learning algorithm. Figure 4.7 shows such a hyperplane. The training examples are represented by circles, the boldly framed ones are the support vectors.

The principle behind Support Vector Machines (SVMs) thus corresponds to a non-linear regression. The vector space is mapped into some other vector space by a non-linear transformation. A so called *kernel function* which needs to be defined then defines the dot product between vectors in the transformed vector space. In the resulting vector space a standard regression is performed to find the maximum-margin hyperplane (compare [Cristianini and Shawe-Taylor, 2000]). In the experiments described in this book, we have used the regression SVMs implemented in TextGarden [Grobelnik and Mladenic, 2006].

Artificial Neural Networks

Artificial Neural Networks (ANNs) are inspired in the human brain and consist of layers of connected artificial neurons [Rosenblatt, 1959, Minsky and Papert, 1969]. Artificial neurons have inputs from other neurons, a weighting function which weights the input of each of these neurons and an aggregation function combining all the weighted inputs. If the result of this combination is over a certain threshold, the neuron is activated and propagates the signal to some other neurons. The most well-known network architecture is the so called *feed forward* network (compare Figure 4.8), in which the neurons are organized in layers: *input, hidden* and *output*. There is no bound on the number of hidden layers or on the number of connections between neurons. In fact, many networks are indeed fully connected in the sense that each neuron

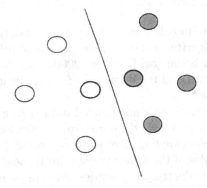

Fig. 4.7. Example for support vectors

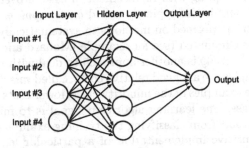

Fig. 4.8. Example for an artificial neural network

is connected to every other neuron in the next layer. The easiest neural network is the so called *Perceptron* consisting merely of an input and an output layer. The model underlying a perceptron is thus a linear one as in the case of SVMs (see before). In case there is at least one hidden layer, we talk about a Multi-Layer Perceptron (MLPER). In the *feed-forward network* the input signals are passed from one layer to the other to the output neurons. The weight of the connection between neurons is typically determined via a learning process, either supervised as in *back propagation* [Rumelhart et al., 1986] or unsupervised as in *Self-Organizing Maps (SOMs)* [Kohonen, 1995]. In back propagation, a labeled training set is needed, and the error is computed for each example in the training set, propagating the error 'backwards' from the output to the input layer, adjusting the weights at each layer to minimize this error rate (compare [Rumelhart et al., 1986]). In the context of this book, we will mainly use the implementation of the back-propagation algorithm available within WEKA [Witten and Frank, 1999].

4.3.1.2 Imbalanced Datasets

Learning in presence of imbalanced data sets is an important issue in machine learning. Learning algorithms incorporate the assumption that maximizing the (overall) accuracy is the goal [Provost, 2000]. However, this does in many cases not meet the goals and requirements of an application and thus results in unsatisfactory classifiers.

A common way to deal with imbalanced data is to artificially change the class distribution, i.e. *rebalancing* the data. Approaches for rebalancing include *oversampling* and *undersampling*. Oversampling consists in replicating some of the training examples of the minority class until the desired class distribution is reached, while undersampling implies removing some training examples of the majority class. There are several techniques for selecting the training examples that should be replicated or deleted. The method used most often is random selection (sampling with replacement in case of oversampling). Sampling with replacement is also typically called *bootstrapping*. A lot of research has been and is still performed on methods to systematically select examples to be replicated or eliminated (see for example [Monard and Batista, 2002]).

Cost-sensitive learning is another approach to deal with imbalanced data. The training examples are assigned relative costs, called *misclassification costs* – high costs for the examples of the minority class, lower costs for the examples of the majority class. The learning algorithm's goal is to minimize the total costs that would result from classifying the training examples. This approach requires a cost-sensitive implementation of a particular learning algorithm. However, appropriate oversampling can have the same effect.

Another method to improve learning in presence of imbalanced data is to vary the threshold of the classifier. Internally, learning algorithms estimate the probability that an example is assigned to a certain class. This is called the *class distribution*. The class having the highest probability is normally assigned. Thus, a binary classifier chooses that class having a probability greater than 0.5. If this value is increased for the majority class, the threshold to assign the majority class is higher and the classifier will more likely assign the minority class.

Each of the approaches presented before have limitations and drawbacks. Oversampling increases the chances for overfitting when exact copies of the training examples are made, undersampling throws away potentially useful data, misclassification costs can only be used with cost-sensitive learning algorithms, and the variation of the threshold does not result in better classifiers for many real-world applications. The question which approach works best for which learning algorithm and type of problem is still subject to recent research. For further reading see for example [Kubat and Matwin, 1997], [Provost, 2000] and [Monard and Batista, 2002].

4.3.2 Unsupervised Learning

Unsupervised learning is typically applied for the exploration of data and does not need any labeled training data. Examples for unsupervised learning techniques are clustering and algorithms for mining association rules (compare [Agrawal and Srikant, 1994]). In the context of this book, we mainly apply clustering as unsupervised learning paradigm. Clustering is generally seen as the task of finding groups or clusters of similar objects in data. It is an unsupervised approach as no classes are given a priori, and there is no labeled data to train from. Clustering approaches can be divided into *hierarchical* and *non-hierarchical* ones. In contrast to non-hierarchical algorithms, which produce a set of groups, hierarchical clustering algorithms additionally order these groups in a tree structure. Clustering algorithms can be further divided into *hard* and *soft* ones. When using a hard clustering algorithm, the assignment of an element to a cluster is functional, while for soft algorithms this assignment is not functional, i.e. typically elements are assigned to clusters with a certain degree of membership. Hierarchical and hard clustering algorithms are for example *hierarchical agglomerative clustering* or Bi-Section-KMeans (see below). KMeans is an example for a non-hierarchical clustering algorithm. Pole-based overlapping clustering (PobOC) [Cleuziou et al., 2004] and Clustering-By-Committee [Pantel and Lin, 2002a] are examples for soft clustering algorithms. In what follows, we describe different clustering algorithms relevant for the work presented in this book in more detail.

4.3.2.1 KMeans

KMeans is a non-hierarchical clustering algorithm mainly consisting of a random selection of k centroids as initialization and an iteration step in which elements are assigned to the centroid which is closest. Then cluster centroids are recomputed on the basis of this assignment (compare the pseudocode in Algorithm 3). KMeans basically implements a hill-climbing procedure which typically ends up in a local optimum. For this reason, KMeans is applied iteratively using different random initializations. Different stopping criteria can be used in combination with KMeans. On the one hand, we can stop in case the centroids or the assignment of elements to centroids do not change (both conditions are in fact equivalent). On the other hand, one can determine a number of iterations beforehand. In practice, both criteria lead to a small number of iterations, such that KMeans can be regarded indeed as a very efficient clustering algorithm. The inner loop is in fact linear in the number of clusters k. For more details the interested reader is referred to [Kaufman and Rousseeuw, 1990] or [Duda et al., 2001].

4.3.2.2 Hierarchical Clustering

Given a set of objects X to cluster, hierarchical agglomerative clustering produces a binary tree (C, E) with the nodes C representing clusters of elements

---

Algorithm 3 KMeans

Input: a set $X = \{x_1, ..., x_n\}$ of objects represented by vectors $\mathbf{x_1}, ..., \mathbf{x_n} \in \mathbb{R}^m$,
    a number of clusters $k \leq n$, as well as
    a distance measure $dist : \mathbb{R}^m \times \mathbb{R}^m \to \mathbb{R}$, and
    a function for computing the centroid of a cluster, i.e., $\mu : 2^{\mathbb{R}^m} \to \mathbb{R}^m$
Output: a set K of k cluster centroids

randomly choose k elements $f_1, ..., f_k$
repeat
    assign each element to the closest f_i with respect to $dist$, i.e.
    $c_i := \{x_j \mid \forall f_l \ dist(x_j, f_i) \leq dist(x_j, f_l)\}$
    recompute the centroids, i.e
    $f_i := \mu(c_i)$
until stopping criterion is true
return $\{f_1, ... f_k\}$

(subsets of X), and the edges $E \subseteq C \times C$ representing inclusion relations. Such a binary tree has to satisfy the following conditions:

$$\forall c, c' \in C \ (c, c') \in E \to (c', c) \notin E \ \textit{(antisymmetric)} \tag{4.45}$$

$$\forall c \in C \ (c, c) \notin E \ \textit{(non-reflexive)} \tag{4.46}$$

$$\forall c, c' \in C \ (c, c') \in E \land (c, c'') \in E \to c' = c'' \ \textit{(functional)} \tag{4.47}$$

$$\forall c \in C \ (c = r \lor \exists c' \ (c, c') \in E) \ \textit{(left total)} \tag{4.48}$$

$$\forall c, c', c'' \in C \ ((c', c) \in E \land (c'', c) \in E \to c = c' \cup c'') \ \textit{(union)} \tag{4.49}$$

$$\forall c, c' \in \ (c, c') \in E \to |c'| > |c| \ \textit{(strict monotonicity in size)} \tag{4.50}$$

$$\forall c \in C \ |c| > 0 \ \textit{(no empty clusters)} \tag{4.51}$$

$$\forall c, c', c'' \in C \ ((c', c) \in E \land (c'', c) \in E \to c' \cap c'' = \emptyset) \ \textit{(disjointness)} \tag{4.52}$$

$$\forall c \in C (\neg \exists c' (c', c) \in E) \lor (\exists c', c'' \ (c', c) \in E \land (c'', c) \in E \land c' \neq c'' \land$$
$$\forall c''' \ (c''', c) \in E \to (c''' = c' \lor c''' = c'')) \ \textit{(binary tree)} \tag{4.53}$$

In particular, axioms *antisymmetric* and *non-reflexive* follow from *strict monotonicity in size*. Finally, the boundary conditions are:

$$\exists c_1, ..., c_n, r \in C \ c_1 := \{x_1\} \land ... \land c_n = \{x_n\} \land r = \{x_1, ..., x_n\}$$

So each cluster c_i contains exactly the element x_i, and there is a root r containing all the elements. The above single-element nodes can not have children as their extension would be empty according to axioms *strict monotonicity in size* and *no empty clusters*. As each cluster besides the root needs to have a father according to the *left total* axiom, and a father has no children or exactly two of them according to *binary tree*, a valid clustering according to the above axiomatization will be built merging two disjoint clusters to yield a cluster representing the union of both until one arrives at the universal cluster which has no father, i.e. the root node r.

The above axioms thus define the search space of all possible cluster trees. A binary cluster tree with disjoint children for n elements has $2n - 1$ nodes and $2(n - 1)$ edges.

From an algorithmic point of view, one can build such a binary cluster tree with disjoint children either bottom-up or top-down. In the first case, the process is called hierarchical agglomerative clustering. In the second case, we talk about divisive clustering. Hierarchical agglomerative (bottom-up) and divisive (top-down) clustering are described more in detail in the following.

Hierarchical Agglomerative (Bottom-Up) Clustering

Hierarchical agglomerative (bottom-up) clustering (HAC) is initialized by creating an own cluster for each element and iterating over the step which merges the most similar clusters. Here an important question is i) how similarity between elements is computed and ii) how similarity between clusters is computed. Actually, the way the similarity between clusters is computed has a strong effect on the complexity of the algorithm (compare [Manning and Schütze, 1999]). We will mention three ways of computing similarity between clusters:

- *Single linkage* defines the similarity between two clusters P and Q as $\max_{p \in P, q \in Q} sim(p, q)$, that means, considering the closest pair between the two clusters.
- *Complete* linkage considers the two most dissimilar terms, i.e. $\min_{p \in P, q \in Q} sim(p, q)$.
- Finally, *average-linkage* computes the average similarity of the terms of the two clusters, i.e. $\frac{1}{|P||Q|} \sum_{p \in P, q \in Q} sim(p, q)$.

The hierarchical agglomerative clustering algorithm is formally given by the pseudocode in Algorithm 4. The pseudocode suggests that the complexity of the algorithm is $O(n^3)$ as the *while loop* ranges over the size of K, which is n at the beginning, and finding the most similar pair takes $O(n^2)$. This is in fact what we will refer to as the naive implementation of HAC. As shown by Manning and Schütze [Manning and Schütze, 1999], some optimization can be done. In particular, the similarities between all the elements can be pre-computed and stored in a $n \times n$ array a in time $O(n^2)$. Depending on the linkage strategy used, the algorithm then differs.

Let us start our discussion with single linkage. The similarities between the n elements in $X = \{x_1, ..., x_n\}$ can actually be stored in a $n \times n$- matrix as depicted in Figure 4.9.

Furthermore, in order to determine the most similar clusters at each step, for each element in the matrix we store the most similar element in a *Best Merges* list. The search for the most similar elements in each iteration can thus be done in $O(n)$.

	x_1	x_2	$\ldots$	x_{n-1}	x_n
x_1		$sim(x_1, x_2)$		$sim(x_1, x_{n-1})$	$sim(x_1, x_n)$
x_2					
$\ldots$	$(\ldots)$	$\ldots$		$\ldots$	
x_{n-1}		$sim(x_{n-1}, x_2)$		$sim(x_{n-1}, x_{n-1})$	$sim(x_{n-1}, x_n)$
x_n		$sim(x_n, x_2)$		$sim(x_n, x_{n-1})$	$sim(x_n, x_n)$

Fig. 4.9. Example similarity matrix

Once the two most similar clusters k_i and k_j (or elements at the beginning) have been identified, a new cluster $k_{new} = k_i \cup k_j$ is built. This cluster needs to be added to the similarity matrix, and the similarity to the other clusters has to be calculated. This is done in $O(n)$ according to the following *update formula*:

$$sim(k_l, k_{new}) = \max(sim(k_l, k_i), sim(k_l, k_j)) \qquad (4.54)$$

The interesting property of single linkage is that the similarity values in the *Best Merges* list never change. This is due to the fact that the max-function is monotonic with respect to cluster merge and the similarity thus never decreases. This means in particular that if k_i or k_j was the most similar element for some cluster k_p, then, after the merge, k_{new} will be the most similar element for k_p. Thus, the *Best Merges* list can be updated in $O(n)$ by replacing the occurrences of k_i and k_j by k_{new}. The complexity of single linkage is thus $O(n^2)$ (see also [Defays, 1977], [Murtagh, 1984] and [Manning and Schütze, 1999]).

For complete-linkage the situation is different. The cluster update function is the following:

$$sim(k_l, k_{new}) = \min(sim(k_l, k_i), sim(k_l, k_j)) \qquad (4.55)$$

So, the similarity here is decreasingly monotonic with respect to cluster merges, such that the invariant property of the values in the *Best Merge* list is violated and consequently we would need to find the new most similar cluster for each element in $O(n^2)$ time, thus leading to an overall complexity of $O(n^3)$. The trick here is to sort the similarity values for each element in the original matrix in $O(n^2 log\, n)$ time and make a priority queue out of the Best Merges list. When a new cluster is formed, the new most similar cluster for each cluster can be found in $O(n\, log\, n)$ as finding the next largest value in a priority queue takes $O(log\, n)$ [Sedgewick, 1984]. Thus, agglomerative clustering with complete linkage has a worst-time complexity of $O(n^2 log\, n)$ (compare [Duda et al., 2001])[5].

---

[5] See also http://www-csli.stanford.edu/~schuetze/ completelink.html on this issue

---

Algorithm 4 Hierarchical Agglomerative (Bottom-Up) Clustering

---

Input: a set $X = \{x_1, ..., x_n\}$ of objects represented by vectors $\mathbf{x}_1, ..., \mathbf{x}_n \in \mathbb{R}^m$ and
a similarity function sim: $\mathbb{R}^m \times \mathbb{R}^m \to \mathbb{R}$

Output: a set K of $2n - 1$ clusters ordered hierarchically
as a binary tree (K, E) with $2(n - 1)$ edges and n leaves

$\forall i \; 1 \leq i \leq n : \; k_i := \{x_i\}$
$K := K' := \{k_1, ..., k_n\}$
$E := \emptyset$
$j := n + 1$
while$(|K'| > 1)$ **do**
    $(k_{u'}, k_{v'}) := \text{argmax}_{(k_u, k_v) \in K' \times K'} \; sim(k_u, k_v)$
    $k_j = k_{u'} \cup k_{v'}$
    $K' := K' \backslash \{k_{u'}\}$
    $K' := K' \backslash \{k_{v'}\}$
    $K' := K' \cup \{k_j\}$
    $K := K \cup \{k_j\}$
    $E = E \cup \{(k_{u'}, k_j), (k_{v'}, k_j)\}$
    j:=j+1
end while
return (K,E)

For average-linkage the overall complexity is $O(n^2)$, assuming that the similarity measure is the cosine and using a special way of calculating average linkage between two clusters (compare [Manning and Schütze, 1999]).

Divisive (Top-Down) Clustering

A binary cluster tree can not only be constructed bottom-up as in hierarchical agglomerative clustering, but also top-down by iteratively partitioning clusters, starting with a universal cluster containing all elements. Here the crucial questions are i) how to select the next cluster to be split, and ii) how to actually split the cluster in two clusters. Concerning the selection of the next cluster to be split, one typically defines a coherence function and selects the least coherent cluster for splitting. Coherence, for example, can be calculated on the basis of the variance in the cluster, thus selecting the cluster with the highest variance for splitting. However, it is also possible to simply select the largest cluster for splitting. Concerning the splitting of the selected cluster, a function *split* needs to be defined. The splitting task is actually again a clustering task consisting of clustering the data points into two clusters. In principle, every clustering algorithm could be used for this purpose. We will see later that Bi-Section-KMeans uses the KMeans algorithm for this purpose. The general algorithm for a top-down clustering is given in Algorithm 5.

Algorithm 5 Top-down hierarchical Clustering

Input: a set $X = \{x_1, ..., x_n\}$ of objects represented by vectors $\mathbf{x_1}, ... \mathbf{x_n} \in \mathbb{R}^m$,
a function coh : $2^{\mathbb{R}^m} \to \mathbb{R}^m$, and
a splitting function $split : 2^{\mathbb{R}^m} \to 2^{\mathbb{R}^m} \times 2^{\mathbb{R}^m}$

Output: a set K of 2n-1 clusters ordered hierarchically
as a binary tree (K, E) with $2(n-1)$ edges and n leaves

$K := K' := \{X\}$
$E := \emptyset$
j:=1
while $\exists k_i \in K'$ such that $|k_i| > 1$ **do**
$\quad k_u := \operatorname{argmin}_{k_v \in K'} \operatorname{coh}(k_v)$
$\quad (k_{j+1}, k_{j+2}) := split(k_u)$
$\quad K' := K' \backslash \{k_u\} \cup \{k_{j+1}, k_{j+2}\}$
$\quad K := K \cup \{k_{j+1}, k_{j+2}\}$
$\quad E := E \cup \{(k_{j+1}, k_u), (k_{j+2}, k_u)\}$
$\quad j := j + 2$
end while
return (K, E)

Bi-Section KMeans

Bi-Section-KMeans is a bisecting top-down clustering algorithm which uses KMeans to partition the cluster selected for splitting into two subclusters (compare Algorithm 6). In fact, the core of the Bi-Section KMeans algorithm is the KMeans algorithm for $k = 2$. The complexity of the inner loop is thus $O(n)$ and consequently the complexity of the outer *for-loop* $O(k\ n)$.

It has often been argued that Bi-Section-KMeans is a very efficient clustering algorithm. Applications for Bi-Section-KMeans can be found, for example, in text clustering [Steinbach et al., 2000].

Algorithm 6 Bi-Section KMeans

Input: a set $X = \{x_1, ...x_n\}$ of objects represented by vectors $\mathbf{x_1}, ..., \mathbf{x_n} \in \mathbb{R}^m$ and
     a function $coh : 2^{\mathbb{R}^m} \to \mathbb{R}$
     a function for computing the centroid of a cluster, i.e., $\mu : 2^{\mathbb{R}^m} \to \mathbb{R}^m$

Output: a set K of clusters with $|K| = 2n - 1$ ordered hierarchically
     as binary tree (K, E) with $2(n - 1)$ edges and n leaves

$K = K' := \{X\}$
$E := \emptyset$
for i=1 to n-1 **do**
    choose the largest or the least coherent cluster $k_u \in K'$, i.e.
    $k_u = \mathrm{argmax}_{k_i \in K'} |k_i|$ or $k_u = \mathrm{argmin}_{k_i \in K'} coh(k_i)$
    choose two data points f_1 and f_2 of k_u as cluster centroids
    repeat
        assign each element in k_u to its closest centroid, i.e.
        $c_1 := \{x \in k_u \mid dist(x, f_1) \leq dist(x, f_2)\}$
        $c_2 := \{x \in k_u \mid dist(x, f_2) \leq dist(x, f_1)\}$
        recompute both centroids, i.e.
        $f_j = \mu(c_j), j \in \{1, 2\}$
    until stopping criterion is true
    $K' := K' \backslash \{k_u\} \cup \{k_1, k_2\}$
    $K := K \cup \{k_1, k_2\}$
    $E := E \cup \{(k_1, k_u), (k_2, k_u)\}$
end for
return (K, E)

5

Datasets

This chapter deals with the different datasets used within this book for the purpose of evaluating the developed algorithms and methods for ontology learning. We describe the manually designed ontologies we use to evaluate our approaches as well as the corresponding corpora used for learning.

5.1 Corpora

This section describes the text corpora used in the diverse experiments conducted. Table 5.1 gives a summary of the main characteristics of the different collections, in particular the number of documents and tokens.

5.1.1 Mecklenburg Vorpommern

The first document collection was acquired from http://www.all-in-all.de and has already been used by Alexander Mädche [Mädche, 2002]. It contains documents describing places, regions, sights, hotels, etc. in *Mecklenburg Vorpommern*, a state in northeast Germany. We will refer to this text collection as Corpus $_{Mecklenburg}$. It consists of 1047 HTML documents which were converted into plain text with about 332.000 tokens.

5.1.2 Lonely Planet

The *LonelyPlanet corpus*[1] consists of 1801 HTML documents containing descriptions of countries, cities, etc. from all continents. The HTML documents have been converted into a corpus consisting of about a million tokens. This corpus has also been used in the experiments conducted by Kavalec and Svátek [Kavalec and Svátek, 2005]. We will refer to this collection as Corpus $_{LP}$.

---

[1] It was originally downloaded from http://www.lonelyplanet.com/destinations in 2003 by Martin Kavalec from the Knowledge Engineering Group (KEG) at the University of Economics, Prague (UEP).

Table 5.1. Corpus statistics

Corpus	Documents	Tokens
Mecklenburg	1.047	332.000
Lonely Planet	1.801	1 Mio.
BNC	4.124	100 Mio.
Reuters	21.578	218 Mio.
OHSUMED	348.556	7.6 Mio.
Genia Corpus	2.000	400.000
Planet Stories	307	n.a.

5.1.3 British National Corpus

The *British National Corpus* (BNC) is a very large corpus of modern English, both spoken and written. The corpus comprises around 100 Mio. words in 4.124 texts.

The development of the corpus was carried out and managed by an industrial/academic consortium lead by Oxford University Press. Work on building the corpus began in 1991, and it was completed in 1994. The Corpus was designed to cover modern British English as far as possible. The written part (90%) includes, for example, extracts from newspapers, periodicals and journals, academic books and popular fiction, letters, essays etc.

The British National Corpus has been annotated with part-of-speech tags and is widely used within NLP research. We will refer to this corpus simply as BNC.

5.1.4 Tourism

The above three corpora, i.e. $Corpus_{Mecklenburg}$, $Corpus_{LP}$ and BNC have been merged into a larger tourism corpus we will refer to as $Corpus_{Tourism}$. The reason for including the BNC corpus in the Tourism corpus is to reach a critical mass of text.

5.1.5 Reuters-21578

The documents in the Reuters-21578 collection[2] appeared on the Reuters newswire in 1987. The documents were assembled and indexed with categories by personnel from Reuters Ltd. and Carnegie Group, Inc. in 1987. In 1990, the documents were made available by Reuters for research purposes. In the context of this book, we have made use of version 1.0 prepared in 1996. In particular, we converted all the documents into plain text files, yielding a text corpus of about 218 Mio tokens. We will refer to this corpus as $Corpus_{Reuters}$.

---

[2] http://www.daviddlewis.com/resources/testcollections/reuters21578/

5.1.6 OHSUMED

The *OHSUMED collection*, initially compiled by Hersh et al. [Hersh et al., 1994], contains a total of 348.566 titles and abstracts from 270 medical journals over the five-year period from 1987 until 1991. Each entry has been manually indexed with a set of descriptors from the MeSH thesaurus (see below). We will refer to this collection as Corpus$_{OHSUMED}$.

5.1.7 Genia Corpus

The *Genia corpus* is developed together with the *Genia ontology* by Tsuji Labs (see the description below). The aim is to create a resource to allow development, training, refinement, etc. of natural language processing applications for the domain of molecular biology, medicine, etc. The corpus contains annotated abstracts taken from the National Library of Medicine's MEDLINE database[3]. The corpus is semantically annotated with respect to categories from the Genia ontology. The current version 3.02 consists of 2000 abstracts which were selected from MEDLINE search results with the keywords (MeSH terms) *human, blood cells* and *transcription factors*. The corpus consists of about 18.546 sentences and 400.000 tokens. We will refer to this corpus as Corpus$_{Genia}$. It can be downloaded at http://www-tsujii.is.s.u-tokyo. ac.jp/~genia/topics/Corpus/.

5.1.8 Planet Stories

The *Planet Stories* corpus, henceforth Corpus$_{Planet Stories}$, has been compiled in 2004 by Victoria Uren from the Knowledge Media institute[4] for an information retrieval experiment with the aim of retrieving topically similar stories for a given story. The *Planet Stories* repository is a collection of stories written by the employees about events, activities or visits at the Knowledge Media institute. The collection consists of 307 HTML documents.

5.2 Concept Hierarchies

In this section, we describe the diverse concept hierarchies with respect to which we will evaluate our ontology learning algorithms.

5.2.1 Tourism and Finance

In the context of this book, we will evaluate our taxonomy induction approaches with respect to two tourism ontologies and one finance ontology. The first ontology, $O_{tourism}$, was developed by an experienced ontology engineer in the context of the study conducted by Mädche and Staab

---

[3] http://www.ncbi.nlm.nih.gov/
[4] http://kmi.open.ac.uk/

Table 5.2. Ontology statistics

	$O_{tourism}$	$O_{Tourism}$	$O_{Finance}$
No. Concepts	293	969	1223
No. Leaves	236	796	861
Avg. Depth	3.99	5.35	4.57
Max. Depth	6	9	13
Max. Children	21	35	33
Avg. Children	5.26	5.87	3.5

[Mädche and Staab, 2002]. In this study, they asked one ontology engineer as well as four students to model a tourism ontology in order to compare the agreement between different subjects on the task of modeling an ontology. They also present measures in order to measure the similarity of the ontologies at the lexical as well as conceptual level. The second ontology, a larger ontology about the tourism domain, i.e. $O_{Tourism}$[5], was developed in the context of the GETESS project also by an experienced ontology engineer. GETESS was a project concerned with information extraction and retrieval from the Web [Staab et al., 1999]. In the same project also a finance ontology was developed. We will refer to this ontology as $O_{Finance}$[6]. The latter two ontologies were translated from German into English by the author of the present book. Concepts which did not have any direct translation into the target language were either rephrased or removed.

Table 5.2 gives some basic facts about the concept hierarchies of the three ontologies. In particular, it shows the number of concepts, the number of leaf concepts, the average depth of the tree, i.e. the average length of the paths from a leaf to the root, the maximal depth, the average number of children for non-leaf concepts as well as the maximal number of children.

5.2.2 Genia

The Genia ontology[7] is developed by Tsuji Labs[8] and is intended to be a formal model of cell signaling reactions in humans. It was designed to be used as a basis for the construction of thesauri and semantic dictionaries for text processing applications such as information retrieval (IR), information extraction (IE), document and term classification, summarization, etc. Furthermore, it is also supposed to provide the basis for an integrated view of multiple databases. The current version of the GENIA ontology, a taxonomy of some entities involved in signaling, has been developed with the aim of semantically annotating the Genia corpus (see Section 5.1).

[5] http://www.aifb.uni-karlsruhe.de/WBS/pci/TourismGoldStandard.isa
[6] http://www.aifb.uni-karlsruhe.de/WBS/pci/FinanceGoldStandard.isa
[7] http://www-tsujii.is.s.u-tokyo.ac.jp/~genia/topics/Corpus/genia-ontology.html
[8] http://sys.pwr.eng.osaka-u.ac.jp/home.html

5.2.3 MeSH

The *Medical Subject Headings* (MeSH) thesaurus is a controlled vocabulary developed by the National Library of Medicine and it is used for indexing, cataloging, and searching for biomedical and health-related information and documents.

It consists of sets of more or less synonymous medical terms arranged under so called *descriptors*, each representing a distinct meaning. The 2004 edition of MeSH used in the context of this book contains more than 22.000 descriptors. These are organized in a hierarchical structure known as *MeSH tree structures*. The most general level of the hierarchy consists of 15 general descriptors such as *anatomy* or *disease*. Each descriptor has attached one or more so called *tree numbers* describing the position of the descriptor within the tree structure. More specific descriptors are found at deeper levels of the hierarchy. The maximum depth of the hierarchy is 11 levels. As an illustrating example, in what follows we give part of the subtree below *abnormalities*:

```
Abnormalities C16.131
    Abnormalities, Drug Induced C16.131.42
    Abnormalities, Multiple C16.131.77
        Alagille Syndrome C16.131.77.65
        Angelman Syndrome C16.131.77.95
```

5.3 Population Gold Standard

In order to evaluate methods for ontology population on the instance level, we created a gold standard as described in what follows. Two subjects were asked to annotate 30 texts from Corpus$_{LP}$. They used a pruned version of the $O_{Tourism}$ ontology. The pruned version consisted of 682 concepts. The subjects were told to annotate instances in the text with the appropriate concept from the ontology. They used the OntoMat Annotizer tool [Handschuh et al., 2001] for this purpose. In what follows, we will refer to these subjects as A and B. Subject A actually produced 436 annotations, and subject B produced 392. There were 277 instances that were annotated by both subjects. For these 277 instances, they used 59 different concepts, and the categorial agreement on these 277 instances as measured by the Kappa statistic was 63.48% (cf. [Carletta, 1996]), which allows to conclude that the annotation task is overall well defined but that the agreement between humans is far from perfect. Furthermore, they had total agreement on 178 instances.

Part II

Methods and Applications

Concept Hierarchy Induction

Concept hierarchies allow to structure information into categories thus facilitating its search, reuse and understanding. Further, they provide a level of generalization which allows to define relationships between data in an abstract and concise way, without having to enumerate all the concrete cases for which the relation or implication in question holds. They form the backbone of any ontology and thus of any knowledge base, allowing to specify axioms, rules and implications between facts in a concise way.

However, as already mentioned in the introduction, it is also well known that any knowledge-based system suffers from the so-called *knowledge acquisition bottleneck*, i.e. the difficulty to actually model the domain in question. This applies in particular to the development of concept hierarchies. In order to partially overcome this problem, we present in this chapter three different methods aiming at acquiring conceptual hierarchies from a text corpus in an automatic fashion. According to the definition of ontology learning tasks in chapter 3, this chapter thus tackles the *concept hierarchy induction* task.

Making explicit the knowledge implicitly contained in texts is a great challenge. Actually, knowledge can be found in texts at different levels of explicitness. Handbooks, textbooks or dictionaries, for example, contain explicit knowledge in form of definitions such as '*a tiger is a mammal*' or '*mammals such as tigers, lions or elephants*'. In fact, some researchers have exploited such regular patterns to discover taxonomic or part-of relations in machine readable dictionaries (compare [Amsler, 1981, Calzolari, 1984, Alshawi, 1987, Dolan et al., 1993]) or texts (see [Hearst, 1992, Charniak and Berland, 1999, Iwanska et al., 2000, Ahmad et al., 2003]). However, it seems that the more technical and specialized the texts are, the less basic knowledge will be found stated in an explicit manner. Thus, an interesting alternative is to derive knowledge from texts by analyzing how certain terms are used rather than to look for their explicit definition. In these lines, the *distributional hypothesis* [Harris, 1968] assumes that terms are similar to the extent to which they share similar linguistic contexts. The distributional hypothesis has been empirically validated in a number of works showing that distributional similarity correlates well with semantic similarity (e.g. [Grefenstette, 1995], [Burgess and Lund, 1997], [Lin, 1998a]). In the following Section 6.1, we discuss in detail these main approaches to learning concept hierarchies.

6.1 Common Approaches

In this section, we review the common approaches to learning concept hierarchies. In particular, we discuss their strengths and weaknesses. After having understood how the common approaches work, the reader should be able to understand the contribution of the approaches described in Sections 6.2, 6.3 and 6.4. We start our overview with methods which have been applied to extract concept hierarchies from machine readable dictionaries. Then, we discuss work related to the application of lexico-syntactic patterns as defined by Hearst to the task at hand. Then we introduce approaches based on distributional similarity, illustrating them with a concrete example. Finally, we discuss methods based on co-occurrence analysis.

6.1.1 Machine Readable Dictionaries

Early work on extracting taxonomies from machine readable dictionaries (MRDs) goes back to the early 80s [Amsler, 1981, Calzolari, 1984]. The core idea is to exploit the regularity of dictionary entries to first of all find a suitable hypernym for the defined word. In many cases, the head of the first NP appearing in the dictionary definition is in fact a hypernym, *genus* [Calzolari, 1984] or *kernel term* [Amsler, 1981]. Consider, for example, the following definitions taken from Dolan et al. [Dolan et al., 1993]:

spring "the <u>season</u> between winter and summer and in which leaves and flowers appear"

nectar "the sweet <u>liquid</u> collected by bees from flowers"

aster   "a <u>garden flower</u> with a bright yellow center"

However, there are also some exceptions to the above rule. On the one hand, the hypernym can be preceded by an expression such as *'a kind of'*, *'a sort of'* or *'a type of'*. Here follow some examples taken from Alshawi [Alshawi, 1987]:

hornbeam   "a type of <u>tree</u> with a hard wood, sometimes used in hedges"

roller coaster "a kind of small <u>railway</u> with sharp slopes and curves, popular in amusement parks"

The above problem is easily solved by keeping an exception list with words such as *'kind'*, *'sort'*, *'type'* and taking the head of the NP following the preposition *'of'* as genus term.

On the other hand, the word can also be defined in terms of a part-of or membership relation as in:

corolla   "the part of a flower formed by the petals, usu. brightly colored to attract insects."

republican "a member of a political party advocating republicanism"

In the above case it is neither possible to derive that *is-a(corolla, part)* or *is-a(republican, member)* nor that *is-a(corolla, flower)* or *is-a(republican, political party)*. In fact, in these cases we are not faced with an is-a relation but a part-of relation. Another important question when determining the genus of a word according to its dictionary entry is what to do with nominal modification. Consider the following examples taken again from Alshawi [Alshawi, 1987]:

launch "a large usu. motor-driven boat used for carrying people on rivers, lakes, harbors, etc."

nail   "a thin piece of metal with a point at one end and a flat head at the other for hammering into a piece of wood, usu. to fasten the wood to something else"

Certainly, we all agree that the adjective modifiers *'large'* and *'motor-driven'* are essential for the definition of a *'launch'*. In the same vein, the adjective modifier *'thin'* and the prepositional complement *'of metal'* are essential characteristics of a *'nail'*. However, it is unclear in how far modifiers should be regarded as part of the genus term. In any case, the above examples also show that we can find a wealth of information other than the genus term of the word defined in the entry. In the definitions of *'launch'* and *'nail'* we also find information about the purpose of the object in question. Alshawi [Alshawi, 1987] as well as Dolan et al. [Dolan et al., 1993] have in fact proposed the extraction of richer structures from dictionary entries.

Alshawi, for example, proposes to extract the following structures for *'launch'* and *'nail'*:

```
(((CLASS BOAT) (PROPERTIES LARGE))
  (PURPOSE
      (PREDICATION (CLASS CARRY) (OBJECT PEOPLE))))

(((CLASS PIECE) (MATERIAL METAL) (PROPERTIES THIN))
  (HAS-PART ((CLASS POINT))))
```

The above examples suggest that one can extract frame-based or feature-like structures from dictionaries containing a wealth of semantic relations linking the different words together.

Of particular interest to our discussion is the work described in [Amsler, 1981], [Calzolari, 1984], [Copestake, 1990] and [Dolan et al., 1993]. These researchers have attempted to build a large network containing taxonomic links between words denoting hypernymy or hyponymy relations. As argued by Dolan et al. [Dolan et al., 1993], such a network has indeed important applications in natural language understanding. An important advantage of using dictionary definitions for building a taxonomy is that dictionaries separate different senses of words. Thus, taxonomic relations are learned between senses of words rather than between the words themselves. However, this only holds if the words used in the definitions of a certain sense of a word are also sense-disambiguated. Though this is partially the case for the LDOCE dictionary used in a lot of research on extracting knowledge bases from MRDs, it is unfortunately not done consistently (compare [Dolan et al., 1993]). Thus, it seems crucial to cope with the ambiguity of words used to define a certain word. To some extent this is alleviated by the LDOCE MRD which restricts the words used to define an entry to a couple of thousands. In general, approaches deriving taxonomic relations from MRDs are quite accurate. Dolan et al. [Dolan et al., 1993], for example, mention that 87% of the hypernym relations they extract are correct. Calzolari [Calzolari, 1984] cites a precision of more than 90%, while Alshawi mentions a precision of 77%. These methods are quite accurate due to the fact that dictionary entries show a regular structure. Furthermore, the methods are quite robust. Montemagni and Vanderwende [Montemagni and Vanderwende, 1992] have even shown that a standard parser can be applied to the task of processing dictionary definitions without decreasing parsing accuracy too much. Dictionary definitions in fact contain quite explicit knowledge compared to arbitrary text and thus provide an interesting basis for ontology learning. We currently see two main drawbacks in using a dictionary-based approach to ontology learning. The first is related to the fact that the acquired knowledge heavily depends on the intrinsic idiosyncrasies related to the writing of the entry. Second, in ontology learning we are mostly interested in acquiring domain-specific knowledge. However, dictionaries are generally domain independent resources. It is thus unclear in how far they could be used to learn a domain-specific ontology.

6.1.2 Lexico-Syntactic Patterns

In her seminal work, Hearst [Hearst, 1992] suggested the application of so-called lexico-syntactic patterns to the task of automatically learning hyponym relations from corpora. In particular, Hearst defined a collection of patterns indicating hyponymy relations. An example of such a pattern used by Hearst is the following:

$$\text{such } NP_0 \text{ as } NP_1,...,NP_{n-1} \text{ (or|and) other } NP_n$$

where NP stands for a noun phrase. If such a pattern is matched in a text, according to Hearst we could derive that for all $0 < i \leq n$

hyponym(lemma(head(NP_i)),lemma(head(NP_0))), i.e. lemma(head(NP_i)) is a hyponym of lemma(head(NP_0))[1], where lemma(head(NP)) denotes the lemma[2] of the nominal heads of NP. For example, from the sentence *'Such injuries as bruises, wounds and broken bones...'*, we could derive the relations: hyponym(bruise, injury), hyponym(wound, injury) and hyponym(broken bone, injury).

The patterns used by Hearst are the following:

Hearst1: *NP* such as {*NP*,}* {(and | or)} *NP*
Hearst2: such *NP* as {*NP*,}* {(and | or)} *NP*
Hearst3: *NP* {,*NP*}* {,} or other *NP*
Hearst4: *NP* {,*NP*}* {,} and other *NP*
Hearst5: *NP* including {*NP*,}* *NP* {(and | or)} *NP*
Hearst6: *NP* especially {*NP*,}* {(and|or)} *NP*

According to Hearst, the patterns should satisfy the following requirements:

1. They should occur frequently and in many text genres.
2. They should accurately indicate the relation of interest.
3. They should be recognizable with little or no pre-encoded knowledge.

Hearst mentions that an important issue is how to treat nominal modification, in particular adjectives prenominally modifying a noun. She does not give a definite answer to this problem, but mentions that the choice here certainly depends on the application in question. Furthermore, Hearst also suggests a procedure in order to acquire such patterns:

1. Decide on a lexical relation R of interest, e.g. hyponymy/hypernymy.
2. Gather a list of terms for which this relation is known to hold, e.g. hyponym(car, vehicle). This list can be found automatically using the patterns already learned or by bootstrapping from an existing lexicon or knowledge base.
3. Find expressions in the corpus where these terms occur syntactically near one another.
4. Find the commonalities and generalize the expressions in 3. to yield patterns that indicate the relation of interest.
5. Once a new pattern has been identified, gather more instances of the target relation and go to step 3.

As mentioned by Hearst, the value of such lexico-syntactic patterns is that they can be identified easily and are quite accurate. Hearst, for example, showed that, out of 106 relations extracted with her method from New York Times texts where the hyponym and hypernym were in Word-Net, 61 were correct with respect to WordNet. Thus, a lower bound for

---

[1] From a linguistic point of view, a term t_1 is a hyponym of a term t_2 if we can say *'a t_1 is a kind of t_2'*. Correspondingly, t_2 is then a hypernym of t_1.

[2] The lemma of a word is its base or normal form, i.e., *cats - cat*, *drove - drive*, etc.

Table 6.1. Tourism domain knowledge as formal context (rep.)

	bookable	rentable	driveable	rideable	joinable
hotel	x				
apartment	x	x			
car	x	x	x		
bike	x	x	x	x	
excursion	x				x
trip	x				x

the accuracy of Hearst patterns is 61/106, i.e. 57.55%. The drawback of the patterns is however that they appear rarely and most of the words related through an is-a relation do not appear in Hearst-style patterns. Thus, one needs to process large corpora to find enough of these patterns. For this reason, recently several researchers have attempted to match these patterns on the Web as a big corpus using some query engine (compare [Markert et al., 2003, Pasca, 2004, Etzioni et al., 2004a]). A further drawback of such an approach based on lexico-syntactic patterns is that we learn lexical relations between word forms rather than between senses of words or concepts. Furthermore, the patterns are typically specified in the form of regular expressions and this imposes limits on the accuracy of the patterns. Given a sentence as *'However, the main historic area of Ordino is a charming village'* most of the approaches based on matching lexico-syntactic patterns would derive: is-a(Ordino, village), which is definitely not correct, i.e. it is the *'main historic area of Ordino'* which is a *'charming village'*, but not *Ordino* itself. In fact, it is language's variety which is difficult to capture merely relying on regular expression power. Further work related to the application of lexico-syntactic patterns is discussed in Section 6.5.

6.1.3 Distributional Similarity

The so called *distributional hypothesis* claims that words are similar to the extent that they share similar context [Harris, 1968]. This hypothesis is also in line with Firth's well known statement that *'you shall know a word by the company it keeps'* [Firth, 1957]. In fact, empirical investigations corroborate the validity of the above hypothesis. Miller and Charles [Miller and Charles, 1991], for example, found in several experiments that humans determine the semantic similarity of words on the basis of the similarity of the contexts they are used in. Grefenstette [Grefenstette, 1994] further showed that similarity in vector space correlates well with semantic relatedness of words. We will explain how the distributional hypothesis can be exploited to derive concept hierarchies by means of the example formal context already described in Section 4.2 and shown again in Table 6.1 for the sake of convenience.

Table 6.2. Similarities for tourism example

	hotel	apartment	car	bike	excursion	trip
hotel	1.0	0.5	0.33	0.25	0.5	0.5
apartment		1.0	0.66	0.5	0.33	0.33
car			1.0	0.75	0.25	0.25
bike				1.0	0.2	0.2
excursion					1.0	1.0
trip						1.0

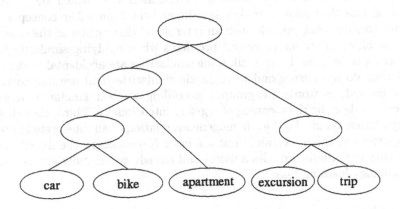

Fig. 6.1. Cluster tree built by agglomerative hierarchical clustering

Assuming that each of the objects o in Table 6.1 is represented by a binary vector with 5 dimensions corresponding to the attributes given in Table 6.1, we can calculate the similarity between the objects, for example by the Jaccard coefficient introduced in Section 4.1.5. The similarities are given in Table 6.2.

Using hierarchical agglomerative clustering, we could now build a cluster tree for the objects in Table 6.2. Let us assume we are using *single linkage* as measure of the similarity between clusters. First, we would cluster *excursion* and *trip* as they have a similarity of 1. We would then cluster *bike* and *car* as this is the next pair with the highest degree of similarity. Then we would build a cluster consisting of *bike*, *car* and *apartment*. Next, we would either join the latter cluster with *hotel* or build a cluster between *hotel* and the already created cluster consisting of *excursion* and *trip*. Assuming that we traverse the similarity matrix from the upper left corner to the lower right one, we would add *hotel* to the cluster consisting of *bike*, *car* and *apartment*. At the top level we would then join the clusters {*hotel, apartment, bike, car*} and {*excursion, trip*} producing a universal cluster containing all elements. The corresponding cluster tree is shown in Figure 6.1.

The cluster tree in Figure 6.1 thus bears some similarity with the lattice produced by FCA for the same tourism example (shown in Figure 4.5). In fact, in the lattice there are corresponding formal concepts with the extensions: {*excursion, trip*}, {*bike, car*}, {*bike, car, apartment*} and {*bike, car, apartment, hotel, excursion, trip*}, respectively. However, there is one crucial difference. While the lattice is based on a sound theory of attribute inheritance and thus represents a concept hierarchy in which attributes are inherited by subconcepts, the cluster tree lacks a clear and formal interpretation. Furthermore, the concept hierarchy produced by FCA also contains an intensional description of the concepts in terms of the attributes which they have in common and thus allows for distinguishing them from other concepts. The cluster tree does not provide such an intensional description of the concepts. In general, one encounters several problems when applying similarity-based clustering techniques. First of all, some similarities are accidental in the sense that they do not correspond to semantic similarities and are due to sparse data. Second, as words are grouped according to their similarity, it seems difficult to describe the meaning of a group intensionally. Third, though similarity is often assumed to be a homogeneous relation often interpreted in terms of equivalence, this is certainly not the case. Nevertheless, the distributional similarity hypothesis provides a useful and already successfully applied model for ontology learning tasks.

6.1.4 Co-occurrence Analysis

Some research has hypothesized that the fact that the occurrence of some word implies the occurrence of some other word in the same sentence, paragraph or document hints at a potential directed relation between both words. Directed means for example a *sub-topic*, *is-a* or *part-of* relation. This notion is related to the one of a *collocation*. We will say that two words form a collocation if they occur together in a paragraph, sentence, document or next to each other more often than predicted by chance. Sanderson and Croft [Sanderson and Croft, 1999] present a document-based definition of subsumption according to which a certain term t_1 is more special than a term t_2 if t_2 also appears in all the documents in which t_1 appears. On the basis of this document-based definition of subsumption, they automatically induce a hierarchy between nouns from a document collection. As shown by Fotzo and Gallinari [Fotzo and Gallinari, 2004], Sanderson and Croft's approach can in fact be generalized by the following definition:

Definition 19 (Document-based Subsumption) *A term x subsumes a term y iff $P(x|y) \geq t$ and $P(y|x) < P(x|y)$, where*
   $n(x, y)$ is the number of documents in which x and y co-occur
   $n(y)$ is the number of documents that contain y
   $P(x|y) = \frac{n(x,y)}{n(y)}$.

In particular, Sanderson and Croft consider the case in which $t = 1$. Though directed co-occurrences seem in fact to indicate some directed relation between the involved words, it is unclear which specific relation actually holds between these. Some research has suggested that depending on the context we consider, i.e. bigrams, sentences, paragraphs or even whole documents, we tend to get different types of relations. However, to our knowledge this hypothesis has not been empirically analyzed.

6.1.5 Road Map

We have seen that there is a wide range of techniques which have been applied to the problem of learning concept hierarchies from textual data. As we are dealing with learning ontologies from domain-specific corpora, the methods based on MRDs are less interesting for our purposes. However, all the other learning paradigms will find application in the book. In fact, in the remainder of this chapter we will present three methods exploiting the above described learning paradigms in some way or the other.

Section 6.2 describes an approach based on Formal Concept Analysis which groups and hierarchically orders words or terms according to their use or behavior in a corpus. The set-theoretical method of FCA is compared to similarity-based clustering techniques, in particular hierarchical agglomerative clustering as well as Bi-Section-KMeans by comparing the different hierarchies generated with respect to a reference concept hierarchy on the basis of a novel evaluation method. In addition to this quantitative evaluation, we also provide a qualitative discussion of the different methods. The contribution here is, on the one hand, the application of set-theoretical methods such as FCA to the problem as well as the systematic comparison of the different approaches along several dimensions. This section is partially based on material already published in [Cimiano et al., 2003a], [Cimiano et al., 2003b], [Cimiano et al., 2004b], [Cimiano et al., 2004c] and [Cimiano et al., 2005a].

However, when applying unsupervised techniques to the generation of concept hierarchies, one encounters different problems we already discussed above, that is, spurious similarities and lack of intensional descriptions. In Section 6.3, we present a novel approach dealing with two problems inherent in similarity-based clustering approaches, i.e. accidental similarities and lack of intensional labels. The approach addresses both issues by guiding the clustering via an hypernym-oracle constructed by other means. In particular, at early phases of the algorithm, words are only clustered if they actually have a common hypernym according to the oracle, reducing the number of accidental clusterings. By labeling the constructed cluster with the common hypernym, the cluster is also described intensionally. This section is partially based on material already published in [Cimiano and Staab, 2005].

We have seen above that each of the learning paradigms has advantages but also disadvantages. Consequently, it is unlikely that one paradigm can produce optimal results. Thus, a combination of techniques seems likely to overcome some of the problems inherent in the different approaches. The third approach described in this chapter is in fact an attempt to combine different learning approaches to increase the quality of the learned taxonomic relations. The approach is inspired by the way humans acquire knowledge. We assume here that humans do not acquire their knowledge from one single source, but from many different sources such as newspapers, text-books, dictionaries, etc. In fact, different types of textual resources contain information at varying levels of explicitness. Whereas text books, dictionaries and educational resources in general may contain very explicit definitions, knowledge can, in most cases, only be derived implicitly from the way words are used in conventional texts such as newspapers, novels, etc. The approach considers different approaches generating evidence for a certain taxonomic relation with different degrees of explicitness and combines these evidences in an optimal way. In particular, well-known techniques from supervised machine learning are applied to learn an optimal combination of the different approaches. The material presented in this section is partially based on the work described in [Cimiano et al., 2004d] and [Cimiano et al., 2005c].

Section 6.5 then presents related work in more detail and Section 6.6 closes this chapter by discussing the main contributions as well as some open issues.

6.2 Learning Concept Hierarchies with FCA

We have seen in the previous chapter that different types of methods have been proposed in the literature to address the problem of (semi-) automatically deriving a concept hierarchy from text relying on the distributional hypothesis. Basically, these methods can be grouped in two classes: the *similarity*-based methods on the one hand, and the *set-theoretical* approaches on the other hand. Both methods adopt a vector-space model and represent a word or term as a vector containing features or attributes derived from a corpus. There is certainly a great divergence in which attributes are used for this purpose, but typically some sort of syntactic dependencies are used, such as conjunctions, appositions [Caraballo, 1999] or verb-argument dependencies (see [Hindle, 1990, Pereira et al., 1993, Grefenstette, 1994, Faure and Nedellec, 1998]). The first type of methods is characterized by the use of a similarity or distance measure in order to compute the pairwise similarity or distance between vectors corresponding to two words or terms in order to decide if they can be clustered or not (compare [Hindle, 1990, Pereira et al., 1993, Grefenstette, 1994, Faure and Nedellec, 1998, Caraballo, 1999]. Set-theoretical approaches partially order the objects according to the inclusion relations between their attribute sets (compare [Petersen, 2002, Sporleder, 2002, Haav, 2003]).

In this chapter, we present a set-theoretical approach based on Formal Concept Analysis (compare Section 4.2). In order to derive attributes from a certain corpus, on the one hand we parse it and extract verb–PP-complement, verb–object and verb–subject dependencies. On the other hand, we also use surface dependencies as described in Section 4.1.4. For each noun appearing as head of these argument positions, we then use the corresponding verbs as attributes for building the formal context and calculate the formal concept lattice on its basis. The use of such syntactic dependencies to represent a term's context have also been suggested by Grefenstette [Grefenstette, 1994], Lin [Lin, 1998a] as well as Gamallo et al. [Gamallo et al., 2005].

Though different methods have been explored in the literature, there is actually a lack of comparative work concerning the task of automatically learning concept hierarchies by applying clustering techniques. However, ontology engineers need guidelines about the effectiveness, efficiency and trade-offs of different methods in order to decide which techniques to apply in which settings. Thus, we present a comparison along these lines between our FCA-based approach, hierarchical bottom-up (agglomerative) clustering, and Bi-Section-KMeans as an instance of a divisive algorithm. In particular, we compare the learned concept hierarchies with handcrafted reference taxonomies for two domains: tourism and finance. In addition, we examine the impact of using different information measures to weight the significance of a given object–attribute pair. Furthermore, we also investigate the use of a smoothing technique to cope with data sparseness. The remainder of this section is structured as follows: In Section 6.2.1, we present the approach in general, whereas in Section 6.2.2 we discuss the details related to the automatic construction of formal contexts from texts. We present our evaluation measures in Section 6.2.3 and the concrete results in Section 6.2.4. We summarize the main results in Section 6.2.5.

6.2.1 FCA for Concept Hierarchy Induction

The overall process of automatically deriving concept hierarchies from text by FCA is depicted in Figure 6.2. First, the corpus is part-of-speech (POS) tagged using TreeTagger [Schmid, 1994] and parsed using LoPar (compare Section 4.1). Then, verb–subject, verb–object and verb–prepositional phrase (PP) dependencies are extracted from these parse trees. In particular, pairs are extracted consisting of the verb and the head of the subject, object or prepositional phrase they subcategorize. Then, the verb and the heads are lemmatized, i.e. assigned to their base form. In case the word is not in our lexicon, it is simply not lemmatized. In order to address data sparseness, the collection of pairs is smoothed, i.e. the frequency of pairs which do not appear in the corpus is estimated on the basis of the frequency of other pairs. The pairs are then weighted according to some statistical measure, and only the pairs above a certain threshold are transformed into a formal context to which Formal Concept Analysis is applied. The lattice resulting from this, $(\mathfrak{B}, \leq)$, is transformed into a partial order $(C', \leq')$ which is closer to a concept hierarchy in the traditional sense. As FCA typically leads to a proliferation of concepts, the partial order is compacted removing abstract concepts, leading

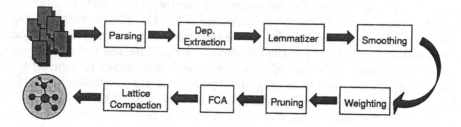

Fig. 6.2. Overall process for concept hierarchy induction with FCA

to a compacted partial order $(C'', \leq'')$ which is the resulting concept hierarchy. More formally, the process is described algorithmically by the pseudocode in Algorithm 7.

Algorithm 7 ConstructConceptHierarchy(D,T)

/* construct a hierarchy for the terms in T on the basis of the documents in D */

Parses = parse(POS-tag(D));
SynDeps = tgrep(Parses);
LemmatizedSynDeps = lemmatize(SynDeps);
SmoothedSynDeps = smooth(LemmatizedSynDeps);
WeightedSynDeps = weigth(SmoothedSynDeps);
SynDeps' = applyThreshold(WeightedSynDeps);
K = getFormalContext(T,SynDeps');
$(\mathfrak{B}, \leq)$ = computeLattice(K);
$(C', \leq')$ = transform($\mathfrak{B}, \leq$);
$(C'', \leq'')$ = compact($C', \leq'$);
return $(C'', \leq'')$;

In order to illustrate the whole process, we will discuss the formal context already introduced in Section 4.2 which is shown again in Table 6.3 for the sake of convenience. The lattice produced by FCA is depicted in Figure 6.3 (left)[3]. It can be transformed into a special type of concept hierarchy as shown in Figure 6.3 (right) by removing the bottom element, introducing an ontological concept for each formal concept (named with the intent) and introducing a subconcept for each element in the extent of the formal concept in question. In order to formally define the transformation of the lattice $(\mathfrak{B}, \leq)$ into the partial order $(C', \leq')$, we assume that the lattice is represented using *reduced labeling* (compare Section 4.2). Now given a lattice $(\mathfrak{B}, \leq)$ of formal concepts

---

[3] The *Concept Explorer* software was used to produce this lattice (see http://sourceforge.net/projects/conexp).

Table 6.3. Tourism domain knowledge as formal context (rep.)

	bookable	rentable	driveable	rideable	joinable
hotel	x				
apartment	x	x			
car	x	x	x		
bike	x	x	x	x	
excursion	x				x
trip	x				x

for a formal context $K = (G, M, I)$, we transform it into a partial order $(C', \leq')$ as follows:

Definition 20 (Transformation of $(\mathfrak{B}, \leq)$ to $(C', \leq')$) *First of all C' contains objects as well as intents (sets of attributes):*

$$C' := G \cup \{B \mid (A, B) \in \mathfrak{B}\}$$

Further:

$$\leq' := \{(g, B_1) \mid \gamma(g) = (A_1, B_1)\} \cup \{(B_1, B_2) \mid (A_1, B_1) \leq (A_2, B_2)\}$$

Finally, as FCA typically produces a high number of concepts, we compress the resulting hierarchy of ontological concepts by removing any inner node the extension of which is the same as the one of its child in terms of leaf nodes subsumed. As a result, we create a partial order $(C'', \leq''_C)$ as follows:

Definition 21 (Compacted Concept Hierarchy $(C'', \leq'')$) *Assuming that $lext(c)$ is the set of leaf nodes dominated by c according to $\leq'_C$:*

$$C'' := \{c_2 \in C' \mid \forall c_1 \in C' \ c_2 \leq'_C c_1 \to lext(c_2) \neq lext(c_1)\}$$

Further:

$$\leq''_C := \leq'_C \mid_{C'' \times C''}$$

i.e. $\leq''_C$ is the relation $\leq'_C$ restricted to pairs of elements of C''.

In the case of the hierarchy depicted in Figure 6.3 (right), we would remove the rideable concept for example.

At a first glance, it seems that the hierarchy shown in Figure 6.3 (right) is odd due to the fact that the labels of abstract concepts are verbs rather than nouns as typically assumed. However, from a formal point of view, concept labels have no meaning at all so that we could just as well have named the concepts with some other arbitrary symbols. The reason why it is handy to introduce 'meaningful' concept identifiers is for the purpose of easier human readability. In fact, if we adopt an extensional interpretation of our hierarchy, we have no problems asserting that the extension of the concept denoted by bike is a subset of the extension of the concept of the rideable objects in our

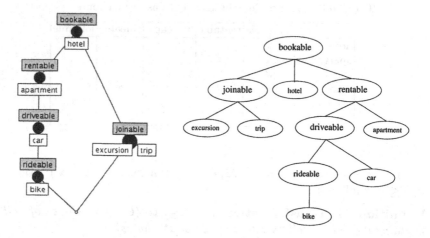

Fig. 6.3. The lattice of formal concepts (left) and the corresponding hierarchy of ontological concepts (right) for the tourism example

world. This view is totally compatible with interpreting the concept hierarchy in terms of formal subsumption as given by the logical formula: $\forall x \; (bike(x) \rightarrow rideable(x))$. We thus conclude that, from an extensional point of view, the verb-like concept identifiers have the same status as any concept identifier based on a noun. From an intensional point of view, there may not even exist a hypernym with the adequate intension to label a certain abstract concept, such that using a verb-like identifier may even be the most appropriate choice. For example, we could easily replace the identifiers **joinable**, **rideable** and **driveable** by **activity**, **two-wheeled vehicle** and **vehicle**, respectively. It is certainly difficult, however, to substitute **rentable** by some appropriate term denoting the same extension, i.e. all the things that can be rented.

It is also important to mention that the learned concept hierarchies represent a conceptualization of a domain with respect to a given corpus in the sense that they represent the relations between terms as they are used in the text. However, corpora represent a very limited view of the world or a certain domain due to the the fact that if something is not mentioned, it does not mean that it is not relevant, but simply that it is not an issue for the text in question. As a result, certain similarities between terms with respect to the corpus are actually accidental - in the sense that they do not map to a corresponding semantic relation - but are due to the fact that texts represent a biased snapshot of a domain. Thus, the learned concept hierarchies have to be merely regarded as approximations of the conceptualization of a certain domain.

The task we are now focusing on is: given a certain number of terms referring to concepts relevant for the domain in question, can we derive a concept hierarchy between them? In terms of FCA, the objects are thus given and we need to find the corresponding attributes in order to build an incidence matrix, a lattice and then transform it into a corresponding concept hierarchy. In the following section, we describe how we acquire these attributes automatically from the underlying text collection.

6.2.2 Context Construction

As already mentioned above, in order to derive context attributes describing the terms we are interested in, we make use of syntactic dependencies between the verbs appearing in the text collection and the heads of the subject, object and PP (prepositional phrase)-complements they subcategorize. In fact, in previous experiments [Cimiano et al., 2004b] we found that using all these dependencies in general leads to better results than any subset of them. In order to extract these dependencies automatically, we parse the text with LoPar (compare Section 4.1).

There are three further important issues to consider:

1. the output of the parser can be erroneous, i.e. not all derived verb–argument dependencies are correct,
2. not all the derived dependencies are 'interesting' in the sense that they will help to discriminate between the different objects, and
3. the assumption of completeness of information will never be fulfilled, i.e. the text collection will never be big enough to find all the possible occurrences (compare [Zipf, 1932]).

To deal with the first two problems, we weight the object–attribute pairs with regard to a certain information measure and consider only those verb–argument relations for which this measure is above some threshold t. In particular, we explore the following three information measures (compare [Cimiano et al., 2003a] and [Cimiano et al., 2004b]):

$$Conditional(n, v_{arg}) = P(n|v_{arg}) = \frac{f(n, v_{arg})}{f(v_{arg})} \qquad (6.1)$$

$$PMI(n, v_{arg}) = log_2 \frac{P(n|v_{arg})}{P(n)} \qquad (6.2)$$

$$Resnik(n, v_{arg}) = S_R(v_{arg}) P(n|v_{arg}) \qquad (6.3)$$

where $S_R(v_{arg}) = \sum_{n'} P(n'|v_{arg}) log \frac{P(n'|v_{arg})}{P(n')}$.

Furthermore, $f(n, v_{arg})$ is the total number of occurrences of a term n as argument arg of a verb v, $f(v_{arg})$ is the number of occurrences of verb v with a corresponding argument and $P(n)$ is the relative frequency of a term n compared to all other terms. The first information measure is simply the conditional probability of the term n given the argument arg of a verb v. The second measure $PMI(n, v_{arg})$ is the pointwise mutual information (compare Section 4.1.5) and was used by Hindle [Hindle, 1990] for discovering groups of similar terms. The third measure is inspired by the work of Resnik [Resnik, 1997] and introduces an additional factor $S_R(v_{arg})$ which takes into account all the terms appearing in the argument position arg of the verb v in question. In particular, the factor measures the relative entropy of the prior and posterior (considering the verb it appears with) distributions of n and thus the *selectional strength* of the verb at a given argument position. It is important to mention that in our approach the values of all the above measures are normalized into the interval [0,1] by the function $f(x) = \frac{x}{max-min}$. For illustration purposes, let us discuss the above measures on the basis of the example verb–object–occurrence matrix given in Table 6.4.

Table 6.4. Occurrences of nouns as objects of verbs

	$book_{obj}$	$rent_{obj}$	$drive_{obj}$	$ride_{obj}$	$join_{obj}$
hotel	10				
apartment	6	5			
car	3	4	5		
bike	2	3	2	2	
excursion	1				3
trip	2				2

First of all, we have a total number of 50 occurrences of nouns as objects of some verbs. Therefore, we get the following prior probabilities for the nouns: P(hotel)=$\frac{10}{50}$=0.2, P(apartment)=$\frac{11}{50}$=0.22 , P(car)=$\frac{12}{50}$=0.24, P(bike)=$\frac{9}{50}$=0.18, P(excursion)=$\frac{4}{50}$=0.08, P(trip)=$\frac{4}{50}$=0.08. The posterior probabilities, i.e. the probability of a noun given the object position of a certain verb, are given in Table 6.5.

Table 6.5. Posterior probabilities

	$P(n|book_{obj})$	$P(n|rent_{obj})$	$P(n|drive_{obj})$	$P(n|ride_{obj})$	$P(n|join_{obj})$
hotel	$\frac{10}{24}$=0.42				
apartment	$\frac{6}{24}$=0.25	$\frac{5}{11}$=0.45			
car	$\frac{3}{24}$=0.13	$\frac{4}{11}$=0.36	$\frac{5}{7}$=0.71		
bike	$\frac{2}{24}$=0.08	$\frac{3}{11}$=0.27	$\frac{2}{7}$=0.29	$\frac{2}{2}$=1	
excursion	$\frac{1}{24}$=0.04				$\frac{3}{5}$=0.6
trip	$\frac{2}{24}$=0.08				$\frac{2}{5}$=0.4

Now, the PMI of hotel and $book_{obj}$ is, for example, $PMI(hotel, book_{obj}) = log_2 \frac{P(hotel|book_{obj})}{P(hotel)} = log_2 \frac{0.42}{0.2} = 1.07$. The selectional strength of $book_{obj}$ should be much lower than the one of $drive_{obj}$ according to our intuitions.

In fact, we get: $S_R(book_{obj}) = 0.42 \cdot log_2(\frac{0.42}{0.2}) + 0.25 \cdot log_2(\frac{0.25}{0.22}) + 0.13 \cdot log_2(\frac{0.13}{0.24}) + 0.08 \cdot log_2(\frac{0.08}{0.18}) + 0.04 \cdot log_2(\frac{0.04}{0.08}) + 0.08 \cdot log_2(\frac{0.08}{0.08}) = 0.25$, and $S_R(drive_{obj}) = 0.71 \cdot log_2(\frac{0.71}{0.24}) + 0.29 \cdot log_2(\frac{0.29}{0.18}) = 1.31$.

We thus get, for example, $Resnik(hotel, book_{obj}) = 0.42 \cdot 0.25 = 0.11$ and $Resnik(car, drive_{obj}) = 0.71 \cdot 1.31 = 0.93$. The above results certainly correspond to our intuitions about the selectional strength of 'book' and 'drive'.

The third problem mentioned above, i.e. the data sparseness, requires smoothing of input data. In fact, when working with text corpora, data sparseness is always an issue [Zipf, 1932]. A typical method to overcome data sparseness is smoothing [Manning and Schütze, 1999], which in essence consists in assigning non-zero probabilities to unseen events. For this purpose, we apply the technique described in [Cimiano et al., 2003b], in which mutually similar terms are clustered with the result that an occurrence of an attribute with one term is also counted as an occurrence of that attribute with the other term. As similarity measures we examine the *Cosine, Jaccard, L1 norm* as well as the *Jensen-Shannon* and *Skew* divergence measures analyzed and described by Lee [Lee, 1999] (compare also Section 4.1.5.3):

$$cos(t_1, t_2) = \frac{\sum_{v_{arg} \in V} P(t_1|v_{arg})P(t_2|v_{arg})}{\sqrt{\sum_{v_{arg} \in V} P(t_1|v_{arg})^2 \sum_{v_{arg} \in V} P(t_2|v_{arg})^2}} \tag{6.4}$$

$$Jac(t_1, t_2) = \frac{|\{v_{arg}|P(t_1|v_{arg}) > 0 \text{ and } P(t_2|v_{arg}) > 0\}|}{|\{v_{arg}|P(t_1|v_{arg}) > 0 \text{ or } P(t_2|v_{arg}) > 0\}|} \tag{6.5}$$

$$L1(t_1, t_2) = \sum_{v_{arg} \in V} |P(t_1|v_{arg}) - P(t_2|v_{arg})| \tag{6.6}$$

$$JS(t_1, t_2) = \frac{1}{2}[D(P(t_1, V) \parallel avg(t_1, t_2)) + D(P(t_2, V) \parallel avg(t_1, t_2)] \tag{6.7}$$

$$SD(t_1, t_2) = D(P(t_1, V) \parallel \alpha \cdot P(t_1, V) + (1 - \alpha) \cdot P(t_2, V)) \tag{6.8}$$

where $D(P_1(V) \parallel P_2(V))$ is the Kullback-Leibler divergence introduced in Section 4.1.5 and $avg(t_1, t_2) = \frac{P(t_1, v) + P(t_2, v)}{2}$. In particular, we implemented these measures using the variants relying only on the elements v_{arg} common to t_1 and t_2 as described by Lee [Lee, 1999]. Strictly speaking, the Jensen-Shannon as well as the Skew divergence are dissimilarity functions as they measure the average information loss when using one distribution instead of the other. We transform them into similarity measures as $k - f$, where k is an appropriate constant and f the dissimilarity function in question. We cluster all the terms which are *mutually similar* with regard to the similarity measure in question, counting more attribute–object pairs than are actually found in the text and thus obtaining also non-zero frequencies for some attribute–object pairs that do not appear literally in the corpus. The overall result is consequently a 'smoothing' of the frequency landscape by assigning some non-zero frequencies to combinations of verbs and objects which were actually not found in the corpus. Here follows the formal definition of mutual similarity:

Definition 22 (Mutual Similarity) *Two terms n_1 and n_2 are mutually similar iff $n_2 = argmax_{n'}\ sim(n_1, n')$ and $n_1 = argmax_{n'}\ sim(n_2, n')$.*

According to this definition, two terms n_1 and n_2 are mutually similar if n_1 is the most similar term to n_2 with regard to the similarity measure in question and the other way round. Similar notions have been proposed by Hindle [Hindle, 1990] and Lin [Lin, 1998b], where these pairs are called *reciprocally similar* and *Respective Nearest Neighbors*, respectively. Figure 6.4 (left) shows an example of a lattice which was automatically derived from a set of texts acquired from the *Lonely Planet* as well as the *Mecklenburg* corpora together. We only extracted verb–object pairs for the terms in Table 6.3 and used the conditional probability to weight the significance of the pairs. For excursion, no dependencies were extracted and therefore it was not considered when computing the lattice. The threshold used was $t = 0.005$. Assuming that car and bike are mutually similar, they would be clustered, i.e. car would get the attribute startable and bike the attribute needable. Accordingly, the result here would be the lattice in Figure 6.4 (right), where car and bike are in the extension of one and the same concept.

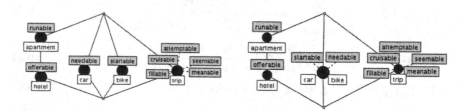

Fig. 6.4. Examples of lattices automatically derived from tourism-related texts without smoothing (left) and with smoothing (right)

6.2.3 Evaluation

In order to evaluate our approach, we need to assess how good the automatically learned ontologies reflect a given domain. One possibility would be to compute how many of the direct sub-/superconcept relations in the automatically learned ontology are correct. This has been done, for example, by Hearst [Hearst, 1992] or Caraballo [Caraballo, 1999]. However, due to the fact that our approach, as well as many others (compare [Hindle, 1990, Pereira et al., 1993, Grefenstette, 1994, Faure and Nedellec, 1998]), does not produce appropriate labels for the generated concepts, it seems difficult to assess the validity of a given sub-/superconcept relation. Another possibility is to compute how similar the automatically learned concept hierarchy is with respect to a given hierarchy for the domain in question.

Here, the crucial question is how to define similarity between concept hierarchies. Though there is a great amount of work in the AI community on how to compute the similarity between trees [Zhang et al., 1992, Goddard and Swart, 1996], concept lattices [Belohlavek, 2000], conceptual graphs [Myaeng and Lopez-Lopez, 1992, Maher, 1993] and conventional graphs [Zhang et al., 1996, Chartrand et al., 1998], it is not clear how these similarity measures also translate to concept hierarchies. An interesting work in these lines is the one presented by Mädche and Staab [Mädche and Staab, 2002], in which ontologies are compared along different levels: semiotic, syntactic and pragmatic. In particular, the authors present measures to compare the lexical and taxonomic overlap between two ontologies. Furthermore, they also present an interesting study in which different subjects were asked to model a tourism ontology. The resulting ontologies are compared in terms of the defined similarity measures, thus yielding the agreement of different subjects on the task of modeling an ontology. The evaluation measures we will use to compare the different automatically derived concept hierarchies are inspired by the work of Mädche and Staab. In what follows, we first present our evaluation measures in Section 6.2.3.1 and then the actual results in Sections 6.2.4.

6.2.3.1 Evaluation Measures

For the purposes of this section, we will introduce a simplified version of an ontology as defined in Section 2 which we will refer to as a *core ontology*:

Definition 23 (Core Ontology) *A core ontology is a structure $O :=$ $(C, root, \leq_C)$ consisting of (i) a set C of concept identifiers, (ii) a designated root element representing the top element of the (iii) upper semi-lattice $(C \cup \{root\}, \leq_C)$ called* concept hierarchy *or* taxonomy.

For the sake of notational simplicity, we adopt the following convention: given an ontology O_i, the corresponding set of concepts will be denoted by C_i and the partial order representing the concept hierarchy by $\leq_{C_i}$.

It is important to mention that in the approach presented here, terms are directly identified with concepts; that means, we neglect the fact that terms can be polysemous. Now, the lexical recall (LR) of two ontologies O_1 and O_2 is measured as follows:[4]

$$LR(O_1, O_2) = \frac{|C_1 \cap C_2|}{|C_2|} \qquad (6.9)$$

Take for example the concept hierarchies O_{auto} and O_{ref} depicted in Figure 6.5. In this example, the lexical recall is $LR(O_{auto}, O_{ref}) = \frac{5}{10} = 50\%$. Note that the root node has been explicitly excluded from C by Definition 23. This holds for the remainder of this section.

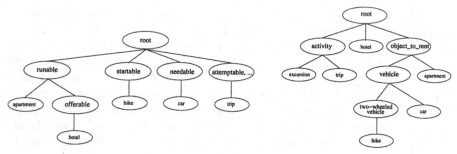

Fig. 6.5. Example for an automatically acquired concept hierarchy O_{auto} (left) compared to the reference concept hierarchy O_{ref} (right)

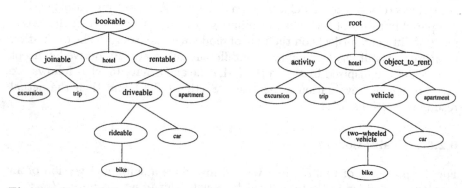

Fig. 6.6. Example for a perfectly learned concept hierarchy $O_{perfect}$ (left) compared to the reference concept hierarchy O_{ref} (right)

In order to compare the taxonomy of two ontologies, we use the *semantic cotopy* (SC) introduced by Mädche and Staab [Mädche and Staab, 2002]. The semantic cotopy of a concept is defined as the set of all its super- and subconcepts:

$$SC(c, O_i) := \{c_j \in C_i \mid c \leq_{C_i} c_j \text{ or } c_j \leq_{C_i} c\} \tag{6.10}$$

In what follows, we illustrate these and other definitions on the basis of several example concept hierarchies. Take for instance the concept hierarchies in Figure 6.6. We assume that the left concept hierarchy has been automatically learned with our FCA approach and that the concept hierarchy on the right is a handcrafted one. Further, it is important to point out that the left ontology is, in terms of the arrangement of the leaf nodes and abstracting from the labels of the inner nodes, a perfectly learned concept hierarchy. This should thus be reflected by a maximum similarity between both ontologies.

---

[4] As we assume that the terms to be ordered hierarchically are given, there is no need to measure the lexical precision, i.e. the ratio $\frac{|C_1 \cap C_2|}{|C_1|}$.

The semantic cotopy of the concept vehicle in the right ontology in Figure 6.6 is for example {car, bike, two-wheeled vehicle, vehicle, object-to-rent} and the semantic cotopy of driveable in the left ontology is {bike, car, rideable, driveable, rentable, bookable}.

It becomes already clear that comparing the cotopies of both concepts will not yield the desired results, that is, a maximum similarity between both concepts. Thus, we use a modified version SC' of the semantic cotopy in which we only consider the concepts common to both concept hierarchies in the semantic cotopy SC' (compare [Cimiano et al., 2004b, Cimiano et al., 2004c]), i.e.

$$SC'(c_i, O_1, O_2) := \{c_j \in C_1 \cap C_2 \mid c_j \leq_{C_1} c_i \lor c_i \leq_{C_1} c_j\} \quad (6.11)$$

By using this *common semantic cotopy* we exclude from the comparison concepts such as runable, offerable, needable, activity, vehicle, etc. which are only in one ontology. So, the common semantic cotopy SC' of the concepts vehicle and driveable is identical in both ontologies in Figure 6.6, i.e. {bike, car}, representing a perfect overlap between both concepts, which certainly corresponds to our intuitions about the similarity of both concepts. However, let us now consider the concept hierarchy in Figure 6.7. The common semantic cotopy of the concept bike is {bike} in both concept hierarchies. In fact, every leaf concept in the left concept hierarchy has a maximum overlap with the corresponding concept in the right ontology. Concerning recall, the problem is even worse, because every concept in the target ontology O_2 will still show a reasonable overlap with a corresponding leaf concept in the automatically learned ontology. The reason for this is the average depth of the ontologies we are considering. The average depth for the tourism ontology is for example 3.99 (compare Chapter 5). We would still get a recall of about 25% when comparing to trivial concept hierarchies. As we are considering only common concepts in the semantic cotopy, this situation is even worse as the average number of concepts in the semantic cotopy is lower than the average depth of the ontology. This is certainly undesirable and leads to very high baselines when comparing such trivial concept hierarchies with a reference standard (compare our earlier results in [Cimiano et al., 2004b] and [Cimiano et al., 2004c]). Thus, we introduce a further modification of the semantic cotopy by excluding the concept itself from its common semantic cotopy, i.e:

$$SC''(c_i, O_1, O_2) := \{c_j \in C_1 \cap C_2 \mid c_j <_{C_1} c_i \lor c_i <_{C_1} c_j\} \quad (6.12)$$

This maintains the perfect overlap between vehicle and driveable in the concept hierarchies in Figure 6.6, while yielding empty common cotopies for all the leaf concepts in the left ontology of Figure 6.7. Now, according to Mädche et al. the taxonomic overlap ($\overline{TO}$) of two ontologies O_1 and O_2 is computed as follows:

$$\overline{TO}(O_1, O_2) = \frac{1}{|C_1|} \sum_{c \in C_1} TO(c, O_1, O_2) \quad (6.13)$$

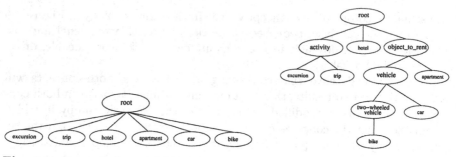

Fig. 6.7. Example for a trivial concept hierarchy $O_{trivial}$ (left) compared to the reference concept hierarchy O_{ref} (right)

where

$$TO(c, O_1, O_2) := \begin{cases} TO'(c, O_1, O_2) & \text{if } c \in C_2 \\ TO''(c, O_1, O_2) & \text{if } c \notin C_2 \end{cases} \quad (6.14)$$

and TO' and TO" are defined as follows:

$$TO'(c, O_1, O_2) := \frac{|SC(c, O_1, O_2) \cap SC(c, O_2, O_1)|}{|SC(c, O_1, O_2) \cup SC(c, O_2, O_1)|} \quad (6.15)$$

$$TO''(c, O_1, O_2) := max_{c' \in C_2} \frac{|SC(c, O_1, O_2) \cap SC(c', O_2, O_1)|}{|SC(c, O_1, O_2) \cup SC(c', O_2, O_1)|} \quad (6.16)$$

So, TO' gives the similarity between concepts which are in both ontologies by comparing their respective semantic cotopies. In contrast, TO'' gives the similarity between a given concept $c \in C_1$ and that concept c' in C_2 which maximizes the overlap of the respective semantic cotopies, i.e. it makes an optimistic estimation assuming an overlap that just does not happen to show up at the immediate lexical surface (compare [Mädche and Staab, 2002]). The taxonomic overlap $\overline{TO}(O_1, O_2)$ between the two ontologies is then calculated by averaging over all the taxonomic overlaps of the concepts in C_1.

In our case it does not make sense to calculate the semantic cotopy for concepts which are in both ontologies, as they will be leaf nodes in our learned ontologies and thus their common semantic cotopies SC'' are empty. This holds only under the assumption that the typical concept labels introduced by our FCA-based approach, i.e. ending with 'able', do not appear in our reference ontology. This assumption is easy to ensure as we could simply introduce a symbol making sure that this will always be the case. We calculate the taxonomic overlap between two ontologies as follows:

$$\overline{TO'}(O_1, O_2) = \frac{1}{|C_1 \backslash C_2|} \sum_{c \in C_1 \backslash C_2} max_{c' \in C_2 \cup \{root\}} TO'''(c, c', O_1, O_2) \quad (6.17)$$

where

$$TO'''(c, c', O_1, O_2) = \frac{|SC''(c, O_1, O_2) \cap SC''(c', O_2, O_1)|}{|SC''(c, O_1, O_2) \cup SC''(c', O_2, O_1)|} \quad (6.18)$$

Finally, as we do not only want to compute the taxonomic overlap in one direction, we introduce the precision, recall and an F-measure calculating the harmonic mean of both:

$$P_{TO}(O_1, O_2) = \overline{TO'}(O_1, O_2) \quad (6.19)$$

$$R_{TO}(O_1, O_2) = \overline{TO'}(O_2, O_1) \quad (6.20)$$

$$F_{TO}(O_1, O_2) = \frac{2 \cdot P_{TO}(O_1, O_2) \cdot R_{TO}(O_1, O_2)}{P_{TO}(O_1, O_2) + R_{TO}(O_1, O_2)} \quad (6.21)$$

The importance of balancing recall and precision against each other will be clear in the discussion of a few examples below. Let us consider the concept hierarchy $O_{perfect}$ in Figure 6.6, for example. In fact, the four non-leaf concepts joinable, rentable, driveable and rideable in the left hierarchy in Figure 6.6 have the same common semantic cotopy as the concepts activity, object_to_rent, vehicle and two-wheeled vehicle in the right hierarchy in Figure 6.6. For joinable and activity, the common semantic cotopy is {excursion, trip}; for rentable and object_to_rent it is {bike, car, apartment}; for driveable and vehicle it is {bike, car}, and for rideable and two-wheeled vehicle it is {bike}, respectively. These perfect correspondences lead to a precision and recall of 100% with respect to the taxonomic overlap. We thus get a precision and a recall of $P_{TO}(O_{perfect}, O_{ref}) = R_{TO}(O_{perfect}, O_{ref}) = \frac{1+1+1+1}{4} = 100\%$ and an F-Measure of $F_{TO}(O_{perfect}, O_{ref}) = 100\%$.

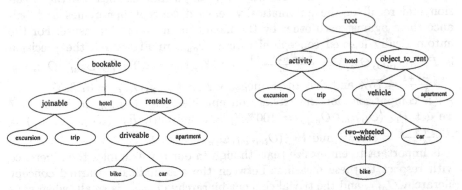

Fig. 6.8. Example for a concept hierarchy with lower recall ($O_{\downarrow_R}$) compared to the reference concept hierarchy O_{ref}

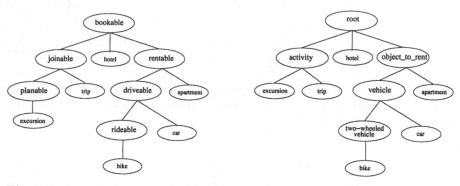

Fig. 6.9. Example for a concept hierarchy with lower precision ($O_{\downarrow P}$) compared to reference concept hierarchy O_{ref}

In the concept hierarchy $O_{\downarrow R}$ shown in Figure 6.8, the precision is still 100% for the same reasons as above, but due to the fact that the rideable concept has been removed there is no corresponding concept for two-wheeled-vehicle. The concept maximizing the taxonomic similarity in O_{ref} for two-wheeled-vehicle is driveable with a taxonomic overlap of 0.5. The recall is thus $R_{TO}(O_{\downarrow R}, O_{ref}) = \overline{TO'}(O_{ref}, O_{\downarrow R}) = \frac{1+1+1+\frac{1}{2}}{4} = 87.5\%$ and the F-measure decreases to $F_{TO}(O_{\downarrow R}, O_{ref}) = 93.33\%$.

In the concept hierarchy of $O_{\downarrow P}$ in Figure 6.9, an additional concept planable has been introduced, which reduces the precision to $P_{TO}(O_{\downarrow P}, O_{ref}) = \frac{1+1+1+1+\frac{1}{2}}{5} = 90\%$, while the recall stays obviously the same at $R_{TO}(O_{O_{\downarrow P}}, O_{ref}) = 100\%$ and thus the F-measure is $F_{TO}(O_{\downarrow P}, O_{ref}) = 94.74\%$. It becomes clear now why it is important to measure the precision and recall of the automatically learned concept hierarchies and balance them against each other by the harmonic mean or F-measure. For the automatically learned concept hierarchy O_{auto} in Figure 6.5 the precision is $P_{TO}(O_{auto}, O_{ref}) = \frac{\frac{2}{5}+\frac{1}{5}+1+\frac{1}{2}+1}{5} = 62\%$, the recall $R_{TO}(O_{auto}, O_{ref}) = \frac{1+\frac{3}{5}+\frac{2}{5}+1}{4} = 75\%$ and thus the F-measure $F_{TO}(O_{auto}, O_{ref}) = 67.88\%$.

As a comparison, for the trivial concept hierarchy $O_{trivial}$ in Figure 6.7 we get $P_{TO}(O_{trivial}, O_{ref}) = 100\%$ (per definition), $R_{TO}(O_{trivial}, O_{ref}) = \frac{\frac{2}{6}+\frac{3}{6}+\frac{2}{6}+\frac{1}{6}}{4} = 33.33\%$ and $F_{TO}(O_{trivial}, O_{ref}) = 50\%$.

It is important to emphasize that, though in our toy examples the difference with respect to these measures between the automatically learned concept hierarchy O_{auto} and the trivial concept hierarchy $O_{trivial}$ is small, when considering concept hierarchies with a much higher number of concepts it is clear that the F-measures for trivial concept hierarchies will be very low (see the results in Section 6.2.4).

Finally, we also calculate the harmonic mean of the lexical recall and the

F-measure as follows:

$$F'(O_1, O_2) = \frac{2 \cdot LR(O_1, O_2) \cdot F_{TO}(O_1, O_2)}{LR(O_1, O_2) + F_{TO}(O_1, O_2)} \qquad (6.22)$$

The reason is that we do not only want to maximize the taxonomic overlap of the learned ontologies but also the lexical recall at the same time. For the automatically learned concept hierarchy O_{auto}, we get:

$$F'(O_1, O_2) = \frac{2 \cdot 50\% \cdot 67.88\%}{50\% + 67.88\%} = 57.58\%.$$

The taxonomic overlap thus assesses the global quality of the learned concept hierarchies. However, we are also interested in knowing how good the clusters produced actually are. While the taxonomic overlap is a global quality criterion for the learned concept hierarchies, we will also measure the local quality by the *local taxonomic overlap*.

In order to introduce the local taxonomic overlap, we will first introduce the siblings of a concept:

Definition 24 (Siblings)

$$Sib(c, O_i) := \{c' \mid \exists c'' \ c \prec_{C_i} c'' \wedge c' \prec_{C_i} c''\}$$

In particular, we only compare common siblings, i.e

Definition 25 (Common Siblings)

$$Sib(c, O_1, O_2) := \{c' \in C_1 \cap C_2 \mid \exists c'' \ c \prec_{C_1} c'' \wedge c' \prec_{C_1} c''\}$$

The local taxonomic overlap (LTO) between two concepts is now defined as:

$$LTO(c, O_1, O_2) := max_{c' \ s.t. \ |Sib(c', O_2, O_1)| > 1} \frac{|Sib(c, O_1, O_2) \cap Sib(c', O_2, O_1)|}{|Sib(c, O_1, O_2) \cup Sib(c', O_2, O_1)|} \qquad (6.23)$$

The average local taxonomic overlap ($\overline{LTO}$) is consequently defined as follows:

$$\overline{LTO}(O_1, O_2) := \frac{1}{|\{c : \ |Sib(c, O_1, O_2)| > 1\}|} \sum_{c \ s.t. \ |Sib(c, O_1, O_2)| > 1} LTO(c, O_1, O_2) \qquad (6.24)$$

So, we can also compute the local taxonomic overlap in two directions and calculate the precision P_{LTO}, recall R_{LTO} and F-measure F_{LTO}.

We evaluate our approach on two domains: tourism and finance. The ontology for the tourism domain is the reference ontology of the comparison study conducted by Mädche and Staab [Mädche and Staab, 2002], which was modeled by an experienced ontology engineer. The finance ontology is basically the one developed within the GETESS project [Staab et al., 1999], i.e. $O_{Finance}$. The tourism domain ontology is the $O_{tourism}$ ontology, consisting of 293 concepts. The finance domain ontology is bigger with a total of 1223 concepts. As domain-specific text collection for the tourism domain we use the *Tourism* corpus consisting of the *Mecklenburg*, *Lonely Planet* and *BNC* corpora. Altogether the corpus size is over 100 Million tokens. For the finance domain we consider the *Reuters-21578* corpus with 218 Million tokens (compare Section 5).

6.2.4 Results

In what follows, we present the results of comparing the different clustering algorithms with respect to the measures defined in this section. Further, in Section 6.2.4.2 we discuss the results of using different information measures and in Section 6.2.4.3 we describe the impact of our smoothing method. Finally, in Section 6.2.4.4, we present results of clustering using pseudo-syntactic dependencies instead of dependencies extracted from full parses.

6.2.4.1 Comparison

The best F-measure for the tourism dataset is $F_{TO}^{FCA,tourism} = 40.52\%$ (at a threshold of $t = 0.005$), corresponding to a precision of $P_{TO}^{FCA,tourism} = 29.33\%$ and a recall of $R_{TO}^{FCA,tourism} = 65.49\%$. For the finance dataset, the corresponding values are $F_{TO}^{FCA,finance} = 33.11\%$, $P_{TO}^{FCA,finance} = 29.93\%$ and $R_{TO}^{FCA,finance} = 37.05\%$.

The lexical recall obviously also decreases with increasing threshold t such that overall the F-measure F' also decreases inverse proportionally to t. Overall, the best results in terms of F' are $F'^{FCA,tourism} = 44.69\%$ for the tourism dataset and $F'^{FCA,finance} = 38.85\%$ for the finance dataset. The reason why the results on the finance dataset are slightly lower is probably due to the more technical nature of the domain (compared to the tourism domain) and also to the fact that the concept hierarchy to be learned is bigger.

In order to evaluate our FCA-based approach, we compare it with hierarchical agglomerative clustering and Bi-Section-KMeans (compare Section 4.3.2). In our experiments, we use three different strategies to calculate the similarity between clusters: *complete, average* and *single*-linkage (compare Section 4.3.2.2). As similarity measure we make use of the cosine measure for all the similarity-based clustering algorithms. Further, it is important to mention that in the case of the similarity-based clustering algorithms, we prohibit the merging of clusters with similarity 0 and rather order them under a fictive universal cluster 'root'. This corresponds exactly to the way FCA creates and orders objects with no attributes in common. In addition, as Bi-Section-KMeans is a randomized algorithm, we produce ten runs and average the

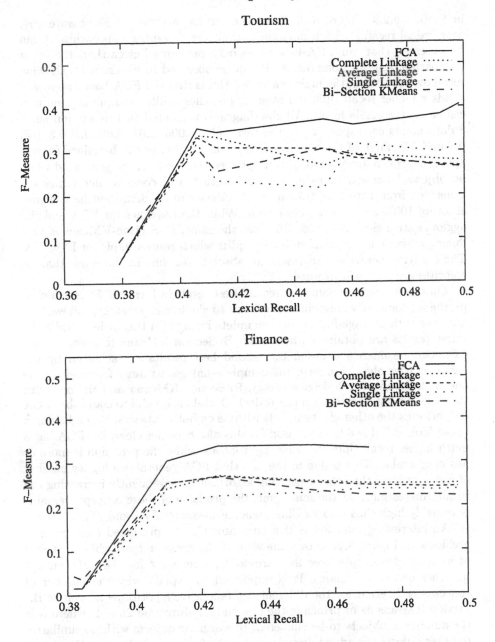

Fig. 6.10. Results for the FCA-based approach: F-measure over lexical recall for the tourism and finance domains

obtained results.

We compare the different approaches along the lines of the measures described in Section 6.2.3. Figure 6.10 shows the results in terms of F-measure F_{TO} over lexical recall for both domains and all the clustering approaches. It can be observed that our FCA-based approach performs better than the other approaches on both domains. As it can be observed in Figure 6.11, showing recall over precision, the main reason for this is that the FCA-based approach yields a higher recall than the other approaches, while maintaining the precision at reasonable levels. All the diagrams presented in this section show 8 data points corresponding to the thresholds 0.005, 0.01, 0.05, 0.1, 0.3, 0.5, 0.7 and 0.9. First of all, it seems important to discuss the baselines for our approach, which are the trivial concept hierarchies which are generated when no objects have attributes in common. Such trivial concept hierarchies are generated from threshold 0.7 on our datasets and by definition have a precision of 100% and a recall close to 0. While the baselines for FCA and the agglomerative clustering algorithm are the same, Bi-Section-KMeans is producing a hierarchy by random binary splits which results in higher F' values. These trivial hierarchies represent an absolute baseline in the sense that no algorithm could perform worse.

On the tourism domain, the second best result in terms of F' is achieved by the agglomerative algorithm with the single-linkage strategy, followed by the ones with average-linkage and complete-linkage (in this order), while the worst results are obtained when using Bi-Section-KMeans (compare Table 6.6). On the finance domain, the second best results are achieved by the agglomerative algorithm with the complete-linkage strategy followed by the one with the average-linkage strategy, Bi-Section-KMeans and the one with the single-linkage strategy (in this order). Overall, it is valid to claim that FCA outperforms the other clustering algorithms on both datasets. When having a closer look at Table 6.6, the reason for this also becomes clear, i.e. FCA has a much higher recall than the other approaches, while the precision is more or less comparable. This is due to the fact that FCA generates a higher number of concepts than the other clustering algorithms, consequently increasing the recall. Interestingly, at the same time, the precision of these concepts remains reasonably high thus also yielding higher F-measures F_{TO} and F'.

An interesting question is therefore how big the produced concept hierarchies are. Figure 6.12 shows the size of the concept hierarchies in terms of number of concepts over the threshold parameter t for the different approaches on both domains. It is important to explain why the number of concepts is different for the different agglomerative algorithms as well as Bi-Section-KMeans as in principle the size should always be $2n - 1$, where n is the number of objects to be clustered. However, as objects with no similarity to other objects are added directly under the fictive root element, the size of the concept hierarchies varies depending on the way the similarities are calculated. In general, the sizes of the agglomerative and divisive approaches are similar, while at lower thresholds FCA yields concept hierarchies with much more concepts. From threshold 0.3 on, the sizes of the hierarchies produced by all the different approaches are quite similar. Table 6.7 shows the results

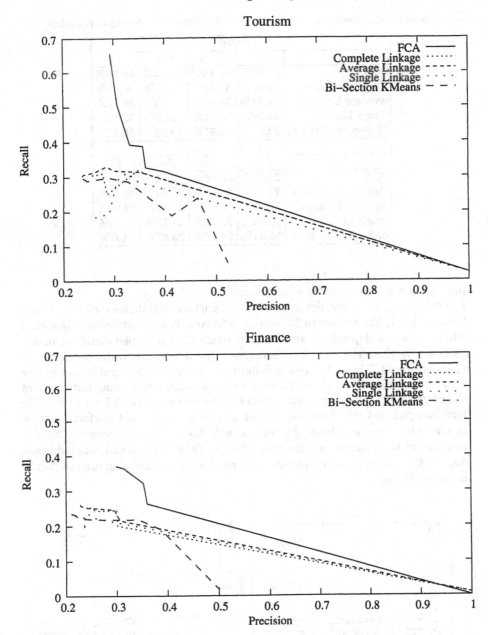

Fig. 6.11. Results for the FCA-based approach: recall over precision for the tourism and finance domains

for all approaches using the thresholds 0.3 and 0.5. In particular, we can conclude that FCA also outperforms the other approaches on both domains when

Table 6.6. Results of the comparison of different clustering approaches

Tourism				
	P_{TO}	R_{TO}	F_{TO}	F'
FCA	29.33%	**65.49%**	**40.52%**	**44.69%**
Complete Linkage	34.67%	31.98%	33.27%	36.85%
Average Linkage	**35.21%**	31.45%	33.23%	36.55%
Single Linkage	34.78%	28.71%	31.46%	38.57%
Bi-Section-KMeans	32.85%	28.71%	30.64%	36.42%
Finance				
	P_{TO}	R_{TO}	F_{TO}	F'
FCA	29.93%	**37.05%**	**33.11%**	**38.85%**
Complete Linkage	24.56%	25.65%	25.09%	33.35%
Average Linkage	29.51%	24.65%	26.86%	32.92%
Single Linkage	25.23%	22.44%	23.75%	32.15%
Bi-Section-KMeans	**34.41%**	21.77%	26.67%	32.77%

producing a similar number of concepts.

In general, we have not determined the statistical significance of the results because FCA, in contrast to Bi-Section-KMeans, is a deterministic algorithm which does not depend on any random seeding. Our implementation of agglomerative clustering is also deterministic given a certain order of the terms to be clustered. Thus, the only possibility to calculate the significance of our results would be to produce different runs by randomly leaving out parts of the corpus and calculating a statistical significance over the different runs. We have not pursued this direction further as the fact that FCA performs better in our setting is clear from the results in Table 6.6. Concerning the results in terms of local taxonomic overlap, given in Table 6.8, we can conclude that our FCA-based approach also outperforms the other clustering approaches in terms of F_{LTO}.

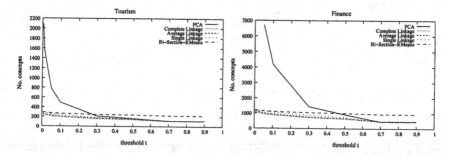

Fig. 6.12. Sizes of concept hierarchies for the different approaches on the tourism and finance domains: number of concepts over threshold t

Table 6.7. Comparison of results at thresholds 0.3 and 0.5 (F')

	Tourism		Finance	
Threshold	0.3	0.5	0.3	0.5
FCA	**37.53%**	**37.74%**	**37.59%**	**34.92%**
Complete Linkage	36.85%	36.78%	33.05%	30.37%
Single Linkage	29.84%	35.79%	29.34%	27.79%
Average Linkage	35.36%	36.55%	32.92%	31.30%
Bi-Section K-Means	31.50%	35.02%	32.77%	31.38%

Table 6.8. Results of the comparison of different clustering approaches (LTO)

Tourism			
	P_{LTO}	R_{LTO}	F_{LTO}
FCA	21.98%	33.82%	**26.64%**
Complete Linkage	23.17%	21.34%	22.22%
Average Linkage	23.48%	23.24%	23.36%
Single Linkage	23.01%	19.63%	21.19%
Bi-Section-KMeans	22.63%	18.52%	20.37%
Finance			
	P_{LTO}	R_{LTO}	F_{LTO}
FCA	21.24%	32.50%	**25.69%**
Complete Linkage	21.84%	21.59%	21.71%
Average Linkage	21.75%	22.56%	22.15%
Single Linkage	22.21%	19.84%	20.96%
Bi-Section-KMeans	21.53%	21.47%	21.49%

6.2.4.2 Information Measures

As already anticipated, the different information measures are also subject of our analysis. Table 6.9 gives the best results for the different clustering approaches and information measures. It can be concluded from these results that using PMI or the *Resnik* measure produces worse results on the tourism dataset, while yielding only slightly better results on the finance dataset for the FCA-based approach. It is also interesting to observe that, compared to the FCA-based approach, the other clustering approaches are much more sensitive to the information measure used. Overall, the use of the conditional probability as information measure seems reasonable. For the local taxonomic overlap LTO this situation is different. As Table 6.10 shows, the choice of the information measure has indeed an influence on the F-measure F_{LTO}. On the finance domain, the best result with FCA is achieved using the *Resnik* measure. In general, the pointwise mutual information seems to produce better results in terms of F_{LTO}.

Table 6.9. Comparison of results for different information measures (F')

	Conditional	PMI	Resnik
FCA			
Tourism	**44.69%**	44.51%	43.31%
Finance	38.85%	**38.96%**	38.87 %
Complete Linkage			
Tourism	**36.85%**	27.56%	23.52%
Finance	**33.35%**	22.29%	22.96%
Average Linkage			
Tourism	**36.55%**	26.90%	23.93%
Finance	**32.92%**	23.78%	23.26%
Single Linkage			
Tourism	**38.57%**	30.73%	28.63%
Finance	**32.15%**	25.47%	23.46%
Bi-Section-KMeans			
Tourism	**36.42%**	27.32%	29.33%
Finance	**32.77%**	26.52%	24.00%

Table 6.10. Comparison of results for different information measures (F_{LTO})

	Conditional	PMI	Resnik
FCA			
Tourism	**26.64%**	26.17%	26.25%
Finance	25.60%	25.86%	**27.02%**
Complete Linkage			
Tourism	22.22%	**24.57%**	21.98%
Finance	21.71%	**21.79%**	21.38%
Average Linkage			
Tourism	23.36%	**23.83%**	21.90%
Finance	22.15%	**23.81%**	21.83%
Single Linkage			
Tourism	21.19%	**22.46%**	21.62%
Finance	**20.96%**	20.23%	20.65%
Bi-Section-KMeans			
Tourism	21.52%	**21.83%**	21.76%
Finance	21.49%	**21.58%**	20.99%

6.2.4.3 Smoothing

We apply our smoothing method described in Section 6.2.2 to both datasets
in order to find out in how far the clustering of terms as a preprocessing step
improves the results of the FCA-based approach. As information measure we
use in this experiment the conditional probability because it was found to perform reasonably well (see Section 6.2.4.2). In particular, we use the following
similarity measures: the cosine measure, the Jaccard coefficient, the L1 norm

as well as the Jensen-Shannon and the Skew divergences (compare Section 4.1.5). Table 6.11 shows the impact of this smoothing technique in terms of the number of object–attribute terms added to the dataset. The *Skew Divergence* is excluded because it did not yield any mutually similar terms. It can be observed that smoothing by mutual similarity based on the cosine measure produces the most previously unseen object–attribute pairs, followed by the Jaccard, L1 and Jensen-Shannon divergence (in this order). Table 6.12 shows the results for the different similarity measures. The tables in sections A.2 and A.3 of the appendix list the mutually similar terms for the different domains and similarity measures. The results show that our smoothing technique actually yields worse results on both domains and for all similarity measures used. The smoothing method thus seems to be grouping terms which are not siblings in our gold standards. We conclude that our smoothing technique did not improve the results of the clustering. This does not mean that smoothing in general does not work in our context, but that other more elaborated methods should be examined. Actually, when having a close look at the pairs shown in Tables A.2 and A.3, it becomes clear that the 'semantic relatedness' of the mutually similar pairs is remarkably high.

Table 6.11. Impact of the smoothing technique in terms of new object–attribute pairs

	Baseline	Jaccard	Cosine	L1	JS
Tourism	525912	531041	534709	530695	528892
		(+ 5129)	(+ 8797)	(+ 4783)	(+ 2980)
Finance	577607	599691	634954	584821	583526
		(+ 22084)	(+ 57347)	(+ 7214)	(+ 5919)

Table 6.12. Results of smoothing (F')

	Baseline	Jaccard	Cosine	L1	JS
Tourism	44.69%	39.54%	41.81%	41.59%	42.35%
Finance	38.85%	38.63%	36.69%	38.48%	38.66%

6.2.4.4 Pseudo-syntactic Dependencies

In a further series of experiments, instead of using syntactic dependencies extracted with a parser, we also make use of the pseudo-syntactic surface dependencies described in Section 4.1.4.

We thus extract more dependencies compared to the method presented above. The dependencies we extract are very much in line with the ones extracted by Grefenstette [Grefenstette, 1994] or Gasperin et al. [Gasperin et al., 2001]. The results of repeating our experiments using pseudo-syntactic surface dependencies are given in Table 6.13 in terms of taxonomic overlap and in Table 6.14 in terms of local taxonomic overlap.

We can observe in Table 6.13 that, on the tourism domain, we yield a best F-measure F' of 48.84% which is more than 4 points above the version of the FCA-based approach relying on syntactic dependencies extracted from parse trees. On the finance domain, we yield a best F-measure of F'= 38.43% which is only slightly below the best F-measure of F'= 38.85% obtained using syntactic dependencies as well as the conditional probability to weight the features. In general, it is important to mention that the FCA-based approach outperforms again all the other clustering approaches. It is also worth mentioning that for both domains agglomerative clustering with single-linkage yields the second best results.

Table 6.14 shows the results in terms of local taxonomic overlap. We can see that the results for the FCA-based approach are slightly worse for both domains compared to using syntactic dependencies (compare table 6.8). However, it is important to emphasize that for all the agglomerative clustering approaches the results are better when using pseudo-syntactic dependencies with respect to taxonomic overlap as well as local taxonomic overlap.

Table 6.13. Results of the comparison of different clustering approaches using pseudo-syntactic dependencies (F')

	Tourism			
	P_{TO}	R_{TO}	F_{TO}	F'_{TO}
FCA	27.02%	68.67%	38.78%	**48.82%**
Complete Linkage	26.44%	32.98%	29.35%	40.60%
Average Linkage	25.22%	34.68%	29.20%	40.72%
Single Linkage	40.40%	28.05%	33.08%	44.85%
Bi-Section-KMeans	22.07%	25.61%	23.66%	34.72%
	Finance			
	P_{TO}	R_{TO}	F_{TO}	F'_{TO}
FCA	23.96%	33.32%	27.88%	**38.43%**
Complete Linkage	20.69%	22.98%	21.77%	32.59%
Average Linkage	19.92%	23.75%	21.66%	32.47%
Single Linkage	26.87%	19.98%	22.92%	33.86%
Bi-Section-KMeans	20.00%	21.53%	20.72%	29.53%

Table 6.14. Results of the comparison of different clustering approaches using pseudo-syntactic dependencies (LTO)

Tourism			
	P_{LTO}	R_{LTO}	F_{LTO}
FCA	19.23%	36.51%	**25.19%**
Complete Linkage	23.03%	25.63%	24.26%
Average Linkage	22.15%	26.36%	24.07%
Single Linkage	23.40%	24.77%	24.07%
Bi-Section-KMeans	19.53%	19.64%	19.58%
Finance			
	P_{LTO}	R_{LTO}	F_{LTO}
FCA	20.03%	35.71%	**25.67%**
Complete Linkage	22.19%	23.24%	22.70%
Average Linkage	22.30%	25.35%	23.73%
Single Linkage	22.89%	20.35%	21.54%
Bi-Section-KMeans	20.87%	21.72%	21.28%

6.2.4.5 Discussion

We have shown that our FCA-based approach is a reasonable alternative to similarity-based clustering approaches, even yielding better results on our datasets with respect to the F' and F_{LTO} measures defined in Section 6.2.3. The main reason for this is that the concept hierarchies produced by FCA yield a higher recall due to the higher number of concepts, while maintaining the precision at comparable levels. Furthermore, we have shown that the conditional probability performs reasonably well as information measure compared to other more elaborate measures such as PMI or the one introduced by Resnik [Resnik, 1997]. Unfortunately, applying a smoothing method based on clustering mutually similar terms does not improve the quality of the automatically learned concept hierarchies. Using pseudo-syntactic surface dependencies yields even better results for almost all methods – except for Bi-Section-KMeans - on the tourism domain as well as comparable results on the finance domain with respect to F'. However, with respect to the local taxonomic overlap extracting contextual features based on pseudo-syntactic dependencies yields slightly worse results for the FCA-based method and Bi-Section-KMeans, but better results for the agglomerative clustering algorithms on both domains. In general, we conclude that pseudo-syntactic dependencies indeed provide a reasonable alternative to extracting contextual features from parse trees, even yielding better results in most cases. A comparison of the results of the best configuration for each algorithm on both domains can be found in Table 6.15. The table in addition highlights the fact that every approach has its own benefits and drawbacks. The main benefit of using FCA is, on the one hand, that on our datasets it performed better than the other algorithms, thus producing better concept hierarchies. On the other hand, it does not only generate clusters — formal concepts to be more specific — but it also provides an intensional description for these clusters, thus contributing to better understanding by the ontology engineer (compare Figure 6.3 (left)). This is in contrast to the similarity-based methods, which do not provide the same level of traceability due to the fact that it is the numerical value of the similarity between two high-dimensional vectors which drives the clustering process and which thus remains opaque to the engineer. The agglomerative and divisive approach are different in this respect as, in the agglomerative paradigm, initial merges of small-size clusters correspond to high degrees of similarity and are thus more understandable, while in the divisive paradigm the splitting of clusters aims at minimizing the overall cluster variance thus being harder to trace. A crucial difference is that, in contrast to the similarity-based clustering approaches, FCA produces concept hierarchies with a sound and formal interpretation in terms of attribute inheritance. A clear disadvantage of FCA is that the size of the lattice can get exponential in the size of the context in the worst case, thus resulting in an exponential time complexity — compared to $O(n^2 \log n)$ and $O(n^2)$ for agglomerative clustering and Bi-Section-KMeans, respectively. The implementation of FCA we have used is the *concepts* tool by Christian Lindig[5], which basically implements Ganter's Next Closure algorithm [Ganter and Reuter, 1991, Ganter and Wille, 1999] as described in Section 4.2 with the extension of Aloui for computing the covering relation described by Godin et al. [Godin et al., 1995]. Figure 6.13 shows the number of seconds over the number of attribute–object pairs it took FCA to compute the lattice of formal concepts compared to the time needed by a naive $O(n^3)$ implementation of the agglomerative algorithm with complete linkage. It can be seen that FCA performs quite efficiently compared to the agglomerative clustering algorithm. This is due to the fact that the object–attribute matrix is sparsely populated. Such observations have already been made before. Godin et al. [Godin et al., 1995], for example, suspect that the lattice size increases linearly with the number of attributes per object. Lindig [Lindig, 2000] presents empirical results analyzing contexts with a fill ratio below 0.1 and comes to the conclusion that the lattice size grows quadratically with respect to the size of the incidence relation I. Similar findings have also been reported by Carpineto and Romano [Carpineto and Romano, 1996]. Figure 6.14 shows the number of attributes over the terms' rank, where the rank is a natural number indicating the position of the word in a list ordered by decreasing term frequencies. It can be appreciated that the amount of (non-zero) attributes is distributed in a Zipfian way (compare [Zipf, 1932]), i.e. a small number of objects have a lot of attributes, while a large number of them have just a few. In particular, for the tourism domain, the term with most attributes is person with 3077 attributes, while on average a term has approx. 178 attributes. The total number of attributes considered is 9738, so that we conclude that the object–attribute matrix contains almost 98% zero

---

[5] http://www.st.cs.uni-sb.de/~lindig/src/concepts.html

values. For the finance domain, the term with highest rank is percent with 2870 attributes, the average being approx. 202 attributes. The total number of attributes is 21542, such that we can state that in this case more than 99% of the matrix is populated with zero-values and thus are much sparser than the ones considered by Lindig [Lindig, 2000]. These figures explain why FCA performs efficiently in our experiments. Concluding, though the worst-time complexity is exponential, FCA is much more efficient than the agglomerative clustering algorithm in our settings.

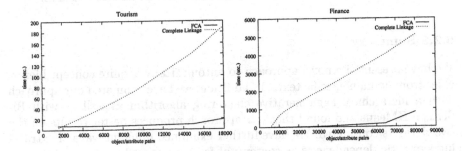

Fig. 6.13. Comparison of the time complexities for FCA and agglomerative clustering for the tourism and finance domains

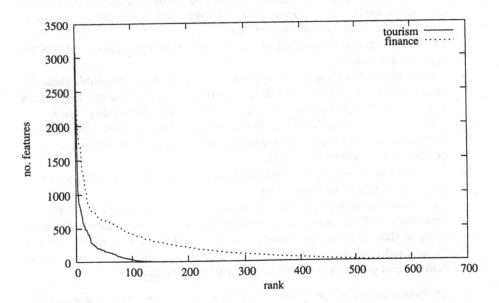

Fig. 6.14. Distribution of features: number of (non-zero) features over word rank

Table 6.15. Trade-offs between different taxonomy construction methods

	Effectiveness (F')		Worst Case Complexity	Traceability	Size
	Tourism	Finance			
FCA	**48.82%**	**38.85%**	$O(2^n)$	**Good**	Large
Agglomerative:					
Complete	40.60%	38.43%	$O(n^2 \log n)$	Fair	**Small**
Average	40.72%	32.92%	$O(n^2)$		
Single	44.85%	32.47%	$O(n^2)$		
Bi-Section-KMeans	36.42%	32.77%	$O(n^2)$	Weak	**Small**

6.2.5 Summary

We have presented a novel approach to automatically acquire concept hierarchies from domain-specific texts. In addition, we have compared our approach with a hierarchical agglomerative clustering algorithm as well as with Bi-Section-KMeans and found that our approach produces better results on the two datasets considered. We have further examined different ways of extracting syntactic dependencies as contextual features as well as various information measures to weight the significance of an attribute–object pair. The main conclusions can be summarized as follows:

- FCA outperforms the similarity-based methods on both domains with respect to global quality of the hierarchies as measured by the taxonomic overlap as well as with respect to local coherence of the clusters as measured by the local taxonomic overlap.
- FCA is efficient in our setting due to the fact that the formal contexts are sparsely populated.
- The results of the FCA-based approach are more understandable than the ones produced by other algorithms. Furthermore, the concept hierarchies have a sound logical interpretation in terms of attribute inheritance.
- The conditional probability yields reasonable results as weighting measure compared to other more elaborate measures such as PMI or the one based on Resnik's selectional strength.
- Our smoothing technique based on the notion of mutual similarity in general does not improve the results.
- Pseudo-syntactic dependencies are an interesting alternative to extracting dependencies from parse trees, as they can be extracted more efficiently using shallow parsing techniques and have yielded better results for our FCA-based and the agglomerative clustering approaches on the tourism domain and comparable results on the finance domain.

As mentioned at the beginning of this chapter, two main challenges remain when using an unsupervised approach to inducing a concept hierarchy. First, as distributional similarity is the criterion driving the clustering process, the methods presented in this section are very sensitive to the frequency of the words. This leads in some cases to the creation of spurious clusters of words which appear to be similar according to their behavior in the corpus, but are actually not similar from a semantic point of view. To some extent, this problem can be addressed by finding a similarity measure which is more sensitive to sparse data, but this does not solve the problem in a principled way. The second challenge is to find appropriate labels describing the intension of the cluster. In some sense, the FCA-based clustering presented in this section has addressed this issue, but also here we encounter problems. First of all, there are a large number of corpus-derived attributes that are considered, thus sometimes also leading to large intensions. Second, instead of a whole set of attributes characterizing the concept in question, sometimes we would like to have one label unambiguously describing the sense or intension of the cluster. The following section presents an approach addressing both challenges in an algorithmic manner.

6.3 Guided Clustering

Most approaches aiming at learning concept hierarchies are based on unsupervised learning paradigms. These approaches rely on the possibility of assessing the semantic similarity between words on the basis of the amount of linguistic context they share in a given corpus. In order to induce a hierarchy between concepts, many approaches exploit clustering algorithms such as the approach of Pereira et al. [Pereira et al., 1993], which uses a soft clustering method relying on deterministic annealing to find lowest distortion sets of clusters. Others use agglomerative clustering (c.f. [Faure and Nedellec, 1998, Caraballo, 1999, Bisson et al., 2000]). As shown in the previous section, divisive algorithms such as Bi-Section-KMeans or conceptual clustering algorithms such as Formal Concept Analysis are also applicable. However, there are two major problems shared by all of these approaches. On the one hand, there is the problem of data sparseness leading to the fact that certain syntactic similarities with respect to the corpus are spurious and due to missing data (cf. [Zipf, 1932]), thus not corresponding to real-world or semantic similarities. On the other hand, all the approaches share the problem of not being able to appropriately label the produced clusters. In this section, we present a new algorithm addressing both issues. The algorithm is a novel guided hierarchical agglomerative clustering algorithm exploiting a hypernym oracle automatically extracted from different resources in a first step. Though there exist approaches making use of hypernyms extracted by other means for labeling the concepts as in the approach of Caraballo [Caraballo, 1999], the principle difference in the approach presented in this section is that, instead of merely post-processing the hierarchy, the hypernyms are directly used to guide the clustering algorithm. In fact, in our guided algorithm, two terms are only clustered if there is a corresponding common hypernym according to the oracle, thus making the clustering less error-prone. We demonstrate this claim by presenting results comparing our approach with Caraballo's algorithm [Caraballo, 1999] on the tourism and finance domains. Further, we also present a comparison between our guided algorithm and Caraballo's method in terms of a human evaluation of the hierarchies produced for the tourism domain.

6.3.1 Oracle-Guided Agglomerative Clustering

In this section, we present the guided agglomerative clustering approach for learning concept hierarchies. The approach relies on the distributional similarity of terms with respect to an underlying corpus. Furthermore, it is guided in the sense that it exploits hypernyms acquired by other means to drive the clustering process. In particular, the approach exploits hypernyms extracted from WordNet as well as an approach matching lexico-syntactic patterns indicating a hypernym-relationship as suggested by Hearst (compare [Hearst, 1992] and Section 6.1.2). The clustering algorithm is then driven by these extracted hypernyms in the sense that, given two terms which are similar according to their corpus behavior, it will either order them as subconcepts, in case one is a hypernym of the other, or – in case they have a common hypernym – add them as siblings under a concept labeled with that hypernym. Figure 6.15 gives an overview of the approach. The figure shows in particular that the hypernym oracle is constructed using information from WordNet, the Web as well as the corpus. The similarity between words is calculated on the basis of the corpus. The clustering algorithm then groups words on the basis of the computed similarities, using the hypernym oracle as a guide. In a first phase, the bottom-up algorithm we present only clusters words which have a common hypernym according to the oracle, thus reducing the number of accidental clusterings. In what follows, we first describe how the similarity between terms is calculated in Section 6.3.1.1. Then we describe our method for extracting hypernyms from different resources in Section 6.3.1.2. After presenting the actual algorithm in Section 6.3.1.3, we discuss an example for illustration purposes in Section 6.3.1.4.

6.3.1.1 Calculating Term Similarities

In order to calculate the similarity between terms, we rely on Harris' distributional hypothesis [Harris, 1968] claiming that terms are semantically similar to the extent to which they share similar syntactic contexts. As it is usual, we formalize the context of a term as a vector mirroring the pseudo-syntactic dependencies automatically extracted from the corpus for the term in question (compare Section 4.1.4.2). On the basis of these vectors, we calculate the similarity between two terms t_1 and t_2 as the cosine between their corresponding vectors. According to the cosine measure (compare Section 4.1.5.2), the following ten pairs of terms are the ten most similar terms of the *tourism* reference taxonomy with respect to our *Tourism corpus* (compare Section 5):

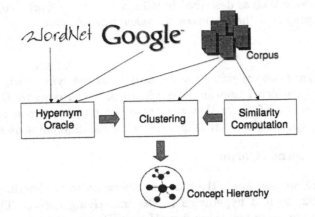

Fig. 6.15. Overview of guided agglomerative clustering (GAC)

(t_1,t_2)	Cosine similarity
(autumn,summer)	0.93
(autumn,night)	0.83
(summer,spring)	0.72
(person,living thing)	0.69
(trip,visit)	0.68
(winter,summer)	0.66
(badminton,tennis)	0.65
(day,morning)	0.64
(tennis,golf)	0.64
(farm,town)	0.62

6.3.1.2 The Hypernym Oracle

The guided agglomerative clustering algorithm relies on an oracle returning possible hypernyms for a given term. Thus, before applying the actual algorithm, the oracle needs to be constructed. In this section, we describe an automatic approach to construct such an oracle which in essence is a function

$$H : String \to 2^{String \times \mathbb{N}}$$

which for a term t returns a set of tuples (h, f), where h is a hypernym and f is the number of times the algorithm has found evidence for it. We also define the first projection $H_1(t)$ returning the set of hypernyms of t:

$$H_1(t) := \{h \mid \exists n \ (h, n) \in H(t)\}$$

In order to find these hypernyms, we make use of three sources: (i) WordNet, (ii) Hearst patterns matched in a corpus, and (iii) Hearst patterns matched in the World Wide Web as described in [Cimiano et al., 2005c]. We briefly show in the following how these sources are taken into account.

WordNet

For each term t, we collect all the hypernyms in the synsets which dominate any synset in which t appears. We add these hypernyms to $H(t)$ together with the number of times that the corresponding hypernym appears in a dominating synset. We are thus ignoring here the different senses of t.

Hearst Patterns (Corpus)

Furthermore, we also apply the lexico-syntactic patterns described by Hearst [Hearst, 1992] to find hypernyms in the underlying corpus. The following patterns we use are in fact taken from Hearst [Hearst, 1992] (compare Section 6.1.2):

(1) NP_0 such as NP_1, NP_2, ..., NP_{n-1} (and|or) NP_n
(2) such NP_0 as NP_1, NP_2, ... NP_{n-1} (and|or) NP_n
(3) NP_1, NP_2, ..., NP_n (and|or) other NP_0
(4) NP_0, (including|especially) NP_1, NP_2, ..., NP_{n-1} (and|or) NP_n

In addition, we also use the following patterns:

(5) NP_1 is NP_0
(6) NP_1, another NP_0
(7) NP_0 like NP_1

Now given two terms t_1 and t_2, we record how many times a Hearst-pattern indicating an *isa*-relation between t_1 and t_2 is matched in the corpus. In order to match the above patterns, we create regular expressions over part-of-speech tags to match NP's. In particular, we use the TreeTagger described in [Schmid, 1994] and match non-recursive NP's consisting of a determiner, an optional sequence of modifying adjectives and a sequence of common nouns constituting the head of the NP.

Hearst Patterns (WWW)

Additionally, we also follow an approach in which web pages are actually downloaded and Hearst patterns are matched offline. For this purpose, we assign one or more functions $f_i : string \rightarrow string$ – which we will refer to as *clues* – to each of the Hearst patterns i to be matched. Given a concept of interest c, we instantiate each of the clues and download a number of pages (100 in our experiments) matching the query $f_i(c)$ using the Google API. For example, given the clue $f(x) = "such\ as" \oplus \pi(x)$ and the concept country, we would download the first 100 Google abstracts matching the query f(country), i.e. "such as countries".[6] For each concept of interest and for each of the correspondingly instantiated clues, we then process the downloaded documents by matching the corresponding pattern, thus yielding its potential superconcepts. The following table gives the clues used as well as the number of the corresponding Hearst pattern:

Clue	Hearst pattern
$f(x) = $ "such as" $\oplus \pi(x)$	(1)
$f(x) = \pi(x) \oplus$ "and other"	(3)
$f(x) = \pi(x) \oplus$ "or other"	(3)
$f(x) = $ "including" $\oplus \pi(x)$	(4)
$f(x) = $ "especially" $\oplus \pi(x)$	(4)
$f(x) = x \oplus$ "is"	(5)

It is important to notice that no clues have been defined for Hearst patterns (2), (6) and (7). Defining a pattern for (2) would require some support for querying regular expressions as, sticking to the country example, we would need to query for an expression like 'such * as countries'. As Google did not provide such a support at the time these experiments were carried out,[7] no clue has been defined for this pattern. Patterns (6) and (7) were found to deliver very noisy results when used on the Web and have not been considered therefore.

The following table shows the results of the above described hypernym extraction process for the term summer. In particular, for each resource it gives the hypernyms as well as the number of times evidence was found in the corresponding resource:

Hearst Corpus	
is-a(summer,heat)	1
is-a(summer,performer)	1
is-a(summer,time)	1
is-a(summer,mind)	1
is-a(summer,tubing)	1
Hearst WWW	
is-a(summer,time)	3
is-a(summer,vacation)	2
is-a(summer,period)	1
is-a(summer,season)	1
is-a(summer,skill)	1
WordNet	
is-a(summer,period)	1

---

[6] Here, $\oplus$ denotes the concatenation operator defined on two strings and $\pi(t)$ is a function returning the correct plural form of t.

[7] Recently, Google has added functionality to issue queries containing wildcards.

In this example, the results of the different resources would add up to 4 for the hypernym time, 2 for the hypernym vacation and 2 for the hypernym period as well as 1 for the rest of the candidate hypernyms in the table.

6.3.1.3 Algorithm

In this section, we describe the guided agglomerative clustering algorithm for inducing concept hierarchies. The algorithm is specified by the pseudocode in Algorithms 8 and 9.

Algorithm 8 Guided Clustering Algorithm (GAC)

---

1. Input: a list T of k terms to be ordered hierarchically
2. Calculate the similarity between each pair of terms ($O(n^2)$) and sort them from highest to lowest ($O(n \log n)$).
   Initialize the set of clustered terms C, i.e. $C := \emptyset$
3. FOREACH pair (t_1, t_2) in the ordered list representing a potential pair to be clustered, if either t_1 or t_2 has NOT been classified as subconcept of some other concept:
   a) IF $(t_1, m) \in H(t_2)$
      i. IF $(t_2, n) \in H(t_1)$ and $n > m$, THEN isa(t_1, t_2)
      ii. ELSE isa(t_2, t_1)
   b) ELSE IF $(t_2, m) \in H(t_1)$
      i. isa(t_1, t_2)
   c) ELSE IF $(h, n) \in H(t_1)$ and $(h, m) \in H(t_2)$ and there is no h' such that $(h', p) \in H(t_1)$ and $(h', q) \in H(t_2)$ and $p + q > m + n$
      i. IF isa(t_1, t'), i.e t_1 is already classified as t'
         A. IF t' == h, THEN isa(t_2, t')
         B. ELSE IF $(h, n) \in H(t')$ and $((t', m) \in H(h) \to m < n)$
            IF t_2 has not yet been classified, THEN isa(t_2, t')
            IF t' has not yet been classified, THEN isa(t', h)
         C. ELSE
            IF t_2 has not yet been classified THEN isa(t_2, h)
            IF h has not yet been classified, THEN isa(h, t')
      ii. ELSE IF isa(t_2, t'), i.e. t_2 is already classified as t'
         /* (analogous case to 3c i) */
         A. IF t' == h, THEN isa(t_1, t')
         B. ELSE IF $(h, n) \in H(t')$ and $((t', m) \in H(h) \to m < n)$
            as t_1 has not yet been classified, THEN isa(t_1, t')
            IF t' has not yet been classified, THEN isa(t', h)
         C. ELSE
            as t_1 has not yet been classified, THEN isa(t_1, h)
            IF h has not yet been classified, THEN isa(h, t')
      iii. ELSE, as neither t_1 nor t_2 have been classified, isa(t_1, h), isa(t_2, h) .
   d) ELSE, as there are no common hypernyms, mark t_1 and t_2 as clustered, i.e.
      $C := C \cup \{(t_1, t_2)\}$

Algorithm 9 Guided Clustering Algorithm (Cont'd)

4. FOREACH term $t \in T$ which has not been processed (because no similar terms were found in the corpus), if there is some other term t' such that r-matches(t,t'), THEN isa(t',t)

5. FOREACH $(t_1, t_2) \in C$
   a) IF there is a t' such that isa(t_1,t') AND t_2 has not been classified, THEN isa(t_2,t')
   b) ELSE IF there is a t' such that isa(t_2,t') AND t_1 has not been classified, THEN isa(t_1,t')
   c) ELSE select the pair $(t', m) \in H(t_1) \cup H(t_2)$ for which there is no $(t'', n) \in H(t_1) \cup H(t_2)$ such that $n > m$ and create the following structures: isa(t_1,t') and isa(t_2,t')

6. FOREACH term $t \in T$ which has not been classified, put it directly under the root concept, i.e. isa(t,root)

7. Output: a labeled concept hierarchy for the terms in T

For each pair (t_1, t_2), the algorithm thus first consults the hypernym oracle to find out if t_1 is a hypernym of t_2 or the other way round, creating the appropriate subconcept relation (3a and 3b). If this is not the case (3c), it consults the oracle for common hypernyms of both terms, selecting the most frequent hypernym h and distinguishes three cases. In case none of the terms has already been classified (3c iii), it creates a new concept labeled with h together with two subconcepts labeled as t_1 and t_2. In case one of the two terms, say t_1, has already been classified as $isa(t_1, t')$, there are three more cases to distinguish. In the first case (3c i.A), if h and t' are identical, the algorithm simply puts a concept t_2 under t' (compare Figure 6.16 (left)). In the second case (3c i.B), if, according to the oracle, h is a hypernym of t', it creates the structure in Figure 6.16 (middle). In case it is not a hypernym (3c i.C), it creates the structure in Figure 6.16 (right). The algorithm proceeds analogously in case t_2 has already been classified. In case there are no common hypernyms, t_1 and t_2 are simply marked as clustered for further processing (3d). This is done for all the similarity pairs, provided that one of the two terms has not been classified yet.

After this process, the algorithm exploits the 'head'-heuristic used by Velardi et al. [Velardi et al., 2001], adding t_2 as subconcept of t_1, in case t_1 r-matches t_2 in the way 'credit card' matches 'international credit card' (compare step 4 of Algorithm 8). More formally, the r-matches relation is defined as follows:

Definition 26 (r-matches) *A term t_1 r-matches a term t_2 iff $\exists x \; x \oplus t_1 = t_2$ where $\oplus$ is the string concatenating operator.*

The x in the above definition typically represents some adjectival or nominal modification of t_1. Then, all the pairs (t_1, t_2) which have been clustered and kept for later processing are considered (compare step 5), and if either t_1 or t_2 has already been classified (5a and 5b), the other term is added under the

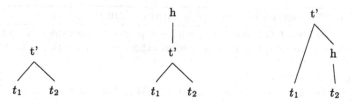

Fig. 6.16. Structures constructed by Guided Agglomerative Clustering in steps 3c i.A and 3c i.B and 3c i.C, respectively

corresponding superconcept. If this is not the case, both terms are added as subconcepts of the most frequent hypernym in $H(t_1) \cup H(t_2)$ according to the oracle (5c). At the end, every unclassified term is added directly under the root concept (6).

The overall time complexity of the algorithm is thus $O(k^2)$ as steps 2, 3, 4 and 5 have complexity $O(k^2)$, and step 6 is even linear in the number of terms $k = |T|$. The algorithm is thus as efficient as agglomerative clustering with single linkage or average linkage and more efficient than agglomerative clustering with complete linkage (compare Section 4.3.2.2). In practice, however, the algorithm is much more efficient because there is no need to update the similarity matrix in each cycle and similarity is always computed between elements and never between clusters.

As already mentioned in the introduction, this algorithm can be considered as guided as it depends on an external hypernym oracle. The obvious benefit is that, by only clustering terms at first steps of the algorithm in case they have a common hypernym according to the oracle, the clustering process is more controlled and less error-prone. This claim is demonstrated experimentally in Section 6.3.2. Furthermore, the approach also allows for labeling abstract concepts in an appropriate way.

It is important to emphasize that the outcome of the algorithm does not simply mirror the hypernym oracle, but is in fact implicitly performing sense disambiguation. Due to the fact that we look up the common hypernym of two terms which are similar with respect to the underlying corpus, we are more likely to find a hypernym (of the many contained in the oracle for both terms separately) which corresponds to the common sense of both terms in the domain in question, thus finding more appropriate labels than when processing each term separately.

6.3.1.4 An Example

In order to illustrate the above algorithm, let us consider again the top ten most similar pairs with respect to the *Tourism* corpus (see section 6.3.2 for details about the dataset), together with their common hypernyms as well as the corresponding occurrences in Table 6.16.

Table 6.16. Common hypernyms with occurrences for the top ten most similar pairs of terms

(t_1,t_2)	Sim	Hypernym	Count
(autumn,summer)	0.93		
		period	3
(autumn,night)	0.83		
		period	5
(summer,spring)	0.72		
		period	3
(person,living thing)	0.69		
(trip,visit)	0.68		
		activity	23
		event	10
		travel	3
		outing	2
(winter,summer)	0.66		
		season	3
(badminton,tennis)	0.65		
		human activity	2
		sport	2
(day,morning)	0.64		
		time	10
		period	9
		day	4
		work	4
		others	2
(tennis,golf)	0.64		
		sport	2
(farm,town)	0.62		
		area	15
		place	9
		entity	6
		landscape	6
		unit	5
		country	2
		structure	2

After the first three iterations of the FOREACH-loop in step 3 of Algorithm 8, autumn, summer, night and spring are added as subconcepts of a concept labeled with period according to steps 3c iii, 3c i.A and 3c i.A, respectively. In the 4th iteration, as living thing is a hypernym of person according to our hypernym oracle, person is added as a subconcept of living thing according to case 3a of our algorithm. In the 5th iteration, trip and visit are added as subconcepts of a concept labeled with activity according to step 3c iii. Interesting is the 6th iteration, in which, as season is not a hypernym of period following the oracle, a new concept season, with winter as subconcept is created as subconcept of period – according to case 3c ii.B. Then, badminton and tennis are added as subconcepts of human activity according to case 3c iii. In the 8th iteration, according to case 3c iii. again, a new concept time is created with day and morning as subconcepts. Finally, as sport is a human activity and not the other way round, golf is added as a subconcept of sport according to step 3c i.B; farm and town are added as subconcepts of a new concept area according to 3c iii.

As all pairs have been processed, then, as activity r-matches human activity, the latter, following step 4, is added as a subconcept of the former thus yielding at the end the concept hierarchy depicted in Figure 6.17. This hierarchy is certainly far from perfect but shows that the results of our algorithm are quite reasonable.

6.3.2 Evaluation

In order to evaluate the automatically produced concept hierarchies, we compare them to a handcrafted reference concept hierarchy but also present the hierarchy to a test person in order to assess its quality more directly. In order to compare the automatically learned hierarchies with a reference hierarchy, we use the taxonomic overlap measures described in Section 6.2.3. However, we make use of the standard definition of the semantic cotopy as proposed by Mädche and Staab [Mädche and Staab, 2002] but with a variant of the taxonomic overlap which is defined as follows:

$$\overline{TO}(O_1, O_2) = \frac{1}{|C_1 \backslash L(C_1)|} \sum_{c \in C_1 \backslash L(C_1)} TO(c, O_1, O_2) \qquad (6.25)$$

where

$$TO(c, O_1, O_2) := \begin{cases} TO'(c, O_1, O_2) & \text{if } c \in C_2 \backslash L(C_2) \\ TO''(c, O_1, O_2) & \text{if } c \notin C_2 \backslash L(C_2) \end{cases} \qquad (6.26)$$

and TO' and TO'' are defined as follows:

$$TO'(c, O_1, O_2) := \frac{|SC(c, O_1, O_2) \cap SC(c, O_2, O_1)|}{|SC(c, O_1, O_2) \cup SC(c, O_2, O_1)|} \qquad (6.27)$$

$$TO''(c, O_1, O_2) := max_{c' \in C_2 \backslash L(C_2)} \frac{|SC(c, O_1, O_2) \cap SC(c', O_2, O_1)|}{|SC(c, O_1, O_2) \cup SC(c', O_2, O_1)|} \qquad (6.28)$$

where $L(C)$ are the leaf nodes with respect to the concept hierarchy $\leq_C$. So we are excluding leaf nodes from the taxonomic overlap computation. The reason for this is the same as explained in Chapter 6.2; that is, the fact that otherwise trivial concept hierarchies having every concept directly subordinated by the root node can be rated very highly in terms of taxonomic overlap compared to a standard hierarchy, especially in terms of recall. The measures used here

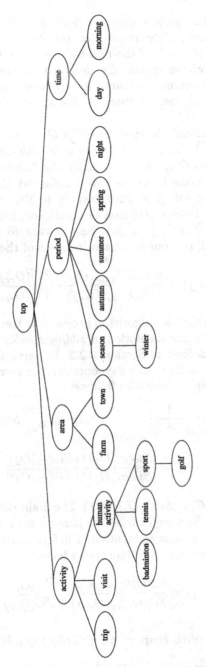

Fig. 6.17. Example for an automatically learned concept hierarchy

are thus similar to the ones introduced in Section 6.2.3, but do not rely on the common semantic cotopy. The reason for introducing the common semantic cotopy was the lack of labels of the non-leaf concepts. Guided agglomerative clustering is an algorithm specifically designed to overcome the lack of labels. Thus, using the common semantic cotopy would make no sense in these settings. Unfortunately, the drawback is that the results can not be directly compared.

Given an automatically learned ontology O_{auto} and a reference ontology O_{ref}, calculating $\overline{TO}(O_{auto}, O_{ref})$ amounts to calculating the precision of O_{auto} with respect to O_{ref} as we calculate the taxonomic overlap for each concept in O_{auto}. In order to assess how satisfactory the coverage of the automatically learned ontology is with respect to the reference ontology, we need to compute the inverse precision or recall, too, i.e. $R_{TO}(O_{auto}, O_{ref}) = P_{TO}(O_{ref}, O_{auto}) = \overline{TO}(O_{ref}, O_{auto})$. As we want to maximize both recall and precision, we evaluate our approach in terms of the F-Measure:

$$F_{TO}(O_{auto}, O_{ref}) = \frac{2\,\overline{TO}(O_{auto}, O_{ref})\,\overline{TO}(O_{ref}, O_{auto})}{\overline{TO}(O_{auto}, O_{ref}) + \overline{TO}(O_{ref}, O_{auto})} \qquad (6.29)$$

To support our claim that our algorithm produces better groupings or clusters of terms, we also introduce the notion of *sibling overlap* (SO) building on the notion of sibling as defined in Section 6.2.3. In particular, we only consider sets of siblings with at least two elements for the comparison; that is, the average sibling overlap is defined as follows:

$$\overline{SO}(O_1, O_2) := \frac{1}{|Sib_{O_1}^{\geq 1}|} \sum_{c_1 \in Sib_{O_1}^{\geq 1}} max_{c_2 \in Sib_{O_2}^{\geq 1}} SO(c_1, c_2, O_1, O_2) \qquad (6.30)$$

$$SO(c_1, c_2, O_1, O_2) := \frac{|Sib(c_1, O_1) \cap Sib(c_2, O_2)|}{|Sib(c_1, O_1) \cup Sib(c_2, O_2)|} \qquad (6.31)$$

where $Sib_{O_i}^{\geq 1} := \{c \in C_i : |Sib(c, O_i)| > 1\}$ The main difference to the sibling overlap introduced in Section 6.2.3 is that here we are not relying on common siblings for the same reasons as mentioned before concerning the taxonomic overlap. We also calculate the F-Measure as follows:

$$F_{SO}(O_{auto}, O_{ref}) = \frac{2\,\overline{SO}(O_{auto}, O_{ref})\,\overline{SO}(O_{ref}, O_{auto})}{\overline{SO}(O_{auto}, O_{ref}) + \overline{SO}(O_{ref}, O_{auto})} \qquad (6.32)$$

6.3.2.1 Evaluation with respect to a Gold Standard

As tourism text collection we use the *Lonely Planet* as well as *Mecklenburg* corpora together with the British National Corpus (BNC). For the finance domain, we use the *Reuters-21578* corpus. The reference ontologies are $O_{tourism}$ and $O_{Finance}$, respectively (compare Section 5).

In order to evaluate our approach, we implemented the method described by Caraballo [Caraballo, 1999], in which first a hierarchy is produced by standard agglomerative clustering and then hypernyms derived from Hearst patterns are attached to each cluster. The most frequent hypernym is then taken as a label for the cluster, provided that it is a valid hypernym for at least two elements in the cluster. Finally, the hierarchy is compressed by removing all clusters without a label. In our implementation of Caraballo's approach, we apply *complete linkage* as strategy to calculate the similarity between clusters, in contrast to Caraballo, who used *average linkage*. In addition, we employ our full hypernym oracle instead of merely the hypernyms derived from Hearst patterns.

Table 6.17 shows the results of comparing the concept hierarchies produced by our guided agglomerative clustering approach and by Caraballo's method with the reference concept hierarchy in terms of the taxonomic overlap measures for the tourism and finance domains. In particular, the table shows results for different combinations of the resources used for the construction of the oracle. The best result for our method on the tourism domain is $F_{TO}^{tourism,GAC} = 21.40\%$ using evidences derived from WordNet and Hearst patterns, compared to a best result of $F_{TO}^{tourism,Caraballo} = 18.29$ obtained with Caraballo's method, only using Hearst patterns.

On the finance domain, the guided agglomerative clustering achieves a best result of $F_{TO}^{finance,GAC} = 18.51\%$ using Hearst patterns only, whereas Caraballo's method yields a best result of $F_{TO}^{finance,Caraballo} = 10.16\%$. Our method thus outperforms Caraballo's approach on both domains. In general, Hearst patterns represent a very reliable resource for the oracle, while using WordNet alone does not yield very satisfactory results in most cases. Overall, it seems valid to conclude that using Hearst patterns alone or in combination with WordNet or the patterns matched in the WWW represents a good oracle configuration. Unfortunately, these observations can not be generalized given the experimental results at hand as no general pattern seems to emerge.

The corresponding results in terms of sibling overlap are given in Table 6.18. On the tourism domain, the guided agglomerative clustering algorithm achieves a best result of $F_{SO}^{tourism,GAC} = 12.91\%$ relying only on Hearst patterns. This compares to a best result of $F_{SO}^{tourism,Caraballo} = 8.04\%$ obtained with Caraballo's method relying on WordNet and the patterns matched on the WWW. On the finance domain, we get corresponding best results of $F_{SO}^{finance,GAC} = 14.62\%$ using Hearst patterns matched in the corpus and on the WWW and $F_{SO}^{finance,Caraballo} = 7.79\%$ using the same oracle configuration. Two conclusions can be drawn here: on the one hand, our method clearly outperforms Caraballo's method in terms of sibling overlap. This demonstrates that our approach is producing better clusters than Caraballo's method. On the other hand, we can state that the oracle configuration using Hearst patterns matched in the corpus and on the Web yields quite satisfactory results. Using WordNet and the WWW Hearst patterns also yields good results, but using WordNet alone produces very bad results for Caraballo's method. The reason is that there are not enough hypernyms, with the result that a lot of unlabeled nodes are removed at the compaction step, leading to very flat hierarchical structures.

These results, unfortunately, can not be compared to the results presented in Section 6.2 as we have not used the modified semantic cotopy here.

Table 6.17. Comparison of results for Guided Agglomerative Clustering and Caraballo's method in terms of $\overline{TO}$ on both domains

Tourism			
	TO(auto,ref)	TO(ref,auto)	F_{TO}(auto,ref)
Guided Agglomerative Clustering			
WWW	17.10%	20.54%	18.67%
Hearst	19.46%	20.94%	20.18%
Hearst + WWW	16.72%	20.43%	18.39%
WordNet	17.76%	18.52%	18.13%
WordNet + WWW	18.24%	20.72%	19.40%
WordNet + Hearst	20.48%	22.41%	**21.40%**
WordNet + Hearst+ WWW	17.05%	21.02%	18.83%
Caraballo's method			
WWW	12.09%	20.25%	15.14%
Hearst	17.65%	18.99%	**18.29%**
Hearst + WWW	11.89%	20.50%	15.05%
WordNet	41.47%	10.03%	16.15%
WordNet + WWW	12.07%	20.18%	15.10%
WordNet + Hearst	17.5%	19.02%	18.23%
WordNet + Hearst + WWW	11.93%	20.46%	15.07%
Finance			
	TO(auto,ref)	TO(ref,auto)	F_{TO}(auto,ref)
Guided Agglomerative Clustering			
WWW	19.46%	17.17%	18.24%
Hearst	18.94%	18.09%	**18.51%**
Hearst + WWW	18.54%	17.76%	18.14%
WordNet	18.21%	16.23%	17.16%
WordNet + WWW	18.12%	16.61%	17.33%
WordNet + Hearst	17%	15.75%	16.35%
WordNet + Hearst + WWW	15.66%	14.27%	14.93%
Caraballo's method			
WWW	10%	9.74%	9.87%
Hearst	9.87	9.7%	9.78%
Hearst + WWW	9.08%	11.42%	10.11%
WordNet	34.78%	2.42%	4.53%
WordNet + WWW	9.96%	9.76%	9.86%
WordNet + Hearst	9.92%	9.71%	9.82%
WordNet + Hearst + WWW	9.1%	11.49%	**10.16%**

Table 6.18. Comparison of results for Guided Agglomerative Clustering and Caraballo's method in terms of $\overline{SO}$ (in percent) on both domains

	Tourism		
	SO(auto,ref)	SO(ref,auto)	F_{SO}(auto,ref)
	Guided Agglomerative Clustering		
WWW	13.5%	10.51%	11.82%
Hearst	14.07%	11.93%	**12.91%**
Hearst + WWW	13.86%	11.48%	12.56%
WordNet	12.19%	9.21%	10.49%
WordNet +WWW	13.74%	11.25%	12.37%
WordNet + Hearst	12.42%	10.12%	11.15%
WordNet + Hearst+ WWW	13.78%	11.28%	12.41%
	Caraballo's method		
WWW	6.89%	9.52%	8%
Hearst	7.67%	5.32%	6.28%
Hearst + WWW	6.79%	9.34%	7.86%
WordNet	7.68%	1.51%	2.52%
WordNet +WWW	6.9%	9.62%	**8.04%**
WordNet + Hearst	7.8%	5.56%	6.49%
WordNet + Hearst + WWW	6.87%	9.43%	7.95%
	Finance		
	SO(auto,ref)	SO(ref,auto)	F_{SO}(auto,ref)
	Guided Agglomerative Clustering		
WWW	16.62%	13.3%	14.77%
Hearst	16.35%	12.36%	14.08%
Hearst + WWW	15.96%	13.48%	**14.62%**
WordNet	17.66%	12.21%	14.44%
WordNet + WWW	16.64%	12.79%	14.47%
WordNet + Hearst	16.1%	12.4%	14.01%
WordNet + Hearst+ WWW	15.52%	12.8%	14.03%
	Caraballo's method		
WWW	7.87%	7.12%	7.47%
Hearst	7.4%	6.1%	6.68%
Hearst + WWW	7.26%	8.41%	**7.79%**
WordNet	8.67%	0.4%	0.76%
WordNet + WWW	7.88%	7.11%	7.48%
WordNet + Hearst	7.28%	6.01%	6.58%
WordNet + Hearst + WWW	7.21%	8.39%	7.76%

6.3.2.2 Human Assessment

As Sabou et al. [Sabou, 2005] have shown, using a gold standard for the evaluation of automatically constructed ontologies is sometimes problematic and may lead to wrong conclusions about the quality of the learned ontologies.

This is due to the fact that if the learned ontology does not mirror the gold standard, it does not necessarily mean that it is wrong or inappropriate. In order to assess the quality of the automatically learned concept hierarchies more directly, we asked a student at our institute to validate the learned *isa*-relations by assigning credits from 3 (correct), over 2 (almost correct) and 1 (not completely wrong) to 0 (wrong). Actually, we did not consider those *isa*-relations classifying a concept directly under root as it seems very difficult to assess what should be directly under root and what not. Then, we calculated the precision of the system counting an *isa*-relation as correct if it received three credits (P_3), at least two credits (P_2) and at least one credit (P_1), respectively. The precision for the versions of our approach using different combinations of the hypernym resources are given in Table 6.19, showing also the number of *isa*-relations evaluated. The results corroborate the claim that the concept hierarchies produced by our method are quite reasonable according to human intuitions. Actually, the fact that 65.66% of the learned relations are considered as totally correct by our evaluator is a very impressive result. The results of the human evaluation for the hierarchies produced by Caraballo's method can also be found in Table 6.19. In general, the results are certainly lower. The highest result of 100% is achieved with a hierarchy with only 4 non-root taxonomic relations compared to 267 taxonomic relations with root as superconcept. The results here have thus to be regarded as an outlier. The four relations were the following:

```
is_a(swimming,human_activity)
is_a(camping,human_activity)
is_a(ferry,vehicle)
is_a(bus,vehicle)
```

6.3.2.3 Discussion

Figure 6.18 summarizes the results in terms of F_{TO} for the Guided Agglomerative Clustering Algorithm as well as Caraballo's method for both domains. While our method in general seems to perform better on the finance domain than Caraballo's method, this does not hold for the tourism domain to the same extent. However, comparing both algorithms with respect to F_{SO} clearly shows that our method performs much better on both domains compared to Caraballo's method in terms of local coherence of the clusters (compare Figure 6.19). The human evaluation conducted on the tourism domain is summarized in Figure 6.20, showing that our method, with the only exception of the outlier concept hierarchy, also yields better results with respect to human intuitions. An important question to clarify here is why we have not evaluated our guided agglomerative clustering approach using the measures described in Section 6.2.3.1. The answer is that the ontologies learned with the guided agglomerative clustering algorithm have indeed only a few concepts which are not contained in the gold standards and the other way round, thus rendering

Table 6.19. Results of the human evaluation of the hierarchies produced by our guided clustering algorithm and Caraballo's method for the tourism domain

Guided Agglomerative Clustering				
	#	P_1	P_2	P_3
WordNet + Hearst + WWW	265	67.17%	**66.04%**	**65.66%**
WordNet + Hearst	233	65.24%	62.23%	62.23%
WordNet + WWW	262	68.32%	65.65%	65.65%
Hearst + WWW	268	**69.03%**	63.43%	63.43%
WordNet	236	58.90%	55.51%	55.08%
Hearst	203	66.50%	64.04%	64.04%
WWW	261	73.18%	64.37%	62.07%
Caraballo's Method				
	#	P_1	P_2	P_3
WordNet + Hearst + WWW	304	45.40%	40.46%	40.46%
WordNet + Hearst	97	41.24%	40.21%	40.21%
WordNet + WWW	295	41.02%	38.64%	37.97%
Hearst + WWW	301	41.20%	37.54%	37.54%
WordNet	4	100%	100%	100%
Hearst	93	45.16%	38.71%	38.71%
WWW	291	51.89	42.61%	41.92%

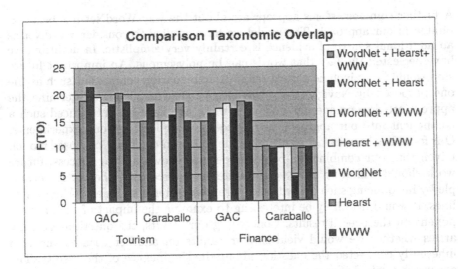

Fig. 6.18. Comparison of guided agglomerative clustering with Caraballo's method in terms of F_{TO} on both domains

meaningless the comparison using the measures introduced in Section 6.2.3.1.

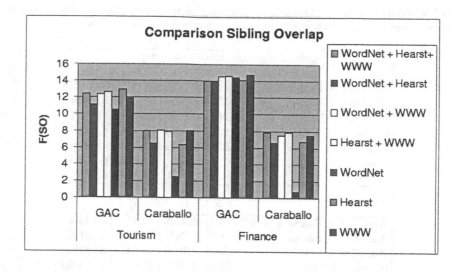

Fig. 6.19. Comparison of guided agglomerative clustering with Caraballo's method in terms of F_{SO} on both domains

A further comment seems appropriate about the way WordNet has been exploited in our approach. The model we have applied to consider WordNet as an additional source of evidence is certainly very simplistic. In addition, we have neglected the fact that words can be polysemous. An important future step would be to include a word sense disambiguation component such as the one proposed by Navigli et al. [Navigli and Velardi, 2004] to determine the appropriate domain-specific sense of a word. We have not introduced such a component into our approach to reduce the complexity of our experiments. Our focus has been in fact to examine the proposed combination-based model. Given that our combination-based model has shown a clear success, future work should definitely improve the different sources of evidence, for example by introducing such a word sense disambiguation component. Along these lines, it would definitely be interesting to examine the impact of such a component on the overall results. Concerning our results, the question certainly arises whether we would yield similar results on another dataset and also inherently connected the question about the significance of the results. The answer is twofold. On the one hand, it has not been possible to determine the significance of our results due to the fact that our as well as Caraballo's algorithm are deterministic given a certain corpus and order of the terms to cluster. As discussed in Section 6.2.4, the only possibility to determine the significance of our results would have been to run the algorithm on different subsets of the corpus, i.e. performing some sort of bootstrapping. However, the introduction of a random factor in this way seems quite artificial given

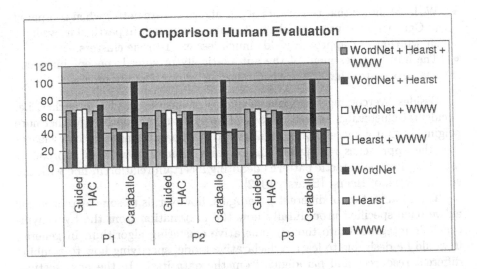

Fig. 6.20. Comparison of the human evaluation of the hierarchies produced by guided agglomerative clustering and Caraballo's method on the tourism domain

that one would never run the algorithm on subsets of the corpus in practice, but use all the available data. This is different for inherently randomized algorithms such as KMeans, in the case of which also in practice we would choose different random seeds and then select the best clustering for further processing.

6.3.3 Summary

We have presented a novel guided agglomerative clustering algorithm with the aim of automatically inducing concept hierarchies from a text corpus. The algorithm exploits an external hypernym oracle to drive the clustering process. Further, we have also described an automatic method to derive such a hypernym oracle from WordNet, a corpus as well as the WWW. The approach has been evaluated by comparing the resulting concept hierarchies with a reference concept hierarchy for the tourism and finance domains. Our contribution and conclusions can be summarized as follows:

- We have provided an original method combining different paradigms for ontology learning.
- With this method, we have successfully addressed the two problems inherent in unsupervised approaches: lack of labels and spurious similarities.
- Further, we have provided a method which is much faster in practice than agglomerative clustering as the similarities are only calculated between single elements and not between clusters.

- We have shown that the results of our algorithm are better when compared to Caraballo's approach on both domains examined. In particular, we have shown that our approach yields much less error-prone clusters.
- The human assessment of the automatically produced concept hierarchy has also shown that the learned relations are reasonably precise.

Besides overcoming two main problems of unsupervised approaches, i.e. accidental clusterings as well as lack of labels, our approach is furthermore original in that it successfully combines two main paradigms to ontology learning: the approaches relying on contextual similarity as well as approaches matching lexico-syntactic patterns denoting a certain relation in line with the seminal work of Hearst [Hearst, 1992].

The combination of different paradigms, however, is to some extent *adhoc* as we have specified procedurally how the information from the hypernym-oracle is integrated into the agglomerative clustering algorithm. In general, it would be desirable to learn a declarative model specifying how to combine different resources and paradigms from the data itself. In the next section, we present an approach relying on supervised machine learning techniques to learn such a combination model directly from our datasets.

6.4 Learning from Heterogeneous Sources of Evidence

We have already discussed the major approaches to learning concept hierarchies in Section 6.1. We have also noted that there has been almost no work on combining different learning paradigms. In this section, we present an approach which combines different paradigms to learn taxonomic relations. The crucial issue herein is to find an optimal combination of the indications provided by different approaches. As any manual attempt to combine these different approaches would certainly be *adhoc*, we resort to a supervised scenario in which an optimal combination is learned from the data itself, and make use of standard classifiers for this purpose. In fact, we learn classifiers which, given two terms as well as the results of all the different approaches considered, decide if they stand in a taxonomic relation or not (compare Figure 6.21). As most of the terms in a given taxonomy do not stand in such a relation, we are thus faced with very unbalanced datasets making it necessary to apply strategies to cope with such skewed distributions as described in Section 4.3.1.2.

In this section, we examine the possibility of learning taxonomic relations by combining the evidence from different sources and techniques using a classification approach. We show, on the one hand, how to convert the different sources of evidence and results of different approaches into numerical first-order features which can be used by a classifier. On the other hand, we also analyze which classifiers perform best on the task as well as which strategies are most suitable to deal with the unbalanced datasets we consider. The structure of this section is as follows: in Section 6.4.1 we discuss the main idea and describe the features used. In Section 6.4.2 we then present a detailed evaluation of the different classifiers and strategies for dealing with unbalanced datasets with respect to the task at hand. A summary in Section 6.4.3 concludes the section.

6.4.1 Heterogeneous Sources of Evidence

In this section, we describe the different sources of evidence we aim at combining via our classification-based approach to learn concept hierarchies. In particular, we discuss how the various sources can be transformed into first-order numerical features which can be used by a classifier. In fact, in this section we present a classification-based approach which classifies pairs of words (t_1, t_2) as *isa*-related or not, given the values of 8 features we describe in the following Section 6.4.1.1. The model induced by the classifier contains no domain-specific information and can, in principle, be applied to other domains. The features are based on state-of-the-art approaches to discover *isa*-relations. In what follows, we describe each of the approaches as well as how the numerical values are calculated, and give the best results of a naive threshold classifier as a baseline. In particular, we give results in terms of precision, recall and F-measure calculated with respect to the transitive closure of the relations in our gold standard concept hierarchy. It is certainly a difficult question what to consider as the set of relations to be learned. This is due to the fact that an approach learning taxonomic relations can not be expected to only learn direct taxonomic relations, as immediate taxonomic dominance is merely a modeling artifact. On the one hand, evaluating our approach with respect to the set of immediate relations would thus penalize our approach for finding non-immediate but correct taxonomic relations. On the other hand, evaluating with respect to the transitive closure of the *isa*-relations in our target ontology will lead to a very low recall as we can not expect our system to learn the complete transitive closure. One possibility would be to consider the transitive closure up to a certain level, but here again choosing some level would represent an *adhoc* solution and an additional parameter in our experiments. In the approach described in this section, we have simply opted for a pragmatic solution and considered the transitive closure as our target set. In the following, we discuss in detail the features considered in our approach. All the single features are evaluated in terms of precision, recall and F-Measure with respect to our target set, i.e. the transitive closure of the isa-relations of our reference ontology. For each of these features, we give the results of a *naive threshold classifier* as baseline which classifies a pair as *isa*-related if the corresponding confidence produced by the approach is above some threshold t, i.e.

Definition 27 (Naive Threshold Classifier) *Classify an example characterized by a single feature as positive if the value of the feature is above some threshold t.*

For each feature, the threshold has been varied from 0 to 1 in steps of 0.01. In what follows, we always report only the best results. The experiments are carried out with the Tourism corpus and evaluated with respect to the concept hierarchy of the $O_{tourism}$ ontology (compare Section 5).

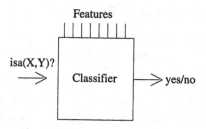

Fig. 6.21. Learning from heterogeneous sources of evidence

6.4.1.1 Hearst Patterns

Matching Patterns in a Corpus (Feature 1)

The first source of evidence we consider are lexico-syntactic patterns matched in a certain corpus in line with the work of Hearst [Hearst, 1992], where the patterns we use are mainly taken from. In particular, here we use the same patterns as well as the same technique to match regular expressions defined over part-of-speech tags as described in Section 6.3.1.2. Given two terms t_1 and t_2, we record how many times a Hearst-pattern indicating an *isa*-relation between t_1 and t_2 is matched in the corpus. We then normalize this value by dividing by the maximum number of Hearst patterns found for t_1, i.e. $isa_{Hearst} = \frac{|patterns(t_1,t_2)|}{|patterns(t_1,*)|}$, where $*$ stands for any other term. For the conference concept for example, we find the following candidate *isa* relations, where the number in the second column gives the normalized value as described above:

$$isa_{Hearst}(\text{conference, event}) \quad 0.36$$
$$isa_{Hearst}(\text{conference, body}) \quad 0.18$$
$$isa_{Hearst}(\text{conference, course}) \quad 0.09$$
$$isa_{Hearst}(\text{conference, weekend}) \quad 0.09$$
$$isa_{Hearst}(\text{conference, meeting}) \quad 0.09$$
$$isa_{Hearst}(\text{conference, activity}) \quad 0.09$$

The first interesting observation here is that despite of using quite a big corpus, Hearst patterns appear relatively rarely. With respect to the naive threshold classifier we get the best F-measure of $F = 10.64\%$ at $t = 0.03$, corresponding to a precision of $P = 25\%$ and a recall of $R = 6.76\%$. The best precision is 60% using a threshold of $t = 0.5$. In fact, using such a threshold, we can reach arbitrarily high precisions at the cost of a very reduced recall. In order to address the low recall, we also use two features based on matching Hearst patterns on the Web; they are described in the following.

Matching Patterns on the Web (Feature 2)

Certainly, when using a corpus we have to cope with typical data sparseness problems. However, some researchers have shown that the World Wide Web is an attractive way of reducing data sparseness (compare [Grefenstette, 1999, Keller et al., 2002, Resnik and Smith, 2003, Markert et al., 2003]). In this line, following Markert et al. [Markert et al., 2003], we use the Google API[8] to count the matches of a certain expression on the Web. In particular, for each pair (t_1, t_2), we generate the following patterns and count the number of hits returned by the Google API:

$$\pi(t_1) \text{ such as } \pi(t_2)$$
$$\text{such } \pi(t_1) \text{ as } \pi(t_2)$$
$$\pi(t_1), \text{ including } \pi(t_2)$$
$$\pi(t_1), \text{ especially } \pi(t_2)$$
$$\pi(t_2) \text{ and other } \pi(t_1)$$
$$\pi(t_2) \text{ or other } \pi(t_1)$$

where $\pi(t)$ returns the plural form of t as described in Section 6.3.1.2. These patterns are indicators for a corresponding taxonomic relation $isa_{WWW}(t_1, t_2)$. Thus, this source of evidence is certainly similar in spirit to the Hearst approach described above, but with the main difference that there the patterns are matched against a corpus and here for each pair (t_1, t_2) a certain number of patterns are generated and then sent as queries to the Google API. The sum of the number of Google hits over all patterns for a certain pair (t_1, t_2) is then normalized by dividing through the number of hits returned for t_1. For instance, in what follows we give the top five matches for the conference concept and other terms in the tourism concept hierarchy we consider; the value in the second column indicates the normalized number of hits returned by the Google API:

$$\begin{array}{ll} isa_{WWW}(\text{conference, service}) & 0.27 \\ isa_{WWW}(\text{conference, event}) & 0.25 \\ isa_{WWW}(\text{conference, area}) & 0.11 \\ isa_{WWW}(\text{conference, organization}) & 0.05 \\ isa_{WWW}(\text{conference, information}) & 0.04 \end{array}$$

It is important to note that due to the simple plural formation we have used, i.e. adding an 's' at the end of the word, we get no information for nouns which do not form their plural regularly, e.g. *activity*. With respect to the

---

[8] http://www.google.com/apis/

naive threshold classifier baseline, the best F-measure here is $F = 18.84\%$ with a precision of $P = 15.77\%$ and a recall of $R = 23.43\%$ when selecting all the relations above a threshold of 0.04. So here we yield a greater recall at the cost of a lower precision, which is due to the fact that the WWW is a very general resource and the pattern-matching approach also yields a considerable amount of errors.

Downloading Web Pages (Feature 3)

Furthermore, as an alternative to the pattern generation approach described above, we also follow an approach in which web pages are actually downloaded and Hearst patterns are matched offline, thus overcoming the idiosyncrasies with the generation of plural forms and allowing to match expressions with a more complex linguistic structure. For this purpose, we assign one or more functions $f_i : string \rightarrow string$ – which we will refer to as *clues* – to each of the Hearst patterns i to be matched. Given a concept of interest c, we instantiate each of the clues and download a number of pages matching the query $f_i(c)$ using the Google API. For example, given the clue $f(x) = "such\ as" \oplus \pi(x)$ and the concept conference, we would download 100 abstracts matching the query f(conference), i.e. "such as conferences". For each concept of interest and for each of the correspondingly instantiated clues, we then process the downloaded abstracts by matching the corresponding pattern, thus yielding its potential superconcepts. As described above, for each pair (t_1,t_2) we calculate the number of times t_1 and t_2 were found to stand in an *isa*-relation divided by the number of times t_1 was matched in a pattern as subconcept, i.e. $isa_{WWW'} = \frac{|patterns_{WWW}(t_1,t_2)|}{|patterns_{WWW}(t_1,*)|}$. Here we use the same patterns and clues as defined in Section 6.3.1.2. The top four pairs for the conference concept are in this case:

$$isa_{WWW'}(\text{conference, event})\quad 0.27$$
$$isa_{WWW'}(\text{conference, activity})\quad 0.17$$
$$isa_{WWW'}(\text{conference, initiative}) \; 0.03$$
$$isa_{WWW'}(\text{conference, function}) \; 0.03$$

Using the naive threshold classifier, we get an F-measure of $F = 17.58\%$ with a precision of $P = 16.12\%$ and a recall of $R = 19.34\%$ at a threshold of $t = 0$.

6.4.1.2 WordNet

As a further source of evidence, we use the hypernymy information from Word-Net[9]. Actually, the information contained in WordNet is so general and domain independent that when exploiting it in the context of a specific domain, it has to be treated as an uncertain source of evidence such as the other sources we consider here.

---

[9] We have used version 1.7.1 for our experiments.

WordNet – All Senses (Feature 4)

Given two terms t_1 and t_2, we check if they stand in a hypernym relation with regard to WordNet. It is important to note that two terms t_1 and t_2 can appear in more than one synset and thus there could be more than just one hypernym path from the synsets of t_1 to the synsets of t_2. We normalize the number of hypernym paths by dividing by the number of senses of t_1, setting 1 as maximum, i.e. we consider the value $isaw_N(t_1, t_2) = min(\frac{|paths(senses(t_1), senses(t_2))|}{|senses(t_1)|}, 1)$. Hereby, a path is simply a sequence of edges connecting two synsets. As Word-Net allows for multiple inheritance, there can even be multiple paths between two synsets. Therefore, we set 1 as maximum in the formula above. For example, in WordNet there are four such different hypernym paths between the synsets of *country* and the ones of *region*. Furthermore, as *country* has 5 senses, this value would be 0.8.

WordNet – First Sense (Feature 5)

Further, we also consider a variant of taking into account the WordNet hierarchy in which we consider only the first and thus most frequent sense of t_1 as specified by the formula $isaw_{N_{first}} = min(|paths(sense_1(t_1), senses(t_2))|, 1)$. This value is obviously 0 or 1. The precision for the *isa* pairs extracted from WordNet is much lower than for the ones from the Hearst patterns. The reason is that WordNet contains so much ambiguity and that it is domain independent. The precision is in fact around $P = 21.6\%$ when considering all senses and regarding all relations with a value above 0.2 as correct and around $P = 30.55\%$ when taking into account only the first sense. While the recall is higher than with Hearst's approach, it is still quite low at $R = 7.23\%$ and $R = 5.19\%$, respectively. The best F-measure for the feature considering all senses is thus $F = 10.84\%$ and $F = 8.87\%$ for the feature considering only the first sense and all the relations with a value over 0 as correct.

It is important to emphasize that this does not mean that the relations found in WordNet are wrong, but that they do not appear in our target ontology. After manual inspection of the relations in WordNet and the ones in the target ontology, we found that certain terms are modeled in a very different manner, which explains why the precision of the relations found in WordNet is so low when compared to the target hierarchy. For example, according to WordNet, presentation is a human activity (most frequent sense), while according to our target ontology, presentation is a business event. Another example here is night, which according to WordNet is a period, while according to our target ontology it is a time. Further, according to WordNet, price list is an information, while according to our target ontology price list is an agreement.

6.4.1.3 'Head'-Heuristic (Feature 6)

In order to identify further *isa* relations, we make use of the *head*-heuristic already described in Section 6.3.1.3. Basically, given two terms t_1 and t_2, if

t_1 r-matches t_2, we derive the relation isa(t_2,t_1). As an example, according to this heuristic we might derive that t_1='conference' and t_2='international conference' are related by an *isa* relation, i.e. isa$_{head}$(international conference, conference). This is similar to the *HeadNounToClass_ModToSubClass* rule used by Buitelaar et al. [Buitelaar et al., 2004]. When evaluating this heuristic on our dataset, we get a precision of 50%, a very low recall of 3.77% and an F-measure of $F = 7.02\%$. So this heuristic is indeed very accurate at the cost of a very low recall.

6.4.1.4 Corpus-based Subsumption (Feature 7)

As a further source of evidence, we introduce a corpus-based notion of subsumption and regard a term t_1 as a subclass of t_2 if all the syntactic contexts in which t_1 appears are also shared by t_2. For this purpose, for each term in question we extract pseudo-syntactic dependencies from the corpus and construct the corresponding term vectors as described in Section 4.1.4. On the basis of these term vectors, we calculate a directed Jaccard coefficient as follows: $isa_{corpus}(t_1, t_2) = \frac{|features(t_1) \cap features(t_2)|}{|features(t_1)|}$, thus computing the number of common features divided by the number of features of term t_1.

So, the measure presented here gives a normalized value within the interval $[0..1]$, indicating in how far $features(t_1)$ is included in $features(t_2)$.
Here follow the top ten superconcepts for *conference* according to this method:

isa$_{corpus}$(conference, congress)	0.44
isa$_{corpus}$(conference, seminar)	0.44
isa$_{corpus}$(conference, masseur)	0.43
isa$_{corpus}$(conference, banquet)	0.34
isa$_{corpus}$(conference, aerobic)	0.37
isa$_{corpus}$(conference, pilgrimage)	0.33
isa$_{corpus}$(conference, elevator)	0.31
isa$_{corpus}$(conference, sanatorium)	0.31
isa$_{corpus}$(conference, brochure)	0.30
isa$_{corpus}$(conference, cabaret)	0.30

Evaluated on our reference taxonomy, the naive threshold classifier yields a relatively high recall of $R = 27.83\%$ but a very low precision and F-measure of $P = 0.92\%$ and $F = 1.78\%$ at a threshold of $t = 0.01$.

6.4.1.5 Document-based Subsumption (Feature 8)

Sanderson and Croft [Sanderson and Croft, 1999] have suggested a document-based notion of subsumption according to which a term t_1 is a subclass of term t_2 if t_2 appears in all documents in which t_1 appears. Instead of computing these results with respect to a corpus, we resort once more the World Wide Web and use the Google API to calculate the number of documents in which

t_1 and t_2 occur, dividing this value by the number of documents in which t_1 occurs. Thus we also yield a value between $[0..1]$. According to this document co-occurrence method, the top ten superconcepts for *conference* are:

$$\text{isa}_{croft}(\text{conference,information}) \quad 0.17$$
$$\text{isa}_{croft}(\text{conference,service}) \quad 0.17$$
$$\text{isa}_{croft}(\text{conference,day}) \quad 0.16$$
$$\text{isa}_{croft}(\text{conference,time}) \quad 0.16$$
$$\text{isa}_{croft}(\text{conference,email}) \quad 0.15$$
$$\text{isa}_{croft}(\text{conference,event}) \quad 0.14$$
$$\text{isa}_{croft}(\text{conference,date}) \quad 0.14$$
$$\text{isa}_{croft}(\text{conference,area}) \quad 0.12$$
$$\text{isa}_{croft}(\text{conference,place}) \quad 0.12$$
$$\text{isa}_{croft}(\text{conference,organization}) \quad 0.11$$

Here the best result of the threshold classifier yields an F-measure of $F = 6.32\%$ at a precision of $P = 13.98\%$ and a recall of $R = 4.09\%$ at a relatively high threshold of 0.6.

6.4.2 Evaluation

Having introduced the different features, we now turn to the description of the diverse classifiers applied to the task. As classifiers, we use a Naive Bayes (NB) classifier, a C4.5 decision tree classifier, a Perceptron (PER) as well as a Multi-layer Perceptron (MLPER) with one hidden layer consisting of as many hidden nodes as input nodes, i.e. eight in our case, corresponding to the eight features described above. We make use of the version of these algorithms implemented in WEKA[10], applying standard settings, and give results averaged over ten runs. In particular, we produce ten runs for each configuration of classifier and rebalancing strategy, applying jackknifing to randomly select partitions of the dataset with a 60%:40% training/testing ratio. Further, in order to address the problem of the unbalanced dataset, we experiment with the following strategies: (i) undersampling, (ii) oversampling, (iii) varying the classification threshold as well as (iv) introducing a cost matrix (compare Section 4.3.1.2). Additionally, we report on results of experimenting with one-class Support Vector Machines, for which we obviously do not need to worry about the unbalanced character of the dataset as they merely make use of positive examples for training. The structure of the remainder of this section is as follows: in Section 6.4.2.1 we discuss the baselines for our approach. In Sections 6.4.2.2 - 6.4.2.5 we discuss the results of our method with respect to different strategies for dealing with the unbalanced character of our dataset. Finally, we present results with the one-class Support Vector Machines in Section 6.4.2.6 and conclude this section with a discussion in Section 6.4.2.7.

---

[10] http://www.cs.waikato.ac.nz/~ml/weka/

6.4.2.1 Baselines

In order to evaluate our machine learning approach, we calculate for each feature the results with respect to our dataset of the simple threshold classifier, which assigns an example to the *isa* class if the value of the corresponding feature is above a threshold t. For each feature we vary the threshold from 0 to 1 in steps of 0.01. The F-measure, precision and recall values for the best threshold parameter t for each feature are summarized in Table 6.21. As a straightforward combination of the features we experiment with two further very simple classifiers, assigning an example to the *isa* class if the average or the maximum of the values of features 1-6 is above a threshold t (compare the results in Table 6.20)[11].

Table 6.20. Results for single features and simple combination strategies

No.	Feature	t	F	P	R
1	isa_{Hearst}	0.03	10.64%	25%	6.76%
2	isa_{WWW}	0.04	18.84%	15.77%	23.43%
3	$isa_{WWW'}$	0	17.58%	16.12%	19.34%
4	isa_{WN}	0.2	10.84%	21.60%	7.23%
5	$isa_{WN_{first}}$	0	8.87%	30.55%	5.19%
6	isa_{head}	0	7.02%	50%	3.77%
7	isa_{corpus}	0.01	1.78%	0.92%	27.83%
8	isa_{croft}	0.6	6.32%	13.98%	4.09%
	Average(1-6)	0.02	21.28%	18.61%	24.84%
	Maximum(1-6)	0.12	21%	19.03%	23.43%

Table 6.21. Results for single features and naive combination

6.4.2.2 Undersampling

Undersampling (compare [Provost, 2000]) consists of removing a number of examples of the majority class, in our case the *non-isa* examples, or which is equivalent, to select only a subset of the examples of the majority class for training. In our experiments, we randomly select a number of negative examples which equals the number of positive examples multiplied by an undersampling factor f_U, i.e. |Negatives| = f_U * |Positives|. We vary the factor f_U from 1 to 30. The results for all classifiers are given in Figure 6.22, which shows the F-measure over the undersampling factor f_U. The best F-measure of $F = 21.50\%$ is obtained with $f_U = 13$ using the Mulitlayer Perceptron (MLPER), thus being slightly over the results obtained with the simple average and maximum strategies (compare Table 6.21).

---

[11] When adding the features 7 and 8 the results are actually worse. Thus, we refrain from using these features when calculating the average and maximum.

6.4.2.3 Oversampling

In contrast to undersampling, oversampling consists of adding additional examples of the minority class (see [Provost, 2000]), in our case the *isa* class. In our experiments, we randomly select a number of positive examples equal to the original number of positive examples multiplied with a factor f_O, i.e. $|Positives'| = |Positives| * f_O$. We vary the oversampling parameter from 0 to 20 in steps of 1. The corresponding results are depicted in Figure 6.22. With this oversampling strategy we get better results than with the undersampling strategy, achieving an F-measure of 22.86% using the Multilayer Perceptron (MLPER) and an oversampling factor $f_O = 11$. These results are only significant at a level of 0.17 according to a Student's t-test and compared to the best results achieved with undersampling and the MLPER. Unfortunately, for the oversampling as well as for the varying cost strategies (see below), we have not been able to perform our experiments with C4.5 decision trees as WEKA reported not to have enough memory.

6.4.2.4 Threshold

Another possibility is to vary the classification threshold of the classifier. All classifiers internally compute for each example a probability of belonging to each target class, assigning the example to the class with the highest probability. In our binary case, an example is thus classified as *isa* if this probability is greater than 0.5. We also vary this threshold from 0 to 1 in steps of 0.05. The corresponding results for all the classifiers are depicted in Figure 6.23. The best F-measure of $F = 18.7\%$ is achieved using the Multilayer Perceptron (MLPER) and a threshold of 0.1. With this strategy we thus do not improve upon the average and maximum strategies (compare Table 6.21).

6.4.2.5 Cost Matrix

In WEKA, it is possible to specify a cost matrix indicating the relative cost for misclassifying an example. In further experiments we make use of this possibility, introducing a factor f_C specifying the relative cost of misclassifying an *isa* example as *non-isa* with respect to misclassifying a *non-isa* as *isa*. We vary this factor from 1 to 10 in steps of 1. The results in terms of F-measure over this factor are given in Figure 6.23. Here the best F-measure of F=20.09% is achieved when using the Multilayer Perceptron and a relative misclassification cost of 6:1. As a result, when using this strategy we do not improve upon the average and maximum strategies (compare Table 6.21).

6.4.2.6 One Class SVMs

Further, we also experiment with one-class Support Vector Machines, which only rely on positive examples for training (compare

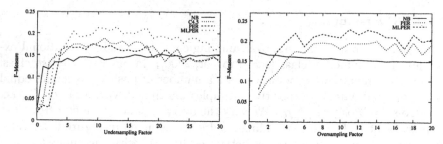

Fig. 6.22. Results for undersampling (left) and oversampling (right)

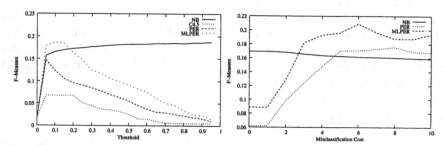

Fig. 6.23. Results for varying the threshold (left) and misclassification cost (right)

[Grobelnik and Mladenic, 2006]). Thus, the unbalanced character of the dataset is not an issue here. In particular, we use the regression SVM implementation of the TextGarden tool suite[12], applying standard settings and performing the evaluation with n-fold cross validation, where n is the number of data splits. We experiment here with different training/test splits obtaining the best result of $F = 32.96\%$ with a split of 2/1. Table 6.22 shows the F-measure, precision and recall values for the different splits used.

Table 6.22. Results of one-class SVM for different test/train splits

Train/Test split	F-measure	precision	recall
1/1	32.72%	36.98%	29.38%
2/1	**32.96%**	37.85%	29.21%
3/1	32.38%	37.65%	28.47%
4/1	32.91%	37.64%	29.35%

---

[12] http://kt.ijs.si/dunja/TextGarden/

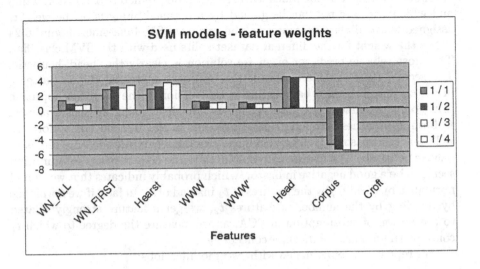

Fig. 6.24. Weight of each feature for the different test/train splits

6.4.2.7 Discussion

The best results achieved with the one-class SVM ($F = 32.96\%$) are more than 10 points above the baseline classifier taking into account the average ($F = 21.28\%$) or the maximum ($F = 21\%$) of the different approaches considered. Furthermore, the best result is also more than 14 points better than the best single-feature classifier using the $isaw_{WWW}$ feature ($F = 18.84\%$). These figures show that our supervised approach to combining different indicators from multiple and heterogeneous sources indeed yields very promising results. The second best results have been achieved using a Multilayer Perceptron as well as oversampling and undersampling as strategies to cope with the unbalanced character of the dataset. However, the results of a Student's t-test showed that there is in fact no significant difference between using undersampling or oversampling. As the baseline used is deterministic, it is not possible to determine whether the difference to the Multilayer Perceptron results is indeed significant. We can thus not claim that the Multilayer Perceptron yields indeed better results compared to the baseline.

Varying the threshold or the misclassification cost does not yield better results compared to the baseline. Furthermore, due to the fact that the results obtained with the Support Vector Machines are more than 10% over the baselines as well as the Multilayer Perceptron classifier, we have not performed a significance test as it is obvious that the results are much better.

A deeper insight about which features are good predictors of an *isa*-relation and which ones are not can be gained by a detailed analysis of the weights assigned to the different features by the one-class SVM classifier. Figure 6.24 shows the weight for the different dataset splits used with the SVM classifier. The most reliable predictor of an *isa*-relation is clearly the 'head'-heuristic. The second most reliable feature is the approach matching Hearst patterns in the corpus. The third best feature is the version of the WordNet approach using only the first sense. The version of WordNet using all senses as well as both approaches matching Hearst patterns in the Web do not perform so well, but still reasonably. The document-based subsumption feature seems to behave neutrally. The feature corresponding to the corpus-based subsumption seems to be a good negative indicator, which probably indicates that we should normalize by dividing by the features of t_2 instead of t_1. In fact, if we normalize by dividing by the number of features t_2, we get a feature strongly related to the notion of subsumption in FCA, as we measure the degree to which t_1 contains the features of its superconcept t_2.

We repeat our experiments with two modifications:

1. We calculated the corpus-based subsumption feature as
   $isa_{corpus}(t_1, t_2) = \frac{|features(t_1) \cap features(t_2)|}{|features(t_2)|}$.
2. For each feature $f(t_1, t_2)$ we also add the inverse feature $f(t_2, t_1)$ to the dataset.

The results are in line with our expectations in the sense that all the positive features $f(t_1, t_2)$ indeed correspond to positive weights in the SVM model, whereas the inverse features $f(t_2, t_1)$ actually yield negative weights. Overall, the results in terms of F-measure also improve as shown in Table 6.23.

Figure 6.25 indicates the weights for the positive features. Again we observe that the features based on the *'head'-heuristic*, on the first sense of WordNet as well as on matching Hearst patterns perform best. The other features are not such good predictors of *isa*-relations. The document-based subsumption feature (Croft) seems to be the weakest predictor.

Further, the one-class SVM has been found to yield the best results. The second best results are achieved by the Multi-layer Perceptron using oversampling. This could hint at the fact that the problem we are considering is not clearly linearly separable.

6.4.3 Summary

We have shown in this section that it is possible and furthermore reasonable to combine different approaches as well as resources using a machine-learning approach. The benefit of such a machine-learning approach is in fact that the weight of the contribution of each approach is not determined in an *ad-hoc* manner, but learned from the data itself. The main contributions of our approach can be summarized as follows:

Table 6.23. Results of one-class SVM for different train/test splits (mod.)

Train/Test split	F-measure	precision	recall
1/1	31.23%	37.41%	27.22%
2/1	**33.71%**	38.82%	29.86%
3/1	33.52	38.21%	29.92%
4/1	33.23%	37.84%	29.75%

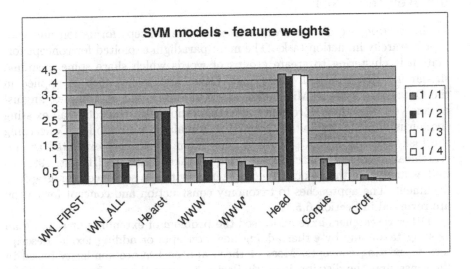

Fig. 6.25. Weight of each feature for the different train/test splits (modified version)

- We have shown that combining different approaches indeed pays off, compared to using only single approaches based only on Hearst patterns, distributional similarity, the 'head'-heuristic, etc.
- We have also shown that the machine-learning based combination performs better compared to a naive combination considering the average or maximum of the confidence produced by the single approaches.
- Our experiments demonstrate that the unbalanced character of the dataset is actually an issue. In fact, beating the naive average and maximum classifiers has turned out to be far from straightforward.
- We have further shown that one-class Support Vector Machines, which are not affected by the unbalanced dataset, deliver the best results.
- Finally, a detailed analysis of the weights of the different features in the models learned with the SVMs have allowed insight in which approaches are the most reliable predictors for the task at hand.

One drawback of the proposed method is that the computation of some of the features is expensive. Further work should clarify if the method actually scales with respect to the number of concepts. In addition, an important question is whether a model trained on one domain, say tourism, can be successfully applied to other domains. Further, when integrating information from a lexical database such as WordNet, lexical disambiguation should definitely be performed.

6.5 Related Work

In this section, we discuss work related to the concept formation and concept hierarchy induction tasks. The main paradigm exploited for concept formation is clustering to create groups of words which share some meaning, similar in spirit to WordNet's synset. Other approaches such as applied in the OntoLearn system [Missikoff et al., 2002] are based on complex linguistic analysis, including word sense disambiguation with respect to an existing thesaurus which is exploited to build a domain-specific model. Concerning the task of constructing a hierarchy, the main approaches exploited are hierarchical clustering, matching of lexico-syntactic patterns [Hearst, 1992] as well as analyzing the co-occurrence of terms within a sentence, paragraph or document. The approaches to taxonomy construction and concept formation are reviewed in Section 6.5.1.

Other researchers have addressed the problem of extending or refining an existing taxonomy by either adding new concepts or adding lexical descriptors to existing concepts. Most of these approaches are similarity-based in the sense that the distributional similarity between the new concept and the concept it is classified to should be maximal. Different algorithms have been exploited for this purpose: kNN or memory-based learning, tree-ascending and tree-descending algorithms. Section 6.5.2 reviews work related to taxonomy refinement.

6.5.1 Concept Formation and Hierarchy Induction

In this section, we describe in more detail work related to the tasks of concept formation and hierarchy induction. We first discuss related work on lexico-syntactic patterns. The seminal work of Hearst on lexico-syntactic patterns has been very relevant for the approaches presented in this chapter. In our work, we have applied Hearst patterns in the approaches presented in Sections 6.3 and 6.4. We also describe in detail related work relying on clustering approaches. A quantitative comparison of the different approaches on clustering is almost impossible and therefore not the purpose of this section. Researchers have presented various types of evaluation on different datasets and used very different techniques. Our aim in this section is to provide the interested reader with an overview of related work on clustering as well as entry points to the relevant literature.

6.5.1.1 Lexico-syntactic patterns

Hearst's seminal work (compare Section 6.1.2) has been reused and refined in a lot of follow-up work as well as applied to different tasks. Iwanska et al. [Iwanska et al., 2000], for example, define additional patterns. Poesio et al. [Poesio et al., 2002] suggested to exploit Hearst patterns for anaphora resolution. Ahmad et al. [Ahmad et al., 2003] applied Hearst patterns to very specific domains, in particular applying them to texts surrounding images. Recent work such as the one of Etzioni et al. [Etzioni et al., 2004a] and Markert et al. [Markert et al., 2003] have shown how these patterns can also be matched on the WWW by using search engine APIs such as the one of Google. Lexico-syntactic patterns have also been applied to the identification of other lexical relations such as part-of [Charniak and Berland, 1999] or causal relations [Girju and Moldovan, 2002, Sanchez-Graillet and Poesio, 2004].

Recently, Cederberg and Widdows [Cederberg and Widdows, 2003] have shown that the precision of Hearst patterns can be improved by filtering the results of the pattern matching using Latent Semantic Analysis. In particular, the assumption is that hyponyms/hypernyms are typically distributionally similar. The results obtained with Hearst patterns are then post-filtered, retaining only those pairs with a similarity over a certain threshold. In their experiments, precision is raised from 40% to 58%, which corresponds to a 30% reduction in error rate.

In order to improve the recall of the patterns, Cederberg and Widdows also exploit a simple heuristic assuming that if there is a lexico-syntactic pattern indicating that A is a hyponym of B and A appears coordinated with C, then C is also a hyponym of B. Their method leads to a five-fold increase in the number of correct relations extracted at a precision of 46%. Further, they also apply the LSA filtering technique to the relations extended by taking into account coordination patterns, achieving a precision of 64% corresponding to a reduction of the error rate by 33%.

Some research has aimed at learning the patterns automatically (see [Agichtein and Gravano, 2000], [Ravichandran and Hovy, 2002] and [Downey et al., 2004]). Morin et al. [Morin and Jacquemin, 1999, Finkelstein-Landau and Morin, 1999] have addressed the automatic generation of patterns via a similarity-based approach in which the patterns are represented as vectors and grouped if they are similar enough, thus leading to generalization of the patterns. In our work, we have not addressed the important issue of learning the patterns themselves, but have compiled a library of patterns from the literature, assuming their availability in our approaches.

6.5.1.2 Clustering

Work on clustering is mainly based on Harris' [Harris, 1968] *distributional hypothesis*, claiming that similar words tend to occur in similar linguistic contexts. Actually, this is the main assumption on which clustering approaches build on. In what follows, we will briefly discuss some seminal but also recent work in the field of clustering words on the basis of text.

Hindle

Hindle [Hindle, 1990] aims at grouping nouns semantically, relying on the distributional hypothesis. He uses his own parser Fidditch to derive verb–subject as well as verb–object dependencies from a 6 million word sample of Associated Press news stories. To weight the association between a verb and the head of the subject or object it subcategorizes, he makes use of the pointwise mutual information:

$$I(x,y) = log_2 \frac{P(x,y)}{P(x)\ P(y)} \tag{6.33}$$

In particular, for a verb v and a head noun n he calculates different mutual information values for the subject and object position, i.e. $I_{subj}(n,v)$ and $I_{obj}(n,v)$. The similarity measure used is defined as follows:

$$sim_{arg}(v, n_1, n_2) := \begin{cases} min(I_{arg}(v, n_1), I_{arg}(v, n_2)) \\ \quad \text{if } I_{arg}(v_{arg}, n_1) > 0 \text{ and } I_{arg}(v, n_2) > 0 \\[2mm] abs(max(I_{arg}(v, n_1), I_{arg}(v, n_2))) \\ \quad \text{if } I_{arg}(v, n_1) < 0 \text{ and } I_{arg}(v, n_2) < 0 \\[2mm] 0 \ \text{otherwise} \end{cases} \tag{6.34}$$

Finally, the similarity is calculated by summing up the subject and object similarity over all verbs:

$$sim(n_1, n_2) = \sum_{v \in V} sim_{subj}(v, n_1, n_2) + sim_{obj}(v, n_1, n_2) \tag{6.35}$$

In contrast to the cosine measure, which is length-normalized, the above measure is proportional to the number of verbs shared by both nouns. Though Hindle does not provide a quantitative evaluation of the clustering, he reports that *"for many nouns, encouragingly appropriate sets of semantically similar nouns are found"*. Interestingly, he also introduces and analyzes the concept of mutually similar nouns - which he calls *reciprocally most similar nouns*. He concludes that considering reciprocally most similar nouns yields *quite a good set of substitutable words, many of which are near synonyms*. Hindle's and our approach have in common the use of syntactic dependencies as features as well as of an information measure, i.e. PMI, to weight the contribution of the features.

Pereira et al.

Pereira et al. [Pereira et al., 1993] present a top-down soft clustering algorithm which uses deterministic annealing to find lowest distortion sets of clusters. The algorithm is soft in the sense that an element can appear in different clusters, thus allowing to account for multiple meanings of words. They evaluate the learned hierarchy in two ways. On the one hand, they present an entropy-based evaluation of the clusters (compare Section 9.1.3.2). On the other hand, they also test the prediction/generalization power of the cluster hierarchy on a decision task, i.e. deciding whether a verb v or a verb v' is more likely to take a noun n as object, where all occurrences (v, n) have been removed before from the training set. The task helps thus in evaluating how well the learned model allows for reconstructing the verb distribution of n from its closest centroids. In contrast to Pereira et al., we have not focused on accounting for the different meanings of words in our FCA-based approach. However, as FCA supports multiple inheritance, in contrast to the agglomerative clustering algorithms, accounting for different meanings of a word is actually possible.

Caraballo

Caraballo [Caraballo, 1999] presents a bottom-up clustering approach to build a hierarchy of nouns. For this purpose, she uses conjunctive and appositive constructions for nouns derived from the Wall Street Journal Corpus using the parser described in [Caraballo and Charniak, 1998]. In particular, she only considers the lemmatized head of the noun phrases in question. As similarity measure she uses the cosine measure as well as average linkage as strategy to compute the similarity between clusters C_1 and C_2, i.e.,

$$sim(C_1, C_2) = \frac{\sum_{w_1 \in C_1, w_2 \in C_2} cos(w_1, w_2)}{|C_1| \times |C_2|} \tag{6.36}$$

Using the above similarity measure, Caraballo first clusters the nouns in a bottom-up fashion, thus yielding an unlabeled hierarchy of nouns.

In order to label the inner nodes of the tree, she extracts appropriate hypernyms from the corpus using the Hearst pattern 'NP, NP,... and other NP'. The hypernyms are added to every leaf node in the tree in form of a vector. For each internal node of the tree, the vectors of its children are aggregated. Finally, for each node the hypernyms are ranked according to frequency, and the best three hypernyms are chosen as cluster label if the hypernym subsumes at least two of the elements in the cluster.

After the clusters have been labeled, the tree is then compressed removing i) every inner node which remains unlabeled, as well as ii) every node with the same hypernyms as its parent. The children are correspondingly raised along the hierarchy to the parent concept.

Caraballo evaluates her approach by randomly selecting 10 internal nodes dominating at least 20 nouns and, for each internal node, randomly selecting

20 nouns under that node which were presented together with the three hypernyms to three human judges for evaluation. Additionally, five 'noise' nouns selected from elsewhere in the hierarchy were also presented to the judges to check that they were not just confirming the results by default. The pairs consisting of the best hypernym of a cluster and some hyponym were accepted by the majority of judges in 33% of the cases, 39% of the cases at least by one judge. Considering any of the three hypernyms for each cluster, 47.5% relations were accepted by the majority, while 60.5% were judged as valid by at least one judge.

We have compared our guided agglomerative clustering method with Caraballo's clustering approach and experimentally demonstrated that we outperform her method with respect to local coherence of clusters as well as with respect to human judgements (compare Section 6.3).

The ASIUM System

ASIUM [Faure and Nedellec, 1998] implements a bottom-up and breadth-first clustering strategy for the purpose of learning a concept hierarchy as well as subcategorization frames with generalized selectional restrictions with respect to this concept hierarchy at the same time.

The first step of the algorithm is to build so called *basic clusters* consisting of nouns appearing at a specific position of a certain verb. In particular, the authors consider the verb's object, subject as well as prepositional complements or adjuncts. For example, given the following verb structures found in a corpus,

```
<to travel> <subject: father> <by: car>
<to travel> <subject: neighbor> <by: train>
<to drive> <subject: friend> <object: car>
<to drive> <subject: colleague> <object: motorbike>
<to drive> <subject: friend> <object: motorbike>
```

ASIUM would generate the following two verb frames:

```
<to travel> <subject: {father(1), neighbor(1)}>
            <by: {car(1), train(1)}>

<to drive> <subject: {friend(2), colleague(1)}>
           <object: {car(1), motorbike(2)}>
```

and would create four basic classes:

```
C1={father(1), neighbour(1)}
C2={car(1), train(1)}
C3={friend(2), colleague(1)}
C4={car(1), motorbike(2)}
```

After this first step, the distance between the different clusters is computed. Clusters with a distance under a certain threshold are merged and the corresponding selectional restrictions of the verb generalized.

The distance measure between clusters C_1 and C_2 is defined as follows (slightly reformulated w.r.t. the presentation in [Faure and Nedellec, 1998]):

$$dist(C_1, C_2) = 1 - \frac{|C_1 \cap C_2| \cdot \left(\frac{\sum_{c \in C_1 \cap C_2} w_{C_1}(c)}{|C_1|} + \frac{\sum_{c \in C_1 \cap C_2} w_{C_2}(c)}{|C_2|} \right)}{\sum_{c \in C_1} w_{C_1}(c) + \sum_{c \in C_2} w_{C_2}(c)} \qquad (6.37)$$

where $w_C(c)$ is the weight of each element c in the cluster C.

For example, the distance between $C2$ and $C4$ is calculated as follows:

$$dist(C2, C4) = 1 - \frac{1 * \left(\frac{1}{2} + \frac{1}{2} \right)}{2 + 3} = 1 - \frac{1}{5} = \frac{4}{5} \qquad (6.38)$$

ASIUM's algorithm is described by the pseudocode in Algorithm 10. According to this algorithm, new clusters are only merged with clusters from lower levels. After each level, the user is asked to validate and label the clusters. Thus, clusters are only processed further if they have been validated by the user, decreasing the amount of noise produced by the algorithm. Furthermore, the user can not only accept the cluster as a whole, but also split it into subclusters or remove some elements. The generalized subcategorization frames can also be adjusted by the user in a similar fashion.

Faure and Nedellec present an evaluation of ASIUM by showing the number of correctly generated clusters in dependence of the size of the corpus used. The best result is a cluster accuracy of 99.53% using 90% of the corpus with an *a posteriori* evaluation of the clusters by a human judge. This result, for example, can not be compared quantitatively to our results as our evaluations have always been conducted with respect to a gold standard, thus leading to much lower values

.

The Mo'K Workbench

The *Mo'K Workbench* [Bisson et al., 2000] is a workbench with the aim of facilitating the experimentation with bottom-up hierarchical clustering algorithms for the purpose of ontology construction. The workbench allows to vary:

- the representation of the context of a word, i.e verb–object, verb–subject, adjectival or nominal modification relations, etc.
- pruning parameters, i.e. the least number of occurrences of an attribute to be taken into account, and
- the similarity or distance function.

Algorithm 10 ASIUM Algorithm

ClustersToAggregate = BasicClusters;
NewClusters = BasicClusters;
Repeat
      CandidateClusters := $\emptyset$
      for all pairs of clusters (C_i, C_j), $C_i \in$ NewClusters and
      $C_j \in$ ClustersToAggregate such that C_i does not subsume C_j
      if dist$(C_i, C_j) <$ Threshold and $C_i \neq C_j$ **then**
         C_{new} = aggregate(C_i, C_j);
         CandidateClusters = CandidateClusters $\cup$ C_{new}
      endfor
      NewClusters = cooperatively validated CandidateClusters
      ClustersToAggregate = ClustersToAggregate $\cup$ NewClusters
      level++;
until NewClusters := $\emptyset$

The authors assess the generalization power of the different approaches by using part of the corpus as training data to calculate similarities and then evaluate newly obtained pairs with respect to the test corpus. The assumption here is that if two words are similar with respect to the training corpus, they can be exchanged to some extent, and artificially created pairs of verb–noun dependencies can be tested for their appearance in the test corpus. This is certainly an interesting form of evaluating the results, which can thus be presented in terms of precision and recall, measuring the generalization accuracy and coverage of the similarity assessment. Concerning some experiments in which different pruning methods were tested, the authors come to the conclusion that pruning can have a very strong effect on the results. They demonstrate that pruning too much can lead to a considerable reduction in performance in terms of precision and recall. Furthermore, they also experiment with three different methods of calculating similarity or semantic relatedness, i.e. the measure of the ASIUM system as described above, the measure described in Dagan et al. [Dagan et al., 1994] as well as a χ^2-based measure. They also conclude here that the effect of the similarity or distance measure can have a strong impact on the results. This has also been corroborated by our experiments with our smoothing technique in Section 6.2. Further, they conclude that ASIUM produces more accurate word classes than the competing methods with respect to a cooking recipe corpus.

Grefenstette

Grefenstette [Grefenstette, 1994], like Hindle, aims at the automatic creation of groups of semantically related words on the basis of a text corpus. He presents the *SEXTANT* approach, which derives features from text using a shallow parsing strategy and calculates the similarity between words using a weighted Jaccard measure. In particular, he presents the probably most thorough analysis and discussion of clustering results on a variety of different domains and corpora conducted so far. Grefenstette uses the following grammatical relations as features:

- verb–subject (SUBJ)
- verb–direct object (DOBJ)
- verb–indirect object (IOBJ)
- adjectival modification
- nominal modification

For example, from the following text:

It was concluded that carcinoembryonic antigens represent cellular constituents which are repressed during the course of differenciation of the normal digestive system epithelium and reappear in the corresponding malignant cells by a process of derepressive dedifferentiation.

the following object/attributes are extracted:

```
antigen carcinoembryonic
antigen repress-DOBJ
antigen represent-SUBJ
constituent cellular
constituent represent-DOBJ
course repress-IOBJ
course differentiation
digestive normal
epithelium normal
system digestive
epithelium digestive
epithelium system
differentiation epithelium
cell correspond-SUBJ
cell malignant
cell reappear-IOBJ
cell process
dedifferentiation derepressive
process dedifferentiation
```

As mentioned above, SEXTANT relies on a weighted Jaccard measure to assess the similarity of two words w_1 and w_2. SEXTANT is evaluated in three different ways:

- **Antonym discovery**: the task here is to reproduce certain antonym pairs - known as *Deese* antonyms - such as cold/hot, dark/light, passive/active, etc. specified by humans. Grefenstette analyzes the rank at which the corresponding antonym appears, concluding that SEXTANT performs successfully on the task.

- **Artificial synonyms**: for this task, synonyms are artificially created, and it is evaluated if SEXTANT can rediscover the artificially created synonyms. In particular, a certain number of occurrences of a given word, say 'cell', are replaced by the upper-case version of the word, i.e. 'CELL'. If the system then lists 'CELL' as the most similar word to 'cell', the task is regarded as successful. This is similar to the evaluation of WSD algorithms proposed by Schütze [Schütze, 1992]. Grefenstette reports results for 20 randomly selected words for each of three different word frequency ranges (*frequent*, *common* and *ordinary*). He analyzes the percentage of artificially created synonyms appearing at a) the 1st or 2nd, b) 3rd to 5th, c) 6th to 10th and d) beyond the 10th position. He states the results varying the percentage of words changed to upper-case. For the frequent words, the results are still reasonable in case 20-50% of the words are changed, while the results drop when changing less words. For the common and ordinary words, the results are much worse. This shows already that similarity-based algorithms are very sensitive to the frequency with which the words in question occur.

- **Comparison with an existing thesaurus**: as a further experiment, Grefenstette compares SEXTANT's results with three thesauri: *Roget*, *Macquarie* and *Webster's 7th*. Grefenstette evaluates if a noun and the corresponding most similar word given by SEXTANT appear under the same topics in the Roget and Macquarie thesauri, respectively. The evaluation with respect to Webster's 7th is performed slightly differently by taking into account the dictionary definition of each of the involved words and regarding the pair as correct in case the corresponding dictionary definitions share at least two common words. Interestingly, for this task Grefenstette compares syntactically motivated features such as used in SEXTANT with a technique using nouns, adjectives and verbs appearing within a 10 word window before or after the word in question and without trespassing sentence boundaries. Grefenstette concludes that for high frequency words, the syntactically motivated features perform best, while for low frequency words they do not provide enough contextual material for an accurate clustering, thus being outperformed by the window-based technique.

Further, Grefenstette presents four applications of SEXTANT to:

- **Query expansion**, reporting an increase in retrieval performance when expanding the original query with words found to be similar by SEXTANT. This will be discussed in more detail in the applications section (compare Section 9).

- **Thesaurus enrichment**, where SEXTANT results are used to find the correct place in a thesaurus for a given word once a certain hyponym/hypernym pair has been found by a Hearst-pattern.
- **Word meaning clustering**, where meanings are created by grouping reciprocally similar words together.
- **Automatic Thesaurus Construction**, where definitions for words are automatically generated containing the word frequency, the most similar words, the most frequent verbs they appear with, etc.

The work of Grefenstette and ours have in common the extensive evaluation of different methods on different datasets as well as the attempt to evaluate automatically produced clusters with respect to existing resources, e.g. thesauri.

Gasperin et al.

Gasperin et al. [Gasperin et al., 2001] present a refinement of Grefenstette's work and suggest using more fine-grained syntactic dependencies than those used by Grefenstette. In particular, Gasperin et al. criticize that Grefenstette does not explicitly distinguish between adjectival, nominal and PP-complement modification of nouns. They suggest to represent a syntactic dependency as a binary relation $r(w_1^{\downarrow}, w_2^{\uparrow})$ where r is the relation, i.e. a preposition, a verb–subject or verb–object relation, etc. Hereby, w_1 is the modified and w_2 the modifying word. So, *possible cause* is represented as ADJ($\downarrow$cause,$\uparrow$possible) and *death cause* as NN($\downarrow$cause,$\uparrow$death). From a compound as *death cause* we would yield two features, one for the modified word *cause*, i.e. <$\uparrow$NN,death> indicating that *death* is the modifier of *cause* in a nominal compound, and one for the modifier *death*, i.e. <$\downarrow$NN,cause>.

For their experiments, Gasperin et al. use the same weighted Jaccard measure as Grefenstette and a Brazilian Portuguese corpus with 1,4 million word occurrences. Though they do not provide any quantitative evaluation, from their experiments they conclude that using more fine-grained information about prepositions as well as not only $\downarrow$-features for the modified noun based on the modifiers, but also $\uparrow$-features for the modifiers, yields more accurate similarity assessments between words.

Reinberger et al.

In the context of the Flemish *OntoBasis* project, Reinberger and colleagues have investigated the application of unsupervised learning techniques to the problem of deriving clusters of related words given a certain corpus. They emphasize that words and concepts should not be collapsed together as concepts are language-independent abstractions.

Their work is based on the *DOGMA* ontology engineering approach [Meersman, 2001]. In the dogma approach, knowledge is represented in form of intuitively plausible facts, represented as context-specific conceptual binary relations, so called *lexons*. These are formalized as a 6-tuple $< \gamma, \lambda :$

$t_1, r, r^{-1}, t_2 >$ where γ uniquely identifies a certain context and λ identifies a specific language such that a triple (γ, λ, t) refers to a unique concept c in the context referred to by γ and lexicalized by the term t in the language λ. A lexon $< \gamma, \lambda : t_1, r, r^{-1}, t_2 >$ then specifies a relation r with its inverse r^{-1} to hold between t_1 and t_2.

The unsupervised approach to word clustering by Reinberger et al. is based on the fact that syntactic roles impose selectional restrictions on their arguments. If we then group together the words sharing the same syntactic positions, this will lead to the formation of groups of words fulfilling similar selectional restrictions and thus to a semantically homogeneous group. As a way to extract syntactic dependencies, Reinberger et al. make use of the memory-based shallow parser Timbl [Daelemans et al., 1999a], which in particular outputs subject-verb-object relations which can be used as a basis to build lexons. Reinberger et al. rank these subject-verb-object dependencies according to frequency and consider the n top ranked structures for clustering. In some cases, the authors additionally extract NP-P-NP constructs from the corpus. In [Reinberger et al., 2004], they use these constructs to filter the subject-verb-object relations by only considering such a relation if the arguments also appear in a NP-P-NP construct. In [Reinberger and Daelemans, 2004] and [Reinberger and Spyns, 2004], groups of nouns appearing as head of the first NP (before the preposition) as well as head of the second NP are compared with the clusters obtained by clustering nouns based on the verb–subj and verb–object positions and eventually merged.

The similarity between two clusters of nouns C1 and C2 is calculated in a quite *adhoc* manner on the basis of the number of elements common to both clusters as well as on the number of elements in C1 not contained in C2 and the other way round. In [Reinberger and Daelemans, 2003], for example, two classes are clustered if they have more than 2 elements in common and not more than 5 different elements. The authors apply their methods to different corpora, i.e. Medline [Reinberger and Spyns, 2004, Reinberger et al., 2003, Reinberger and Daelemans, 2003], SwissProt [Reinberger et al., 2004] or a corpus with EU VAT directives [Reinberger et al., 2004]. The clusters are evaluated by comparing their precision and recall with respect to pairs related in WordNet by synonymy, hypernymy, hyponymy or meronymy (compare [Reinberger and Daelemans, 2003, Reinberger et al., 2003]). In other experiments, the clusters are evaluated with respect to the UMLS thesaurus (compare [Reinberger and Daelemans, 2004] and [Reinberger and Spyns, 2004]). In [Reinberger et al., 2003], an alternative qualitative evaluation is presented in which experts in the biological domain were asked to rate the clusters. In addition, the authors examine the following parameters or variations of their approach:

- **Parsing vs. bigrams:** in [Reinberger and Daelemans, 2003], the authors compare the results when using the shallow parser with considering bigrams. Their conclusion is that using the shallow parser yields better results both in terms of recall and precision (negative recall) of the produced clusters.

- **Hard vs. soft clustering:** in [Reinberger et al., 2003], they analyze a soft clustering as well as a hard clustering version of their method. The soft clustering method groups classes of nouns appearing in certain syntactic positions, thus allowing nouns to appear in different clusters. In the hard clustering approach, nouns are clustered in a bottom-up fashion on the basis of the verb–subject and verb–object contexts they share. The authors conclude that while the hard clustering method produces less clusters, thus yielding a smaller recall than the soft clustering method, it is twice as precise as its counterpart. By using an additional version of the method in which both techniques are combined by only selecting the clusters produced with the soft variant which show a certain degree of similarity with clusters built by the hard clustering method, the authors demonstrate an improvement over both methods.

- **Weighting measures:** in [Reinberger and Daelemans, 2004], the authors compare different measures to weight the significance of the verb–object and verb–subject relations. They use a simple frequency measure as a baseline, as well as the conditional probability, PMI and Resnik measures described in Sections 4.1.5 and 6.2.2. They do not provide a definite answer to the question which measure performs best due to too much variation in the results depending on other parameters. This shows indeed that the choice of an appropriate weighting measure is a non-trivial problem. In general, it is worth emphasizing that the simple measures did not perform notably worse than the PMI or Resnik measures.

As in our work, the weighting measures are thus also in the focus of examination in Reinberger et al.'s work. Interestingly, they come to similar conclusions, i.e. that the simple measures do not perform notably worse than more elaborated ones.

Lin et al.

Lin et al. have addressed the derivation of classes of words from natural language texts. For this purpose, Lin has conducted an empirical comparison of different similarity measures with respect to the task of finding similar nouns (see [Lin, 1998a]). Dependency triples extracted with Minipar [Lin, 1993] are used as features. The similarity measures analyzed are: Hindle's measure using verb–object and verb–subject dependencies as well as the cosine, Dice and Jaccard measures (compare Section 4.1.5). Furthermore, an extended version of Hindle's measure, which takes into account more syntactic dependencies, is also considered. Finally, Lin also introduces an additional similarity measure based on the mutual information:

$$\frac{\sum_{(r,w)\in T(w_1)\cap T(w_2)}(I(w_1,r,w) + I(w_2,r,w))}{\sum_{(r,w)\in T(w_1)} I(w_1,r,w) + \sum_{(r,w)\in T(w_2)} I(w_2,r,w)} \tag{6.39}$$

where $T(w)$ returns pairs (r, w') whereby r is a dependency relation by which w is related to w'. $I(w_1, r, w_2)$ is then the pointwise mutual information between w and w' with respect to the dependency relation r. For each noun, a list with the most similar nouns is produced, which is then evaluated by comparing it to lists automatically derived form WordNet and Roget's thesaurus. For details about how these lists are derived the reader is referred to [Lin, 1993]. Lin argues, on the one hand, that the extended Hindle measure performs better than the original measure, thus allowing to conclude that using more syntactic dependencies yields better results. On the other hand, a statistical significance test shows that Lin's measure outperforms the extended Hindle measure, which in turn is better than the cosine measure. In general, the differences between the cosine, Jaccard and Dice measures are shown to be very small.

In further experiments described by Lin and Pantel [Lin and Pantel, 2001c], the aim is to discover semantic classes instead of merely similar words. For this purpose, the authors present a novel algorithm consisting of two main components: the CLIMAX and UNICON algorithms. The CLIMAX algorithm has as input a similarity matrix and calculates cliques for each element, whereby a clique is a set of words such that each element is among the top n most similar words of the other words. These cliques are thus very homogeneous groups of words which are then fed into the UNICON algorithm. The UNICON algorithm first computes the centroid of each clique. Then, CLIMAX is again applied to group the cliques themselves into cliques of cliques on the basis of the similarity between their centroids. The cliques of cliques are then merged, removing the corresponding cliques from the original set of cliques and the whole process iterated. The algorithm is described more in detail by the pseudocode in Algorithm 11.

Algorithm 11 UNICON algorithm in pseudocode

Input: a collocation database D, a similarity matrix M for a list of words E and a natural number n

1: $C \leftarrow CLIMAX(M, E, n)$
2: for each cluster $c \in C$, compute its centroid
3: compute the similarity matrix M' between all centroids
4: $S \leftarrow CLIMAX(M', C, n)$ where S is a set of subsets of C.
5: for each element in S (i.e., a subset of C), merge the different clusters and remove them from C
6: go to step 2 unless S is empty
7: compute the centroids of all the clusters in C and add them as pseudo-words in D
8: compute the similarity of the original words in E to the pseudo-words and add them to the corresponding clusters
9: Finally, remove words from clusters for which the similarity is lower than 90% of the highest similarity with the other clusters it has been assigned to

Output: The list C of clusters

The approach is evaluated by presenting the learned clusters to human judges for two different domains: news and medicine. The judges were asked to rate the clusters with a score from 1 to 5. The clusters produced have an average score of 4.26 on the news corpus and 3.37 on the MEDLINE corpus.

Furthermore, Pantel and Lin also tackle the problem of discriminating between different senses of a word and present a clustering approach based on committees. They present an algorithm called *clustering by committees* (CBC) in which, at a first step, the similarity between elements is calculated using an optimized procedure by taking advantage of the fact that the features are indexed, thus being able to retrieve elements which share a certain feature. At a second step, the elements are first clustered using average-linkage clustering. Then the clusters are iteratively added to committees if their similarity to the committee is below a certain threshold θ_1. Otherwise a new committee is created. Those elements in E for which the similarity to every committee is below a threshold θ_2 are added to a residue list R and the clustering algorithm iterated using R instead of E. The crucial step of the algorithm is the one in which each element e is assigned to its most similar cluster, removing the features from e which overlap with the cluster's centroid. In the next iteration, e can then be assigned to another cluster corresponding to another meaning. The approach is evaluated by calculating the precision and recall of the clusters with respect to WordNet as well as via a manual evaluation. Pantel and Lin conclude that CBC outperforms UNICON as well as soft versions of Bi-Section-KMeans, KMeans, bucket shot as well as clustering based on average linkage.

Pantel and Lin's CBC algorithm thus focuses on capturing different meanings of words, an aspect which we have neglected in the approaches presented in this chapter.

CobWeb

CobWeb [Fisher, 1987] is a system for incremental concept formation which represents concepts probabilistically. It carries out a hill-climbing search in the space of possible concept hierarchies guided by the notion of *category utility*. The concept hierarchy is initialized with a single category representing the features of the first instance. For each further instance, the algorithm moves through the tree to find its appropriate position. At each level the algorithm has to take a decision whether to:

- classify the new object with respect to the current category,
- create a new class,
- merge two existing classes, or
- split a class into several subclasses.

Crouch et al.

Crouch et al. [Crouch, 1988, Crouch and Yang, 1992] present a clustering-based approach to thesaurus construction. They apply hierarchical agglomerative clustering with complete linkage to build a cluster tree of documents. The intersection of the low-frequency word in every subcluster of a given cluster is then used to label it. Crouch et al. present results on an information retrieval task in which documents are indexed with respect to the learned thesaurus and user queries expanded with respect to it. Crouch and Yang [Crouch and Yang, 1992] report results on four different datasets and conclude that *"the results indicate that the algorithm can be used to produce useful thesauri, substantially improving retrieval effectiveness"*. The crucial difference to our clustering approach described in Section 6.2 is that Crouch et al. cluster documents instead of words.

Haav

Haav has also applied Formal Concept Analysis to the task of automatically learning concept hierarchies on the basis of textual input [Haav, 2003]. The technique is similar in spirit to our FCA-based approach with the main difference that (i) the method is applied to small text snippets coming from a dictionary or advertisements, ii) all the noun phrases appearing in the snippet are used as attributes, i.e. no syntactic dependencies are used, and (iii) no evaluation of the method is presented.

Curran et al.

Curran and Moens [Curran and Moens, 2002] have investigated different similarity and feature weighting measures on the task of discovering synonyms given a certain corpus. The results are evaluated with respect to WordNet. The authors' results show that the best similarity measures are the binary measures Jaccard and Dice, and the best weighting measure the t-test. Further, they suggest an approach for comparing the similarities more efficiently by considering only the most interesting k features as well as choosing for each element at most p elements for which the full similarity is computed. This approximation is demonstrated to be useful as results only decrease by 3.9%, while the time to compute the similarity is reduced by 89%.

Further, Curran [Curran, 2002] experiments with a method combining different sources of evidence for the task of finding synonyms. Curran in particular examines different ways of extracting context features relying on word windows as well as three methods based on syntactic dependencies: one method based on MINIPAR, one method using the chunker CASS as well as the SEXTANT approach introduced by Grefenstette (see above). The similarities extracted with the different methods are first evaluated on their own, but also combined with the following methods:

- **MEAN**: calculating the mean of each term's rank with respect to the different extraction methods
- **HARMONIC**: calculating the harmonic mean with respect to the different extraction methods

- **MIXTURE**: calculating the mean score (non-normalized)

It is important to mention that the latter method is only applicable if all the scores are comparable, that means, if all the methods use the same similarity and weighting function. The authors conclude in general that their combination method outperforms each single extractor, in particular SEXTANT, which was identified to be the best single extractor. Though the task is certainly a different one, the combination approach of Curran bears some resemblance with our approach presented in Section 6.4. However, we have also shown that more sophisticated combination methods than calculating the mean can indeed deliver better results.

Terascale Knowledge Acquisition

Some researchers have addressed the challenge of ontology learning from very large text collections in the magnitude of terabytes, therefore the name *terascale*. Pantel et al. [Pantel et al., 2004], for example, present an approach to learn lexico-syntactic patterns from large text collections relying on a modified edit distance defined between patterns, which is used as a basis to unify them. The edit distance is calculated using different levels of analysis, such as surface appearance, part-of-speech tags, etc. The approach is compared to the co-occurrence based approach used by Pantel and Ravichandran [Pantel and Ravichandran, 2004] in terms of the ability to generate correct hyponymy pairs. The authors find that, whereas the co-occurrence based approach is more precise given a certain critical mass of text, their pattern-based approach achieves a six-fold increase in recall on smaller datasets with respect to the co-occurrence method. On smaller datasets, the co-occurrence based approach has a higher recall but a lower precision. Furthermore, the pattern-based approach shows a relatively constant precision, while yielding a much higher recall on smaller datasets. Overall, the gain in performance is impressive: 47 days of processing for the co-occurrence based method vs. 4 days for the pattern-based approach on a 6GB text collection.

Recently, Ravichandran et al. [Ravichandran et al., 2005] have attempted to speed up traditional clustering techniques to group similar nouns on the basis of very large corpora. They notice that every similarity-based method needs at least to build a similarity matrix which takes $O(n^2 k)$ time, where n is the number of nouns and k is the number of features considered. Thus, if one wishes to have an algorithm which is linear in the number of nouns, one has to avoid calculating the whole similarity matrix using traditional techniques. Ravichandran et al. [Ravichandran et al., 2005] propose to use so called *Locality Sensitive Hash (LSH)* functions, which are randomized and probabilistic, thus optimizing the similarity computation by creating short signatures for each vector and comparing their fingerprints. The computation of the similarity matrix is thus reduced to $O(nk)$. In particular, Ravichandran et al. [Ravichandran et al., 2005] use a local sensitive hash function approximating the cosine similarity measure. Whereas they run their approach on a 138GB corpus, they compare their results with the method of Pantel and Lin (see above) to induce lists of similar nouns on a 6GB corpus, concluding that their method reproduces 70% of the gold standard similarity list. In our approaches, we have glossed over aspects related to efficiency to a large extent The reason is that we have used corpora of up two 218 million words only, in contrast to big corpora downloaded from the Web as used by Ravichandran et al.

6.5.1.3 Linguistic Approaches

The approaches discussed in this section can in fact be called linguistic in the sense that they directly exploit linguistic analysis to derive taxonomic relations. They differ from the clustering approaches described above in that linguistic analysis is not merely exploited for feature extraction, but in a more direct manner.

OntoLT

OntoLT [Buitelaar et al., 2004] is an ontology learning plugin for the Protégé[13] ontology editor. The approach is based on performing linguistic annotation of part-of-speech, chunks as well as grammatical relations using a shallow parser. The annotations can be used to define complex patterns which are then mapped to ontological structures. Examples of such mapping rules are for instance:

- **HeadNounToClass_ModToSubClass**, which maps a common noun to a concept or class, creating a subclass by adding nominal modifiers at the front.
- **SubjToClass_PredToSlot_DObjToRange**, which maps a predicate – typically a verb – into a relation, setting the head of the subject as domain and the direct object as range of the relation.

OntoLearn

OntoLearn (compare [Velardi et al., 2001], [Missikoff et al., 2002], [Navigli and Velardi, 2004] and [Velardi et al., 2005]) is a system extracting relevant terminology for a certain domain from a domain-specific textual corpus. It is unique due to the fact that it attempts to analyze multi-word terms compositionally with respect to an existing semantic resource. OntoLearn relies on WordNet and derives the meaning of a complex term from the meaning of each of the subterms with respect to WordNet. Their approach thus requires disambiguation of terms with respect to WordNet. For this purpose, they present an algorithm called SSI (Structural Semantic Interconnection), performing word sense disambiguation on the basis of patterns representing paths in WordNet (the reader is referred to

---

[13] http://protege.stanford.edu/

[Navigli and Velardi, 2004] for details). In addition, a classification-based approach is used to label the relation between the synset corresponding to the meaning of each of the subterms. OntoLearn also includes a gloss generation component in order to generate natural language descriptions for the complex concepts constructed. The generation is performed via a number of rules combining the WordNet glosses of the different senses identified for a complex term. A detailed evaluation of the system, especially of the word sense disambiguation procedure as well as of the gloss generation component is presented in [Velardi et al., 2005]. The OntoLearn system is embedded in a methodology consisting of i) automatic extraction of knowledge, ii) validation and iii) maintenance and extension within an ontology management system (compare [Missikoff et al., 2002]). OntoLearn is probably the only system generating intensional descriptions of concepts in natural language, in contrast to the rather formal intension consisting of sets of attributes produced by our approach (compare Section 6.2). In general, the approaches to concept hierarchy induction presented in this chapter would clearly benefit from a word sense disambiguation component as implemented in OntoLearn.

Morin et al.

Morin et al. [Morin and Jacquemin, 1999] tackle the problem of projecting semantic relations between single terms to multiple terms. For example, one would like to project the *isa*-relation between *apple* and *fruit* to an *isa*-relation between *apple juice* and *fruit juice*. Such a projection is called *transfer* by Morin. *Specialization* is then the inverse relation in which, for example, an *isa*-relation between *apple* and *fruit* is transferred to a relation between *dried apples* and *dried fruit*. In an empirical evaluation, Morin et al. show that *transfer* is more frequent than *specialization* and that the former is more precise (P=83.3%) compared to the latter (P=58.4%).

Sanchez and Moreno

Sanchez and Moreno present an approach to automatically learn a taxonomy from the WWW given a certain seed word [Sanchez and Moreno, 2004b, Sanchez and Moreno, 2004a, Sanchez and Moreno, 2005]. Their procedure is defined as follows:

1. Issue the seed word as query to Google and download the first n pages returned by Google.
2. Search the original word in the downloaded pages, process their neighborhood linguistically and extract the adjective or noun to the left and right of the seed word. The word to the left is potentially a modifier of the seed word and can be used to create a specialized concept by concatenating it with the seed. Let us assume that the seed word is *cancer* and *breast* is found as the word to the left in one document. *Breast* is then considered as a *candidate concept* which can be concatenated with *cancer* to form the more special concept *breast cancer*.

3. Apply different statistics to verify that a candidate concept can indeed be used as modifier to create a more specialized concept (these statistics include computing the number of occurrences as well as the number of different pages the potential modifier occurs in, a PMI-like measure of the degree of relationship between the seed word and the modifier, etc.)

4. Iterate this procedure for each valid candidate concept.

The result of the procedure is a tree in which modifiers are monotonically added to the seed word level by level of the taxonomy. Additional heuristics are used to (i) detect named entities, (ii) distinguish several senses of the seed word by clustering as well as (iii) collapse different classes standing in a taxonomic relationship if the corresponding modifiers were retrieved from URLs which overlap to a considerable extent. Sanchez and Moreno evaluate their approach by comparing their automatically produced taxonomies with the web directories of Yahoo, Clasty or AlltheWeb. However, it remains very vague how precision and recall are calculated exactly.

Sabou

Sabou [Sabou, 2005] has recently applied ontology learning techniques to the task of inducing concept hierarchies for the purpose of modeling web services. Sabou performs extraction of terms as well as of taxonomic relations. Taxonomic relations are extracted relying on the 'head'-heuristic also used by OntoLearn [Missikoff et al., 2002] and OntoLT [Buitelaar et al., 2004], which is shown to be very reliable. Two case studies are presented: the first on a corpus describing RDF(S) storage tools, the second on a corpus consisting of descriptions of bioinformatics services. The automatically produced hierarchies are evaluated by comparing them to hand-crafted concept hierarchies for each of the domains. The method is unique in that it applies methods not to full text, but to Java-documentation of web services.

6.5.2 Taxonomy Refinement and Extension

In this section, we present approaches for the refinement and extension of concept hierarchies as defined in Section 3.1. Though refinement has not been tackled in the present thesis, we nevertheless provide an overview of relevant approaches for the sake of completeness. Further, some of the approaches for refinement presented in this Section are highly related to our approach to ontology population presented in Section 8.2.

Most approaches regard the process of refinement as the one of classifying unknown words with respect to the existing concept hierarchy. Such a refinement is monotonic in the sense that it adds new concepts, but leaves the remaining structure unmodified. The different approaches differ in i) the contextual features used, ii) the way the most appropriate position for the new term is chosen, and iii) the evaluation method used. Mainly, three different means of evaluating the choice can be distinguished. All approaches evaluate the decision in terms of accuracy, i.e. the number of times the algorithm chooses the position of the new term as specified in a gold standard. Other approaches report results with respect to a *lenient accuracy*, which either defines a choice as correct if it is validated a posteriori by a human judge as in the approach of Alfonseca et al. (see below), or in case the chosen subconcept is subsumed – up to a certain level – by the correct concept in the gold standard as in the approach of Widdows (see below). Further, some researchers also evaluate their approaches with respect to the learning accuracy of Hahn et al. [Hahn and Schnattinger, 1998a]. This is the case of the approaches of Alfonseca et al. as well as Mädche et al. (see below). Besides discussing approaches for the refinement of concept hierarchies, we also briefly discuss work related to the extension of lexical description of concepts.

6.5.2.1 Refinement

We start our discussion of approaches for refining taxonomies by discussing the seminal work of Hearst and Schütze, which relies on the *word space* approach described by Schütze [Schütze, 1993]. We then discuss the more recent extension of this model by Widdows [Widdows, 2003b]. Finally, we also discuss the related approaches of Mädche et al. as well as Alfonseca et al. The results of the different algorithms are shown in Table 6.24. Though the results are not actually comparable, they clearly show that all the approaches achieve between 15% and 17.39% in terms of accuracy. These low values show that refinement is in fact a difficult task as the choice of the ideal superconcept in the gold standard mirrors subjective choices of the human annotators. Some distinctions are probably quite idiosyncratic and thus difficult to account for with an automatic approach.

Hearst and Schütze

Hearst and Schütze [Hearst and Schütze, 1993] rely on the *word space* method introduced by Schütze [Schütze, 1993] consisting in collecting co-occurring words for the target word within a given window size. Latent semantic analysis (LSA) is used to reduce the dimension of the co-occurrence matrix. Hearst and Schütze use letter fourgrams instead of words as units and derive a 5000-by-5000 matrix from a corpus consisting of five months of the New York Times. The collocation matrix of fourgrams is collected such that the entry $a_{i,j}$ counts the number of times that fourgram i occurs at most 200 fourgrams left of fourgram j. The resulting matrix is densely populated with only 2% zero values. LSA is then applied to reduce the matrix dimension from 5000 to 97. Semantic similarity is calculated as the cosine of the two vectors in question.

At a second step, a further collocation matrix is calculated containing the co-occurrence count of 50.000 words from the New York Times with the 5000 predefined fourgrams of the first matrix. Co-occurrence between a word and the fourgrams was calculated using a window of 1001 fourgrams centered around the target word. The context vector of a word is then the sum of all the fourgram vectors appearing within 1001 fourgrams. The resulting word vectors consequently also have 97 dimensions. This representation is called *word space* by Schütze [Schütze, 1993].

The procedure to assign a new word to a new category is now as follows:

For each word w in *word space*:
1. collect the 20 nearest neighbors in space using the cosine measure,
2. compute the score s_i of category i for w
   as the number of nearest neighbors that are in i, and
3. assign w to the highest scoring category.

In order to test the algorithm, 1000 medium frequency words were selected. When assessing the quality of the results obtained when assigning new words to WordNet synsets, Hearst and Schütze state that 63% of the words are assigned correctly, 19% are assigned to related synsets, and 19% are misassigned.

Table 6.24. Comparison of word classification approaches

Method	Strict Accuracy	Lenient Accuracy	Learning Accuracy
tree-ascending + kNN (SD)	15.74%		39.46%
Alfonseca et al.	17.39%	28.26%	38%
Hearst and Schütze	n.a.	63%	n.a.
Widdows	15%	up to 80.8%	

Widdows

Widdows [Widdows, 2003b] extends the method described by Hearst and Schütze [Hearst and Schütze, 1993], modifying steps 3 and 4 of their algorithm. He aims at finding the place in the given taxonomy where nearest neighbors are most concentrated. Thus, the chosen position for the new concept is not necessarily one of the nearest neighbors with respect to *word space*, but can, for example, be a hypernym subsuming all or part of the neighbors. Widdows in fact relies on the *word space* model but uses word co-occurrence instead of fourgram co-occurrence. In the approach of Widdows [Widdows, 2003b], *word space* is constructed selecting 1000 frequent words from the British National Corpus and computing co-occurrence on the basis of a 15 word window, yielding a sparse matrix to which latent semantic analysis is applied. The dimension of the matrix is reduced from 1000 to 100. Similarity between words is then defined as the cosine between their vectors in *word space*. The algorithm suggested by Widdows is as follows:

- For a target word w, find words from the corpus which are similar to those of w. Consider these corpus-derived neighbors $N(w)$.
- Map the target word w to the place in the taxonomy where the neighbors $N(w)$ are 'most concentrated'.

Here the crucial question here is to define 'the place where the neighbors are most concentrated'. For this purpose, Widdows first introduces the set H consisting of all the hypernyms of the neighbors N(w), i.e.,

$$H = \bigcup_{w' \in N(w)} H(w') \qquad (6.40)$$

where $H(w)$ are all the hypernyms for a word w. The task is now to choose the most appropriate synset for the new word w out of the set H. For this purpose, Widdows defines a so called affinity function which quantifies the trade-off between choosing a too general and a too specific synset:

$$\alpha(w,h) := \begin{cases} f(dist(w,h)) & \text{if } h \in H(w) \\ -g(w,h) & \text{if } h \notin H(w) \end{cases} \qquad (6.41)$$

where $dist(w,h)$ is a measure of the distance between w and h, f is some positive monotonically decreasing function and g is some positive function. Intuitively speaking, $f(dist(w,h))$ is the higher, the closer w and h are with respect to the hierarchy, while $-g(w,h)$ subtracts penalty points if h does not subsume w.

Overall, the assignment of the target word to the most appropriate synset can be formulated as a maximization problem as given by the equation:

$$h_{max} = max_{h \in H} \sum_{w' \in N(w)} \alpha(w',h) \qquad (6.42)$$

Widdows in particular uses the following functions f and g:

$$f = \frac{1}{dist(w,h)^2}$$

$$g = 0.25$$

where $dist(w,h)$ is the number of levels in the taxonomy between h and w. The best result of this approach, considering an answer only as correct if it exactly reproduces the classification of WordNet, yielded an accuracy of 15%. This result is achieved with a version considering 3 neighbors and including part-of-speech information to distinguish between the different syntactic categories of a word. Using a more lenient version of the learning accuracy considering a prediction as valid if it is subsumed by the correct concept up to a certain number of levels, the approach achieves an accuracy of up to 80.8% at a maximal distance of 10 levels.

Mädche, Pekar and Staab

Mädche, Pekar and Staab [Mädche et al., 2002] present a comparison of different approaches for classifying a new word under the correct concept of a given concept hierarchy, given distributional data obtained from the corpus. They present the following techniques for the classification task:

- tree-descending,
- tree-ascending,
- k-nearest neighbors (kNN), and
- combination of tree-ascending with kNN.

The tree descending algorithm consists in starting from the top category of the concept hierarchy and moving down to the leaves, always choosing that child concept which maximizes the distributional similarity with the unknown word. Here, an important question is how the context vectors of the inner nodes of the tree are calculated. Mädche et al. suggest aggregating the vectors of the child nodes until a fixed depth and then either normalizing the vector (*category-based method*) or calculating the centroid by dividing by the number of aggregated vectors (*centroid-based method*).

The tree ascending method bears some similarity with the method of Widdows [Widdows, 2003b] as described above. In fact, the tree ascending method also aims at finding the most appropriate superconcept which subsumes all or at least part of the nearest neighbors. The voting of each inner node is calculated using the taxonomic similarity as defined by Mädche et al. [Mädche et al., 2002], relying on the notion of the least common superconcept of two concepts a and b:

$$lcs(a, b) := c \ such \ that \ \delta(a, c) + \delta(b, c) + \delta(top, c) \ is \ minimal, \qquad (6.43)$$

where $\delta(a, b)$ is the distance between a and b in terms of the number of edges which need to be traversed.

Now the taxonomic similarity σ between two concepts is defined as:

$$\sigma(a, b) := \frac{\delta(top, c) + 1}{\delta(top, c) + \delta(a, c) + \delta(b, c) + 1}$$

where $c = lcs(a, b)$.

The voting weight for a certain node is then calculated as:

$$W(n) := \sum_{h \in H(n)} sim(t, h) \cdot \sigma(n, h) \qquad (6.44)$$

where t is the target word to be classified and H is the set of hyponyms of node n, namely its children.

The k-nearest neighbor method consists in calculating the distributional similarity of the new word with all the concepts in the hierarchy. The k most similar concepts are considered further, letting them vote for the new word proportionally to the corresponding similarity. The majority vote then decides about which concept the new word is classified to. The obvious drawback of such a method is that concepts higher in the hierarchy are chosen rarely.

Mädche et al. experiment with the corpus used in the GETESS project [Staab et al., 1999]. As context they use the three stemmed words to the left and right of the target word, excluding stopwords and without trespassing sentence boundaries. The construction of a hypernym vector is performed by aggregating the hyponyms up to three levels.

Overall, Mädche et al. achieve the best results using a combination of the tree-descending algorithm to pick out a certain concept and kNN to choose one of its subconcepts. They also explore three different similarity measures, the Jaccard Coefficient, the L1 norm and the Skew divergence, achieving the best result of an accuracy of 15.74% as well as a Learning Accuracy as defined in [Hahn and Schnattinger, 1998a] of 39.46% using the Skew divergence.

Alfonseca et al.

Alfonseca et al. [Alfonseca and Manandhar, 2002] also present an approach based on the distributional similarity of words. They consider for each word w the following topic signatures:

- the *topic signature* is the list of words that co-occur with the target word w in the same sentence,
- the *subject signature* is the list of verbs for which w appears as subject,
- the *object signature* is the list of verbs and prepositions, for which w appears as argument, as well as
- the *modifier signature* is the list of adjectives and determiners that modify w in a noun phrase.

Overall, the procedure to classify a new word w' with respect to WordNet is as follows:

1. Take all the synsets which could be a potential superconcept for w'.
2. For each synset, aggregate the frequencies of the vectors of all hyponyms and smooth the frequencies by adding 1 to every value.
3. For each synset, use the other synsets as contrast to measure the weight of each word in the vector using χ^2.
4. Calculate the similarity between the target word and each synset as the dot product of the corresponding vectors.
5. Assign the new word to the concept maximizing the similarity as calculated in 4.

Given a target word w, a similarity is calculated for each concept in the ontology with respect to each signature as the dot product, i.e. the cosine measure without normalization by vector length. The result of the similarity with respect to the different signatures is then combined in a linear way as given by the following formula:

$$P(s_i) = \sum_{j=0}^{m} w_j P_{sig_j}(s_i), \qquad (6.45)$$

where (s_i) is a WordNet synset. The authors experiment, on the one hand, with a uniform combination using a factor of $w_j = \frac{1}{m}$, where m is the number of signatures considered (4 in this case). On the other hand, they also determine the factors experimentally using a simulated annealing procedure to calculate the weights such that the distance between the final combined distribution P and each of the distributions P_{sig_j} is uniform with respect to the relative entropy or Kullback-Leibler distance. The weights are initialized to $w_j = \frac{1}{m}$ and modified until the relative entropies $D(P_{sig_j}||P)$ converge. The authors successfully show that the learned combination of signatures yields better results compared to the uniform combination.

The authors use a variety of measures to report the results, among them the *strict accuracy, lenient accuracy* and the *learning accuracy* of [Hahn and Schnattinger, 1998a]. In terms of direct accuracy, the best result of 17.39% is achieved using only the object signatures. The best lenient accuracy of 28.26% is obtained twice using only object signatures as well as combining the topic, subject and object signatures using the entropy-driven simulated annealing procedure. The conclusion in this line should thus be that combining the different methods does not pay off. The authors do also conclude that the modifier signature performed very bad in general.

6.5.2.2 Lexical Extension

For many applications in natural language processing and information retrieval, it is crucial to establish a link between a conceptual model as specified in an ontology and the way the entities defined in the model appear in a corpus. Such approaches aim at establishing a link between a given ontology and the symbols used in a corpus to refer to the domain-specific concepts contained therein (compare [Buitelaar et al., 2006]). We discuss in particular the work of Agirre et al. on deriving topic signatures, which can be used for many applications within NLP (compare [Lin and Hovy, 2000]). We also discuss the work of Faatz et al. on enriching a given ontology with lexical descriptors for concepts as well as the related work of Turner on finding synonyms.

Agirre et al.

Agirre et al. [Agirre et al., 2000] present an approach to automatically derive so called topic signatures for the concepts of an ontology. Topic signatures can be seen as a collection of words contextually related to a given target word. Agirre et al. [Agirre et al., 2000] define a procedure to download topic signatures for WordNet synsets from the World Wide Web using automatically created search engine queries. When creating these queries, attention is paid to ensure that words of other synsets corresponding to other senses of the word in question are excluded. This is done by using the Altavista NOT operator in the queries. The downloaded documents then form the basis for the generation of topic signatures for each synset, whereby each word is weighted using the χ^2 measure with respect to the document collection for the other synsets as a contrastive corpus. The topic signatures derived in this way are then successfully used in a word sense disambiguation experiment. It is well known though that WordNet suffers from a proliferation of word senses in some cases. Thus, in a second experiment, the authors attempt to derive more coarse-grained senses for a certain word by hierarchically clustering the document collections for each sense of a given word. The idea is then that the more abstract clusters represent more coarse-grained sense for the word. In a further experiment, the authors perform word sense disambiguation directly using the generated cluster tree and achieve better results at all levels: fine, medium and coarse sense distinction.

Faatz and Steinmetz

Faatz and Steinmetz [Faatz and Steinmetz, 2003] present an approach for enrichment of ontologies with additional lexical descriptors for its concepts. Interesting is the fact that the lexical enrichment of an ontology is seen as an optimization problem with the aim of minimizing the difference between the corpus-based dissimilarity between two concepts and their corresponding distance in the taxonomy. The dissimilarity between two vectors representing the context of a concept in the corpus is calculated component-wise by a function f_k, for which an optimal configuration is searched which minimizes the average squared error with respect to distance in the taxonomy. In [Faatz and Steinmetz, 2003] the results of the method are only discussed qualitatively, while in [Faatz and Steinmetz, 2005] a more formal evaluation framework is presented.

Turney

Turney [Turney, 2001] addresses the task of finding synonyms for given words. For this purpose, he relies on the pointwise mutual information (PMI) measure to discover strongly related words.

Given a word w_1, the score of word w_2 as synonym is measured as follows:

$$score(w_2) = log_2 \frac{P(w_1, w_2)}{P(w_1)\, P(w_2)} \tag{6.46}$$

As $P(w_1)$ is the same for all the different synonyms to be checked, this reduces to:

$$score(w_2) = log_2 \frac{P(w_1, w_2)}{P(w_2)} \qquad (6.47)$$

Turney computes the PMI between two words w_1 and w_2 relying on the number of pages returned by a search engine such as Altavista for certain queries. In order to calculate the PMI, Turner presents different measures relying on the NEAR and AND Altavista operators:

$$score(w_2) = \frac{hits(w_1 \ AND \ w_2)}{hits(w_2)} \qquad (6.48)$$

$$score(w_2) = \frac{hits(w_1 \ NEAR \ w_2)}{hits(w_2)}$$

The NEAR operator returns all documents in which w_1 occurs within a distance of up to 10 words to w_2. Further measures with the aim of ruling out antonyms and taking into account context are also presented. The approach is evaluated on the TOEFL synonym finding task achieving an accuracy of 73.75%. He also shows that his method performs better than latent semantic analysis using an encyclopedia and calculating similarity between words as the cosine between their corresponding context vectors, yielding an accuracy of 64.4%.

6.6 Conclusion and Open Issues

The present chapter has contributed to the state-of-the-art in concept hierarchy induction in several ways. In Section 6.2, we have systematically compared different hierarchical clustering approaches with respect to effectiveness, speed and traceability by the ontology engineer. The main conclusions here were that set-theoretic approaches as FCA can in fact compete and even outperform similarity-based approaches in terms of quality of the produced hierarchies, speed and traceability. The better quality is mainly due to a higher recall of the FCA-based approach. Though FCA is theoretically exponential in the size of the formal context, we have shown that in our settings, where the contexts are typically sparsely populated, FCA performs quite efficiently compared to an agglomerative clustering algorithm. On the other hand, we have also provided an evaluation method based on Mädche's taxonomic overlap, in which automatically learned concept hierarchies are evaluated by comparing them to a reference concept hierarchy. We have in particular presented measures evaluating the global quality of the hierarchy as well as the local quality or coherence of the clusters.

In Section 6.3, we have presented a novel and efficient bottom-up clustering algorithm exploiting an external hypernym oracle to guide the clustering process. The algorithm is theoretically and practically more efficient than agglomerative clustering as it does not need to update the similarity matrix for newly formed clusters, relying only on the similarity of single elements. We have shown that, in terms of cluster coherence, our algorithm produces more reliable clusters compared to other methods such as the one of Caraballo. As a byproduct, the algorithm also automatically labels clusters with the appropriate hypernym. A human evaluation of the produced hierarchies has shown that the learned *isa*-relations correspond to human intuitions.

Finally, we have also addressed the important question of combining different paradigms and approaches to learning taxonomic relations from text and presented a novel and unique approach using machine learning techniques to derive a model combining the different approaches in an optimal way. We have examined different classifiers as well as methods for addressing problems related to the unbalanced character of our datasets. Our experiments have demonstrated that the learned model indeed outperforms all single approaches considered as well as naive combinations of them.

Fortunately, there remain a lot of open issues.

On the one hand, the issue which similarity or weighting measure to choose still remains an open problem. To some extent, this question can only be answered with respect to a given dataset. For sure, the question can be answered only empirically by comparing different similarity measures and feature weighting measures over many different domains. It does also remain an open question which features to consider to represent a certain word or term. Our results have shown that the more features one considers, the better is the quality of the learned concept hierarchies. An interesting question is whether features can be aggregated somehow to represent a term at a more abstract level. One possibility, for example, would be to map a verb to WordNet top levels or to verb classes as described in Levin [Levin, 1993]. Another possibility is to also cluster the features themselves, possibly by using co-clustering techniques [Dhillon, 2001]. Dimension reduction techniques could also be applied, thus clustering on reduced vectors (compare [Landauer and Dumais, 1997]). Again, only the evidence from empirical investigations will shed light on these questions.

On the other hand, there remains the problem of modeling polysemy of terms. We have argued that our FCA-based approach supports multiple inheritance and can thus, in principle, represent various meanings of a term. However, this should be definitely verified, also using other soft clustering techniques such as PoBOC (Pole-Based Overlapping Clustering) [Cleuziou et al., 2004] or Clustering-By-Committee [Pantel and Lin, 2002a]. The question of how to evaluate if a certain method has captured all the relevant senses for a term in a certain domain is certainly a difficult and open question.

Another important issue seems the automatic induction of lexico-syntactic patterns. Though there have already been initial blueprints in the works of Agichtein and Gravano [Agichtein and Gravano, 2000], Ravichandran and

Hovy [Ravichandran and Hovy, 2002], Snow et al. [Snow et al., 2004] Downey et al. [Downey et al., 2004], and recently also Pennacchiotti and Pantel [Pennacchiotti and Pantel, 2006], the problem of fully automatic and unsupervised induction of lexico-syntactic patterns conveying a certain relation of interest seems still unsolved.

Finally, though we have provided a first step towards combining different approaches in a non-adhoc way, there remains a lot of work for the future. On the one hand, other models allowing for combination should be examined. On the other hand, a crucial question is how to compute the confidences for different approaches. Another important question is whether a model learned for a certain domain can be successfully applied to other domains too. Finally, we have also argued for the inclusion of a word sense disambiguation component when integrating evidence from a lexical resource or thesaurus such as WordNet.

7

Learning Attributes and Relations

Besides being described by their position in a taxonomy, concepts are also characterized by attributes as well as by relations to other concepts. In the context of this book, we will restrict ourselves to binary relations establishing a connection between different concepts at the schema level. In order to provide useful inferences, these relations need to be further axiomatically defined and combined with other relations or concepts in the form of rules. The learning of corresponding axioms or rules is, however, out of the scope of this book. We will focus on learning relations at the schema level. In what follows, we first present the most common approaches to learning relations from text in order to situate our work in the context of the state-of-the-art in the field.

7.1 Common Approaches

In this section, we first give an overview of the main techniques applied for extracting ontological relations from corpora. We first introduce techniques based on collocation analysis, which can be understood as producing 'anonymous' relations without a label. Second, we will briefly introduce approaches relying on syntactic dependencies, especially dependencies between verbs and their arguments. Finally, we also discuss approaches based on matching lexico-syntactic patterns in the tradition of Heart's seminal work [Hearst, 1992].

7.1.1 Collocations

A great amount of work on the topic of extracting relations from text is based on the notion of a collocation. Let us recall that a collocation is a pair of words which occur together more often than expected by chance within a certain boundary, that is, within a certain window of words, a sentence, a paragraph or even a document. In order to detect such collocations, researchers have used statistical tests such as the Student's t-test or the χ^2-test (see Section 4.1.5). A collocation thus typically reveals a strong but unknown relation between words. Examples for such techniques can be found, for instance, in the work of Mädche and Staab [Mädche and Staab, 2000], Yamaguchi [Yamaguchi, 2001] or Heyer et al. [Heyer et al., 2001]. These approaches are discussed in more detail in Section 7.5.

7.1.2 Syntactic Dependencies

Other research has exploited syntactic dependencies, in particular the dependencies between a verb and its arguments. For example, from a sentence like *'A person works for some employer'* we could derive the existence of a relation *work_for* between the concept **person** and the concept **employer**. This simple idea has been explored by several researchers (e.g. [Gamallo et al., 2002, Buitelaar et al., 2004, Kavalec and Svátek, 2005, Ciaramita et al., 2005, Schutz and Buitelaar, 2005]). An important issue herein is to find the right level of generalization for the verb's arguments with respect to a given concept hierarchy. This issue has also received considerable attention in the computational linguistics community in the context of the acquisition of so called *selectional restrictions* [Ribas, 1995, Resnik, 1997, Clark and Weir, 2002]. Another important issue is to detect verbs denoting the same ontological relation. One possibility here is for example to cluster verbs semantically taking into account their arguments. Such an approach is pursued by Schulte im Walde [Schulte im Walde, 2000], for example. Finally, a further interesting issue is how to order relations hierarchically. Not much effort has been devoted to this issue though.

7.1.3 Lexico-syntactic patterns

Lexico-syntactic patterns as originally defined by Hearst [Hearst, 1992] can be applied in the context of relation discovery to the task of learning the domain-specific extension of very specific relations such as *part-of, cause, purpose*, etc. Charniak and Berland have applied, for example, the following patterns to discover part-of relations:

Charniak 1: NN_{whole}'s$\{POS\}$ NN_{part}
Charniak 2: NN_{part} of$\{PREP\}$ $((the|a)\{DET\}$ $\{JJ|NN\})$* NN_{whole}
Charniak 3: NN_{part} in$\{PREP\}$ $((the|a)\{DET\}$ $\{JJ|NN\})$* NN_{whole}
Charniak 4: NN_{part} of$\{PREP\}$ NN_{whole}
Charniak 5: NN_{part} in$\{PREP\}$ NN_{whole}

The above expressions should be interpreted as regular expressions in the following way: words are supposed to be matched explicitly in the text in the indicated order. A part-of-speech tag in curly brackets '{' and '}' poses the additional constraint that the word preceding it should belong to the corresponding syntactic category. Further, as in standard regular expression notation, elements are grouped using standard brackets '(' and ')', whereas '|'

stands for a disjunction. Further, as usual, + stands for 1 or more occurrences and * for none or more. The part-of-speech tags will be hereby expressed relying on the frequently used Penn Treebank tagset. The tagset can be found in Appendix A.4.

Other patterns have been applied to derive causation (see [Girju and Moldovan, 2002]) or *telic* (purpose) relations (compare [Yamada and Baldwin, 2004]). Research on extraction of lexical knowledge bases from MRDs has also attempted to derive purpose and part-of relations using a specific set of patterns. Consult, for example, the structures extracted by Alshawi's approach [Alshawi, 1987] in Section 6.1.1.

7.1.4 Road Map

We have reviewed the main techniques for deriving relations from text. In the remainder of this chapter, we will present three approaches to learning relations. The first and second approaches are based on learning relations relying on syntactic dependencies. The first approach aims at learning attributes relying on the syntactic relation between a noun and its modifying adjectives. The second approach follows the tradition of learning relations on the basis of verbs and their arguments, focusing specifically on the issue of finding the right level of generalization for the arguments given a concept hierarchy. The third approach is based on matching lexico-syntactic patterns and aims at learning *qualia structures* for nouns. The remainder of this chapter addresses the following issues:

Learning Attributes

Section 7.2 presents an approach to derive attributes from a text corpus. In particular, we derive attributes with a finite set of values as range consisting of adjectives found in the corpus. WordNet is used in order to find an appropriate intensional description of the attribute which the different adjectives refer to. We present a human evaluation of the automatically learned attributes and arrange the concepts in a lattice according to their attributes using FCA.

Learning the Appropriate Generalization Level for Relations

In Section 7.3, we present an approach to discover ontological relations from text on the basis of verb structures found in the corpus. In particular, the focus is on analyzing different statistical measures for the purpose of selecting the proper domain and ranges for the relation in question. We restrict ourselves here to binary relations and make the naive assumption that the domain and range of a relation can be generalized independently of each other. Experiments are conducted on the Genia corpus and using the Genia ontology[1] [Ohta et al., 2002]. The results are evaluated with respect to a gold standard

---

[1] http://www-tsujii.is.s.u-tokyo.ac.jp/~genia/topics/corpus/

provided by a biologist. This section is based on joint work with Matthias Hartung and Esther Ratsch, which has been partially previously published in [Cimiano et al., 2006].

Learning Qualia Structures

Section 7.4 deals with the acquisition of a well-defined set of relations, i.e. so called *qualia roles*, which typically apply to objects in general. In particular, we present an approach to learning qualia structures from the Web. Some of these qualia roles correspond to ontological relations which are well understood in artificial intelligence and philosophy, i.e. taxonomic and mereological relations. This section is due to joint work with Johanna Wenderoth published in [Cimiano and Wenderoth, 2005].

7.2 Learning Attributes

Attributes are defined as relations with a datatype as range. Typical attributes are, for example, name or color with a *string* as range, date with a *date* as range or size with an *integer* or *real* as range. In this section, we will deal with the issue of acquiring attributes automatically from text. Attributes are typically expressed in texts using the preposition *of*, the verb *have* or genitive constructs, e.g.

- the color **of** the car
- every car **has** a color
- the **car's** color
- Peter bought a new car. **Its** color [...]

However, we are not only interested in learning the domain (e.g. car) and name for an attribute (e.g. color), but also its range. In fact, values of attributes are expressed in texts in quite different ways, for instance using copula constructs, adjectives or expressions specific to the attribute in question:

- the car **is** red / his name **is** Peter (copula + value)
- Peter **is** 176 cm **tall** (copula + value + adjective)
- the car **is** 3 meters **long** (copula + value + adjective)
- the **red** car (adjective)
- the car is **painted** red / he is **called** Peter / the baby **weighs 3kg** (specific expressions)

In order to systematize the above, in what follows we suggest a classification of attributes according to their range. This classification is given in Table 7.1. We give examples and describe how the attribute and its domain as well as the range of the attribute are typically expressed in texts.

To some extent, the classes are self-explanatory. For the sake of completeness, we will nevertheless give some brief explanations for each class. The

Table 7.1. Classification of attributes

Type	Domain + Attribute	Range
discrete + finite (e.g. *gender, legal status*)	of/have/genetive	copula + adj. /adj. mod. *the man is single* *the single man*
discrete + enumerable (e.g. *name, ssn*)	of/have/genetive	copula / specific *his ssn is* *he is called Peter*
numeric (continuous/discrete) (e.g. *height, weight, size, temperature*)	of/have/genetive	copula + value / copula + value + adj. specific *its height is 5 m* *the car is 3 m long* *the baby weights 3 kg*
fuzzy usage (e.g. *color*)	of/have/genetive	copula + adj. / adj. mod *the car is red / the blue sky*
inherently fuzzy (e.g. *niceness, conventionality*)		copula + adj /adj. mod *a nice man* *a conventional wedding*

class *discrete + finite* describes attributes which have a discrete and finite set as range. This is the case of gender with the set {*male, female*} as well as legal status with the set {*single, married, divorced, widowed*} as range. The class *discrete + enumerable* describes attributes which have a discrete, possibly infinite, but enumerable set as range, such as name or ssn. An exception is the set of integers, which we assign to the *numeric* class consisting of attributes with a numeric scale as range, either continuous or discrete. The most common sets here are the set of integers or the set of the real values. With *fuzzified usage* we denote continuous variables which are 'fuzzified' in natural language such as height, weight, size or temperature for which we typically use adjectives such as tall, heavy, big or hot to express their values, respectively, as well as attributes which are measured via a numeric and continuous scale, but are used exclusively in a fuzzy way by humans. For example, though we know that color is not an intrinsic property of objects, but a function of the human visual system and can be measured by the amplitude of the light's wave, nobody would say something like: '*the color of the car is 580nm*'. The category *inherently fuzzy* contains attributes which can not be measured by a scale, but are inherently fuzzy. Examples for such attributes are, for instance, niceness, conventionality, etc.

When extracting attributes from text corpora, we are faced with different problems which we briefly discuss in the following.

As discussed by Poesio and Almuhareb [Poesio and Almuhareb, 2005], constructs involving the preposition '*of*', the verb '*to have*' as well as genitive constructs are highly ambiguous, indicating a wide range of semantic relations. In fact, the preposition *'of'* can relate an attribute to its concepts, a part to its whole, an agent to its activity, an activity to its patient or beneficiary, such as in the following examples:

- the color of the car (attribute)
- the hood of the car (part-whole)
- the repairing of the car (activity-patient)
- the driver of the car (agent-patient)

On the other hand, some artificial attributes such as niceness are not likely to appear in expressions like the above. Certainly, it is a debatable question whether we want to consider qualities such as niceness or conventionality as attributes (compare the discussion in [Almuhareb and Poesio, 2004]). Our position here is that niceness and conventionality are perfectly reasonable 'fuzzy' attributes with a discrete and finite set as range, which we also aim at acquiring.

So far, we conclude that expressions like the above are, on the one hand, ambiguous with respect to the relation they express. On the other hand, there are a lot of 'fuzzy' attributes which are not likely to be mentioned in similar constructions, such as niceness or conventionality. Thus, instead of learning attributes in an intensional way, in this section we present an approach aiming at learning attributes given information about their values in the form of adjectives.

In language, adjectives typically convey qualities of the nouns they modify. In particular, they denote the fuzzy values of a certain quality. However, as argued by Raskin and Nirenburg [Raskin and Nirenburg, 1996], not all adjectives denote an attribute, a quality or a property of a noun. There are, for example, the following exceptions:

- **attitude adjectives**, expressing the opinion of the speaker such as in *'good house'*,
- **temporal adjectives**, such as the *'former president'* or the *'occasional visitor'*,
- **membership adjectives**, such as the *'alleged criminal'*, a *'fake cowboy'*, and
- **event-related adjectives**, such as *'abusive speech'*, in which either the agent of the speech is abusive or the event itself.

In our approach, we will find the corresponding intensional description for the adjective by looking up its corresponding attribute in WordNet and only consider those adjectives which do have such an attribute relation (compare Section 4.1.8), thus decreasing the probability that we are considering an adjective which does not denote the value of some attribute, quality or property.

It is important to mention that with our approach, we only yield attributes with a finite discrete set of fuzzy values as range as this is the way values of attributes are expressed in natural language through adjectives. We will thus in principle not be able to distinguish between the classes *discrete+finite*, *fuzzy usage* and *inherently fuzzy*. We draw here the analogy to fuzzy logic, where we have so called linguistic variables such as *temperature* together with fuzzy values such as *hot, cold*, etc. representing a characteristic function of a fuzzy set in the sense that membership is measured with a certain degree (compare [Zadeh, 1975]). In fact, in natural language the values of an attribute or variable such as temperature are expressed in a fuzzy way. The reasons for this are obvious; on the one hand, people do often not know the exact value of a certain variable such as the temperature and therefore can not express it. On the other hand, using a fuzzy value is often totally sufficient for the purpose of communicating some message as well as reasoning on the basis of known information.

7.2.1 Approach

In our approach to learning attributes, we first tokenize and part-of-speech tag the corpus using TreeTagger [Schmid, 1994]. Then we apply suitable regular expressions to match the following two patterns and extract adjective/noun pairs.

- (\w+{DET})? (\w+{NN})+ is{VBZ} \w+{JJ}
- (\w+{DET})? \w+{JJ} (\w+{NN})+

For the same reasons as described in Section 6.2, these pairs are weighted using the conditional probability, i.e.

$$Cond(n, a) := \frac{f(n, a)}{f(n)} \tag{7.1}$$

where $f(n, a)$ is the joint frequency of adjective a and noun n and $f(n)$ is the frequency of noun n. For the noun *car* we get, for example, 436 different adjectives as modifiers. Using a threshold of 0.01 on the above conditional probability, we get the adjectives shown in Table 7.2 from our tourism corpus.

At a second step, for each of the adjectives we look up the corresponding attribute in WordNet, further considering only adjectives which actually have an attribute. For car, with our method we get the following attributes and ranges (t=0.01):

car:

        age is one of {new, old}
        value is one of {black}
        numerousness/numerosity/multiplicity is one of {many}
        otherness/distinctness/separateness is one of {other}
        speed/swiftness/fastness is one of {fast}
        size is one of {small, little, big}

Table 7.2. Adjectives extracted from the tourism corpus for *car* with a conditional probability above 0.01

Adjective	Cond
new	0.11
own	0.05
other	0.04
old	0.03
private	0.03
steal	0.03
first	0.03
fast	0.02
small	0.02
big	0.02
little	0.02
many	0.01
unmarked	0.01
second	0.01
red	0.01
black	0.01
diesel	0.01

In the above example, adjectives such as *'own'*, *'private'*, *'steal'*, *'first'*, *'unmarked'*, *'second'*, *'red'* and *'diesel'* have not been considered as WordNet 1.7.1 does not specify a corresponding attribute.

7.2.2 Results

Our approach to automatically derive attributes from a text corpus has been applied to the *Tourism* corpus and evaluated along the following lines:

- human evaluation of the produced domain–attribute–value structures,
- evaluation of taxonomies created on the basis of the attributes in terms of TO and LTO compared with the tourism reference ontology in Section 6.2 when using attributes or adjectives as features, and
- a qualitative discussion of a lattice automatically derived on the basis of the attributes.

We discuss the results of these evaluations more in detail in the following subsections.

7.2.2.1 Human Evaluation

In order to evaluate the learned attributes, we presented the different attributes grouped with respect to their domain concepts to a human assessor.

We asked this assessor to evaluate for every domain concept (i) its attributes and (ii) their corresponding ranges by assigning them a rate from '0' to '3'. Hereby, '3' means that the attribute or its range is totally reasonable and correct, while '0' means that the attribute or the range does not make any sense. The results of this evaluation are given in Table 7.3 showing for each concept in the $O_{tourism}$ ontology the number of attributes derived as well as the average rating of the attribute and its range. We see that on average almost 6 attributes have been derived for each concept in the tourism ontology. The learned attributes were rated with almost 2 credits on average and their ranges with about 2.5 credits on average. The attributes derived thus seem indeed reasonable and the corresponding ranges even more.

Table 7.3. Average credits per attribute

	No. attr	Avg. attr. credits	Avg. value credits
address	10	1.1	2.7
aerobic	3	2	3
afternoon	6	1.83	2.83
animation	5	1.8	3
autumn	1	3	3
banquet	5	2.4	3
bill	6	1.5	2.5
booking	5	2.4	3
bus	7	2.71	3
camping	5	3	3
car	6	2	2.17
caravan	12	1.92	2.5
castle	7	2	2.57
category	6	2	2.5
cheque	5	2.4	3
contract	10	1.7	2.4
day	7	1.29	1.86
drier	4	1.5	2.25
equipment	7	2.29	2.14
ferry	10	2.4	3
football	3	3	3
gym	7	3	3
holiday	7	1.71	2.57
inn	4	3	3
iron	12	1.25	2
journey	6	2.17	2.83
kayak	6	0.5	1.17
kitchenette	4	2.5	3
law	6	2.5	3
lounge	7	2.57	2.57
massage	10	1.9	2.7
menu	6	3	3
organization	5	1.8	2.4
panorama	6	2	3
park	4	2.25	2.25
party	3	1	2
period	3	2	2.67
plant	5	2.2	2.4
port	6	2	2.5
presentation	4	3	3
promenade	10	2.1	3
region	6	1	2.17
rental	4	3	3
ruin	7	2.29	2.57
sauna	12	1.75	2.83
sight	7	1.71	2.57
spring	3	2.33	3
station	5	1.2	2.4
steamer	3	2	3
swimming	5	1.8	3
tennis	15	1.67	2.47
terrace	6	2	2.67
time	5	0.6	2.4
tree	6	2.5	2.5
vehicle	6	2	2.5
view	5	3	3
wedding	9	1.67	2.33
average	5.82	1.91	2.52

7.2.2.2 Taxonomy Induction

We create concept hierarchies with our FCA-based method as presented in Section 6.2, using the attributes derived with the method described in this section, and compare the generated hierarchies with our tourism reference hierarchy in terms of taxonomic overlap and local taxonomic overlap. In particular, we compare using the adjectives themselves as formal attributes with respect to using the attributes derived from WordNet. The results are shown in Tables 7.4 and 7.5 for different thresholds. The reason why results are reported for a threshold from 0.03 on when using attributes is that our compaction procedure ended prematurely due to an out-of-memory exception for lower thresholds (compare Section 6.2 for details on the lattice compaction procedure). From a certain threshold on, no formal attributes remain and thus no lattices are constructed, which by definition have a precision of 100% and a recall of 0%. When using adjectives as formal attributes, this situation is reached at a threshold of 0.7. When using attributes, the corresponding threshold is 0.5.

The results show that using adjectives leads to better results in terms of taxonomic overlap compared to using attributes at different thresholds. At a threshold of $t = 0.03$ the results are comparable though. In general, using attributes yields a much higher local taxonomic overlap for different thresholds, but comparable results at a threshold of $t = 0.03$. Overall, the results on the taxonomy induction tasks are worse than the results obtained with FCA using syntactic dependencies or pseudo-syntactic surface dependencies.

7.2.2.3 Qualitative Discussion

Finally, we discuss our attribute extraction method by highlighting some interesting structures in the concept lattice produced by FCA on the basis of the attribute information and using a threshold of 0.04. Figures 7.1 - 7.5 show interesting fragments of the generated lattice. In Figure 7.1, it can be appreciated that FCA has grouped together entities having a temperature, such as seasons, i.e. *summer, spring, winter*, but also a *whirlpool*, a *buffet*, an *iron*, a *shower*, etc. Figure 7.2 shows a big cluster of entities which have an *age*. Interesting are the time-related concepts consisting of entities having a certain *regularity, timing* or *duration/length* which are depicted in Figures 7.3, 7.4 and 7.5, respectively. In general, the formal concepts produced by FCA seem indeed reasonable and correspond to our intuitions.

Table 7.4. Results of comparison with the tourism reference taxonomy in terms of $\overline{TO}$

	P_{TO}	R_{TO}	F_{TO}	F'
Adjectives				
0.01	22.74%	43.35%	29.83%	**37.41%**
0.02	22.32%	41.07%	28.88%	36.66%
0.03	21.19%	33.70%	25.79%	33.91%
0.04	20.40%	29.64%	23.73%	31.86%
0.05	20.67%	28.06%	22.96%	30.57%
0.1	24.06%	6.50%	9.85%	14.53%
0.3	83.33%	1.36%	2.60%	2.95%
0.5	100%	0.69%	1.37%	0.55%
0.7	100%	0%	0%	0%
0.9	100%	0%	0%	0%
Attributes				
0.03	27.00%	25.89%	26.43%	**33.41%**
0.04	28.90%	25.17%	26.91%	32.26%
0.05	32.94%	8.72%	13.79%	19.41%
0.1	49.17%	3.54%	6.61%	8.98%
0.3	100%	1.72%	3.38%	0.62%
0.5	100%	0%	0%	0%
0.7	100%	0%	0%	0%
0.9	100%	0%	0%	0%

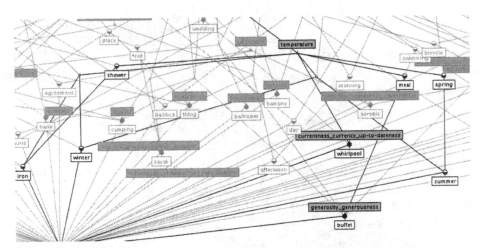

Fig. 7.1. Attribute-based concept lattice: objects with temperature

Table 7.5. Results of comparison with the tourism reference taxonomy in terms of $\overline{LTO}$

	P_{LTO}	R_{LTO}	F_{LTO}
	Adjectives		
0.01	21.54%	44.71%	**29.07%**
0.02	21.37%	34.69%	26.45%
0.03	22.55%	30.21%	25.82%
0.04	21.99%	27.81%	24.56%
0.05	22.44%	24.45%	23.40%
0.1	26.00%	24.88%	25.43%
0.3	50%	16.67%	25%
0.5	100%	0%	0%
0.7	100%	0%	0%
0.9	100%	0%	0%
	Attributes		
0.03	23.96%	26.95%	25.37%
0.04	22.15%	22.25%	22.20%
0.05	25.10%	22.52%	23.74%
0.1	32.34%	27.27%	**29.59%**
0.3	100%	0%	0%
0.5	100%	0%	0%
0.7	100%	0%	0%
0.9	100%	0%	0%

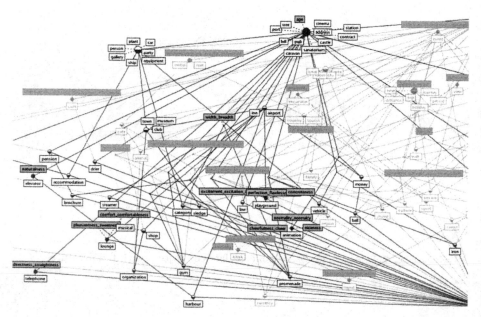

Fig. 7.2. Attribute-based concept lattice: objects with age

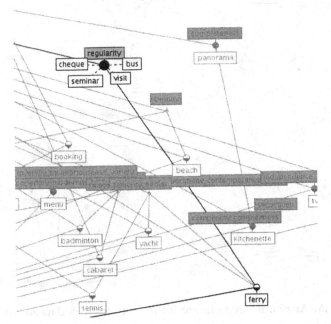

Fig. 7.3. Attribute-based concept lattice: objects with regularity

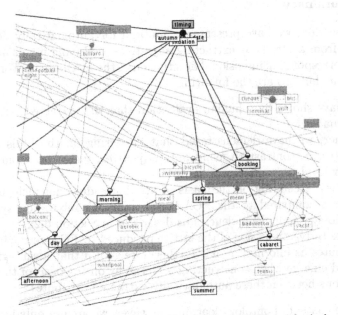

Fig. 7.4. Attribute-based concept lattice: objects with timing

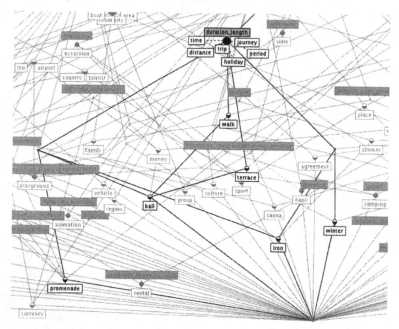

Fig. 7.5. Attribute-based concept lattice: objects with duration or length

7.2.3 Summary

In this section, we have presented a method for automatically deriving attributes from a corpus by extracting adjectives modifying nouns and looking up the corresponding intensional description of the attribute in WordNet. The main contributions are the following:

- We have shown by a human evaluation that the extracted attributes are reasonable.
- Further, we have demonstrated that clustering on the basis of the attributes, in contrast to using only adjectives, yields taxonomies with a better local taxonomic overlap.
- However, clustering on the basis of attributes does not yield better taxonomies compared to the FCA-based approach relying on syntactic or pseudo-syntactic dependencies as described in Section 6.2.
- A qualitative discussion of the lattice produced by FCA on the basis of the attributes as information has furthermore shown that meaningful groups indeed emerge when constructing a hierarchy on the basis of the inclusion relations between these automatically extracted attributes.

In the context of ontology learning, however, we are not only interested in acquiring attributes, but also in learning general relations between concepts.

Whereas quite a lot of work in ontology learning has tackled the problem of learning relations based on verb structures found in the corpus, not as much research has addressed the question of determining the most appropriate domain and range for the extracted relations. We address this issue in the following section.

7.3 Learning Relations from Corpora

In this section, we tackle the task of learning relations from corpora based on verbal expressions. The approach thus follows the tradition of the works of Gamallo [Gamallo et al., 2002], Buitelaar et al. [Buitelaar et al., 2004], Schutz and Buitelaar [Schutz and Buitelaar, 2005] or Ciaramita et al. [Ciaramita et al., 2005], but focuses on the appropriate generalization of the arguments of a relation with respect to a given taxonomy. For example, given the relation *work_for*, while *work_for(man,department)*, *work_for(employee,institute)*, *work_for(woman,store)* are certainly valid signatures, from an ontology engineering point of view we are interested in finding the most general signature describing all the instances of the relations, possibly *work_for(person,organization)* in this case. We analyze different statistical measures with respect to their generalization behavior. In particular, we examine the conditional probability, the pointwise mutual information (PMI) as well as a measure based on the χ^2-test. We apply our approach to the Genia corpus using the Genia ontology [Ohta et al., 2002] to generalize the verb slots. The different measures are evaluated with respect to a gold standard provided by a biologist. The structure of this section is as follows: in Section 7.3.1, we introduce our approach to extracting binary relations based on verbs using shallow linguistic processing as well as to generalizing the domain and range with respect to a given concept hierarchy. We present the evaluation of the approach in Section 7.3.4, concluding with a summary in Section 7.3.5.

7.3.1 Approach

In our approach, verb frames are extracted using Steven Abney's chunker CASS [Abney, 1996] (compare Section 4.1.2). From CASS's output, we extract tuples NP-V-NP and NP-V-P-NP. We construct binary relations from these tuples, using the lemmatized verb V (with the preposition P if applicable) as corresponding relation label and the head of the NP phrases as concepts for the domain and range of the relation. In particular, we only consider nouns as concepts which also appear in the Genia ontology. Our aim is then to find the most general and appropriate concept for the domain and range of the relation on the basis of the different examples found in the corpus. For illustration purposes, let us consider the input sentences marked with (a) and the CASS output in (b), and the binary relations we extract relying on the corpus annotation in (c):

Example 1. a. This bipartite motif consists of an N-terminal POU-specific domain.
b. consist(subj:bipartite motif, of: N-terminal POU-specific domain)
c. consist_of(substructure_of_protein,domain_or_region_of_DNA)

Example 2. a. The virus leads to severe acute disease in macaques.
b. lead(subj:virus, to:disease, in: macaque)
c. lead_to(virus,other), lead_in(virus,organism)

Example 3. a. Lipoarabinomannan releases IL-6 in a dose-response manner.
b. release(subj:Lipoarabinomannan, obj:IL-6, in:dose-response manner)
c. release(substance,substance)

While the NP-V-NP pattern can generally be mapped to Subj-V-Obj structures without producing too many errors, the NP-V-P-NP pattern generates substantial noise due to PP-attachment ambiguities. Particularly, CASS does not differentiate between PPs functioning as oblique arguments of the verb (as in (1) and (2)) and facultative adjuncts (as in (3)). However, we decided to keep this pattern and assume that every PP attaches to the preceding verb. For each of these patterns, we then create binary relations labeled with the verb V (and the preposition P if applicable), relying on the semantic annotations of the Genia corpus to map the arguments to corresponding concepts for the domain and range of the relation. The result of this process are the binary relations 1-3 (c). Note that the relation lead_in is a consequence of the spurious attachment of *in macaques* to *leads*. Further, for example (3) no second binary relation has been extracted as *dose-response manner* does not map to any concept in the Genia ontology.

7.3.2 Generalizing Verb Frames

Having thus collected a number of labeled relations from the corpus, our aim is to find the most appropriate generalization for the concepts within the domain and the range of each relation on the basis of the different examples found in the corpus. For this purpose, we experiment with three different measures:

- the conditional probability of a concept given a verb slot,
- the pointwise mutual information between a concept and a verb slot,
- a χ^2-based measure.

We briefly describe the three measures in the following section and illustrate them on the basis of an example.

7.3.3 Measures

As an illustrating example, let us consider the object position of the verb *activate*. Let us further assume that the objects appearing in the corpus for *activate* together with their frequencies are the following:

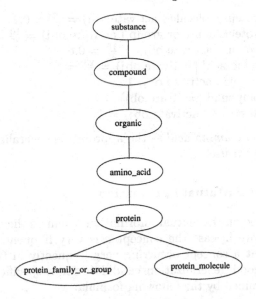

Fig. 7.6. Part of the Genia ontology

protein_molecule: 5
protein_family_or_group: 10
amino_acid: 10

The above example reflects the empirically observed frequencies of concepts in the respective argument position before the propagation of frequencies along the taxonomy. In order to find the appropriate concept for a certain slot with respect to the hierarchy, we examine three measures which are described in the following and illustrated according to this example.

7.3.3.1 Conditional Probability

The first method examined calculates for a certain slot s of a verb v the conditional probability that a concept c appears in this slot, propagating the frequencies along the concept hierarchy (see Figure 7.6), and then chooses the concept maximizing this value:

$$c_{v_s} := argmax_c \ P(c|v_s)$$

If there are several concepts with the same value, we choose the most specific ones, leaving out the concepts which subsume them. For our example we would get:

$P(\text{protein\_molecule} \mid \text{activate\_obj}) = \frac{5}{25} = 0.2$

$P(\text{protein\_family\_or\_group} \mid \text{activate\_obj}) = \frac{10}{25} = 0.4$

$P(\text{protein} \mid \text{activate\_obj}) = \frac{15}{25} = 0.6$

$P(\text{amino\_acid} \mid \text{activate\_obj}) = \frac{25}{25} = 1$

$P(\text{organic} \mid \text{activate\_obj})$ 1

$P(\text{compound} \mid \text{activate\_obj}) = 1$

$P(\text{substance} \mid \text{activate\_obj}) = 1$

So we would choose *amino_acid* as the appropriate generalization for the object position of *activate*.

7.3.3.2 Pointwise Mutual Information

The method based on the mutual information penalizes the conditional probability value above in case the concept c is very frequent. The underlying hypothesis is that a concept occurring very frequently in the context of all verbs is not a good generalization candidate for a specific verb. The best concept is determined by the following formula:

$$c_{v_s} = argmax_c \; PMI(c, v_s)$$
$$= argmax_c \; log_2 \frac{P(c|v_s)}{P(c)}$$

Now assuming a probability $P(amino\_acid) = \frac{825}{3050} = 0.27$ for *amino_acid* occurring as the object of *activate* and $P(protein) = \frac{415}{3050} = 0.14$ for *protein* (compare Tables 7.6 and 7.7), we would get:

$PMI(\text{protein}|\text{activate\_obj}) = log_2 \frac{0.6}{0.14} = 2.1$

$PMI(\text{amino\_acid}|\text{activate\_obj}) = log_2 \frac{1}{0.27} = 1.89$

According to the PMI-measure, we would thus choose *protein* as the most appropriate generalization.

7.3.3.3 A χ^2-based measure

The measure based on the χ^2-test substantially differs from the other measures in the sense that it does not compare conditional probabilities but contingencies between two variables. The procedure performs a test whether the two variables are statistically independent or not. The null hypothesis H_0 thus is that both variables are unrelated and the aim is to reject this hypothesis in favor of the hypothesis that they are actually statistically dependent. In order to apply the χ^2 test we assume that the deviations between observed and expected values are normally distributed as well as that both variables have the same underlying distribution (compare Section 4.1.6). The most critical assumption is certainly the one that the samples are randomly generated as we are dealing with textual data which is never generated by a

Table 7.6. 2-by-2 χ^2 table for protein as range of activate

	range(activate)	range($\neg$ activate)
protein	15	400
$\neg$ protein	35	2600

Table 7.7. 2-by-2 χ^2 table for amino_acid as range of activate

	range(activate)	range($\neg$ activate)
amino_acid	25	800
$\neg$ amino_acid	25	2200

purely random process. However, this assumption is typically made in corpus linguistics such that χ^2 and other hypothesis tests are applicable (compare [Manning and Schütze, 1999]).

We apply χ^2 as proposed by Clark and Weir [Clark and Weir, 2002], testing the contingencies between v_s and the concept c as well as its possible generalizations $c'_1, ... c'_n$ in an iterative manner. The assumption is that we can generalize c to c'_i if the χ^2-test reveals v_s and c'_i to be statistically dependent. A result is considered significant with regard to a significance level $\alpha = 0.05$ if the χ^2 value within our 2×2 χ^2-matrix exceeds the typically assumed critical value of 3.84. The generalization stops when encountering the first significant result. In contrast to the other approaches, when applying the χ^2-based generalization we do not yield any ties as we stop when encountering a first appropriate generalization.

The formula used for the χ^2 test is:

$$\chi^2 = \sum_{i,j} \frac{(O_{ij} - E_{ij})^2}{E_{ij}}$$

where O_{ij} are the so called *observed frequencies* as calculated on the basis of the corpus and given in row i and column j in Tables 7.6 and 7.7 and E_{ij} are the expected frequencies calculated under the assumption of independence between v_s and c'_i.

For the 2×2 case we have (compare [Manning and Schütze, 1999]):

$$\chi^2 = \frac{N(O_{11}O_{22} - O_{12}O_{21})^2}{(O_{11} + O_{12})(O_{11} + O_{21})(O_{12} + O_{22})(O_{21} + O_{22})}$$

where N is the sum of all the frequencies in the table. For the examples in Table 7.6 and 7.7 we thus yield:

$$\chi^2(range(activate), protein) = \frac{3050(15 * 2600 - 400 * 35)^2}{415 \times 50 \times 3000 \times 2635} = 11.62$$

$$\chi^2(range(activate), amino\_acid) = \frac{3050(25 * 2200 - 800 * 25)^2}{825 \times 50 \times 3000 \times 2225} = 13.57$$

In both cases we get a significant result at a level of $\alpha = 0.05$. As appropriate generalization we would choose *protein* as it is the first concept yielding a significant result.

The variations in the predicted concept for the range of *activate* show that the measure chosen can indeed have a decisive impact on the results.

7.3.4 Evaluation

In order to evaluate the different measures we propose, we applied our preprocessing to the Genia corpus [Ohta et al., 2002]. Overall, the corpus contains 18.546 sentences with 509.487 words and 51.170 verbs. We use the semantic annotations of the Genia corpus to map the subject and object of verb phrases to the Genia ontology. The domain and range of the extracted relations are then generalized with respect to the Genia ontology using the measures described above. For the evaluation of the different measures, a biologist specified the ideal domain and range for 100 binary relations corresponding to the 100 most frequent patterns extracted with the approach based on CASS as described above. The average frequency of occurrence for the verbs of these 100 patterns is around 17.51, with a minimum of 3 and a maximum of 148 occurrences. Out of these 100 relations, 15 were regarded as inappropriate by our evaluator, such that the evaluation was carried out on the remaining 85 relations.

The biologist specified a number of concepts from the Genia ontology as the best generalization for the domain and range of each relation denoted by the verb. In some cases, she was also able to specify one single 'best concept' out of several possible candidates. In general, however, she specified a set of concepts generalizing each argument position. The output of our approach is compared with this gold standard using the different measures described above in terms of:

- direct matches for domain and range (DM),
- average distance in terms of number of edges in the taxonomy between correct and predicted concept (AD), and
- a symmetric variant of the Learning Accuracy (LA) defined by Hahn and Schnattinger [Hahn and Schnattinger, 1998b].

The different measures are formalized in the following:

$$\overline{DM} = \frac{direct\ matches\ for\ domain + direct\ matches\ for\ range}{2\,|R|}$$

$$\overline{AD} = \frac{\sum_{r\in R} \delta(dom_S(r), dom_G(r)) + \delta(range_S(r), range_G(r))}{2\,|R|}$$

$$\overline{LA} = \frac{\sum_{r\in R} LA(dom_S(r), dom_G(r)) + LA(range_S(r), range_G(r))}{2\,|R|}$$

Here, R denotes the set of relations in the output of our system. Further, for $r \in R$ we define $dom_S(r)$ as the domain produced by our system and $dom_G(r)$ as the domain as specified in the gold standard; $range_S(r)$ and $range_G(r)$ are defined analogously. Please note that these functions return sets. The system returns more than one concept in case there is a tie, and our annotator used more than one concept in most cases, indicating the most appropriate wherever possible. We will refer to this most appropriate concept for a relation r as $dom_G^*(r)$ or $range_G^*(r)$, depending if we are considering the domain or range od the relation.

The reason for measuring the average distance as well as the learning accuracy is that, in general, the system can not be expected to predict exactly the same concept as specified by the human evaluator. Therefore, we need a measure to evaluate how good the prediction actually is, given that it is not the same as specified in the gold standard. The interpretation of the average distance is clear, i.e. the lower the average distance, the better are the predictions of our system. The learning accuracy LA is inspired by the corresponding measure introduced by Hahn and Schnattinger [Hahn and Schnattinger, 1998b]. However, we consider a slightly different formulation of the learning accuracy as defined by Mädche and Staab [Mädche and Staab, 2000]. The measure of Hahn et al. and our learning accuracy measure are not totally equivalent. The main difference is that we measure the distance between nodes in terms of edges – instead of nodes as in Hahn's version – and we do not need any case distinction considering whether the classification was correct or not. Additionally, in contrast to Hahn's learning accuracy, our measure is symmetric. The learning accuracy between two concepts is defined as:

$$LA(a,b) := \frac{\delta(top,c) + 1}{\delta(top,c) + \delta(a,c) + \delta(b,c) + 1}$$

where $c = lcs(a,b)$, i.e. c is the least common subsumer of a and b in the taxonomy, and δ measures the distance between two nodes as the number of edges between them. In particular, the distance is defined as following:

$$\delta(a,b) := \delta(a, lcs(a,b)) + \delta(b, lcs(a,b))$$

where δ measures the distance in terms of edges and obviously $\delta(a,a) = 0$.

Due to the fact that our system as well as the annotator specified a set of possible concepts as domain and range of the relations, we decided to consider three evaluation modes: i) *optimistic*, ii) *average*, and iii) *pessimistic*.

The *optimistic* version compares that concept our system predicts for a certain position of a relation with the concept in the gold standard yielding the best result with respect to the given evaluation measure. The *pessimistic* version chooses the concepts in the output of the system and the gold standard yielding the worst results, whereas the *average* averages the results of the evaluation measures for all combinations of concepts in the system's output and the gold standard. In all cases, we will compare to $dom_G^*(r)$ or $range_G^*(r)$ if they have been specified. Otherwise we will compare the output of the system to the whole set of concepts specified by our annotator. In case of the DM measure, we count as a direct match all those cases in which one concept in the output of the system is the same as one of the concepts specified by the annotator. Table 7.8 summarizes our results. It shows, for each measure, the percentage of direct matches, as well as the optimistic, average and pessimistic variants of the average distance and learning accuracy. The main conclusion is that the conditional probability consistently outperforms all other measures with respect to all evaluation modes.

Table 7.8. Results for the different measures

	DM	AD			LA		
		opt.	avg.	pess.	opt.	avg.	pess.
Conditional	33.53%	1.21	1.76	22.22	70.40%	60.57%	53.24%
PMI	13.53%	3.28	3.76	4.19	48.65%	43.06%	38.62%
χ^2	26.79%	2.63	3.44	4.15	56.71%	46.19%	38.48%

7.3.5 Summary

Our results have shown that the conditional probability is a reasonable measure to find the correct level of generalization with respect to a given concept hierarchy for verb-based relations extracted from a corpus. The conditional probability, on the one hand, outperforms the other methods in terms of direct matches, average distance and learning accuracy. The χ^2-based measure, on the other hand, outperforms the point-wise mutual similarity measure. An important observation is that in many cases our human evaluator has chosen abstract concepts, which are in general disfavored by the PMI-measure. This explains why the PMI measure performs so badly. The contribution of this section is a systematic analysis of different probabilistic and statistical measures for the purpose of finding the appropriate generalization level for ontological relations extracted from a corpus with respect to a given taxonomy. Our conclusion is that the conditional probability performs better than other measures such as PMI or a χ^2-test. We have so far conducted experiments on the Genia corpus and ontology. In general, we have also observed that it seems quite difficult to find the appropriate generalization due to the fact that the Genia ontology is very small and lacks a reasonable hierarchical structure. Therefore, it remains an open question if our results would transfer to ontologies with a richer structure. The main drawback of our approach is that it is currently restricted to binary relations. Furthermore, the domain and range of a relation can actually not be regarded as independent from each other. However, according to our current observations, an approach to generalizing domain and range dependently could be seriously affected by data sparseness in the Genia corpus. Concerning the approximation of the conditional probabilities, some more elaborate linguistic analysis or even smoothing techniques should be explored. Finally, other structures than verb frames could be considered for deriving relations.

7.4 Learning Qualia Structures from the Web

In this section, we deal with the automatic acquisition of so called *qualia structures* from the Web. Qualia structures are relevant for ontology learning as they describe a fixed set of relations which every object possesses. As we will see below, qualia structures describe the formal properties of an object, its components or parts, its purpose as well as the act of creation by which it came into existence. Once we have identified the qualia structure for a given object, we have in fact also identified important ontological properties of this object. Some of the qualia relations have been extensively studied in the artificial intelligence community, especially the *part-whole* and *subclass-of* relations (compare [Artale et al., 1996, Guarino and Welty, 2000]).

Qualia structures have been originally introduced by Pustejovsky [Pustejovsky, 1991] and are used for a variety of purposes in natural language processing such as the analysis of compounds [Johnston and Busa, 1996], co-composition and coercion [Pustejovsky, 1991] as well as for bridging reference resolution [Bos et al., 1995]. Further, it has also been argued that qualia structures and lexical semantic relations in general have applications in information retrieval [Pustejovsky et al., 1993, Voorhees, 1994]. One major bottleneck however is that, currently, qualia structures need to be created by hand, which is probably also the reason why there are no practical systems using qualia structures, but a lot of systems using publicly available resources such as WordNet [Fellbaum, 1998] or FrameNet[2] as source of lexical/world knowledge. The work described in this section addresses this issue and presents an approach to automatically learning qualia structures for nominals from the Web. The approach is inspired in recent work on using the Web to identify instances of a relation of interest such as in [Markert et al., 2003] and [Cimiano and Staab, 2004]. These approaches are in essence a combination of the usage of lexico-syntactic patterns conveying a certain relation of interest [Hearst, 1992, Charniak and Berland, 1999,

---

[2] http://framenet.icsi.berkeley.edu/

Iwanska et al., 2000, Poesio et al., 2002] with the idea of using the web as a big corpus [Grefenstette, 1999, Keller et al., 2002, Resnik and Smith, 2003]. The idea of learning qualia structures from the Web is not only a very practical, but in fact a principled one. While single lexicographers creating qualia structures - or lexicon entries in general - might take very subjective decisions, the structures learned from the Web do not mirror the view of a single person, but of the whole world as represented on the World Wide Web. Obviously, on the other hand, using an automatic web based approach also yields a lot of inappropriate results which are due to 1) errors produced by the linguistic analysis (e.g. part-of-speech tagging), 2) idiosyncrasies of ranking algorithms of search machines, 3) the fact that the Web and especially search engines are to a great extent commercially biased, 4) the fact that people also publish erroneous information on the Web, and 5) lexical ambiguities. Because of these reasons, our aim is in fact not to replace lexicographers, but to support them in the task of creating valid qualia structures on the basis of those learned automatically.

This section is structured as follows: Section 7.4.1 introduces qualia structures and describes the specific qualia structures we aim to acquire. Section 7.4.2 describes our approach in detail, and Section 7.4.3 presents a quantitative and qualitative evaluation of the approach.

7.4.1 Qualia Structures

According to Aristotle, there are four basic factors or causes by which the nature of an object can be described (cf. [Kronlid, 2003]):

- the *material cause*, i.e. the material an object is made of,
- the *agentive cause*, i.e. the source of movement, creation or change,
- the *formal cause*, i.e. its form or type, and
- the *final cause*, i.e. its purpose, intention or aim.

In his Generative Lexicon (GL) framework, Pustejovsky [Pustejovsky, 1991] reused Aristotle's basic factors for the description of the meaning of lexical elements. He introduced so called *qualia structures* by which the meaning of a lexical element is described in terms of four roles:

- *constitutive*: describing *physical properties* of an object, i.e. its weight, material as well as parts and components,
- *agentive*: describing factors involved in the *bringing about* of an object, i.e. its creator or the causal chain leading to its creation,
- *formal*: describing that *properties which distinguish an object* in a larger domain, i.e. orientation, magnitude, shape and dimensionality, and
- *telic*: describing the *purpose or function* of an object.

Most of the qualia structures described by Pustejovsky [Pustejovsky, 1991], however, seem to have a more restricted interpretation. In fact, in most examples the *constitutive* role seems to describe the parts or components of an object, while the *agentive* role is typically described by a verb denoting an action which typically brings the object in question into existence. The *formal* role normally consists in typing information about the object, i.e. its hypernym or superconcept. Finally, the *telic* role describes the purpose or function of an object either by a verb or nominal phrase. The qualia structure for *'knife'*, for example, could look as follows (cf. [Johnston and Busa, 1996]):

```
Formal:        artifact_tool
Constitutive:  blade,handle,...
Telic:         cut_act
Agentive:      make_act
```

Our understanding of *qualia structure* is in line with this restricted interpretation of the qualia roles. Our aim is to automatically acquire qualia structures from the Web for an arbitrary nominal, looking for (i) nominals describing the type of the object, (ii) verbs defining its agentive role, (iii) nominals describing its parts or components and (iv) nouns or verbs describing its intended purpose. The approach is described in detail in what follows.

7.4.2 Approach

Our approach to learning qualia structures from the Web is based on the assumption that certain semantic relations can be learned by matching certain lexico-syntactic patterns more or less reliably conveying the relation of interest in line with the seminal work of Hearst [Hearst, 1992] (compare Section 6.1.2). However, it is well known that Hearst-style patterns occur rarely, such that it seems intuitive to match them on the Web. In our case, we are not only looking for the hypernym relation (comparable to the *formal*-relation) but for similar patterns conveying a *constitutive, telic* or *agentive* relation. As currently there is no support for searching using regular expressions in standard search engines such as Google or Altavista[3], our approach consists of 5 phases (compare Figure 7.7):

1. Generate for each qualia role a set of so called *clues*, i.e. search engine queries indicating the relation of interest.
2. Download the snippets of the 10 first Google hits matching the generated clues[4].
3. Part-of-speech-tag the downloaded snippets.
4. Match regular expressions conveying the qualia role of interest.

---

[3] An exception is certainly the Linguist's Search Engine [Resnik and Elkiss, 2003]. At the time of writing, Google has even enhanced search functionality by wildcards.

[4] The reason for using only the 10 first hits is to maintain efficiency. With the current settings, the system needs between 3 and 10 minutes to generate the qualia structure for a given term

5. Weight the returned qualia elements according to some measure.

The outcome of this process are then so called *weighted qualia structures* (WQSs) in which every qualia element in a certain role is weighted according to some measure. The patterns in our pattern library are actually tuples (p, c) where p is a regular expression defined over part-of-speech tags and c a function $c : string \rightarrow string$ called the *clue*. Given a term t and a clue c, the query $c(t)$ is sent to the Google API, and we download the abstracts of the first n documents matching this query and then process the abstracts to find instances of the pattern p. For example, given the clue $f(x) = "such\ as\ " \oplus \pi(x)$ and the concept *computer*, we would download n abstracts matching the query f(computer), i.e. "such as computers". Hereby $\pi(x)$ is a function returning the plural form of x. We implemented this function as a lookup in a lexicon in which plural nouns are mapped to their base form. With the use of such clues, we download a number of Google-abstracts in which a corresponding pattern will probably be matched, thus restricting the linguistic analysis to a few promising pages. The downloaded abstracts are then part-of-speech tagged using QTag [Tufis and Mason, 1998]. Then, we match the corresponding pattern p in the downloaded snippets, yielding candidate qualia elements as output. In our approach we then calculate the weight of a candidate qualia element e for the term t we want to compute the qualia structure for by the *Jaccard coefficient*:

$$\frac{GoogleHits(e \oplus t)}{GoogleHits(e) \oplus GoogleHits(t) - GoogleHits(e \oplus t)} \tag{7.2}$$

Though other more elaborate statistical measures such as PMI as well as a t-test or χ^2-test could have been applied, we have opted here for a measure which is easy to implement and efficient to compute to reduce the number of queries to the Google API. The result is then a *weighted qualia structure* (WQS) in which for each role the qualia elements are weighted according to this Jaccard coefficient. In what follows, we describe in detail the procedure for acquiring qualia elements for each qualia role and especially the clues and lexico-syntactic patterns used. The patterns have been crafted by hand, testing and refining them in an iterative process, paying attention to maximize their coverage but also accuracy (compare [Hearst, 1992]). It is important to mention that by this approach we are not able to detect and separate multiple meanings of words, that means, to handle polysemy, which is appropriately accounted for in the framework of the Generative Lexicon [Pustejovsky, 1991].

7.4.2.1 The Formal Role

To derive qualia elements for the *formal* role, we first download for each of the clues in Table 7.9 the first 10 abstracts matching the clue and then process them offline matching the patterns defined over part-of-speech-tags, thus yielding up to 10 different qualia element candidates per clue. The patterns

Word ➡

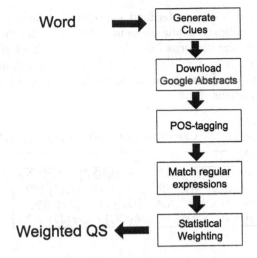

Weighted QS ⬅

Fig. 7.7. General approach for learning qualia structures

are specified in the form of regular expressions, whereby the part-of-speech tags are always given in curly brackets after the token. Besides using the traditional regular expression operators such as +, * and ?, we also use Perl-like symbols such as $\backslash w$ denoting any alphabetic character as well as [a-z] denoting the set of all lower case letters. We use the part-of-speech tags of the Penn Treebank tagset given in Appendix A.4.

As there are 4 different clues for the *formal* role, we thus yield up to 40 qualia elements as potential candidates to fill the *formal* role. In general, we have paid attention to create clues relying on indefinite articles as we found out that they produce more general and reliable results than when using definite articles. In order to choose the correct indefinite article – *a* or *an* – or even using no article at all, we implemented some ad-hoc heuristics checking if the first letter of the term in question is a vowel and checking if the term is used more often with an article or without an article on the Web by a set of corresponding Google queries. The alternative '(a/an/?)' means that we use either the indefinite articles 'a' or 'an' or no article at all depending on the results of the above mentioned Google queries.

A general question already raised by Hearst [Hearst, 1992] is how to deal with nominal modification. Hearst's conclusion is that this depends on the application. In our case, we mainly remove adjective modifiers, keeping only the heads of noun phrases as candidate qualia elements. The lemmatized heads of the NP_F noun phrase are considered as qualia role candidates for the *formal* role. These candidates are then weighted using the above defined *Jaccard coefficient* measure. Hereby, a noun phrase is an instance matching the following regular expression:

$$NP := [a\text{-}z] + \{DT\}? \ ([a\text{-}z] + \{JJ\})^* \ (\underline{[a\text{-}z] + \{NN(S?)\}}) +,$$

where the head is the underlined expression, which is lemmatized and considered as a candidate qualia element. After some initial experiments, we decided not to use the patterns 'X is Y' and 'X is a kind of Y' such as in *'a book is an item'* or *'a book is a kind of publication'* as well as the pattern *'Y, including X'* (compare [Hearst, 1992]) as we found that, in our settings, they delivered quite spurious results.

Table 7.9. Clues and patterns for the *formal* role

Clue	Pattern
such as $\pi(t)$	NP_F ,? such{DT} as{IN} NP
especially $\pi(t)$	NP_F ,? especially{RB]} NP
$\pi(t)$ or other	NP or{CC} other{JJ} NP_F
$\pi(t)$ and other	NP and{CC} other{JJ} NP_F

7.4.2.2 The Constitutive Role

The procedure for finding elements of the *constitutive* role is similar to the one described above for the *formal* role. The corresponding clues and patterns are given in Table 7.10. As for the *formal* role, the candidate qualia elements are the lemmatized heads of the noun phrase NP_C.

Table 7.10. Clues and patterns for the *constitutive* role

Clue	Pattern
(a/an)? t is made up of	NP is{VBZ} made{VBN} up{RP} of{IN} NP_C
$\pi(t)$ are made up of	NP are{VBP} made{VBN} up{RP} of{IN} NP_C
(a/an)? t is made of	NP are{VBP} made{VBN} of{IN} NP_C
$\pi(t)$ are made of	NP are{VBP} made{VBN} of{IN} NP_C
(a/an)? t comprises	NP comprises{VBZ} NP_C
$\pi(t)$ comprise	NP comprise{VBP} NP_C
(a/an)? t consists of	NP consists{VBZ} of{IN} NP_C
$\pi(t)$ consist of	NP consist{VBP} of{IN} NP_C

As an additional heuristic, we test if the lemmatized head of NP_C is an element of the following list containing nouns denoting an indication of amount: *'variety'*, *'bundle'*, *'majority'*, *'thousands'*, *'million'*, *'millions'*, *'hundreds'*, *'number'*, *'numbers'*, *'set'*, *'sets'*, *'series'*, *'range'* and, furthermore, this NP_C is followed by the preposition *'of'*. In that case we would take the head of the noun phrase after the preposition *'of'* as potential candidate of the *constitutive* role. For example, when considering *'a conversation is made up of a series of observable interpersonal exchanges'*, we would take *'exchange'* as a potential qualia element candidate instead of *'series'*.

7.4.2.3 The Telic Role

The *telic* role is in principle acquired in the same way as the *formal* and *constitutive* roles with the exception that the qualia element is not only the head of a noun phrase, but also a verb followed by a noun phrase. Table 7.11 gives the corresponding clues and patterns. The returned candidate qualia elements are the lemmatized underlined expressions in PURP:=\w+{VB} NP | NP | be{VB} \w+{VBD}).

Table 7.11. Clues and patterns for the *telic* role

Clue	Pattern
purpose of a t is	purpose{NN} of{IN} NP_0 is{[VBZ]} (to{TO})? PURP
purpose of $\pi(t)$ is	purpose{NN} of{IN} NP_0 is{VBZ} (to{TO})? PURP
(a/an)? t is used to	(A|a|An|an) NP_0 is{VBZ} used{VBN} to{TO} PURP
$\pi(t)$ are used to	NP_0 are{VBZ} used{VBN} to{TO} PURP

7.4.2.4 The Agentive Role

As discussed by Hearst [Hearst, 1992], it is not always as straightforward to find lexico-syntactic patterns reliably conveying a certain relation. In fact, we did not find any patterns reliably identifying qualia elements for the *agentive* role. Certainly, it would have been possible to find the source of the creation by using patterns such as X *is made by* Y or X *is produced by* Y. However, we found that these patterns do not reliably convey a verb describing how an object is brought into existence. The fact that it is far from straightforward to find patterns indicating an *agentive* role is further corroborated by the research described by Yamada and Baldwin [Yamada and Baldwin, 2004], in which only one pattern indicating an agentive relation is used, namely 'NN BE V[+en]' in order to match passive constructions such as *'the book was written'*. On the other hand, it is clear that constructing a reliable clue for this pattern is not straightforward given the current state-of-the-art concerning search engine queries. Nevertheless, in order to also get results for the *agentive* role, we apply a different method here. Instead of issuing a query which is used to search for possible candidates for the role, we take advantage of the fact that the verbs which describe how something comes into being, particularly artificial things, are often quite general phrases like *'make'*, *'produce'*, *'write'*, *'build'*, etc. So instead of generating clues as above, we calculate the value

$$\frac{GoogleHits(agentive\_verb \oplus ``a" \oplus t)}{GoogleHits(t)} \tag{7.3}$$

for the term t we want to acquire a qualia structure for as well as the following agentive verbs: *build, produce, make, write, plant, elect, create, cook, construct* and *design*. If this value is above an experimentally determined threshold of 0.0005, we assume that it is a valid filler of the *agentive* qualia role. For example, if we wanted to know how good the agentive verb *'write'* is for a *'book'*, we would issue the queries "write a book" as well as "book" and calculate the ratio $\frac{GoogleHits(\text{``write a book''})}{GoogleHits(\text{``book''})}$.

7.4.3 Evaluation

We evaluate our approach for the lexical elements *'knife'*, *'beer'* and *'book'*, which are also discussed by Johnston and Busa [Johnston and Busa, 1996] or [Pustejovsky, 1991], as well as *'computer'*, an abstract noun, i.e. *'conversation'*, as well as two very specific multi-term words, i.e. *'natural language processing'* and *'data mining'*. We give the automatically learned weighted qualia structures for these entries in Figures 7.8, 7.9, 7.10 and 7.11. The evaluation of our approach consists, on the one hand, of a discussion of the weighted qualia structures, in particular comparing them to the ideal structures from the literature. On the other hand, we also asked a student at our institute to assign credits to each of the qualia elements from 0 (incorrect) to 3 (totally correct), whereby 1 credit means 'not totally wrong' and 2 means 'still acceptable'.

7.4.3.1 Quantitative Evaluation

The distribution of credits for each qualia role and term is given in Table 7.12. It can be observed that, with the three exceptions: *beer→formal*, *beer→constitutive* as well as *book→agentive*, '3' is the mark assigned in most cases to the automatically learned qualia elements. For almost every term and qualia role, at least 50% of the automatically learned qualia elements have a mark of '2' or '3' – the only exceptions being *beer→formal* with 45.45%, *book→agentive* with 33.33% and *beer→constitutive* with 28.57%. In general, this shows that the automatically learned qualia roles are indeed reasonable. Considering the average over all the terms ('All' in the table), we observe that the qualia role which is recognized most reliably is the *telic* one with 73.15% assignments of credit '3' and 75.93% of credits '2' or '3', followed by the *agentive* role with 71.43% assignments of credit '3'. The results for the *formal* and *constitutive* role are still reasonable with 62.09% assignments of credit '3' and 65.36% assignments of credits '2' or '3' for the *formal role*; and respectively 63.64% and 64.65% for the *constitutive* role. The worst results are achieved for the *formal* role due to the fact that 28.10% of the qualia elements are regarded as totally wrong. The results for the *constitutive* role are not much better though. Table 7.13 supports the above claims and shows the average credits assigned by the human evaluator per term and role. It shows again that the roles with the best results are the *agentive* and *telic* roles, whereas the *formal* and *constitutive* roles are not identified as accurately. This is certainly due to the fact that the patterns for the *telic* role are much less ambiguous than the ones for the *formal* and *constitutive* roles.

Table 7.12. Distribution of credits for each qualia role and term

	Formal			
	0	1	2	3
Book	2/17 (11.76%)	4/17 (23.52%)	1/17 (5.88%)	10/17 (58.82%)
Computer	8/28 (28.57%)	1/28 (3.57%)	2/28 (7.14%)	17/28 (60.71%)
Knife	3/16 (18.75%)	0/16 (0%)	0/16 (0%)	13/16 (81.25%)
Beer	12/22 (54.54%)	0/22 (0%)	2/22 (9.09%)	8/22 (36.36%)
Data Mining	6/25 (24%)	0/25 (0%)	0/25 (0%)	19/25 (76%)
NLP	2/15 (13.33%)	1/15 (6.66%)	0/15 (0%)	12/15 (80%)
Conversation	10/30 (33.33%)	4/30 (13.33%)	0/30 (0%)	16/30 (53.33%)
All	43/153 (28.10%)	10/153 (6.54%)	5/153 (3.27%)	95/153 (62.09%)
	Agentive			
Book	0/3 (0%)	2/3 (66.66%)	0/3 (0%)	1/3 (33.33%)
Computer	0/1 (0%)	0/1 (0%)	0/1 (0%)	1/1 (100%)
Knife	0/3 (0%)	0/3 (0%)	0/3 (0%)	3/3 (100%)
Beer	0/3 (0%)	1/3 (33.33%)	0/3 (0%)	2/3 (66.66%)
Data Mining	0/1 (0%)	0/1 (0%)	0/1 (0%)	1/1 (100%)
NLP	0/1 (0%)	0/1 (0%)	0/1 (0%)	1/1 (100%)
Conversation	1/2 (50%)	0/2 (0%)	0/2 (0%)	1/2 (50%)
All	1/14 (7.14%)	3/14 (21.43%)	0/14 (0%)	10/14 (71.43%)
	Constitutive			
Book	8/29 (27.58%)	4/29 (13.79%)	1/29 (3.44%)	16/29 (55.17%)
Computer	6/26 (23.07%)	1/26 (3.84%)	0/26 (0%)	19/26 (73.07%)
Knife	4/15 (26.66%)	0/15 (0%)	0/15 (0%)	11/15 (73.33%)
Beer	5/7 (71.42%)	0/7 (0%)	0/7 (0%)	2/7 (28.57%)
Data Mining	0/1 (0%)	0/1 (0%)	0/1 (0%)	1/1 (100%)
NLP	n.a.	n.a.	n.a.	n.a.
Conversation	3/21 (14.28%)	4/21 (19.04%)	0/21 (0%)	14/21 (66.66%)
All	26/99 (26.26%)	9/99 (9%)	1/99 (1.01%)	63/99 (63.64%)
	Telic			
Book	3/22 (13.63%)	2/22 (9.09%)	3/22 (13.63%)	14/22 (63.63%)
Computer	0/27 (0%)	3/27 (11.11%)	0/27 (0%)	24/27 (88.88%)
Knife	5/18 (27.77%)	0/18 (0%)	0/18 (0%)	13/18 (72.22%)
Beer	n.a.	n.a.	n.a.	n.a.
Data Mining	2/22 (9.09%)	4/22 (18.18%)	0/22 (0%)	16/22 (72.72%)
NLP	1/6 (16.66%)	0/6 (0%)	0/6 (0%)	5/6 (83.33%)
Conversation	6/13 (46.15%)	0/13 (0%)	0/13 (0%)	7/13 (53.84%)
All	17/108 (15.74%)	9/108 (8.33%)	3/108 (2.78%)	79/108 (73.15%)

7.4.3.2 Qualitative Evaluation

In this section, we provide a more subjective evaluation of the automatically learned qualia structures by comparing them to ideal qualia structures discussed in the literature wherever possible. We discuss more in detail the qualia structure for *'book'*, *'knife'* and *'beer'* and leave the detailed assessment of the qualia structures for *'computer'*, *'natural language processing'*, *'data mining'*

Table 7.13. Average credits for each qualia role

	Formal	Agentive	Constitutive	Telic
Book	2.12	1.67	1.86	2.27
Computer	2	3	2.23	2.78
Knife	2.44	3	2.2	2.17
Beer	1.27	2.33	0.96	n.a.
Data Mining	2.28	3	3	2.36
Natural Language Processing	2.47	3	n.a.	2.5
Conversation	1.73	1.5	2.19	1.62
All	1.99	2.36	2.02	2.33

and 'conversation' to the interested reader.

For 'book' (compare Figure 7.9), the first four candidates of the *formal* role, i.e. 'product', 'item', 'publication' and 'document' are very appropriate, but allude to the *physical object* meaning of book as opposed to the meaning in the sense of *information container* (compare [Pustejovsky, 1991]. As candidates for the *agentive* role we have 'make', 'write' and 'create', which are appropriate, 'write' even being the ideal filler of the *agentive* role according to Pustejovsky [Pustejovsky, 1991]. For the *constitutive* role of 'book' we get – besides 'it' at the first position, which could be easily filtered out – 'sign' (2nd position), 'letter' (3rd position) and 'page' (6th position), which are quite appropriate. The top four candidates for the *telic* role are 'give', 'select', 'read', and 'purchase'. It seems that 'give' is emphasizing the role of a book as a gift, 'read' is referring to the most obvious purpose of a book as specified in the ideal qualia structures of Pustejovsky [Pustejovsky, 1991] as well as Johnston and Busa [Johnston and Busa, 1996], and 'purchase' denotes the more general purpose of a book, that is, to be bought.

Unfortunately, the first element of the *formal* role of 'knife' (compare Figure 7.8) denotes the material it is typically made of, i.e. 'steel', but the next 5 elements are definitely appropriate: 'weapon', 'item', 'kitchenware', 'object' and 'instrument'. The ideal element *tool* (compare [Johnston and Busa, 1996]) can be found at the 10th position. The results are interesting in that, on the one hand, the most prominent meaning of 'knife' according to the web is the one of a weapon. On the other hand, our results are more specific, classifying a knife as 'kitchenware' instead of merely as a *tool*. Very interesting are the specific and accurate results at the end of the list. The reason why they appear at the end is that the Jaccard coefficient ranks them lower because they are more specific, thus appearing less frequently. This shows that using some other measure less sensitive to frequency could yield more accurate results. The fillers of the *agentive* role 'produce', 'make' and 'create' seem all appropriate, whereby 'make' corresponds exactly to the ideal filler for the *agentive* role as mentioned by Johnston and Busa [Johnston and Busa, 1996]. Not only do the results for the *constitutive* role include parts, but also materials a knife is made of, thus containing more information than the typical qualia structures assumed in the literature. The best results are (in this order) *'blade'*, *'metal'*, *'steel'*, *'wood'* and *'handle'* at the 6th position. In fact, in the ideal qualia structure mentioned by Johnston and Busa [Johnston and Busa, 1996] *'blade'* and *'handle'* are mentioned as fillers of the *constitutive* role, while there are no elements describing the materials which a knife is made of. Finally, the top four candidates for the *telic* role are *'kill'*, *'slit'*, *'cut'* and *'slice'*, whereby *'cut'* corresponds to the ideal filler of the qualia structure for *'knife'* (compare [Johnston and Busa, 1996]).

Considering the qualia structure for *'beer'* (compare Figure 7.8), it is surprising that no purpose has been found. The reason is that currently no results are returned by Google for the clue *'a beer is used to'*, and the four snippets returned for *'the purpose of a beer'* contain expressions of the form *'the purpose of a beer is to drink it'*, which is not matched by our patterns as *'it'* is a pronoun and not matched by our NP pattern (unless it is matched by error as in the qualia structure for *'book'* in Figure 7.9). Considering the results for the *formal* role, the elements *'drink'* (1st), *'alcohol'* (2nd) and *'beverage'* (4th) are much more specific than *'liquid'* as specified by Pustejovsky [Pustejovsky, 1991], while *'thing'* at the 3rd position is certainly too general. Furthermore, according to the automatically learned qualia structure, *'beer'* is made of *'rice'*, *'malt'* and *'hop'*, which are perfectly reasonable results. Very interesting are the results *'concoction'* and *'libation'* for the *formal* role of *'beer'*, which unfortunately were rated low by our evaluator due to the fact that English is not her mother tongue and these words seemed odd to her (compare Figure 7.8).

Overall, the discussion has shown that the results produced by our method are reasonable when compared to the qualia structures from the literature. In general, our method produces in some cases additional qualia candidates, such as those describing the material a knife is typically made of. In other cases, it discovers more specific candidates, such as for example *'weapon'* or *'kitchenware'* as elements of the *formal* role for *'knife'* instead of the general term *artifact_tool*.

Knife		
	Jaccard	Eval.
Formal		
steel	3.8666	3
weapon	3.4876	3
item	1.7458	3
kitchenware	1.6840	3
object	1.6025	3
instrument	1.2963	3
utensil	1.2886	3
court	1.1441	0
equipment	0.9479	3
tool	0.7090	3
action	0.7028	0
time	0.6590	0
cutting instrument	0.0739	3
cutting instruments	0.0551	3
emergency items	0.0383	3
cutting weapons	0.0232	3
Agentive		
produce		3
make		3
create		3
Constitutive		
blade	5.4618	3
metal	5.0205	3
steel	3.8666	3
wood	2.9699	3
person	2.6829	0
handle	1.9223	3
tang	1.6784	3
gold	1.6609	0
alloy	1.2466	3
dragonfly	0.8742	3
model	0.7513	3
tool	0.7090	0
quality	0.6575	3
group	0.5764	0
rotating discs	0.0062	3
Telic		
kill	3.7626	3
slit	3.4829	3
cut	3.4373	3
slice	3.2499	3
begin	2.4192	0
split	1.7241	3
avoid	1.3190	0
score	1.0204	0
an instrument	0.8137	0
process	0.5327	3
prune	0.4505	3
incise	0.0573	3
cut things	0.0545	3
remove moisture	0.0479	3
add details	0.0361	0
cut a flap	0.0264	3
split a cake	0.0010	3
slit a wide variety	0.0004	3

Beer		
	Jaccard	Eval.
Formal		
drink	9.6677	3
alcohol	4.6006	3
thing	4.0028	3
beverage	3.6182	3
adventure	3.0825	0
mistake	2.7014	0
matter	2.6533	0
style	2.1583	0
delight	1.9198	3
people	1.4465	0
creation	1.2201	0
can	0.9433	3
list	0.8432	0
product	0.8224	3
refreshment	0.5328	3
concoction	0.4851	0
libation	0.1147	0
summery	0.0872	0
adult beverages	0.0848	2
speciality beers	0.0269	2
looney things	0.0002	0
Agentive		
produce		3
make		3
create		1
Constitutive		
rice	2.9871	0
malt	2.5724	3
hop	2.1744	3
bottom	2.1179	0
continuum	0.4808	0
puree	0.3563	0
stoneware	0.3325	0

Fig. 7.8. Weighted qualia structures for *knife* and *beer*

Book	Jaccard	Eval.
Formal		
product	34.6238	3
item	33.8573	3
publication	20.2621	3
document	14.4778	3
history	12.7262	1
project	8.9809	2
material	8.6704	3
reader	8.3890	0
resource	7.7259	3
source	7.6739	3
piece	7.6131	3
format	7.2203	0
tool	6.1124	1
object	3.7705	3
specifics	0.5374	1
library materials	0.1468	3
library property	0.0026	1
Agentive		
make		1
write		3
create		1
Constitutive		
it	21.5785	0
sign	21.0870	3
letter	18.7778	3
part	11.7830	1
individual	11.4043	0
page	10.9202	3
collection	10.7901	0
teaching	10.7004	2
language	9.6041	1
period	9.4002	0
paper	9.3551	3
table	8.7089	3
material	8.6704	3
word	8.1424	3
piece	7.6131	0
chapter	7.4746	3
presentation	7.0955	3
detail	6.8218	3
minute	5.3550	0
sheet	4.4369	3
lie	3.0866	1
ticket	2.3198	0
ink	2.2769	3
dot	1.7427	3
leather	1.1162	1
leaf	1.0266	3
title page	0.3639	3
peice	0.0530	0
dedication page	0.0076	3
Telic		
give	14.8954	1
select	12.9594	0
read	12.4937	3
purchase	9.0372	3
support	8.0204	3
identify	7.9388	1
represent	5.7829	2
inspire	1.7292	3
convey	1.3940	3
present information	0.0728	3
provide additional information	0.0368	3
convey information	0.0260	3
filch	0.0101	3
share a story	0.0081	3
commit crime	0.0061	0
contain words	0.0055	3
introduce concepts	0.0038	2
traprock	0.0015	0
stock libraries	0.0009	3
hold a collection	0.0008	3
fund special projects	0.0007	2
support teachings	0.0001	3

Computer	Jaccard	Eval.
Formal		
technology	20.3667	3
information	20.2418	0
network	14.8052	3
hardware	14.6539	3
service	13.9161	3
office	12.2881	0
equipment	7.4594	2
machine	7.0099	3
item	6.7469	3
device	5.6259	3
medium	4.0503	3
fix	3.9188	0
piece	3.5898	3
notebook	2.1126	3
circuit	1.8663	0
consumer electronics	1.1544	0
appliance	1.0045	3
toy	0.7934	3
office equipment	0.4055	3
datum	0.3262	0
computer clipart	0.3156	1
mentality	0.1158	0
network device	0.0343	3
artefact	0.0339	3
data stores	0.0133	3
display screen equipment	0.0042	2
library equipment	0.0037	3
complex computer processes	0.0001	0
Agentive		
build		3
Constitutive		
software	25.5230	3
hardware	14.6539	3
part	14.6224	1
electronics	9.6139	3
individual	9.3791	0
memory	8.9683	3
man	5.9584	0
device	5.6259	3
unit	5.2078	3
component	4.3808	3
switch	4.2159	3
mix	3.8996	0
string	1.8896	3
circuit	1.8663	0
silicon	1.7717	3
actor	1.2127	0
processing unit	0.1444	3
individual components	0.1122	3
hardware components	0.1087	3
centra	0.0530	0
computer codes	0.0463	3
plastic case	0.0167	3
data storage device	0.0077	3
transistors	0.0022	3
Telic		
make	16.9616	1
access	15.5691	3
control	12.2216	3
run	8.6411	3
assist	4.1410	3
publish	3.0015	3
solve	2.9701	3
facilitate	2.8860	3
insight	2.2718	3
combine	1.9592	1
calculate	1.2977	3
execute	1.2792	3
translate	1.2530	3
suppose	1.1340	3
provide information	0.8969	3
access data	0.1025	3
imitate	0.0998	1
provide feedback	0.0900	3
human freedom	0.0065	3
teach children	0.0266	3
enable people	0.0255	3
manage information	0.0231	3
process words	0.0009	3
support program goals	0.0003	3
reduce analysis time	0.0002	3
perform useful computations	0.0001	3

Fig. 7.9. Weighted qualia structures for *book* and *computer*

Conversation		
	Jaccard	Eval.
Formal		
concept	6.6834	3
expression	5.8487	3
context	5.2338	3
object	4.6343	0
sound	4.4566	0
function	4.1414	0
material	4.1324	0
place	3.7806	0
employee	3.4710	0
skill	3.3323	3
interaction	3.1092	3
communication	3.0006	3
activity	2.9859	3
people	2.9027	0
label	2.7427	3
time	2.6158	1
source	1.6782	0
text	1.5877	1
transmission	1.2251	3
information	1.2182	3
contact	1.1309	3
utterance	0.9499	1
transaction	0.9412	3
school activities	0.2094	3
datum	0.1462	3
mannerism	0.0635	0
communication difficulties	0.0412	1
ambient audio	0.0148	3
official forms	0.0140	3
priceless tidbits	0.0002	0
Agentive		
make		3
create		0
Constitutive		
relationship	6.1848	3
silence	5.7213	3
answer	5.6855	3
question	4.8714	3
sentence	4.8663	3
story	4.4669	3
laughter	3.1766	1
unit	2.9359	1
tree	2.7633	0
contribution	2.6421	3
world	2.1804	0
sequence	1.8986	3
requests	1.4969	3
repetition	1.4267	3
token	1.2746	1
bonus	1.2155	1
pauses	1.1568	3
utterance	0.9499	0
cliches	0.2556	3
interpersonal exchanges	0.0082	3
brief debates	0.0003	3
Telic		
exchange	4.2769	3
establish	3.3530	3
further	3.2694	0
allow	3.2489	3
create	2.7141	0
generate	2.0107	0
get	1.9484	0
gloss	0.4780	0
exchange information	0.2313	3
exchange ideas	0.1896	3
enable people	0.1151	3
pass time	0.0469	0
teach skills	0.0171	3

Fig. 7.10. Weighted qualia structure for *conversation*

Data Mining		
	Jaccard	Eval.
Formal		
data analysis	2.1492	3
intelligence	1.4242	0
analysis	1.2009	3
tool	1.1987	3
prediction	0.9682	3
approach	0.7279	3
speciality	0.6245	3
system	0.6018	3
application	0.5209	3
functionality	0.3974	3
process	0.3840	3
mechanism	0.3503	3
type	0.3372	0
practice	0.3310	3
technology	0.3240	3
activity	0.3207	3
employment	0.2565	0
use	0.2128	3
name	0.1944	3
area	0.1856	0
datum	0.1701	0
data warehousing technologies	0.1497	3
subject	0.1403	0
information process	0.0498	3
information process techniques	0.0005	3
Agentive		
design		3
Constitutive		
knowledge	0.7062	3
Telic		
connect	0.5949	0
achieve	0.3651	3
uncover	0.3460	3
research	0.3374	3
answer	0.2122	3
support	0.2025	3
look	0.1834	0
provide information	0.1527	3
search	0.1451	3
tell	0.1099	1
identify patterns	0.0959	3
discover patterns	0.0934	3
identify trends	0.0765	3
provide a foundation	0.0620	1
improve services	0.0559	3
gain business intelligence	0.0048	3
explore knowledge	0.0045	3
detect dependencies	0.0036	3
gain business	0.0223	1
analyse large volumes	0.0022	1
find new prospects	0.0011	3
analyse disparate customer data	0.0002	3

Natural Language Processing		
	Jaccard	Eval.
Formal		
linguistics	1.0047	3
technique	0.4983	3
intelligence	0.3559	3
method	0.2748	3
model	0.1847	3
aspect	0.1380	3
scheme	0.1258	3
system	0.0750	1
research	0.0636	3
application	0.0603	3
science	0.0536	3
technology	0.0414	3
area	0.0373	0
product	0.0337	0
document processing applications	0.0174	3
Agentive		
design		3
Constitutive		
Telic		
build	0.1037	3
keep track	0.0820	3
understand	0.0662	3
soften	0.0501	0
provide	0.0384	3
build tailored knowledge base	0.0008	3

Fig. 7.11. Weighted qualia structure for *data mining* and *NLP*

7.4.4 Summary

We have presented an approach to automatically learning qualia structures from the Web. Such an approach is especially interesting for lexicographers aiming at constructing lexicons, but even more for natural language processing systems relying on deep lexical knowledge as represented by qualia structures. We have in particular shown that the qualia structures learned by our system are reasonable. Overall, it is valid to claim that our system is the first one automatically producing complete qualia structures for a given term. Such an approach is important for ontology learning as it yields ontological relations relevant for at least all physical objects.

7.5 Related Work

The problem of learning conceptual relations from text has not been addressed to the same extent as the problem of learning synonyms, taxonomic or meronymic relations. The most prominent approach to learning conceptual relations is the discovery of collocations. These collocations can be based on syntactic dependencies (compare [Mädche and Staab, 2000, Gamallo et al., 2002, Ciaramita et al., 2005, Schutz and Buitelaar, 2005]), but can also be defined on the basis of word windows as well as at the sentence or document-level [Sanderson and Croft, 1999]. In what follows, we discuss work related to the acquisition of ontological relations from a corpus. We will see that most research has indeed focused on binary relations. We also discuss work related to the acquisition of attributes as well as of qualia structures. Finally, some preliminary work on defining a calculus to combine ontology learning results is also discussed.

Mädche and Staab

Mädche and Staab [Mädche and Staab, 2000] present an approach using a generalized association rules algorithm [Agrawal and Srikant, 1994] to find conceptual relations between words at the appropriate level of abstraction with respect to a given taxonomy. In their approach, transactions are defined in terms of words occurring together in certain syntactic dependencies. The shallow parser SMES is used to extract such syntactic dependencies from the German version of the *Mecklenburg Vorpommern* corpus (compare Section 5). The syntactic dependencies are transformed into transactions which serve as input for the generalized association rules algorithm. Association rule discovery algorithms have been used especially for data mining of customer behavior in supermarkets. The aim here is to find patterns such as '*snacks are purchased together with drinks*' or '*peanuts are purchased with soda*', which describe the shopping behavior of customers and can thus be used to optimize product placement, advertising or pricing. In order to describe the approach in more detail, we first introduce the notions of a *transaction, association rule* as well as *confidence* and *support* for such an association rule.

A transaction t_i is a set of items which occur together in some context, i.e. $t_i := \{a_{i,1}..., a_{i,m}\}$. Hereby, Mädche and Staab [Mädche and Staab, 2000] define transactions over the concepts C of a given ontology. In the following, we will assume a set T of transactions $T := \{t_i, ...t_n\}$. An association rule now has the form $X \Rightarrow Y$, where X and Y are sets of concepts, i.e. $X, Y \subseteq C$ and furthermore are disjoint $X \cap Y = \emptyset$. Now we can compute the *support* and *confidence* of association rules as follows:

$$support(X, Y) := \frac{|\{t_i \mid X \cup Y \subseteq t_i\}|}{|T|} \tag{7.4}$$

$$confidence(X, Y) := \frac{|\{t_i \mid X \cup Y \subseteq t_i\}|}{|\{t_i \mid X \subseteq t_i\}|} \qquad (7.5)$$

Mädche and Staab consider the extension of Srikant and Agrawal [Srikant and Agrawal, 1997] to determine the associations at the appropriate level of generalization with respect to a given taxonomy. Each transaction t_i is extended to include each superconcept of an item $a_{i,j}$, i.e. $t_i' := t_i \cup \{a_{i,s} \mid a_{i,j} \leq_C a_{i,s} \text{ and } a_{i,j} \in t_i\}$. Further, in line with Srikant and Agrawal [Srikant and Agrawal, 1997], they exclude rules $X \Rightarrow Y$ where Y contains a subconcept of some element in X and also eliminate rules $X \Rightarrow Y$ which are subsumed by an 'ancestral' rule $X' \Rightarrow Y'$ in the sense that X' only contains superconcepts for all the concepts in X and analogously for Y and Y'.

Mädche and Staab in particular apply the following four steps to derive binary conceptual relations using the above generalized rule association algorithm:

1. Determine binary associations $T := \{\{a_{1,1}, a_{1,2}\}, ..., \{a_{n,1}, a_{n,2}\}\}$ where there was a syntactic dependency between $a_{i,1}$ and $a_{i,2}$ found in the corpus.
2. From the binary transactions t_i build a set T' of extended transactions using the concept hierarchy as defined above.
3. Determine the confidence and support for all the association rules $X \Rightarrow Y$ where $|X| = |Y| = 1$.
4. Output the association rules which exceed a user defined confidence and support and which are not subsumed by some rule $X' \Rightarrow Y'$.

The conceptual relations computed in this way are then evaluated in terms of precision and recall compared to the relations in a gold standard ontology. As the results yielded this way are very coarse, the authors additionally define the *Generic Relation Learning Accuracy (RLA)* introducing a gray-scale between completely wrong and totally correct. The $\overline{RLA}$ is computed by averaging over all the discovered relations D, i.e.

$$\overline{RLA}(D, R) = \frac{1}{|D|} \sum_{d \in D} RLA(d, R) \qquad (7.6)$$

Furthermore, the RLA of a discovered relation d is calculated as follows:

$$RLA(d, R) = max_{r \in R} \, max(MA(d, r), MA(d, r^{-1})) \qquad (7.7)$$

where r^{-1} is the inverse relation of r and MA is defined as follows:

$$MA((a_1, a_2), (b_1, b_2)) := \sqrt{CLA(a_1, b_1) \cdot CLA(a_2, b_2)} \qquad (7.8)$$

The CLA is defined as:

$$CLA(a, b) := \frac{\delta(lcs(a, b), top)}{\delta(lcs(a, b), top) + \delta(a, b)} \qquad (7.9)$$

The best results achieved by Mädche and Staab are an average generic relation learning accuracy of $\overline{RLA} = 0.67$, corresponding to a precision $P = 11\%$ and a recall $R = 13\%$.

Kavalec and Svátek

Kavalec and Svátek [Kavalec and Svátek, 2005] have recently extended the model of Mädche and Staab by introducing the 'above expectation' (AE) heuristic to measure the association between a verb and a pair of concepts. If the measure is above some threshold, the verb is considered a good candidate to label the relation between the two concepts. The AE measure suggested by Kavelec et al. is defined as

$$AE(c_1, c_2|v) = \frac{P(c_1, c_2|v)}{P(c_1|v)\ P(c_2|v)} \tag{7.10}$$

It computes the ratio between the observed joint frequency of c_1 and c_2 given the fact that we have seen the verb v and the joint frequency estimated under independence assumption.

Gamallo et al.

Gamallo et al. [Gamallo et al., 2002] present an approach to map syntactic dependencies to semantic relations. As a first step, they use a shallow parser together with some basic attachment heuristics to derive syntactic dependencies between words in a corpus. In a second step, different syntactic positions are clustered on the basis of the words appearing at this position, thus yielding, on the one hand, classes of similar syntactic positions as well as, on the other, classes of similar words which appear at these positions and thus fulfill the selectional restrictions of these. The mapping from the syntactic to the semantic level is accomplished by a set of interpretation rules which map syntactic structures into certain regions in the space of semantic relations. These semantic relations are for example: *agent, theme, cause, mode, locator, posessor, possessed, effect, purpose, function, hyponymy, meronymy,* etc. This mapping remains completely underspecified, underlying some constraints. As discussed by Gamallo et al., this mapping is to a great extent domain-dependent and can be further constrained by considering the nature of the argument appearing at the syntactic position.

Ciaramita et al.

Ciaramita et al. [Ciaramita et al., 2005] present an unsupervised approach to automatically derive conceptual relations from the GENIA corpus [Ohta et al., 2002]. First, a statistical dependency parser [Charniak, 2000] is used to extract the following syntactic relations from the corpus:

- SUBJECT–VERB–DIRECT_OBJECT

- SUBJECT–VERB–INDIRECT. OBJECT

whereby the indirect and direct object can be additionally modified by a noun such as in *'protein molecule stimulation'* where *stimulation* is modified by *'protein molecule'* or by a prepositional phrase as in *'overproduction of a protein'*. These syntactic collocations are then tested for their significance using a χ^2-test (compare Section 4.1.6), and only the collocations significantly occurring more often than by chance are kept. At a further step, the arguments of the relations are generalized with respect to the hierarchy of the Genia ontology. The authors rely on the approach of Clark and Weir [Clark and Weir, 2002] to determine whether using a hypernym instead of the hyponym leads to significantly different probabilities. They compare the probability $p(r|c, s)$ with $p(r|c', s)$ where c' is a superconcept of c. If $p(r|c', s)$ and $p(r|c, s)$ do not significantly differ, c' is regarded as an appropriate generalization. The authors present a twofold evaluation of their approach. On the one hand, they present the learned relations to a biologist for manual validation, coming to the conclusion that 83.3% of the learned relations are correct, and furthermore 53.1% of the generalized relations have been generalized appropriately. On the other hand, they align some top classes of Genia to DOLCE, an upper level ontology in order to detect inconsistencies. They conclude that the number of inconsistencies is small and consequently the relations learned can be regarded as reasonable. To our knowledge, Ciaramita et al.'s as well as Mädche et al.'s work is in addition to ours the only work aiming at appropriately generalizing relations with respect to the underlying taxonomy.

Heyer et al.

Heyer et al. [Heyer et al., 2001] suggest an approach relying on the extraction of collocations from a large text corpus as a basis to derive conceptual or ontological relations. Heyer et al. argue that collocations can denote a variety of relations (hyponymy, cohyponymy, instance-of, agent/action, etc.) with very different properties (symmetry, anti-symmetry, transitivity). Interestingly, they suggest that certain properties of the relation can be identified from the organization of collocations. They also examine an iterative approach in which the collocations for collocation sets are computed. This is what the authors call *second-order collocations*. In fact, the authors show that calculating higher-order collocations leads to more homogeneous classes.

Finally, they also present some very interesting ideas about how to combine partial ontology learning results. They suggest the definition of a set of heuristic rules as follows:

> There is a certain relation r between A and B, and
> There is some strong but (unknown) relation between A and B
> (given by collocation computation)

---

r holds with more evidence

There is a certain relation r between A and B
B is similar to B'
There is some strong but unknown relation between A and B'

There is a relation r between A and B'

A has a certain important property P
B is similar to A

B has the same property p

Definitely, it is appealing to reason on the basis of different results with a calculus as suggested by Heyer et al. However, the rules suggested are definitely *adhoc* and have no clear motivation. In fact, it is our view that such rules have to be automatically learned and thus grounded with respect to a given dataset. The interesting question then is in how far the automatically learned rules correspond to our intuitions.

Ogata and Collier

Ogata and Collier [Ogata and Collier, 2004] present a pattern-based approach to derive subclass relations from text using similar patterns as used by Hearst [Hearst, 1992]. Interestingly, they also present a non-monotonic and 'modal' calculus to reason on the extracted results. The rules, for example, look as follows:

must_properSubtype(X,Y)

---

properSubtype(X,Y)

So, if X *must* be a subclass of Y, then it certainly is.

evidential_properSubtype(X,Y)
not(must_properSubtype(Y,X))

---

properSubtype(X,Y)

Thus, if we have evidence that X is a subclass of Y and no evidence that Y *must* be a subclass of X, then we conclude that X is actually a subclass of Y.

may_properSubtype(X,Y)
not(must_properSubtype(Y,X))
not(evidential_properSubtype(Y,X))

---

properSubtype(X,Y)

Thus, X is a subclass of Y if it *may* be the case that X is a subclass of Y and it is not the case that Y *must* be a subclass of X nor do we have evidence that Y is a subclass of X.

most(X,Y)
not(most(Y,X))
not(must_properSubtype(Y,X))

---

properSubtype(X,Y)

So, we have evidence for the fact that X is a subclass of Y if most of the elements of X are contained in Y and not the other way round.

Furthermore, the authors include other more specific and to some extent proprietary rules to derive *properSubType*, *may_properSubtype* as well as *evidential_properSubtype* statements.

Here the interesting questions are how *must*, *may* and *evidential* as well as the negation *not* are interpreted, but, unfortunately, there is no discussion in the paper on these issues. The authors do not evaluate the impact of such a calculus but only present results of the pattern-matching on biochemical texts. In general, the same comments as for Heyer et al.'s approach apply here. While the idea of using such a calculus is definitely interesting, the rules need to be derived from existing data, for instance by using inductive techniques to approximate the target ontology to be learned.

Yamaguchi

Yamaguchi [Yamaguchi, 2001], besides addressing the learning of taxonomic relations by an algorithm pruning WordNet, also applies Schuetze's *word space* method to find similar terms and suggest potential relations to a user. He presents a variant of Schuetze's *word space* approach using 4-grams, i.e. a four word window, instead of four-letter-grams as used by Schütze [Schütze, 1993] (compare Section 6.5.1). The computation of similarity between words is then performed calculating the cosine of the angle between the word vectors. If the similarity is above a certain threshold, the system suggests a potential (anonymous) conceptual relation between both words. Using a threshold of 0.9993 on a legal corpus, the approach extracts 90 relations of which 53 are judged as correct by a domain expert, while 23 are considered as inappropriate. This gives a precision of 53 / 90 = 58.89%.

Buitelaar et al.

Buitelaar et al.'s OntoLT system [Buitelaar et al., 2004] (compare Section 6.5.1.3) also provides a mapping for the purpose of learning relations, that means, slots with their corresponding domain and range. They propose the **SubjToClass_PredToSlot_DObjToRange** rule which maps a subject to the domain, the predicate or verb to a slot or relation and the object to its range. The method of Buitelaar et al. requires manual inspection and validation of the generated relations and does not tackle the problem of finding the most appropriate and general domain and range with respect to a given concept hierarchy. Recently, Schutz and Buitelaar [Schutz and Buitelaar, 2005] have also presented an approach in which they evaluate their approach in terms of recall and precision with respect to a gold standard, achieving a precision between 9.1% and 11.9%, depending on the evaluation set used.

Poesio and Almuhareb

Poesio and Almuhareb [Poesio and Almuhareb, 2005] address the problem of classifying attributes into the six categories: *quality, part, related-object, activity, related-agent* and *non-attribute*. They train a classifier to recognize the above categories on the basis of (i) morphological information, (ii) the results of clustering the attributes in an unsupervised fashion, (iii) results of issuing certain question-like queries to a search engine as well as (iv) certain heuristics to distinguish between attributive and conceptual uses. On the one hand, using a binary classifier distinguishing attributes from non-attributes, they achieve an F-measure of 89.2% for the attribute class and 41.7% for the non-attribute class. On the other hand, with a 5-way classifier, they achieve an F-measure of 53.8% on the non-attribute class and F-measure between 81-95% on the other 4 classes. The reason why five classes are considered is that the *part* and *related-object* classes have been joined due to the fact that they were found difficult to discriminate. Poesio and Almuhareb further show that clustering nouns on the basis of their attributes instead of the values of these attributes such as specified by adjectives leads in general to more accurate clusters (see [Almuhareb and Poesio, 2004] and [Poesio and Almuhareb, 2004]).

Yamada and Baldwin

Yamada and Baldwin [Yamada and Baldwin, 2004] present an approach to learning *telic* and *agentive* relations from corpora analyzing two different approaches: one relying on matching certain lexico-syntactic patterns as well as a second approach consisting in training a maximum entropy model classifier on the basis of syntactic dependencies extracted with a dependency parser. They evaluate both approaches using 30 nouns as well as 50 verbs as potential fillers of a qualia role. The approaches are evaluated by comparing the output with two hand-crafted gold standards in terms of a variant of Spearman's rank correlation. Their conclusion is that the results produced by the classification approach correlate better with the two gold standards. The patterns used by Yamada and Baldwin [Yamada and Baldwin, 2004] differ substantially from the ones used in our approach due to the fact that we have been using the Web as a corpus with a search engine as interface, not allowing to query for regular expressions.

Claveau et al.

Claveau et al. [Claveau et al., 2003] use Inductive Logic Programming (ILP) [Lavrac and Dzeroski, 1994] to learn whether a given verb is a qualia element or not. A supervised approach is presented, which relies on part-of-speech and semantic tags for words, but also on information about the relative position of the words as features to derive rules indicating a qualia relation between a noun and a verb. The outcome is a set of nine rules predicting a corresponding qualia relation between a noun and a verb. They present a theoretical, empirical as well as linguistic evaluation of their method. From a theoretical point of view (actually empirical in our view), the results are evaluated by cross-validation in terms of precision, recall and Pearson's coefficient with respect to the gold standard. Empirically, they present the positive and negative pairs to four Generative Lexicon experts for a posteriori evaluation. The results are presented in terms of true positives, true negatives, false positives and false negatives and in terms of Pearson's coefficient. The method is found to perform better than simply using a χ^2-test assessing the correlation between the nouns and verbs as a baseline. From a linguistic point of view, the authors conclude that *"it appears that the clauses give very general surface clues about the structures that are favored in the corpus for the expression of qualia relations"*. In general, their approach does not go as far as learning the complete qualia structure for a lexical element in an unsupervised way as presented in our approach (compare Section 7.4). In fact, in their approach they do not distinguish between different qualia roles and restrict themselves to verbs as potential fillers of qualia roles.

Pustejovsky et al.

Pustejovsky et al. [Pustejovsky et al., 1993] present an interesting framework for the acquisition of semantic relations from corpora, not only relying on statistics, but guided by theoretical lexicon principles. Their framework is embedded in the theory of the Generative Lexicon, and one of their main aims is to acquire qualia structures by analyzing machine readable dictionaries as well as corpora. In particular, they suggest combining co-occurrence information or collocational analysis as well as linguistic phenomena such as metonymy and polysemy for knowledge acquisition of lexical items.

7.6 Conclusion and Open Issues

In this chapter, we have addressed several issues related to the acquisition of attributes and relations from a corpus. Concerning the learning of attributes, we have presented an approach relying on adjective modification of nouns which finds an intensional description of the attribute by resorting to Word-Net. We have further presented results of a human evaluation and with respect to the concept hierarchy induction task. Further, we have qualitatively discussed concept lattices built on the basis of the automatically extracted attributes. The different evaluations have shown that the attributes derived are indeed reasonable.

Concerning the discovery of relations, we have on the one hand addressed the task of finding the appropriate level of generalization for the slots of properties derived from the verbal structures appearing in a corpus. Here we have shown that the conditional probability works well enough. To some extent, this result may be a consequence of the fact that the Genia ontology is very shallow. More experiments on different domains and corpora are needed to clarify which measure indeed works best. In general, it is important to emphasize that there is a substantial difference between *a priori* and *a posteriori* evaluations. In *a priori* evaluations, the gold standard is constructed independently of the results of the system, and the system is then evaluated with respect to the gold standard in a strict way. In *a posteriori* evaluations, the results of a system are presented to the evaluator, who then classifies the results of the system. In the first case, the system can be penalized still if its results are reasonable and just because an answer diverges from the one in the gold standard. *A posteriori* evaluation differs in this respect as the results merely depend on how inclined the evaluator is to regard the suggestions of the system as correct. The difference between *a priori* and *a posteriori* evaluation is illustrated by Schutz and Buitelaar, who present their results both in terms of *a priori* as well as *a posteriori* evaluation. With respect to the *a posteriori* evaluation, they report an average precision between 17.7% and 23.9%, yielding approx. 10% higher results compared to the *a priori evaluation*. Examples for *a priori* evaluations are those of Mädche et al., Schutz and Buitelaar as well as ours. Examples for *a posteriori* evaluations are those of Ciaramita et al., Yamaguchi, but also Schutz and Buitelaar. With respect to the directly comparable approach of Mädche and Staab, our approach gets much higher results in terms of precision or direct matches, i.e. 33.53% compared to 11%. The best *a priori* precision of Schutz and Buitelaar (11.9%) is comparable to that obtained by Mädche et al. However, the focus of the latter approach was not on learning the right level of generalization.

On the other hand, we have also presented an approach to learn specific relations typically occurring in ontologies and describing the nature of objects. In particular, we have presented an approach to learning qualia structures and shown that the results are indeed promising. Our results are not directly comparable to the approaches of Poesio et al., Yamada and Baldwin or Claveau et al. as each of the approaches aims at learning different types of relations. Nevertheless, it is certainly valid to claim that our approach is the only one known to us learning complete qualia structures.

Future work should address the question whether relations can also be learned from non-verbal structures, e.g. from noun phrases. Concerning the learning of qualia structures, a few issues remain open. On the one hand, it would be important to have a clear interpretation of the different qualia roles. It could even be considered to extend the approach to learning other specific relations. On the other hand, an important issue is to be able to distinguish between different senses of a given word. Finally, in order to improve the current approach, a gold standard of qualia structures will definitely need to be constructed.

As mentioned several times in the discussion of related work, a calculus being able to reason on partial results from the ontology learning process, combining these results into a big picture, is certainly highly appealing and desirable. In this respect, it would be necessary to define an inductive approach, possibly using machine learning techniques, to automatically derive the rules underlying the calculus from existing data.

Finally, with respect to learning relations, ontology learning should exploit the whole range of lexical semantic theories available to constrain the process according to linguistic principles.

8

Population

In this chapter, we address the population of ontologies on the basis of text documents. According to the definitions of Section 2, population of an ontology involves finding instances of relations as well as of concepts. The problem of finding instances of relations is indeed a very difficult one and practically requires full understanding of natural language. This is clearly out of the scope of this thesis. A more modest target is the extraction of a set of predefined relations. This is the aim of the information extraction task as originally defined in the context of the Message Understanding Conferences (MUC).

In the context of this thesis, we do not deal with the acquisition of instances of relations, but restrict ourselves to the detection of instances of concepts. To some extent, this has also been the aim of the named entity recognition task, typically considered as a subtask of information extraction. Named entity recognition deals with the recognition of named entities in texts as well as their classification to the correct class. State-of-the-art named entity recognition systems are characterized by the fact that they typically only consider (i) a fixed and (ii) small number of classes. The MUC named entity task [Hirschman and Chinchor, 1997], for example, distinguishes three classes: person, location and organization, and the CoNLL[1] task adds one more: misc, while the ACE framework[2] adds two more: GPE (Geo-Political-Entity) and facility. However, the set of categories still remains fixed and small.

Some researchers have addressed the challenge of classifying named entities with respect to a larger number of classes. Fleischman and Hovy [Fleischman and Hovy, 2002], for example, take into account 8 classes: athlete, politician/government, clergy, businessperson, entertainer/artist, lawyer, doctor/scientist and police. Evans [Evans, 2003] considers a totally unsupervised scenario in which the classes themselves are derived from the documents. Hahn and Schnattinger [Hahn and Schnattinger, 1998b] con-

---

[1] http://cnts.uia.ac.be/conll2003/ner/
[2] http://www.itl.nist.gov/iaui/894.01/tests/ace/phase1/index.htm

sider an ontology with 325 concepts, and Alfonseca and Manandhar [Alfonseca and Manandhar, 2002] consider 1200 WordNet synsets.

In this line, we tackle the classification of named entities with regard to hundreds of classes as specified within an ontology. The remainder of this chapter is structured as follows: in Section 8.1 we first give an overview of the main approaches to named entity classification and ontology population. In Sections 8.2 and 8.3 we present our own approaches to the task. The chapter concludes with a discussion of related work in Section 8.4 as well as with a brief summary in Section 8.5.

8.1 Common Approaches

In this section, we provide an overview of the main techniques used for populating an ontology with concept instances. We first, once again, briefly discuss approaches based on lexico-syntactic patterns. Then we present similarity or memory-based techniques and finally discuss supervised approaches such as applied for named entity recognition or information extraction.

8.1.1 Lexico-syntactic Patterns

Lexico-syntactic patterns can also be used to extract instance-of relations in case we assume that the NP at the hyponym position is actually an instance. This straightforward idea is exploited by a number of systems which match these patterns on the Web (compare [Evans, 2003, Etzioni et al., 2004a, Pasca, 2004]). These approaches are discussed in more detail in Section 8.4, but consult also Sections 6.1 and 6.5, where approaches based on lexico-syntactic patterns are discussed in detail.

8.1.2 Similarity-based Classification

Similarity or memory-based approaches typically are based on Harris' distributional hypothesis and thus in line with other approaches in which the context of a phrase is used to disambiguate its sense [Yarowsky, 1995, Schütze, 1998] or class [Lin, 1998c] or to discover other semantically related terms [Hindle, 1990]. The basic similarity-based assignment of an instance to its concept is formally described in Algorithm 12. The algorithm assigns an instance i represented by a certain context vector v_i to that concept c maximizing the similarity to the corresponding vector v_c.

Different formulations of such an algorithm exist. We have seen in Section 6.5.2 that Widdows rephrases the problem as one of finding the k nearest neighbors of the new word in the taxonomy and then choosing the place in the taxonomy where these neighbors are 'most concentrated'. The problem is formulated in a similar fashion by Mädche and Staab [Mädche et al., 2002],

---

Algorithm 12 Similarity-based instance classification algorithm

classify(set of instances I, corpus T, set of concepts C)
{
    foreach c in C
    {
        v_c = getContextVector(c,T);
        doFeatureWeighting(v_c)
    }
    foreach i in I
    {
        v_i = getContextVector(i,T);
        class(i)=argmax$_c$ sim(v_c,v_i);
    }
    return class;
}

---

where the k-nearest neighbors can vote for the new candidate with respect to some measure.

Algorithm 12 is the simplest we can imagine, being quite inefficient at the same time, as we have to iterate through all concepts in the ontology for each instance. Clever optimizations can be used here. On the one hand, one can use feature indexing strategies to retrieve all the examples having at least one feature in common with the instance to be classified. On the other hand, if the concepts are ordered hierarchically, the search space can be explored in a more intelligent fashion either traversing the concept hierarchy top-down or bottom-up (compare [Mädche et al., 2002]). A crucial question for such similarity-based approaches is how to define the context of a certain word. Though most approaches represent the context of a phrase as a vector, there are great differences in which features are used, ranging from simple word windows [Yarowsky, 1995, Schütze, 1998] to syntactic dependencies extracted with a parser [Hindle, 1990, Pereira et al., 1993, Grefenstette, 1994]. A second crucial question is how to construct the context vectors for classes by aggregating the vectors of their subclasses.

The main problem of such similarity-based approaches is, however, data sparseness. In fact, the contextual vectors are to some extent idiosyncratic representations of the context of a word. In many cases, the similarities in vector space thus also correspond to semantic similarities. In other cases, a higher similarity in vector space has to be regarded as accidental and due to sparse data.

8.1.3 Supervised Approaches

Supervised approaches predict the category of a certain instance with a model induced from training data using machine-learning techniques. Such supervised approaches have been exploited, for example, in the context of the named entity recognition (NER) task. Bikel et al. [Bikel et al., 1999] and Zhou and Su [Zhou and Su, 2002], for instance, apply Hidden Markov Models, while Borthwick et al. [Borthwick et al., 1998] and Chieu and Ng [Chieu and Ng, 2003] use a Maximum Entropy-based approach. Sekine et al. [Sekine et al., 1998] and Karkaletsis et al. [Karkaletsis et al., 2000] learn a decision tree classifier, while Isozaki and Kazawa [Isozaki and Kazawa, 2002] and Kazama et al. [Kazama et al., 2002] present an approach using Support Vector Machines. Hendrickx and van den Bosch [Hendrickx and van den Bosch, 2003] make use of memory-based learning. However, when considering hundreds of concepts as possible tags, a supervised approach requiring thousands of training examples seems quite unfeasible. The use of handcrafted resources such as gazetteers or pattern libraries (compare [Maynard et al., 2003]) is deemed to be equally unfeasible due to the high cost involved in creating and maintaining such resources for hundreds of concepts. Interesting and very promising are approaches which operate in a bootstrapping-like fashion, using a set of seeds to derive more training data such as the supervised approach using Hidden Markov Models of Niu et al. [Niu et al., 2003] or the unsupervised approach of Collins and Singer [Collins and Singer, 1999].

The information extraction task can be defined as the one of instantiating a set of templates on the basis of text analysis and is thus also very relevant to the ontology learning population task. Hereby, templates are predefined target knowledge structures to be extracted by the system. Typical target knowledge structures have been joint ventures and microelectronics product announcements (MUC-5), management succession events (MUC-6) as well as airline crashes and launch events (MUC-7). As the early information extraction systems were customized for a certain domain and typically difficult to port to another, recent efforts have concentrated on developing adaptive systems, usually at the cost of reducing expressiveness of the extraction rules or by making strong assumptions, such as what can be called the *one-template-and-occurrence-per-document* assumption. In fact, most of the state-of-the-art systems are able to extract exactly one instance of a specific template from one document.

Several supervised machine learning based techniques have been proposed to automate the information extraction as well as the annotation process of documents (compare [Soderland, 1999, Freitag and Kushmerick, 2000, Ciravegna, 2001, Califf and Mooney, 2004]). However, machine learning approaches inducing extraction rules for each concept from training data do typically not scale to large numbers of concepts as ontologies typically consist of. Second, in order to annotate with respect to a few hundred concepts, a training set in the magnitude of thousands of examples needs to be provided[3], an effort that probably not many people are willing to make.

---

[3] Our experiences with the Amilcare system in [Ciravegna, 2001] showed that at least ten examples for each concept to be extracted are necessary.

Third, machine learning based approaches rely on the assumption that documents have a similar structure as well as content, an assumption which seems quite unrealistic considering the heterogeneity of the current web. Thus, several researchers have started to look at totally unsupervised approaches such as Etzioni et al. [Etzioni et al., 2004a] as well as approaches performing a first unsupervised step and then using the results of this first step to induce new extraction rules in a bootstrapping manner (see [Brin, 1998, Ciravegna et al., 2003, Etzioni et al., 2004b]). Summarizing, the obvious drawback of supervised approaches is that one has to provide labeled data from which to train. In case we are considering hundreds of possible target classes, such an endeavor is deemed to be unfeasible.

8.1.4 Knowledge-based and Linguistic Approaches

Some approaches essentially see the population task as a disambiguation problem and thus as a byproduct of natural language understanding. Hahn et al. [Hahn and Schnattinger, 1998b], for example, present an approach in which, for each unknown named entity, hypothesis spaces containing the diverse ontological categories the entity could belong to are created. The different hypotheses are then refined or discarded iteratively while the text is linguistically analyzed. A so called *qualification calculus* in the background makes use of linguistic evidence as well as of a domain-specific ontology to weight, discard and refine the different hypotheses in the hypothesis space. We discuss this approach in more detail in Section 8.4. Another approach heavily relying on linguistic analysis is the one by Shamsfard and Barforoush [Shamsfard and Barforoush, 2004]. They present a system called *HASTI* exploiting a great variety of linguistic expressions to derive ontological relations formalized as tuples. Interesting aspects of HASTI are that the system is able to reason and detect inconsistencies between already extracted results and that it proceeds, similar to Hahn et al.'s system, iteratively, constantly refining the acquired ontology as more text is processed. The drawback of such knowledge-based and linguistic approaches is certainly that either one needs a relatively complex knowledge base or ontology as in Hahn et al.'s approach, or a set of very accurate tools for linguistic processing, i.e. domain-specific POS-taggers, parsers, etc., as in HASTI.

8.1.5 Road Map

So far, we have discussed the main approaches to ontology population. We conclude that supervised approaches are not a feasible option for the task of classifying entities with respect to an ontology consisting of hundreds of classes. Though knowledge-based approaches are indeed very interesting and promising, it is not our goal to provide our system with a detailed and complex ontology beforehand. We thus opt for similarity-based and semi-supervised approaches. In the remainder of this chapter, we present two different approaches addressing the classification of named entities with respect to an ontology consisting of several hundreds of categories. The task we are addressing is much more challenging than the standard named entity recognition task, requiring to scale to large numbers of concepts and thus rendering the task much harder. At the same time, the goal is to keep the system portable to another domain by allowing to exchange the underlying ontology and corpus. It should be clear from this discussion that a supervised system is simply not suitable for the task.

The first approach presented in Section 8.2 is a standard similarity-based approach in which a named entity is assigned to that entity showing the highest degree of distributional similarity. The approach in itself is certainly not novel. The contribution of our analysis lies in the systematic exploration of certain parameters as well as techniques by which the performance of such a similarity-based approach can be increased. Part of the material has been published previously in [Cimiano and Völker, 2005] and constitutes joint work with Johanna Völker.

The second approach described in Section 8.3 is actually semi-supervised in the sense that Hearst-style patterns are given as input to the system. However, these patterns do not vary from domain to domain so that, from the usage point of view, the system is unsupervised as no training data needs to be provided to apply the system in a specific domain. This second approach, called *Learning by Googling*, is inspired by novel social studies showing that collective knowledge is much more powerful than individual knowledge (cf. [Surowiecki, 2004]). The approach uses the massive amount of implicit knowledge on the Web to derive conclusions about a certain entity. This material is to a great extent based on the material previously published in [Cimiano et al., 2004a], [Cimiano and Staab, 2004] and [Cimiano et al., 2005b].

8.2 Corpus-based Population

Having briefly discussed the traditional named entity recognition task, in this section we propose a more challenging one, the classification of named entities with regard to a large number of classes specified by an ontology or more specifically by a concept hierarchy. Our approach aims at being domain independent in the sense that the underlying ontology and the corpus can be replaced. As already argued above, in our view this aim can only be accomplished if one resorts to an unsupervised system, since providing labeled training data for a few hundred concepts as we consider in our approach is often unfeasible.

We present an unsupervised approach which - as many others - is based on the assumption that words are semantically similar to the extent to which they share syntactic contexts (compare Section 6.5).

In this section, we explore varying different parameters with respect to Algorithm 12. We investigate the impact of using different feature weighting measures and various similarity measures described by Lee [Lee, 1999]. Further, to address data sparseness problems, we examine the influence of (i) anaphora resolution in the hope that it will yield more context information as speculated by Grefenstette [Grefenstette, 1994], (ii) downloading additional textual material from the Web as in the approach of Agirre et al. [Agirre et al., 2000] and (iii) making use of the structure of the concept hierarchy or taxonomy in calculating the context vectors for the classes as in the works of Hearst and Schütze [Hearst and Schütze, 1993], Resnik [Resnik, 1993] or Pekar and Staab [Pekar and Staab, 2002]. The section is organized as follows: Section 8.2.1 presents the approach in detail and Section 8.2.2 describes the evaluation measures. In Section 8.2.3 we present our experiments analyzing the impact of varying the above mentioned parameters step by step, starting with a window-based approach as a baseline. A brief summary concludes this section.

8.2.1 Similarity-based Classification of Named Entities

We examine an approach to named entity classification in line with Algorithm 12. It is already clear from the description of the algorithm that at least three functions need to be specified. First, we need to specify how the context vectors are constructed. Second, we need to fix the measure according to which the vectors will be weighted. Third, we need to choose some similarity measure. In our experiments we examine in fact different context models, different feature weighting strategies as well as similarity measures.

We start our analysis by comparing context extraction techniques relying on word windows as well as on pseudo-syntactic dependencies extracted by means of regular expressions defined over part-of-speech tags (compare Section 4.1.4.2). We analyze the impact of different similarity and feature weighting measures. As they were found to perform particularly well by Lee [Lee, 1999], we use the following similarity measures: the *cosine* and *Jaccard* measures, the *L1 norm* as well as the *Jensen-Shannon* and *Skew* divergences. In order to weight the features, we use the following measures:

$$Conditional(n, feat) = P(n|feat) = \frac{f(n, feat)}{f(feat)} \qquad (8.1)$$

$$PMI(n, feat) = log\frac{P(n|feat)}{P(n)} \qquad (8.2)$$

$$Resnik(n, feat) = S_R(feat)\, P(n|feat) \qquad (8.3)$$

where $S_R(feat) = \sum_{n'} P(n'|feat)\, log\frac{P(n'|feat)}{P(n')}$.

Further, $f(n, feat)$ is the number of occurrences of a term n with feature $feat$, $f(feat)$ is the number of occurrences of the feature $feat$ and $P(n)$

is the relative frequency of a term n compared to all other terms. The PMI and Resnik measures have already been described in Section 6.2.2.

8.2.2 Evaluation

As mentioned by Collins and Singer [Collins and Singer, 1999], the named entity recognition task essentially consists in learning a function from an input string (a proper name or named entity) to its class. We evaluate our approach on the tourism population dataset described in Section 5.3. Our goal is to learn a function f_S which approximates the functions f_A and f_B specified by the two annotators. We assume that these functions are given as sets $C_X := \{(e, c) | e \in dom(f_X) \wedge f_X(e) = c\}$. While f_A and f_B are total functions, f_S is a partial one as our system does not always produce an answer. In fact, if the distributional similarity between the entity to be tagged and all the concepts in the ontology is minimal, the system will give no answer. Thus, it is not only important to measure the recall, but also the precision of the system. We evaluate the system with the standard measures of precision, recall and F-measure by averaging the results for both annotators:

$$P_A = \frac{|C_A \cap C_S|}{|C_S|} \quad P_B = \frac{|C_B \cap C_S|}{|C_S|} \quad P = \frac{P_A + P_B}{2}$$

$$R_A = \frac{|C_A \cap C_S|}{|C_A|} \quad R_B = \frac{|C_B \cap C_S|}{|C_B|} \quad R = \frac{R_A + R_B}{2}$$

$$F_A = \frac{2 * P_A * R_A}{P_A + R_A} \quad F_B = \frac{2 * P_B * R_B}{P_B + R_B} \quad F = \frac{F_A + F_B}{2}$$

As named entities can be tagged at different levels of detail, and there is certainly not only one correct assignment of a concept, we also consider how close the assignment of the system is with respect to the assignment of the annotator by using the *learning accuracy* originally introduced by Hahn and Schnattinger [Hahn and Schnattinger, 1998b]. However, we consider a slightly different formulation of the learning accuracy in line with the measures defined by Mädche et al. [Mädche et al., 2002]. The measure of Hahn et al. and our learning accuracy measure are not totally equivalent. The main difference is that we measure the distance between nodes in terms of edges – instead of nodes as in Hahn's version – and we do not need any case distinction considering whether the classification is correct or not. Additionally, in contrast to Hahn et al.'s learning accuracy, our measure is symmetric. Section A.1 of the appendix formally explains the differences between both measures. The learning accuracy between two concepts is defined as:

$$LA(a, b) := \frac{\delta(top, c) + 1}{\delta(top, c) + \delta(a, c) + \delta(b, c) + 1} \tag{8.4}$$

where $c = lcs(a, b)$, i.e. c is the least common subsumer as defined in Section 2.

8.2.3 Experiments

In what follows, the results of our extensive experiments are presented. In Section 8.2.3.1 we report about experiments using words appearing within a certain window of words from the target word. We then describe the results using pseudo-syntactic dependencies as context to build the vectors describing words in Section 8.2.3.2. We discuss different methods addressing data sparseness in Section 8.2.3.3.

8.2.3.1 Using Word Windows

In a first experiment, we use the n words to the left and right of a certain word of interest excluding so called stopwords and without trespassing sentence boundaries. Here n is the so called window size. The advantage of such an approach is that no preprocessing is necessary to extract context information. However, it also has the drawback that context vectors become larger compared to using syntactic dependencies. As a result, the similarity calculation becomes less efficient (cf. [Grefenstette, 1994]). Consider, for example, the following discourse:

Mopti is the biggest city along the Niger with one of the most vibrant ports and a large bustling market. Mopti has a traditional ambience that other towns seem to have lost. It is also the center of the local tourist industry and suffers from hard-sell overload. The nearby junction towns of Gao and San offer nice views over the Niger's delta.

Here we would extract the following vectors for concepts when using a window-size of 3, excluding stopwords and without trespassing sentence boundaries:

city: biggest(1), Niger(1)
port: vibrant (1), large(1)
market: bustling(1), large(1)
ambience: traditional(1), town(1)
town: ambience(1), seem(1)
center: local(1)
overload: suffer(1), hard-sell(1)
tourist industry: suffer(1), local(1)
junction town: nearby(1), Gao(1), San(1)
view: San(1), offer(1), nice(1), Niger(1)
delta: Niger(1)

as well as the following vectors for instances:

Table 8.1. Results for different word window sizes (in percent).

	Standard		Conditional		PMI		Resnik	
	F	LA	F	LA	F	LA	F	LA
3 Word Window								
Cosine	9.52	53.69	12.78	56.21	11.78	52.57	9.77	50.11
JS	7.27	41.86	6.77	39.66	3.51	30.05	1.5	25.54
Jaccard	1.51	22.51	1.51	22.51	0.5	21.31	0.5	21.31
L1	13.03	62.91	13.53	56.78	11.03	52	9.52	47.55
Skew	13.53	61.67	12.53	58.2	12.03	51.88	12.53	54.04
5 Word Window								
Cosine	13.22	57.46	16.96	60.26	13.47	49.41	13.22	48.25
JS	8.73	43.24	10.47	39.76	4.49	23.06	2.74	20.59
Jaccard	0	22.06	0	22.06	0.5	21.66	0.5	21.66
L1	16.21	63.37	16.96	62.22	13.47	49.29	13.47	49.36
Skew	16.21	64.16	16.71	62.13	17.46	56.11	18.2	56.26
10 Word Window								
Cosine	13.97	57.54	13.97	56.34	11.22	44.14	13.72	48.18
JS	8.98	43.65	7.23	34.75	2	21.7	1	17.61
Jaccard	0.25	18.23	0.25	18.23	0.25	17.41	0.25	17.41
L1	14.46	63.12	16.21	60.79	10.97	43.05	13.72	47.61
Skew	14.96	64.49	16.21	62.78	17.46	54.18	**19.7**	**57.78**

Mopti: traditional(1), biggest(1)
Niger: city(1), delta(1), view(1)
Gao: San(1), offer(1), town(1), junction(1)
San: offer(1), view(1), Gao(1), nice(1)

For our example, we would get the following similarities between named entity vectors and concept vectors with respect to the Jaccard measure:

Named Entity	Concept	Jaccard Similarity
Mopti	city	0.33
	ambience	0.33
Niger	n.a.	n.a.
Gao	view	0.33
	ambience	0.2
San	view	0.33
	junction town	0.14

These similarities do not correspond to our intuitions and seem in fact quite idiosyncratic, hinting at the fact that a context model based on word windows is a rather poor one. Of course, if we would compute the vectors for a larger corpus and possibly using a window size greater than three, we would yield similarities which correspond more to our intuitions. However, the interpretation of a context model based on word windows remains rather unclear.

Nevertheless, we implemented this approach as a baseline in order to verify whether syntactic dependencies actually perform better in our setting. We vary the similarity measure, the feature weighting strategy and experiment with the three different window sizes: 3, 5 and 10 words, thus producing $5 \times 4 \times 3 = 60$ runs of the similarity-based classification algorithm. The results of the different runs are given in Table 8.1. The best result is an F-measure of 19.7% and a learning accuracy of 57.78%. It was achieved when using the Skew divergence as similarity measure, the mutual information as feature weighting measure and a window size of 10.

8.2.3.2 Using Pseudo-syntactic Dependencies

Instead of merely using the words occurring within a given window size before and after the word in question, we also experiment with pseudo-syntactic dependencies as defined in Section 4.1.4.2. These dependencies are not really syntactical as they are not obtained from parse trees, but from a very shallow method consisting in matching certain regular expressions over part of speech tags. Using pseudo-syntactic dependencies, we would get the following vectors for the above discourse:

city: biggest(1)
port: vibrant(1)
market: bustling(1)
ambience: traditional(1)
town: seem_subj(1)
center: of_tourist_industry(1)
tourist industry: center_of(1), local(1)
overload: hard-sell(1)
junction towns: nearby(1)
view: nice(1), offer_obj(1)

and the following ones for named entities:

Mopti: is_city(1), has_ambience(1)
Niger: has_delta(1)
Gao: junction_of(1)
San: offer_subj(1)

It can be observed clearly that using pseudo-syntactic dependencies in general yields smaller vectors. For our example, we would in fact get no reasonable similarities for the short text considered. We need to resort to a much bigger text collection to yield similarities corresponding to our intuitions. However, the context model based on syntactic relations seems easier to interpret. Table 8.2 shows the results for the version of the classification algorithm making use of the pseudo-syntactic dependencies as well as the different similarity and feature weighting measures (Standard). The best result was an F-measure of 19.58% corresponding to a learning accuracy of 60.03%. The overall best learning accuracy was 60.44%. Though the results are comparable to the version using word windows as context, as the length of the vectors is much smaller and thus the computation of the similarities is faster, we conclude that using the pseudo-syntactic dependencies is an interesting alternative and present the results of further modifications to our algorithm with respect to the version using this sort of dependencies. In what follows, we present the different methods to address data sparseness.

8.2.3.3 Dealing with Data Sparseness

Using Conjunctions

In order to address the problem of data sparseness, we exploit conjunctions of named entities in the sense that if two named entities appear linked by the conjunctions 'and' or 'or', we count any occurrence of a feature with one of the named entities also as an occurrence of the other. As the results in Table 8.2 show (see Conjunctions), this simple heuristic improves the results of our approach considerably. The top results are F-measures of 22.8% (Cosine), 22.57% (L1 norm) and 22.57% (Skew divergence) with corresponding learning accuracies of 61.23%, 61.4% and 62.7%, respectively. The best overall learning accuracy was 65.19% obtained with no feature weighting and the Skew divergence.

Exploiting the Taxonomy

An interesting option discussed by Resnik [Resnik, 1993], Hearst and Schütze [Hearst and Schütze, 1993] as well as Pekar and Staab [Pekar and Staab, 2002] is to take into account the taxonomy of the underlying ontology to compute the context vector of a certain term by considering the context vectors of its subconcepts. This is in fact a delicate issue as some studies have shown that this does not work, while other have shown the contrary. We adopt here a conservative strategy and take only into account the context vectors of direct subconcepts to compute the vector of a certain term. In fact, the context vector of a concept will be the sum of the context vectors of all its direct subconcepts (this version is simply referred to as *Ontology* in Table 8.2). However, the aggregated vectors can also be normalized. In fact, we experiment with the two possibilities also discussed by Pekar and Staab [Pekar and Staab, 2002]: (i) standard normalization of the vector or (ii) calculating its centroid (compare [Pekar and Staab, 2002] and [Hearst and Schütze, 1993]). In the latter case, the only difference is that we calculate an average vector by dividing through the number of direct subconcepts. As the results in Table 8.2 show, only the version with the centroid

Table 8.2. Results for pseudo-syntactic dependencies (in percent)

	No weighting		Conditional		PMI		Resnik	
	F	LA	F	LA	F	LA	F	LA
Standard								
Cosine	13.29	55.77	16.78	58.47	19.11	58.93	15.38	56.33
JS	2.56	39	6.29	41.86	5.13	40.25	4.9	38.12
Jaccard	1.4	29.99	1.4	29.99	1.4	29.99	1.4	29.99
L1	15.62	59.45	18.65	59.31	17.72	57.29	18.18	58.91
Skew	14.45	59.41	17.02	58.71	**19.58**	60.03	19.35	**60.44**
Conjunctions								
Cosine	18.51	61.25	20.77	60.87	**22.8**	61.23	21.22	60.32
JS	10.16	52.06	11.06	43.46	10.84	42	10.61	43.1
Jaccard	11.54	44.22	11.54	44.22	11.54	44.37	11.54	44.37
L1	18.28	63.58	21.9	63.27	22.57	61.4	22.12	61.71
Skew	21.9	**65.19**	22.12	63.41	22.57	62.7	22.35	62.92
Conjunctions + Ontology								
Cosine	5.42	63.12	5.64	64.04	6.32	64.17	5.42	62.52
JS	10.61	51.18	10.84	46.09	10.61	43.59	11.06	44.88
Jaccard	11.09	44.93	11.09	44.93	11.09	44.81	11.09	44.81
L1	5.42	66.82	5.64	64.46	5.87	63.59	5.87	62.78
Skew	5.42	65.82	5.64	64.99	5.87	63.43	5.87	63.39
Conjunctions + Ontology (Category)								
Cosine	10.16	47.84	3.16	42.84	5.87	45.76	5.19	43.16
JS	10.61	51.18	10.84	46.09	1.36	38.65	0.9	34.92
Jaccard	11.09	44.93	11.09	44.93	11.09	44.81	11.09	44.81
L1	13.77	55.78	5.42	49.7	9.71	44.03	6.55	49.14
Skew	14.67	59.79	6.77	58.04	7.9	53.71	6.32	59.06
Conjunctions + Ontology (Centroid)								
Cosine	22.35	63.57	22.12	61.05	22.12	60.66	20.99	60.62
JS	10.61	51.18	10.84	46.09	10.38	42.33	10.61	43.39
Jaccard	11.09	44.93	11.09	44.93	11.09	44.81	11.09	44.81
L1	23.02	63.27	22.8	62.53	22.8	61.72	22.12	61.89
Skew	13.54	62.63	**23.02**	64.11	19.86	63.47	21.9	**64.33**
Conjunctions + Ontology (Centroid) + Anaphora Resolution								
Cosine	22.25	64.8	22.7	62.19	22.92	61.69	22.25	61.06
JS	10.11	49.12	11.01	45.58	11.24	43.6	10.36	43.16
Jaccard	10.59	42.8	10.59	42.8	10.59	43.1	10.59	43.1
L1	23.15	**65.45**	23.37	63.92	23.6	63.32	23.37	63.42
Skew	15.28	65.17	**23.82**	65.04	18.88	64.49	23.37	64.69
Conjunctions + Ontology (Centroid) + Web Crawling								
Cosine	25.4	65.43	25.6	64.46	25.6	63.94	24.4	61.9
JS	6.25	45.61	3.63	39.72	3.43	23.63	1.81	20.17
Jaccard	12.1	51.01	12.1	51.01	10.08	50.4	10.08	50.4
L1	24.4	64.22	25.81	64.43	25.81	63.72	24.6	62.41
Skew	9.07	64.68	**26.21**	**65.91**	12.1	64.31	25.2	65.18

method does indeed yield better results, whereas the standard (no vector normalization) and the category method (standard vector normalization) actually make the results worse. The best result with the centroid method is an F-measure of 23.02% and a learning accuracy of 64.11% (using the Skew divergence and the conditional probability weighting). The best overall learning accuracy of 64.33% is obtained with the weighting based on Resnik's measure and the Skew divergence.

Anaphora Resolution

As another approach to overcome the problem of data sparseness, we explored the impact of anaphora resolution on the task of named entity recognition. Based on MINIPAR (cf. [Lin, 1993]) and the work by Lappin and Leass [Lappin and Leass, 1994], we implemented an algorithm for identifying intra-sentential antecedents of personal pronouns which replaces each (non-pleonastic) anaphoric reference by the grammatically correct form of the corresponding antecedent as shown in the following example:

*The port capital of Vathy is dominated by **its** fortified Venetian harbor.*

which is converted into:

*The port capital of Vathy is dominated by **Vathy's** fortified Venetian harbor.*

Or the following one:

*Holiday hooligans used to head to nearby Benitses, until **it** was ruined, so now **they** head north to cut a swathe through the coastline's few remaining unspoilt coves and fishing villages.*

which is transformed into:

*Holiday hooligans used to head to nearby Benitses, until **Benitses** was ruined, so now **the hooligans** head north to cut a swathe through the coastline's few remaining unspoilt coves and fishing villages.*

In order to improve the detection of pleonastic occurrences of *it*, we used a modified set of patterns developed by Dimitrov [Dimitrov, 2002]. Although our implementation seems to perform a bit worse than the one by Lappin and Leass (maybe due to the very noisy data set) the evaluation yielded a remarkable precision of about 79% and a recall of approximately 70%.

As shown by Table 8.2, the use of anaphora resolution even improves the results we obtained by exploiting the taxonomy, leading to an F-measure of

23.82% and a learning accuracy of 65.04% (Skew divergence). The overall best learning accuracy of 65.45% is obtained with no feature weighting and using the L1 norm as similarity measure.

Downloading Documents from the Web

Since named entities tend to occur less often than common nouns representing possible classes, they are to a particularly high degree affected by the problem of data sparseness. We address this issue by downloading from the web a set of at most 20 additional documents D_i for each named entity i. Moreover, in order to make sure that each $d \in D_i$ belongs to the correct sense of i, we compare d with all documents in the original corpus containing at least one occurrence of i. The decision whether to keep d or not is made by creating bag-of-words style vector representations for each of the involved documents, computing their cosine and only considering the document if the similarity is over an empirically determined threshold of 0.2. Table 8.2 shows that this way of extending the corpus with documents from the web notably improves all previous results. With the Skew divergence, we achieved an F-measure of 26.21% and a learning accuracy of 65.91%, which is also the overall best learning accuracy. It is important to emphasize that the anaphora resolution component has not been applied to the documents downloaded from the Web, so that the results for the Anaphora Resolution (AR) and Web Crawling (WC) versions are reported separately in the following.

8.2.3.4 Post-processing

Finally, we also examine a post-processing step in which the k best answers of the system (ranked according to their corresponding similarities from highest to lowest) are checked for their statistical plausibility on the Web. For this purpose, inspired by the work of Markert et al. [Markert et al., 2003], for each named entity e and the top k answers $c_1, .., c_k$ we generate the following Hearst-style [Hearst, 1992] pattern strings and count their occurrences on the Web by using the Google Web API:

$\pi(c_i)$ such as e
e and other $\pi(c_i)$
e or other $\pi(c_i)$
$\pi(c_i)$, especially e
$\pi(c_i)$, including e

where $\pi(w)$ is the result of looking up the plural form of the word w in the lexicon containing word forms delivered with LoPar (see Section 4.1). The number of hits of the above pattern strings are normalized by dividing through the number of hits of the underlined parts. At the end, that answer of the k best is chosen which maximizes the sum of these coefficients. We experimented with different values for k, i.e. 3, 5 and 10. This extension is efficient as we only need to generate $k + 1$ queries per pattern to the Google Web API for each named entity. Table 8.3 gives the results of this step when post-processing the results produced with the versions of our system using anaphora resolution and crawling documents from the Web. The results show that the F-measures increase considerably when using our post-processing step. The best result is an F-measure of 32.6% with a precision of 36.82%, a recall of 29.24% and a learning accuracy of 69.87% for the version of our system including this post-processing step.

Table 8.3. Results of the post-processing step on the Anaphora Resolution and Web Crawling versions (in percent)

	F	P	R	LA
Baseline				
AR (Anaphora Resolution)	23.82	31.55	19.13	65.04
WC (Web Crawling)	26.21	29.68	23.47	65.91
Post-processing				
k=3				
AR + Post-processing	29.15	38.46	23.47	71.04
WC + Post-processing	30.58	34.54	27.44	67.71
k=5				
AR + Post-processing	28.7	37.87	23.1	71
WC + Post-processing	30.78	34.77	27.62	68.52
k=10				
AR + Post-processing	30.72	40.53	24.73	71.71
WC + Post-processing	**32.6**	36.82	29.24	**69.87**

8.2.3.5 Discussion

The best result of our approach is an F-measure of 32.6%, which is more than 32 points above the naive baseline of F= 0.15%, consisting in randomly assigning a class to an instance. Further, our results are almost 20 points over the majority-class-baseline of F=12.64%, calculated assuming that all instances are assigned to the class most frequently used by the annotators, i.e. country. With respect to the word-window based approach, we have yielded an absolute improvement of 12.9 points. The best version of our approach, crawling additional texts from the Web and using the post-processing step achieves a precision of 36.82%, a recall of 29.34% as well as a learning accuracy of almost 70%. Given the difficulty of the task, these results are very encouraging.

8.2.4 Summary

We have addressed the problem of tagging named entities with regard to a large set of concepts as specified by a given concept hierarchy. In particular, we have presented an approach relying on Harris' distributional hypothesis as well as on the vector-space model which assigns a named entity to that concept which maximizes the contextual similarity with the named entity in question. The aim has not been to present a fully fledged system performing this task, but to investigate the impact of varying a number of parameters. In this line we have shown that the pseudo-syntactic dependencies we have considered are an interesting alternative to window-based approaches as they yield a higher learning accuracy and also allow for a more efficient computation of the similarities. To address the typical data sparseness problem one encounters when working with corpora, we have examined the impact of (i) exploiting conjunctions, (ii) factoring the underlying taxonomy into the computation of the concept vectors as in the approach of Pekar and Staab [Pekar and Staab, 2002], (iii) getting additional context by applying an anaphora resolution algorithm developed for this purpose, and (iv) downloading additional documents from the World Wide Web as done by Agirre et al. [Agirre et al., 2000], showing that with the correct settings, all these techniques improve the results of our approach both in terms of F-measure and learning accuracy. Finally, we have also presented a post-processing step by which the system's k most highly ranked answers are checked for their statistical plausibility on the Web, which notably improves the results of the approach. In general, the best results were achieved using the conditional probability as feature weighting strategy and the Skew divergence as similarity measure, thus confirming the results obtained by Lee [Lee, 1999]. Especially successful has been our post-processing step in which certain classification hypotheses are validated with respect to their statistical plausibility with respect to the Web. In the following section, we present an approach relying on the statistical distribution of lexico-syntactic patterns matched in the Web with the help of a standard web search engine.

8.3 Learning by Googling

Inspired by current social studies such as the one of Surowiecki [Surowiecki, 2004], in which it is argued that collective knowledge is much more powerful than individual knowledge, we present in this section a new paradigm of dealing with the problem of automatically populating ontologies. In very general terms our paradigm *Learning by Googling* is based on the idea that collective knowledge is gathered as a first step and then as a second step filtered, either automatically or manually by a knowledge engineer. In fact, if the collective knowledge is presented to a knowledge engineer, he can then effectively and efficiently customize this collective knowledge with regard to the specific context of interest. In this model, the purpose of general knowledge is to compensate the potential lack of knowledge of an individual with respect to a certain topic, while the role of the individual is to filter the collective knowledge with regard to a specific context. With respect to the task of populating ontologies, our *Learning by Googling* paradigm would collect evidence from the Web for the different concepts a given instance could belong to. The evidence collected can then be used either to find the concept with the maximal evidence automatically, or be presented to a knowledge engineer who selects the most appropriate concept given a certain context. This abstract model is instantiated by our PANKOW (Pattern-based Annotation through Knowledge on the Web) approach [Cimiano et al., 2004a] as well as by its successor C-PANKOW [Cimiano et al., 2005b]. The core of PANKOW is a pattern generation mechanism which creates pattern strings out of a certain pattern schema conveying a specific semantic relation, an instance to be annotated and all the concepts from a given ontology. It counts the occurrences of these pattern strings on the Web using the Google™ API. The ontological instance in question is then annotated semantically according to what could be termed *principle of maximal evidence*, that means, with the concept having the largest number of hits. The approach is in principle semi-supervised as a set of patterns is provided. However, these patterns do not vary from domain to domain such that from a practical point of view the system is actually unsupervised in the sense that it needs no training data to adapt to a new domain.

PANKOW has originally been conceived to support a web-page annotator in the task of assigning the instances appearing in a web page to the appropriate concept in a given ontology in line with the CREAM framework [Handschuh, 2005]. In particular, PANKOW generates instances of lexico-syntactic patterns indicating a certain semantic relation and counts their occurrences in the World Wide Web using the Google™ API. The statistical distribution of instances of these patterns then constitutes the collective knowledge which is taken into account by the annotator to decide which concept to annotate the instance with in the particular context.

Let us assume, for example, that the string *'Niger'* appears on a web page and we have no idea about how to annotate it. Figure 8.1 shows the collective knowledge about which concept *'Niger'* belongs to. This collective knowledge is the result of aggregating the counts for different patterns conveying an instance-of relation between Niger and the concepts displayed. Intuitively, given these figures, we would naturally tend to annotate *'Niger'* as a river as it seems to be its most prominent meaning on the Web.

Figure 8.2, for example, shows a screenshot of OntoMat Annotizer [Handschuh and Staab, 2002], depicting a dialog in which the user is presented with the top 5 suggestions from the collective knowledge about how to annotate the instance *Niger*, i.e. as a river, as a country, etc. The advantage of such an approach combining collective and individual knowledge to overcome the knowledge-acquisition bottleneck seems thus obvious: even if the individual

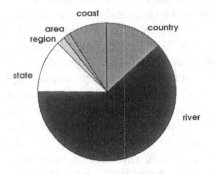

Fig. 8.1. Collective knowledge about Niger

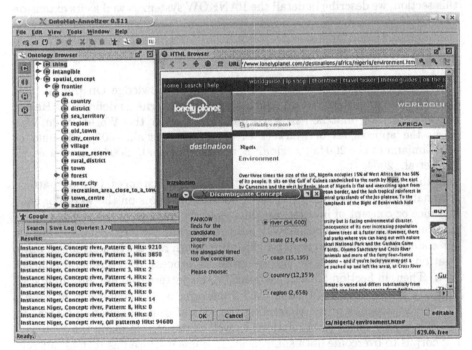

Fig. 8.2. PANKOW within an annotation scenario (interactive mode)

has never heard about the instance in question, together with the collective knowledge and the local context in which the instance appears, he might get a fairly accurate idea of the concept it belongs to.

This illustrates the fact that formal (semantic) annotations can be approximated to a certain extent by considering the statistical distribution of certain syntactic structures over the web. In this line, in [Cimiano et al., 2004a] we presented our vision of a 'Self-Annotating Web' in which globally available syntactic resources are considered to support metadata creation. The main idea herein is to approximate semantics by considering information about the statistical distribution of certain syntactic structures over the Web.

However, as Niger can be a country or a river depending on the context in which it appears, the example also shows that ambiguity is an important problem we need to deal with in such an approach. C-PANKOW [Cimiano et al., 2005b], as a further development of PANKOW, tackles — among others — the issue of ambiguity by taking into account the page on which the entity in question appears as context in order to select its most relevant sense or meaning. Furthermore, it also reduces the querying complexity of PANKOW, thus making it scalable to larger ontologies. In the remainder of this section, we describe in detail the PANKOW system as well as its extension C-PANKOW.

8.3.1 PANKOW

PANKOW (Pattern-based ANnotation through Knowledge On the Web) is based on the idea that certain lexico-syntactic patterns as defined by Hearst can not only be matched in a corpus, but also in the World Wide Web as in the approaches of Markert et al. [Markert et al., 2003], Cimiano et al. [Cimiano et al., 2004a], Etzioni et al. [Etzioni et al., 2004a] or Cui et al. [Cui et al., 2004].

For this purpose, PANKOW generates pattern instances out of pattern schemata and counts the hits of these pattern instances on the web. For each instance or concept of interest, we thus yield the number of times it is related to other entities in the specific way indicated by the pattern schema. Thus we get a *statistical web fingerprint* for this object with respect to a given semantic relation. In what follows, we first describe the process from a general point of view. Then, in Section 8.3.1.2, we describe the patterns we use and finally we formally define what a statistical web fingerprint is and how it can be used.

The approach is novel, combining the idea of using linguistic patterns to identify certain ontological relations as well as the idea of using the Web as a big corpus to overcome data sparseness. It is unsupervised as it does not rely on any training data annotated by hand, and it is pattern-based in the sense that it makes use of linguistically motivated regular expressions to identify instance-concept relations in text. The driving principle behind PANKOW is that of *disambiguation by maximal evidence* in the sense that, for a given instance, it proposes the concept with the maximal evidence derived from Web statistics. This section is structured as follows: Section 8.3.1.1 presents the process of PANKOW, which instantiates the abstract model of *Learning by Googling*, in particular describing the pattern library used. Section 8.3.1.3

formally introduces statistical web fingerprints as used in PANKOW. Section 8.3.1.4 describes the evaluation of PANKOW and Section 8.3.3 concludes this section with a brief summary.

8.3.1.1 The Process of PANKOW

The process of PANKOW, which instantiates our *Learning By Googling* paradigm, consists of three steps:

Input: a set of entities (instances or concepts) to be classified with regard to an ontology.

Step 1: The system iterates through the set of entities to be classified and generates instances of patterns, one for each concept in the ontology. For example, the instance South Africa and the concepts country and hotel are composed using a pattern schema of our pattern library (see 8.3.1.2) and resulting in pattern instances like ''*South Africa is a country*'' and ''*South Africa is a hotel*'' or ''*countries such as South Africa*'' and ''*hotels such as South Africa*''.

Result 1: A set of pattern instances generated as described above.

Step 2: Then, Google™ is queried for the pattern instances through its Web service API. The API delivers as its results:

Result 2: the counts for each pattern instance.

Step 3: The system sums up the query results to a total for each concept.

Result: The *statistical web fingerprint* for each entity, that is, the results of aggregating for each entity the number of Google™ counts for all pattern instances conveying the relation of interest.

The statistical web fingerprint then represents the collective knowledge about the potential concepts an instance could belong to or about the potential superconcepts of a certain concept. Given the tasks of (i) classifying instances with regard to an ontology or (ii) finding an appropriate superconcept for a new concept, a knowledge engineer could be presented with the most relevant *view* of a statistical web fingerprint in order to take a final decision.

Figure 8.3 depicts an example of how PANKOW can be employed in an annotation scenario. The figure illustrates the principle of disambiguation by maximal evidence within an annotation scenario.

8.3.1.2 The Pattern Library

In the following, we describe the patterns we use and give a corresponding example. It is important to emphasize that the pattern library in the case of PANKOW consists of plain strings which are sent to the Google API as search queries.

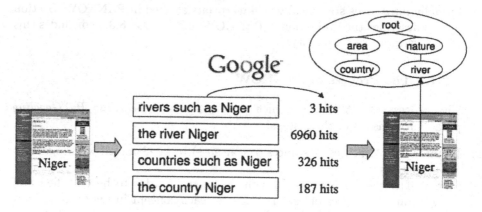

Fig. 8.3. PANKOW within an annotation scenario (automatic mode)

Hearst Patterns

The first four patterns have been used by Hearst to identify *isa*-relationships between the concepts referred to by two words in the text. However, they can also be used to spot *instance-of*-relations. In fact, in PANKOW they are used as indicating *subclass* as well as *instance-of* relations, depending on whether the entity to be classified is an instance or a concept. Correspondingly, we formulate our patterns using the variable i standing for the name of an instance and the variables c_{sup} and c_{sub} standing for the name of a concept from the given ontology. The plural of c is denoted by $\pi(c)$ as usual and is generated in the context of these experiments by a simply heuristic, that is, adding an 's' at the end of the word.

The patterns reused from Hearst are:

HEARST1: $\pi(c_{sup})$ such as $(i \mid c_{sub})$

HEARST2: such $\pi(c_{sup})$ as $(i \mid c_{sub})$

HEARST3: $\pi(c_{sup})$, (especially|including) $(i \mid c_{sub})$

HEARST4: $(i \mid c_{sub})$ (and | or) other $\pi(c_{sup})$

Depending on whether we are attempting to classify an instance or a concept, we would then either derive: instance-of(i,c_{sup}) or subconcept(c_{sub},c_{sup}). The above patterns would match the following expressions:

continents such as Asia (HEARST1)
vehicles such as cars (HEARST1)
such continents as Africa (HEARST2)
such cars as cabriolets (HEARST2)

presidents, especially George Washington (HEARST3)
vehicles, especially motor-bikes (HEARST3)
the Eiffel Tower and other sights in Paris (HEARST4)
motor-bikes and other two-wheeled vehicles (HEARST4)

Definites

The next patterns are about *definites*, that means, noun phrases introduced by the definite determiner *'the'*. Frequently, definites actually refer to some entity previously mentioned in the text. In this sense, a phrase like *'the hotel'* does not stand for itself, but it points anaphorically to a unique hotel occurring in the preceding text. Nevertheless, it has also been shown that in common texts more than 50% of all definite expressions are non-referring [Poesio and Vieira, 1998], i.e. they exhibit sufficient descriptive content to enable the reader to uniquely determine the entity referred to from the global context. For example, the definite description *'the Hilton hotel'* has sufficient descriptive power to uniquely pick-out the corresponding real-world entity for most readers. One may deduce that *'Hilton'* is the name of the real-world entity of type hotel to which the above expression refers.

Consequently, we apply the following two patterns to categorize an instance by definite expressions:

DEFINITE1: the i c

DEFINITE2: the c i

The first and the second pattern would, for example, match the expressions *'the Hilton hotel'* and *'the hotel Hilton'*, respectively. It is important to mention that in our approach these patterns are only used to categorize instances with respect to the ontology, but not concepts.

Apposition and Copula

The following pattern makes use of the fact that certain entities appearing in a text are further described in terms of an apposition as in *'Excelsior, a hotel in the center of Nancy'*. The pattern capturing this intuition looks as follows:

APPOSITION: $(i \mid c_{sub})$, a c_{sup}

The most explicit way of expressing that a certain entity is an instance or a subconcept of a certain concept is by the verb *'to be'* in a copula construction as *'The Excelsior is a nice hotel in the center of Nancy'*, for example. The pattern is defined as follows:

COPULA: $(i \mid c_{sub})$ is a c_{sup}

8.3.1.3 Statistical Web Fingerprints

Having defined these patterns, one could match them in a corpus and propose the corresponding relations. However, it is well known that the above patterns occur rarely and consequently one will need a sufficiently big corpus to find a significant number of matches.

Thus, PANKOW resorts to the biggest corpus available: the World Wide Web. In fact, several researchers have shown that using the Web as a corpus is an effective way of addressing the typical data sparseness problem one encounters when working with corpora (compare [Grefenstette, 1999], [Keller et al., 2002], [Markert et al., 2003], [Resnik and Smith, 2003]). We subscribe to the principal idea by Markert *et al.* [Markert et al., 2003] of exploiting the Google^{TM} API. As in their approach, rather than actually downloading web pages for further processing, we just take the number of web pages in which a certain pattern appears as an indicator for the strength of the pattern.

Given a candidate entity we want to classify with regard to an existing ontology, we instantiate the above patterns with each concept from the given ontology. For each pattern instance, we query the Google^{TM} API for the number of documents that contain it. The function *count* models this query:

$$count : E \times C \times P \to \mathbb{N} \qquad (8.5)$$

Thereby, E, C and P stand for the set of all entities to be classified, for the concepts from a given ontology and for a set of pattern schema, respectively. Thus, $count(e, c, p)$ returns the number of hits of pattern schema p instantiated with the entity e and the concept c. We define the sum over all the patterns conveying a certain relation r:

$$count_r(e, c) = \sum_{p \in P_r} count(e, c, p) \qquad (8.6)$$

where P_r is the set of pattern schemata denoting a certain relation r.

Now we formally define the statistical web fingerprint of an entity e with respect to a relation r and a set of concepts C:

$$SF(e, r, C) := \{(c, n) \mid c \in C \land n = count_r(e, c)\} \qquad (8.7)$$

Instead of considering the complete statistical web fingerprints, we consider views of these such as defined by the following formulas. The first formula defines a view of the statistical web fingerprint which only contains the concept with maximal number of hits:

$$SF_{max}(e, r, C) := \{(c, n) \mid c := argmax_{c' \in C} \, count_r(e, c') \land$$
$$n = count_r(e, c)\} \qquad (8.8)$$

Here we assume that *argmax* breaks ties randomly so that SF_{max} is a singleton set. We extend this to consider the top-m concepts with maximal count:

$$
\begin{aligned}
SF_m(e,r,C) := \{(c,n) \mid{} & C = \{c_1, c_2, ..., c_{|C|}\} \wedge \\
& count_r(e, c_1) \le ... \le count_r(e, c_{|C|}) \wedge \\
& c \in \{c_1, ..., c_m\} \wedge n = count_r(e, c)\} \; if \; m \le |C| \quad (8.9)
\end{aligned}
$$

Finally, we also define a view that takes into account only those concepts having hits over a certain threshold θ:

$$
SF_\theta(e,r,C) := \{(c,n) \mid count_r(e,c) \ge \theta \wedge n = count_r(e,c)\} \quad (8.10)
$$

We can now combine these views by set operations. For example, we yield the set of the m top concepts having hits over a threshold θ as follows:

$$
SF_{m,\theta}(e,r,C) = SF_m(e,r,C) \cap SF_\theta(e,r,C) \quad (8.11)
$$

As an example of such a view, let us consider again the visualization of the SF_6 view of the statistical web fingerprint for Niger with regard to the *instance-of* relation in Figure 8.1.

8.3.1.4 Evaluation

We evaluate our approach with respect to the LonelyPlanet dataset as described in Section 5.3. In particular, we compare the answers of our system with the reference standards for subjects A and B and also evaluate PANKOW using the precision, recall and F_1 measure, averaging over both annotators as described in 8.2.2. It is important to mention that we only take into account the 59 concepts used by the annotators as possible categories. Hereby, I stands for the set of instances to be assigned to an appropriate concept.

As answers $S_{max,\theta}$ of the system we consider the following set:

$$
S_{max,\theta} := \{(i,c) \mid i \in I \wedge \{(c,n)\} = SF_{max,\theta}(i, instance\text{-}of, C)\} \quad (8.12)
$$

where $SF_{max,\theta} = SF_{max} \cap SF_\theta$.

Precision, recall and F_1-Measure are defined as follows:

$$
P_y = \frac{|\text{correct answers}|}{|\text{total answers}|} = \frac{|S_{max,\theta} \cap C_y|}{|S_{max,\theta}|} \quad (8.13)
$$

$$
R_y = \frac{|\text{correct answers}|}{|\text{answers in reference standard}|} = \frac{|S_{max,\theta} \cap C_y|}{|C_y|} \quad (8.14)
$$

$$F_{1,y} = \frac{2 * P_y * R_y}{P_y + R_y} \qquad (8.15)$$

Furthermore, in our experiments we average the results for both annotators as given by the following formulas:

$$P_{avg} = \frac{P_A + P_B}{2} \qquad (8.16)$$

$$R_{avg} = \frac{R_A + R_B}{2} \qquad (8.17)$$

$$F_{1,avg} = \frac{F_{1,A} + F_{1,B}}{2} \qquad (8.18)$$

To get an upper bound for the task we are looking at, we also calculate the F_1-Measure of $Standard_A$ measured against $Standard_B$ and the other way round, yielding F_1=62.09% as average. This value thus represents an upper bound for any system attempting to find the correct class for an unknown instance.

Table 8.4 shows the top 50 $SF_{max}(i,\text{instance-of}, C)$ values for different instances i. Whereas some classifications are definitely spurious, it can be appreciated in general that the results are quite reasonable. Figure 8.4 shows the precision, recall and F_1-Measure values for different thresholds θ within the interval $[0..1000]$, averaged over both reference standards: $Standard_A$ and $Standard_B$. Obviously, the precision increases roughly proportionally to the threshold θ, while the recall and F_1-Measure values decrease. It can be observed that P=R=F at $\theta = 0$. The best $F_{1,avg}$-Measure was 28.24% at a threshold of $\theta = 60$, and the best recall (R_{avg}) was 24.9% at a threshold of $\theta = 0$.

In a second version of the experiment, instead of merely choosing the concept with maximal count with respect to the statistical web fingerprint, we considered the top 5 concepts, i.e. the view $SF_{5,\theta} = SF_5 \cap SF_\theta$, and considered the answer as correct if the annotator's answer was in this view. The results in terms of the same measures are given in Figure 8.5. The qualitative behavior of the three measures is similar as in the first experiment, but obviously the results are much better. The best F_1-Measure of 51.64% was reached at a threshold of $\theta = 50$, corresponding to a precision of 66.01% and a recall of 42.42%. Concluding, these results mean that in 66% of the cases the correct concept for an instance is among the top 5 suggestions and, on the other hand, for more than 40% of the instances the system is able to suggest up to 5 concepts, one of which is the correct one. This is certainly a very satisfactory result and a good proof that using our PANKOW methodology to gather collective knowledge in the form of statistical web fingerprints and presenting certain views of these to a user would drastically help to reduce the time taken to annotate a given web page. Though the results seem very promising, there are two main drawbacks of the system. On the one hand, the number

Table 8.4. Top 50 instance-concept relations

Instance	Concept	# Google^{TM} Matches
Atlantic	city	1520837
Bahamas	island	649166
USA	country	582275
Connecticut	state	302814
Caribbean	sea	227279
Mediterranean	sea	212284
South Africa	town	178146
Canada	country	176783
Guatemala	city	174439
Africa	region	131063
Australia	country	128607
France	country	125863
Germany	country	124421
Easter	island	96585
St Lawrence	river	65095
Commonwealth	state	49692
New Zealand	island	40711
Adriatic	sea	39726
Netherlands	country	37926
St John	church	34021
Belgium	country	33847
San Juan	island	31994
Mayotte	island	31540
EU	country	28035
UNESCO	organization	27739
Austria	group	24266
Greece	island	23021
Malawi	lake	21081
Israel	country	19732
Perth	street	17880
Luxembourg	city	16393
Nigeria	state	15650
St Croix	river	14952
Nakuru	lake	14840
Kenya	country	14382
Benin	city	14126
Cape Town	city	13768
St Thomas	church	13554
Niger	river	13091
Christmas Day	day	12088
Ghana	country	10398
Crete	island	9902
Antarctic	continent	9270
Zimbabwe	country	9224
Central America	region	8863
Reykjavik	island	8381
Greenland	sea	8043
Cow	town	7964
Expo	area	7481
Ibiza	island	6788

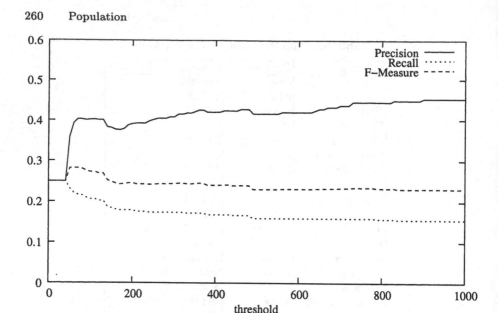

Fig. 8.4. Precision, recall and F_1-Measure for $S_{max,\theta}$ over threshold θ (instance classification)

of queries issued to Google™ is proportional to the number of concepts in the ontology, thus not allowing the system to scale to very large ontologies with hundreds of concepts. In our experiments, we have therefore restricted the number of possible categories to the 59 used by the annotators.

On the other hand, the pattern matching is quite limited due to the problems related to the correct generation of plural forms and the limits of using a keyword based search engine for matching the patterns. Recall that the patterns used in PANKOW are merely plain strings which are sent to the Google API as queries. In particular, no sophisticated linguistic analysis to match more complex noun phrases can be performed in these settings. In the following section, we present the successor of PANKOW – called C-PANKOW – which partially alleviates these problems.

8.3.2 C-PANKOW

C-PANKOW [Cimiano et al., 2005b] has been developed to address some of the shortcomings of PANKOW. First, due to the restrictions of the pattern generation process, a lot of actual instances of the pattern schemata are not found. In particular the approach exhibits problems generating the correct plural forms of concept labels as well as matching more complex linguistic structures such as noun phrases including determiners, noun modifiers, etc. We overcome this problem in C-PANKOW by actually downloading the pages, analyzing them linguistically and matching the patterns instead of merely

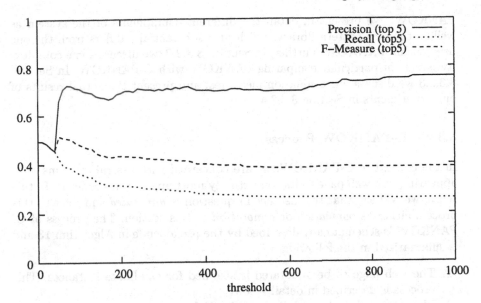

Fig. 8.5. Precision, recall and F_1-measure and recall for $S_{5,\theta}$ over threshold θ (instance classification)

generating plain strings and counting their Google™ hits. The results of the pattern-matching are also linguistically normalized, that means, words are mapped to their base forms, thus completely solving the problem with the generation of plural forms.

At the same time, we overcome the second problem in this way, i.e. the large number of queries sent to the Google™ Web API. In fact, by downloading the pages and processing them locally, we reduce network traffic. PANKOW issues a number of Google™ queries proportional to the size of the ontology considered. PANKOW does therefore not scale to larger ontologies. In C-PANKOW, we generate only a constant number of queries per instance to classify. As a result, C-PANKOW is able to annotate using very large ontologies. PANKOW was already able to take into account more concepts than standard named entity recognition systems, but C-PANKOW is able to consider even more concepts than PANKOW and furthermore achieves a better runtime behavior.

Third and most importantly, we contextualize the pattern matching by distinguishing between relevant and non-relevant pages. Hereby, relevance assessment boils down to calculating the similarity of the involved pages. We present an evaluation of our system analyzing the impact of our notion of contextual relevance as well as varying the number of pages downloaded. The remainder of this section is structured as follows: Section 8.3.2.1 presents the process underlying C-PANKOW, which substantially differs from the one of

PANKOW. We present in detail the different components of the system as well as the new pattern library, which also substantially differs from the one used within PANKOW. Further, in Section 8.3.2.2, we discuss some complexity issues, in particular comparing PANKOW with C-PANKOW. In Section 8.3.2.3 we discuss our evaluation measures, and present the actual results of our experiments in Section 8.3.2.4.

8.3.2.1 C-PANKOW Process

In the context of C-PANKOW, we are concerned with assigning an instance appearing in a web page to its contextually most appropriate concept. In this sense, we will say that the instance in question is *annotated* and refer to this process either as *population* or *annotation* in this section. The process of C-PANKOW is schematically described by the pseudocode in Algorithm 13 and is summarized in the following.

1. The web page to be annotated is scanned for candidate instances. This process is described in detail below.
2. Then, for each instance i discovered and for each clue–pattern pair in our pattern library P (described in detail below), an automatically generated query is issued to Google™ and the abstracts or snippets of the n first hits are downloaded.
3. Then the similarity between the document to be annotated and the downloaded abstract is calculated. If the similarity is above a given threshold t, the actual pattern found in the abstract reveals a phrase which may possibly describe the concept that the instance belongs to in the context in question. The way the similarity is computed is described below.
4. The pattern matched in a certain Google™ abstract is only considered if the similarity between the original page and this abstract is above a given threshold. In this way the pattern-matching process is contextualized.
5. Finally, the instance i is annotated with that concept c having the largest number as well as most contextually relevant hits.

In what follows, we describe in detail every important step of the algorithm, such as the procedure to recognize named entities in web pages as well as the process of downloading Google™ abstracts. We also describe how the similarity is computed as well as our pattern library. Finally, some complexity issues are discussed and the whole process is illustrated by means of a running example. In particular, all process steps will be discussed with respect to the web page depicted in Figure 8.6.

Instance Recognition

In order to detect candidate instances in a web page, first the complete HTML markup is eliminated and the text body of the page extracted. This step is necessary because a part-of-speech tagger is applied to assign word categories

---

Algorithm 13 C-PANKOW's process in pseudocode

```
C-PANKOW(document d, threshold t)
{
    /* recognize all the instances in input document */
    I = recognizeInstances(d);
    foreach i ∈ I
    {
        foreach (p,c) ∈ P
        {
            /* download the n first Google^TM abstracts
            matching the exact query c(i) */
            Abstracts = downloadGoogleAbstracts(c(i),n);
            foreach a in Abstracts
            {
                /* calculate the similarity between the
                document d and the Google^TM abstract a */
                sim = calculateSimilarity(a,d);
                if (sim > t)
                {
                    if (p.matches(a))
                    {
                        c = p.getConcept();
                        Hits[c] = Hits[c] + 1;
                    }
                }
            }
        }
    }
    annotate(i,maxarg_c Hits[c]);
}
```

---

to every token of the extracted text and the tagger is not able to handle HTML markup.[4] Then the text is split into sentences, and every string which matches the following pattern is interpreted as an instance:

INSTANCE := (\w+{DT})? ([a-z]+{JJ})? PRE (MID POST)?

PRE := POST := (([A-Z][a-z]*){NNS|NNP|NN|NP|JJ|UH})+

MID := the{DT} | of{IN} | −{−} | '{POS} |
  (de|la|los|las|del){FW} | [a-z]+{NP|NPS|NN|NNS}

---

[4] We use the QTag part-of-speech tagger in http://web.bham.ac.uk/O.Mason/ software/tagger/. QTag's part-of-speech tagset can be found at http://www. ling.ohio-state.edu/~ntyson/tagset/english-tagset.txt.

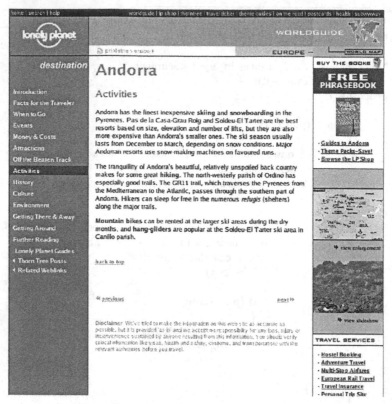

Fig. 8.6. Lonely Planet destinations description of Andorra from http://www.lonelyplanet.com/destinations/europe/andorra/activities.htm

These expressions are intended to be interpreted as standard regular expressions over words and their corresponding part-of-speech tags, which are indicated in curly brackets. Paraphrasing, INSTANCE matches each optional sequence of arbitrary characters (\w+) tagged as a determiner (DT), followed optionally by a sequence of small letters ([a-z]+) tagged as an adjective (JJ), followed by an expression matching the regular expression denoted by PRE, which in turn can be optionally followed by an expression matching the concatenation of MID and POST. Thereby, PRE and POST match a sequence of tokens in which the first character is capitalized and tagged either as a plural proper noun (NPS), a plural common noun (NNS), a common noun (NN), a proper noun (NP), an adjective (JJ) or an interjection UH[5]. MID matches a sequence of determiners *'the'*, prepositions *'of'*, the possessive marker ', a hyphen *'-'*, a foreign word FW such as *'de'*, *'del'*, *'las'*, *'los'*, *'las'*, a lower

---

[5] This is important for processing Asian names which sometimes are tagged as 'UH' by the part-of-speech tagger.

case singular or plural proper and common nouns. For example, the tagged sequence Pas{NP} de{FW} la {FW} Casa{NP} (compare Figure 8.6) would be recognized as an instance, whereby *'Pas'* would match the PRE, *'de la'* the MIDDLE and *'Casa'* the POST part of the above regular expression. The instances discovered this way in our running example web page are given in Table 8.5 as a cross 'X' in the S(system) column.

Downloading Google™ Abstracts

The patterns in C-PANKOW's pattern library are actually tuples (p, c) where p is a regular expression defined over part-of-speech tags as described above, and c a function $c : string \rightarrow string$ called the *clue* (compare the approach to learning qualia structures described in Section 7.4). Given an instance $i \in I$ and a clue c, the query $c(i)$ is sent to the Google™ API, and the abstracts of the first n documents matching this query are downloaded and processed to find instances of pattern p. For example, given the clue $f(x) = "such\ as\ " \oplus x$ and the instance *Seville*, n abstracts matching the query f(Seville), i.e. "such as Seville".[6] would be downloaded. Using such clues, a number of pages are downloaded, in which a corresponding pattern will probably be matched, consequently restricting the linguistic analysis to a few promising pages.

Similarity Assessment

As described in our pseudocode algorithm in Algorithm 13, the similarity between each downloaded abstract and the web page in question is calculated. For this purpose, stopwords from both documents are first removed and vectors representing the count for each word in the document in line with the bag-of-words model [Salton and McGill, 1983] are created. The cosine measure is used to calculate the similarity between the abstract and the document to be annotated. In particular, the similarity between the Google™-snippet and the document is measured as the cosine of the angle between their vectors (compare Section 4.1.5.2). Hereby, only those pages are considered relevant for which this similarity is over the threshold t, contextualizing the pattern-matching process as a result. Therefore, a certain instance can be annotated with a different concept in different contexts, i.e. web pages. In general, the intuition behind this is to yield more accurate annotations and to choose the contextually most appropriate sense or concept for a given instance in case it is ambiguous. As a byproduct, we only need to linguistically analyze those Google™ abstracts which seem relevant for the context in question. In Section 8.3.2.4, we also present the results of further experiments with different threshold values.

The Pattern Library

In what follows, we present the pattern library P we use and briefly describe the intuition behind each pattern. The patterns are in principle the same

---

[6] As usual, $\oplus$ denotes the concatenation operator defined on two strings.

as used in PANKOW (compare Section 8.3.1.2), but they are here extended with the corresponding clues. Furthermore, in contrast to PANKOW's pattern library, the patterns here are not plain string but tuples (p, c) where p is a regular expression defined over part-of-speech tags and c is a string issued as query to Google and used to download a number of snippets in which the pattern p is matched offline.

Hearst Patterns

Also in C-PANKOW we reuse the following patterns defined by Marti Hearst ([Hearst, 1992]):

HEARST1:= CONCEPT such{DT} as{IN} (INSTANCE ,?)+
         ((and|or){CC} INSTANCE)?

HEARST2:= CONCEPT ,? especially{RB}
         (INSTANCE ,?)+ ((and|or){CC} INSTANCE)?

HEARST3:= CONCEPT ,? including{RB}
         (INSTANCE ,?)+ ((and|or){CC} INSTANCE)?

HEARST4:= (INSTANCE ,?)+ and{CC} other{JJ} CONCEPT

HEARST5:= (INSTANCE ,?)+ or{CC} other{JJ} CONCEPT

where CONCEPT := (\w+{DT})? (\w+{JJ})? ([a-z]+{NN(S)?})+,
and the corresponding clues are:

$\text{clue}_{HEARST1}(x) =''\ such\ as''\oplus x$
$\text{clue}_{HEARST2}(x) =''\ especially''\oplus x$
$\text{clue}_{HEARST3}(x) =''\ including''\oplus x$
$\text{clue}_{HEARST4}(x) = x\oplus ``and\ other''$
$\text{clue}_{HEARST5}(x) = x\oplus ``or\ other''$

Definites

The following pattern is used to capture definite expressions:
DEFINITE: the{DT} (\w+{JJ})? INSTANCE CONCEPT,

whereby the corresponding clue is $\text{clue}_{DEFINITE}(x) =''\ the''\oplus x$. Note that we have not applied the dual pattern used in PANKOW (compare Section 8.3.1.2) due to the fact that it is difficult to define a reasonable clue given the actual search support of web search engines.

Copula

In order to match copula constructs, we use the following pattern:
INSTANCE \w+{BE(D?)(Z|R)} CONCEPT,

where *is, are, was* and *were* are tagged by the part-of-speech tagger as BEZ, BER, BEDZ and BEDR, respectively. The corresponding clue is $clue_{COPULA}(x) = x \oplus "is"$.

8.3.2.2 Complexity

The runtime complexity of C-PANKOW is $O(|I| \cdot |P| \cdot n)$, where $|I|$ is the total number of instances to be annotated, $|P|$ the number of patterns we use and n the maximum number of pages downloaded. As $|P|$ and n are constant and a document of size $|D|$ contains at most $|D|$ instances, the overall complexity of C-PANKOW is thus linear in the size of the document, i.e. $O(|D|)$. As the Google™ API does not allow to retrieve more than 10 documents per query, the number of queries sent to the Google™ API is $|P| \cdot (n \ div \ 10)$ per instance. In our special settings, ($|P| = 7$) we thus issue $7n \ div \ 10$ queries per instance independently of how big the ontology actually is. This is an important reduction of the number of queries compared to PANKOW, in which $|P'| * |C|$ queries are issued per instance, where $|C|$ indicates the number of concepts the ontology comprises. For a small set of concepts with $|C| = 59$ as well as $|P'| = 10$ this meant 590 queries per instance to be annotated. As C-PANKOW is independent of the size of the ontology, we can thus consider even larger ontologies than PANKOW, which already provided annotation based on much larger ontologies than most other approaches.

8.3.2.3 Evaluation

C-PANKOW has been evaluated on the same dataset and using the same evaluation measures as PANKOW with the crucial difference that the C-PANKOW system uses the 682 concepts of the pruned *Tourism* ontology as possible tags. For C-PANKOW, we additionally evaluate, on the one hand, the accuracy on the task of actually recognizing named entities in HTML pages. On the other hand, we also present results with respect to the learning accuracy introduced in Section 8.2.2.

Instance Detection

In order to detect potential instances in a web page to be annotated, we make use of the method described in Section 8.3.2.1. We apply this method to the dataset described above and compare the instances discovered by our system with the instances annotated by the annotators in terms of precision, recall and F-measure. More formally, let $I_{A,d}$ and $I_{B,d}$ be the set of instances annotated by subjects A and B in the document d, and let $I_{S,d}$ be the set of instances detected by the system in the same document d, then precision, recall and F-measure are defined as follows, where X stands proxy for A or B:

$$P^I_{X,d} = \frac{|I_{X,d} \cap I_{S,d}|}{|I_{S,d}|} \tag{8.19}$$

$$R^I_{X,d} = \frac{|I_{X,d} \cap I_{S,d}|}{|I_{X,d}|} \tag{8.20}$$

$$F^I_{X,d} = \frac{2 * P^I_{X,d} * R^I_{X,d}}{P^I_{X,d} + R^I_{X,d}} \tag{8.21}$$

For all measures reported in this section, i.e. precision, recall, F-Measure and learning accuracy, we average the results over both annotators, i.e.:

$$M_d = \frac{M_{A,d} + M_{B,d}}{2} \tag{8.22}$$

$$M = \sum_{d \in D} \frac{M_d}{|D|} \tag{8.23}$$

In our running example web page, the system detected 11 instances, while subject A found 9 and subject B 7 (compare Table 8.5). The system coincided with subjects A and B in 6 and 5 instances, respectively. This leads to the following results for our running example: $P^I_{A,d} = \frac{6}{11} = 54.55\%$, $P^I_{B,d} = \frac{5}{11} = 45.45\%$, $R^I_{A,d} = \frac{6}{9} = 66.67\%$, $R^I_{B,d} = \frac{5}{7} = 71.43\%$ and thus $F^I_{A,d} = 60\%$, $F^I_{B,d} = 55.55\%$. Thus, $P^I_d = 50\%$, $R^I_d = 69.05\%$ and $F^I_d = 57.78\%$. For the whole dataset, the system achieved a precision of $P^I = 43.75\%$, a recall of $R^I = 57.20\%$ and a F-measure of $F^I = 48.39\%$. In order to get an upper limit on the task, we also compared the precision, recall and F-measure of subject A against subject B and vice versa, yielding $F^I_{human} = 70.61\%$ as human performance on the task. While we are still quite far away from the human performance on the task, the results are as desired in the sense that we have a higher recall at the cost of a lower precision. This is useful as some of the spurious instances will be filtered out by the instance classification step due to the fact that if no patterns are found, the instance will not be assigned to any concept. Thus, the precision can be increased by the instance classification step, while the recall needs to be reasonably high as it can not be increased later.

Instance Classification

We evaluate the approach using the precision, recall and F-measures described in Section 8.3.1.4, but restricting the evaluation to the set of instances which both annotators annotated. Furthermore, we measure the results in terms of the learning accuracy described in Section 8.2.2.

Table 8.5. Results of the instance detection algorithm

Instance	A	B	S
Andorra	X	X	X
Andorra Activities Andorra			X
Atlantic	X	X	X
Canillo	X	X	X
GR11	X		X
Lonely Planet World			X
Major Andorran			X
Mediterranean	X	X	
Ordino	X	X	X
Pas de la Casa	X		
Pyrenees	X	X	X
Roig			X
Soldeu	X		
Soldeu-El Tarter			X
Traveler		X	

To illustrate this measure, let us consider the annotations for *Canillo* and *Ordino* with respect to our system (S in Table 8.6). Annotator A annotated *Canillo* as a town, while the system proposed the more general annotation area. The least common superconcept of town and area is area according to the ontology in Figure 8.7. Further, the distance in terms of edges between top and area is $\delta(top, area) = 2$, the distance between area and area is $\delta(area, area) = 0$, and the distance between town and area is $\delta(town, area) = 1$. Thus, $LA(town, area) = \frac{2+1}{2+1+0+1} = \frac{3}{4} = 0.75$ with respect to annotator A.

For *Ordino*, A, B and the system produced annotations as region, area and valley, respectively. The least upper superconcept of region and valley as well for area and valley is in both cases area. Further, the distance between top and area is $\delta(top, area) = 2$; the distances between region and area as well as valley and area are $\delta(region, area) = 1$ and $\delta(valley, area) = 2$, respectively. Thus, $LA(region, valley) = \frac{2+1}{2+1+2+1} = \frac{3}{6} = 0.5$ and $LA(area, valley) = \frac{2+1}{2+1+0+2} = \frac{3}{5} = 0.6$. C-PANKOW's classification of *Ordino* as valley is consequently better with respect to annotator B than to annotator A. On average, we would get a learning accuracy of 0.55.

8.3.2.4 Experiments

We conducted experiments varying i) the number of downloaded pages, ii) the strategy to choose the most appropriate concept as well as iii) the similarity threshold. Three different strategies to choose the most appropriate concept for an instance i have been implemented:

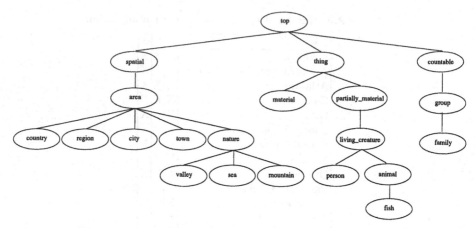

Fig. 8.7. Small excerpt of the GETESS tourism ontology

Table 8.6. Annotations by subjects A, B and the system (S)

Instance	A	B	S
Andorra	country	country	country
Atlantic	sea	sea	fish
Canillo	town	area	area
GR11	walking_trail		
Mediterranean	sea	sea	
Ordino	region	area	valley
Pas de la Casa	town		
Pyrenees	mountain	mountain	mountain
Roig			family
Soldeu	town		
Traveler		person	

- **Hits**: this strategy chooses the concept with the most hits, i.e. $maxarg_c\ Hits(c)$
- **Jaccard**: this strategy chooses the concept maximizing the following Jaccard coefficient, i.e. $maxarg_c\ \dfrac{GoogleHits(c \oplus i)}{GoogleHits(i)+GoogleHits(c)-GoogleHits(c \oplus i)}$
- **Combination**: this strategy combines the above two methods as follows: $maxarg_c\ \dfrac{GoogleHits(c \oplus i)}{GoogleHits(i)+GoogleHits(c)-GoogleHits(c \oplus i)} * Hits(c)$

The different strategies thus represent different alternatives for the *annotate*-statement in Algorithm 13. Tables 8.7 and 8.8 show the results for the various strategies, different numbers of downloaded pages, i.e. 10, 50, 100, 200, 300, 500, as well as different similarity thresholds. As the results heavily depend on Google's index and page rank, we repeated each experiment five times[7] and report averaged results. The results shown in tables 8.7 and 8.8 are grouped according to the number of pages considered, whereby the best recall, F-Measure and learning accuracy of each group are highlighted. There are several interesting conclusions to draw from these results. First, introducing a threshold makes the results worse in almost all cases, such that we have to conclude that our notion of contextual relevance seems too simplistic for the task at hand. Second, the version of our system taking into account the direct hits of the patterns performs better than the statistical measure based on the Jaccard measure as well as the combination of the two methods, whereby the combination of both measures still performs better than the Jaccard measure alone. Third, we also observe that the recall increases proportionally to the number of pages processed, while the precision remains at a more or less constant level. It even seems that the recall is reaching a plateau between 300 and 500 processed pages. To assess the significance of the results, a Student's t-test (compare Section 4.1.6) has been applied to compare the results of the versions of C-PANKOW using the Hits measure as well as no similarity threshold. We thus assume our data to be normally distributed. The null hypothesis here is that different samples of data have been generated by the same random process, i.e. they stem from the same distribution. In case this hypothesis is rejected, we can then conclude that the differences observed between the samples compared are actually significant and not simply due to chance.

The version using 500 pages for example differs from the versions using 100 and 200 pages at a significance level of $\alpha = 0.15$. However, the t-test also reveals that the differences between our version using 500 pages and the one using 300 pages are due to chance with a high probability of 0.92. This corroborates the conclusion that processing more than 300 pages does not pay off. On the other hand, the difference between our versions using 10 and 50 pages is statistically significant at a level of 0.02, while the differences between using 100 or 200 pages with respect to using only 50 are due to chance with a high probability of over 0.75. We conclude thus that using around 50 pages seems to represent an optimum between performance and cost, while moving beyond 300 pages does for sure not pay off with respect to the cost of processing more pages.

8.3.3 Summary

We have presented our paradigm *Learning By Googling* as well as two concrete instantiations thereof, PANKOW and C-PANKOW, the latter being an extension of the first. Both are based on the idea that lexico-syntactic patterns indicating some semantic relation can be matched on the World Wide Web. PANKOW exploits a brute-force approach in which patterns are generated

---

[7] These experiments were conducted between the 25th October 2005 and the 15th January 2006.

Table 8.7. C-PANKOW results for different numbers of downloaded pages, similarity thresholds and strategies (in percent)

	P	R	F	LA
10 pages				
no threshold				
Hits	46.36	**16.86**	**24.41**	**71.88**
Jaccard	46.31	16.25	23.78	71.89
Combination	46.57	16.39	23.97	72.04
sim $\geq$ 0.05				
Hits	44.4	13.61	20.5	71.59
Jaccard	44.25	13.54	20.4	71.76
Combination	44.32	13.54	20.41	70.91
sim $\geq$ 0.1				
Hits	43.55	5.2	9.16	70.51
Jaccard	43.55	5.2	9.16	71.01
Combination	43.55	5.2	9.16	70.19
sim $\geq$ 0.3				
Hits	20	0.14	0.29	40
Jaccard	20	0.14	0.29	40
Combination	20	0.14	0.29	40
50 pages				
no threshold				
Hits	46.52	**22.56**	**30.22**	71.31
Jaccard	40.42	18.81	25.52	67.59
Combination	44.69	20.9	28.31	70.19
sim $\geq$ 0.05				
Hits	43.24	18.99	26.17	72.24
Jaccard	43.15	18.48	25.61	70.58
Combination	45.62	19.64	27.17	72.35
sim $\geq$ 0.1				
Hits	43.64	10.11	16.29	72.53
Jaccard	47.72	10.8	17.44	74.04
Combination	48.51	10.98	17.74	**74.5**
sim $\geq$ 0.3				
Hits	43.33	0.36	0.72	71.67
Jaccard	43.33	0.36	0.72	71.67
Combination	43.33	0.36	0.72	71.67
sim $\geq$ 0.5				
Hits	40	0.14	0.29	40
Jaccard	40	0.14	0.29	40
Combination	40	0.14	0.29	40

	P	R	F	LA
100 pages				
no threshold				
Hits	44.95	**23.32**	**30.6**	71.24
Jaccard	37.37	18.77	24.88	65.79
Combination	42.87	21.59	28.59	68.62
sim $\geq$ 0.05				
Hits	46.1	15.02	21.19	**74.2**
Jaccard	32.56	12.74	17.26	66.28
Combination	34.14	13.61	18.37	67.26
sim $\geq$ 0.1				
Hits	46.43	8.59	13.7	73.15
Jaccard	34.83	8.12	12.69	65.6
Combination	35.92	8.45	13.19	66.06
sim $\geq$ 0.3				
Hits	30	0.29	0.57	67.33
Jaccard	30	0.29	0.57	67.33
Combination	30	0.29	0.57	67.33
sim $\geq$ 0.5				
Hits	60	0.22	0.43	60
Jaccard	60	0.22	0.43	60
Combination	60	0.22	0.43	60
200 pages				
no threshold				
Hits	44.84	23.64	**30.88**	70.45
Jaccard	36.13	18.45	24.35	64.81
Combination	41.1	21.08	27.77	68.71
sim $\geq$ 0.05				
Hits	46.11	23.18	30.67	72.75
Jaccard	43.15	21.37	28.4	69.82
Combination	47.22	**23.65**	31.3	72.76
sim $\geq$ 0.1				
Hits	44.42	14.66	21.98	71.71
Jaccard	44.18	14.4	21.66	70.64
Combination	46.24	15.13	22.73	72.15
sim $\geq$ 0.3				
Hits	44	0.58	1.14	**74.8**
Jaccard	41	0.5	1	73.53
Combination	41	0.5	1	73.53
sim $\geq$ 0.5				
Hits	40	0.14	0.29	40
Jaccard	40	0.14	0.29	40
Combination	40	0.14	0.29	40

Table 8.8. C-PANKOW results for different numbers of downloaded pages, similarity thresholds and strategies (in percent) (Cont'd)

	P	R	F	LA		P	R	F	LA
	300 pages					**500 pages**			
	no threshold					no threshold			
Hits	46.18	**25.85**	**33.09**	71.5	Hits	45.46	**25.92**	**32.97**	70.88
Jaccard	35.86	19.68	25.37	63.68	Jaccard	33.79	18.81	24.13	62.09
Combination	43.57	24.08	30.96	69.27	Combination	44.37	24.94	31.89	69.44
	sim ≥ 0.05					sim ≥ 0.05			
Hits	46.09	23.9	31.32	73.14	Hits	45.75	24.81	32.08	72.37
Jaccard	39.57	20.14	26.54	67.25	Jaccard	38.03	20.4	26.48	65.84
Combination	46.58	23.97	31.47	72.81	Combination	46.41	25.2	32.57	72.06
	sim ≥ 0.1					sim ≥ 0.1			
Hits	46.8	16.17	23.94	73.44	Hits	48.01	18.02	26.09	73.7
Jaccard	44.86	15.31	22.73	71.09	Jaccard	45.28	16.57	24.09	71.79
Combination	48.19	16.57	24.56	73.55	Combination	48.13	17.73	25.73	73.28
	sim ≥ 0.3					sim ≥ 0.3			
Hits	44	0.58	1.14	**74.8**	Hits	54	0.58	1.14	**79.8**
Jaccard	44	0.58	1.14	74.8	Jaccard	54	0.58	1.14	79.8
Combination	44	0.58	1.14	74.8	Combination	54	0.58	1.14	79.8
	sim ≥ 0.5					sim ≥ 0.5			
Hits	40	0.14	0.29	40	Hits	60	0.22	0.43	60
Jaccard	40	0.14	0.29	40	Jaccard	60	0.22	0.43	60
Combination	40	0.14	0.29	40	Combination	60	0.22	0.43	60

taking into account all the concepts of the ontology in question and counts the Google™ -hits of each pattern, aggregating the results for each concept and annotating the instance with the concept having the maximal number of hits. C-PANKOW is based on the same principle, but instead of counting the number of occurrences of a pattern, it downloads a number of pages matching certain automatically generated clues, and processes the abstracts offline. It thus reduces the number of queries sent to the Google™ API, while allowing to match more complex expressions at the same time. In particular, it allows for the application of natural language processing techniques to the downloaded documents. We have also presented a first approach towards creating more contextually appropriate annotations by calculating the similarity of the original page to be annotated and the downloaded abstracts. The main conclusions supported by our experiments are:

- C-PANKOW outperforms PANKOW both in terms of efficiency and quality of the results.
- Considering the number of hits for each concept as well as downloading around 50 pages represents some sort of optimal configuration with respect to the performance–cost trade-off and provides a quite good baseline system difficult to outperform.

- The results can be improved by considering more pages and thus increasing the recall at the cost of processing more pages. Beyond 300 pages, however, the results show no significant improvement with respect to using fewer pages.
- Unfortunately, our notion of contextual relevance and the usage of a similarity threshold does not improve the results.

8.4 Related Work

In this section, we discuss work related to the population of ontologies. We focus in particular on systems going beyond the traditional named entity recognition task using three target classes.

Fleischman and Hovy

Fleischman and Hovy [Fleischman and Hovy, 2002] go beyond the coarse classification into three entities and aim at classifying instances of persons into 7 fine-grained categories: athlete, politician/government, clergy, businessperson, entertainer/artist, lawyer, doctor/scientist and police. They explore a supervised setting in which classifiers are trained to recognize each of these classes. As features for the classifier, Fleischman and Hovy use the frequency of the unigrams, bigrams as well as trigrams occurring within a window of 3 words from the named entity in question. They also derive topic signatures for each of the subcategories of person and compute a topic signature score for each instance indicating how good the context of the instance fits the overall context of the subcategory as given by the topic signature.

To address the problem that various mentions of one and the same entity can be classified in different ways, Fleischman et al. also define a post-processing step, called *MemRun*, in which different hypothesis are re-ranked according to the evidences produced by the classifier. In particular, if the confidence level of the classifier's decision is above a threshold t_1, the hypothesis is entered into the space of final hypotheses together with the number of times it was derived. Coreferences between different entities are resolved here and considered as one entity. In a second step, all the hypotheses having a confidence below a threshold t_2 are discarded. Finally, the instance is assigned to the class with the highest confidence multiplied by the number of times the corresponding hypothesis was derived.

The authors train different classifiers (a C4.5 decision tree classifier, a feed forward neural network with 50 hidden nodes, a kNN algorithm with k=1 and a Support Vector Machine using a linear kernel), achieving the best accuracy of 70.4% using the decision tree classifier and the post-processing by *MemRun*. Examining subsets of the feature set, they come to the conclusion that using all the features leads to the best results.

Evans

Evans [Evans, 2003] considers a totally unsupervised scenario in which the classes themselves are derived from the texts. For each entity appearing in the text, a set of Google queries similar to the clues described in Section 8.3 are issued to derive possible hypernyms for each instance. The instances are clustered bottom-up using the web occurrence counts of the hypernyms as features. The nodes in the cluster tree are labeled using the most specific hypernym of all words in the cluster. These labeled clusters thus constitute the set of classes which the named entities are assigned to. A named entity i with hypernyms $\{c_{i_1}, ..., c_{i_n}\}$ with frequencies $f_{c_{i_1}} ... f_{c_{i_n}}$ is assigned to that cluster t with hypernyms $\{t_1, ..., t_m\}$ which maximizes the following formula:

$$\sum_{j=1}^{m} \sum_{k=1}^{n} \theta(t) \; g(c_{i_k}, t_j) \; f_{c_{i_k}} \tag{8.24}$$

where $\theta(t)$ is a coefficient inversely proportional to the level of t in the cluster tree and $g(c_{i_k}, t_j)$ is a function returning 1 if c_{i_k} is identical to t_j and 0 otherwise. Using this classification procedure, Evans achieves an accuracy between 20% - 70.27% depending on the document considered as well as an overall accuracy of 41.41%.

Widdows

Widdows [Widdows, 2003b] also applies the technique described in Section 6.5.2 to the classification of named entities, achieving much lower results than compared to classifying common nouns. The best result when classifying proper nouns is an accuracy of 10.6%.

Alfonseca et al.

Alfonseca et al. [Alfonseca and Manandhar, 2002] also address the classification of named entities with respect to an ontology. As described in Section 6.5.2, the classification of common nouns and entities is, however, mixed so that it is not possible to assess the accuracy w.r.t. classifying common nouns and proper names separately. Nevertheless, for comparison purposes, we will assume an accuracy of 17.39% on the task of classifying named entities for the approach of Alfonseca et al. (see Table 8.9).

Tanev and Magnini

Recently, Tanev and Magnini [Tanev and Magnini, 2006] have extended our approach described in Section 8.2 by providing seed examples for every class to the system. These seed examples are used to derive contextual features for the class vector. Tanev and Magnini have demonstrated that a significant improvement over our baseline can be achieved with their extension.

Hahn and Schnattinger

Hahn and Schnattinger [Hahn and Schnattinger, 1998a] present an approach based on a *qualification calculus* where several hypotheses about which concept a new named entity belongs to are created, maintained in parallel and iteratively refined or discarded. The hypotheses are created using linguistic evidence from appositive or other constructs as well as by considering what Hahn and Schnattinger call *case frames*, which in essence are selectional restrictions expressed with respect to the concept hierarchy and which allow to create or rule-out certain hypotheses. Interesting is that the different hypotheses get assigned quality labels corresponding to the way they have been created. From the expression *'the printer HP4000'* a hypothesis would, for example, be created according to which HP4000 is a printer. This hypothesis would yield the label APPOSITION. An expression like: *'The Itoh-Ci-8 has a size of...'* would lead to the creation of a hypothesis space in which Itoh-Ci-8 is a physical_object as only physical objects have sizes. This hypothesis space would be labeled with the label CASE FRAME as it is the selectional restriction of the size-of frame which has lead to its creation.

Besides these linguistic quality labels, also conceptual labels are attached to the different hypotheses spaces. The quality label M-DEDUCED, for example, is assigned to multiple derivations of the same concept hypothesis in different hypotheses spaces. The label C-SUPPORTED is assigned to a relation r between two instances if another relation already exists in the knowledge base involving the same instances in the reverse order. The quality-based classification works as described in Algorithm 14.

Algorithm 14 Selecting hypotheses in Hahn et al's approach:

Input: a set of hypothesis $H := \{h_1, ..., h_n\}$
Output: a set of hypothesis $H' := \{h'_1, ..., h'_m\}$

$H' := \{h \in H|$ such that h has the highest number of APPOSITION labels $\}$

if $(|H'| > 1)$
$H' := \{h \in H'|$ such that h has the highest number of CASE FRAME labels$\}$

if $(|H'| > 1)$
$H' := \{h \in H'|$ such that h has the highest number of M-DEDUCED labels$\}$

if $(|H'| > 1)$
$H' := \{h \in H'|$ such that h has the highest number of C-SUPPORTED labels$\}$

return H';

Finally, the returned set H contains the best hypothesis for the assignment of the instance to the appropriate concept. Hahn et al. evaluate their approach in terms of recall, precision and parsimony, the latter being defined as the number of cases in which H' is a singleton set containing the correct concept divided by the number of instances in the test set, and thus corresponds more or less to the accuracy of the other systems described in this chapter. Hahn et al. also measure the degree to which a certain predicted concept is correct by taking into account the distance in the taxonomy between the predicted and the correct concept. They define the learning accuracy in which our version of learning accuracy is inspired as follows:

$$LA := \sum_{i \in I} \frac{LA_i}{|I|} \tag{8.25}$$

$$\alpha(w, h) := \begin{cases} \frac{CP_i}{SP_i} & \text{if } FP_i = 0 \\ \frac{CP_i}{FP_i + DP_i} & \text{if } h \in H(w) \end{cases} \tag{8.26}$$

where SP_i specifies the length of the shortest path (in terms of the number of nodes being traversed) from the TOP node of the concept hierarchy to the maximally specific concept subsuming the instance to be learned. CP_i specifies the length of the path from the TOP node to that concept node which is common both to the shortest path and the path to the predicted concept. FP_i specifies the length of the path from the TOP node to the predicted node in case the prediction is wrong, and $FP_i = 0$ in case the prediction is correct. Finally, DP_i denotes the node distance between the predicted false node and the most specific common concept which is on the path from the TOP node to the predicted false node and still correctly subsumes the predicted node (compare Appendix A.1 for a more detailed discussion of the learning accuracy).

Different versions of Hahn et al.'s system obtain the results shown in Table 8.9, where *baseline* is the system using only the terminological reasoning component, TH is the version of the system using the linguistic quality labels to filter out certain hypothesis, and CB is the version of the system additionally using the conceptual quality labels to filter the hypotheses.

Craven et al.

Craven et al. have addressed the population of ontologies using machine-learning techniques in the context of the Web→KB project [Craven et al., 2000]. They address the population of a small ontology about computer science departments with instances of concepts and relations. They assume that only web pages stand for certain instances, and hyperlinks between different web pages represent instances of relations between these. In this line, they treat the problem of discovering instances of concepts as a text classification task and report experiments using Naive Bayes classifiers and different text representation models, i.e. a simple bag-of-words model, a model relying on the title and heading of the web page as well as a model using the words occurring around hyperlinks. Further, they also examine a ILP-based approach [Lavrac and Dzeroski, 1994] to classify web pages into their corresponding ontological class. They make use of the FOIL algorithm [Quinlan, 1990] for this purpose as well as in order to find instances of relations.

Etzioni et al.

Etzioni et al. [Etzioni et al., 2004a, Etzioni et al., 2004b, Etzioni et al., 2005] have developed KnowItAll, an approach similar in spirit to PANKOW, which does not assign a given instance to the appropriate concept, but aims at determining the complete extension of a given concept. Etzioni et al. also apply Hearst-style patterns to generate search engine queries, download a number of documents, process them linguistically, match the fully fledged patterns and extract a number of candidate instances for the concept in question. The main difference here is that the patterns are correspondingly used in 'reverse mode', i.e. to find instances and not concepts. Each instance is then ranked according to a PMI-like measure:

$$PMI(i,d) := \frac{Hits(d+i)}{Hits(i)} \tag{8.27}$$

where i is the instance in question and d is a so called *discriminator phrase*. Given the concept *actor* and the candidate instance *Robert de Niro* as well as the discriminator phrase *'actors such as'*, the PMI would here amount to calculating

$$PMI(Robert\ de\ Niro, actor) = \frac{\text{``actors such as Robert de Niro''}}{\text{``Robert de Niro''}}$$

These PMI values are calculated for each of the different Hearst-pattern-inspired discriminator phrases and fed into a Bayesian classifier learning the optimal thresholds for the different PMI values to produce an optimal classification of the instances. In order to create training data for this classifier, Etzioni et al. apply a bootstrapping approach in which the m instance/concept pairs with the highest PMI values are used as training examples for the classifier. The authors report their results in terms of recall and precision measured with respect to the TIPSTER Gazetteer for different classes such as US states, cities, countries, actors or films. The results get even better when using different techniques aimed at increasing the recall of the system, such as i) automatically learning new patterns from examples, ii) using similar techniques to find subclasses and calculate the extension of the subclasses, as well as iii) wrapping lists in which some of the already classified instances are encountered to find additional instances (compare [Etzioni et al., 2005]).

8.5 Conclusion and Open Issues

We have presented several approaches tackling the problem of populating large ontologies with named entities representing instances. The problem of assigning named entities to their appropriate ontological class with respect to a large number of classes is currently addressed by a handful of researchers at most. The work presented in this section thus represents a significant contribution to the state-of-the-art in the field of large-scale named entity recognition or ontology population. We have presented a corpus-based approach relying on vector space similarity to assign a named entity to the most similar concept according to the corpus. The contribution here has been the systematic exploration of parameters which can improve such a similarity-based approach. We have in particular shown that there are a number of techniques which, applied in the appropriate way, can indeed enhance the performance of such an approach. It remains an open issue to explore each of the techniques in more detail. As an example, whereas in our experiments we have used an anaphora resolution algorithm developed for this purpose, it would be definitely interesting to explore and compare different state-of-the-art anaphora resolution tools with respect to their ability to improve the results on the task. In general, more thorough experiments are needed to explore the different parameters and techniques in order to allow meaningful conclusions. The contribution of this book is thus to provide a first step in this direction, identifying such techniques which have the potential to improve the results on the task of categorizing named entities with respect to a large number of classes.

Concerning PANKOW and C-PANKOW, the contribution is to show that such a web-based approach to named entity recognition and ontology population is indeed feasible and worth exploring. Though other researchers have presented similar systems (compare [Brin, 1998], [Pasca, 2004], [Etzioni et al., 2005]) we are not aware of any system finding possible classes for a given named entity on the one hand as well as tackling the issue of selecting the contextually most relevant concept on the other. SemTag [Dill et al., 2003], for example, merely addresses the second task, whereby the possible classes for the named entity are given by the TAP lexicon, thus reducing the task to selecting the contextually most relevant meaning of the entity. A systematic exploration of different parameters of PANKOW and C-PANKOW has also lead us to find reasonable settings for both systems. Further research should clarify if it is possible to improve the system along the following lines:

- contextual relevance of annotations,
- precision of the patterns, and
- scalability.

Indeed, it would be necessary to explore more sophisticated techniques for word meaning disambiguation as proposed in the word sense disambigua-

Table 8.9. Comparison of results

System	#concepts	Rec/Acc	LA
MUC	3	>90%	n.a
Evans	2-8	41.41%	n.a.
Hovy et al.	8	70.4%	n.a.
PANKOW	59	24.9%	58.91%
Hahn et al. (Baseline)	325	21%	67%
Hahn et al. (TH)	325	26%	73%
Hahn et al. (CB)	325	31%	76%
Corpus Similarity	682	29.24%	69.87%
C-PANKOW	682	25.85%	71.5%
Alfonseca et al.	1200	17.39%	44%

tion literature (compare [Ide and Veronis, 1998]) as well as by Dill et al. [Dill et al., 2003]. The precision of the patterns would also need to be increased by filtering out spurious concepts at earlier stages, thus making the task easier for the disambiguation step. Downloading hundreds of pages for each pattern used is still the bottleneck of the system. Techniques to avoid downloading and processing such an amount of pages should be explored to make the system even more scalable.

We conclude this section by comparing different systems discussed in Section 8.4 with our three approaches. Table 8.9 summarizes the comparison along the lines of (i) number of classes considered, (ii) accuracy and (iii) learning accuracy. The table illustrates in particular the trade-off between classes considered as well as the accuracy and learning accuracy achieved. The comparison is in a strict sense not meaningful. This is due to the fact that the systems have been applied to different datasets as well as using different evaluation measures or modes which are not comparable. For example, the learning accuracy as defined in the context of this book is not equivalent to the one introduced by Hahn et al. (compare Appendix A.1). Nevertheless, the table allows to conclude that the approaches developed fit well in the state-of-the-art of the field and provide a significant contribution.

9

Applications

In this section, we discuss applications for ontologies learned from text as well as methods for automatically populating them. Besides typical applications of ontologies such as

- agent communication [Finin et al., 1994],
- data integration [Wiederhold, 1994, Alexiev et al., 2005],
- description of service capabilities [Ankolekar et al., 2002] for matching and composition purposes [Paolucci et al., 2002, Sirin et al., 2002],
- formal verification of process descriptions [Ankolekar et al., 2004] or
- unification of terminology across communities,

there are also applications in text processing or information retrieval such as

- information retrieval (e.g. for query expansion)
- clustering and classification of documents,
- semantic annotation, e.g. for knowledge management or semantic retrieval, and
- natural language processing.

The main difference here is that traditional applications require ontologies to have a well-defined model-theoretic semantics as well as to be consistent with respect to these semantics and furthermore represent the product of an agreement between a group of people. Applications of ontologies within text mining differ in this respect in that the requirement of totally correct, consistent and shared ontologies is not given. The reason is that most text mining algorithms are themselves inherently fuzzy, often relying on similarity measures defined over vector space. This is in fact the case of most of the applications mentioned above. *Query expansion*, for example, addresses the so called *vocabulary mismatch* encountered in information retrieval, that is, the problem that the vocabulary of the document and the user query can differ, even if the semantic content is the same. Query expansion thus aims at expanding a user query with synonyms or related terms in order to overcome the vocabulary mismatch problem. An automatically learned ontology can obviously be applied for this purpose. Another way of tackling the problem is to enhance the representation of the documents themselves by abstracting over the plain words occurring in the document and adding conceptual information to the document representation. There also seems to be a potential for applying automatically learned ontologies in this respect.

In the same vein, classification and clustering approaches can also make use of such an enhanced and conceptual document representation. We will come back to this issue below. In natural language processing, on the one hand, several methods have been suggested exploiting the structure of a thesaurus for the tasks of word sense disambiguation as well as the classification of new words (see below). Both tasks could thus make use of an automatically generated ontology. On the other hand, named entity recognition systems relying on gazetteers could obviously make use of automatically populated ontologies.

In this chapter, we demonstrate the benefit of automatic ontology construction and population in two applications which are described in detail in the remainder of this chapter. Thus, in contrast to previous sections of this book, in which ontologies are evaluated with respect to a gold standard or a posteriori by a judge, in this chapter we propose a task-based evaluation of ontologies in line with Porzel and Malaka [Porzel and Malaka, 2005]. The main requirements for such a task-based evaluation are that:

- the output of the algorithm performing the task can be measured quantitatively,
- there is a potential for exploiting background knowledge for the task,
- the ontology can be seen as an additional parameter to the system performing the task, and
- changes in performance can be traced back to the ontology if other parameters remain fixed.

Figure 9.1 illustrates the principle of a task-based evaluation of ontologies. Such a task-based evaluation allows evaluating in terms of their performance on the task:

- different hand-crafted ontologies,
- different systems for automatically learning ontologies,
- automatically learned ontologies compared to hand-crafted ones, or
- a baseline system not using any ontological knowledge.

The task-based evaluation of ontologies and ontology learning approaches is indeed very important as it also allows to gain insight into the real potential of ontologies for certain applications. In fact, task-based evaluations assess the value of a certain ontology *in vivo* in the context of some application, in contrast to *in vitro* experiments comparing ontologies with a gold standard. Such

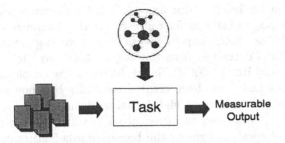

Fig. 9.1. Task-based evaluation of ontologies

task-based evaluations will ultimately allow meaningful conclusions about the usefulness of ontologies as well as of ontology learning systems from an application point of view. In this section, we present two task-based evaluations: one involving automatically learned ontologies and another considering automatically populated ones. In Section 9.1, we describe experiments in which automatically learned ontologies have been successfully used as background knowledge within text clustering and classification tasks. We compare the systems using no ontology, different automatically learned ontologies as well as hand-crafted ontologies. This section is based on joint work with Stephan Bloehdorn and Andreas Hotho (compare [Bloehdorn et al., 2005]). Further, in Section 9.2 we discuss an application of named entity classification/annotation to the browsing of document collections, comparing a version of the browsing approach using automatically extracted facts with one version using standard lexica as a baseline. In particular, we show that support to the user in the form of highlighting named entities in different colors according to their types can actually help to accomplish certain information gathering tasks. This section is based on joint work with Victoria Uren, Enrico Motta and Martin Dzbor from the *Knowledge Media Institute (KMi)* (compare [Uren et al., 2005]). The corresponding user study was carried out jointly by Victoria Uren and the author of this book in November 2004 in the context of the Dot.Kom project[1]. The descriptions in Section 9.1 and 9.2 are thus partially based on material published in [Bloehdorn et al., 2005] and [Uren et al., 2005], respectively.

9.1 Text Clustering and Classification

Text clustering and classification are two important approaches supporting users in organizing their textual information. State-of-the-art clustering and classification systems typically rely on the so called bag-of-words model known

---

[1] http://nlp.shef.ac.uk/dot.kom/

from information retrieval [Salton and McGill, 1983], where single terms or term stems are used as features for representing the documents.

Recent work has shown improvements in text mining tasks by means of conceptual features extracted from ontologies (compare [Hotho et al., 2003] and [Bloehdorn and Hotho, 2004]). So far, however, the ontological structures employed for this task have been created manually by knowledge engineers and domain experts, requiring a high initial modeling effort.

In this section, we report on experiments in which we use automatically constructed ontologies to augment the bag–of–words feature representations of texts with features based on concepts. We compare the obtained results with respect to (i) the baseline given by the plain bag-of-words representation and (ii) results based on the MeSH Tree Structures as a manually engineered medical ontology (compare Chapter 5). We show that both types of conceptual feature representations outperform the bag-of-words model and that results based on the automatically constructed ontologies can actually compete with those obtained with the manually engineered MeSH Tree Structures.

The structure of this section is as follows: in Section 9.1.1 we describe how the concept hierarchies are automatically constructed. In Section 9.1.2 we describe the concept-based extension of the bag–of–words model and in Section 9.1.3 we present our experimental results.

9.1.1 Building Hierarchies

We have conducted extensive experiments using the OHSUMED text collection [Hersh et al., 1994] (compare Chapter 5), which was also used for the TREC-9 filtering track[2]. For the sake of comparison, the hierarchies are built using the terms appearing in the MeSH thesaurus. The terms appearing in the MeSH thesaurus have been sorted according to their frequency in the OHSUMED corpus, and the 7000 or 14000 most frequent terms from this list have been considered in order to build a hierarchy. The hierarchy is built using hierarchical clustering as described in Section 6.2. In the experiments described here, hierarchical agglomerative clustering with complete linkage as well as Bi-Section-KMeans have been used (compare Section 4.3.2). Similarity between vectors is measured as the cosine of their angle in both cases. As contextual features to describe the terms we use pseudo-syntactic dependencies as described in Section 4.1.4. The automatically extracted ontologies are built using the 1987 portion of the collection, i.e. a total of 54,708 documents. In what follows, we give some examples for the features extracted from different syntactic constructions for illustration purposes. Hereby, a:b ++ means that the count for attribute b of a term a is incremented by 1:

adjective modifiers: *alveolar macrophages*
    macrophages: alveolear++

---

[2] http://trec.nist.gov/data/t9_filtering.html

```
prepositional phrase modifiers: a defect in cell function
    defect: in_cell_function ++
    cell function: defect_in ++
possessive modifiers: the dorsal artery's distal stump
    dorsal artery: has_distal_stump ++
noun phrases in subject or object position:
    the bacterium suppresses various lymphocyte functions
    bacterium: suppress_subj ++
    lymphocyte function: suppress_obj ++
prepositional phrases following a verb:
    the revascularization occurs through the common penile artery
    penile artery: occurs_through ++
copula constructs: the alveolar macrophage is a bacterium
    alveolar macrophage: is_bacterium ++
verb phrases with the verb to have:
    the channel has a molecular mass of 105 kDa
    channel: has_molecular_mass ++
```

On the basis of the extracted pseudo-syntactic dependencies, we can construct a context vector for each term in order to calculate similarity between terms by the cosine measure as well as clustering these hierarchically as described in Section 6.2.

9.1.2 Conceptual Document Representations

In the approach of Hotho et al. [Hotho et al., 2003] as well as Bloehdorn and Hotho [Bloehdorn and Hotho, 2004], background knowledge is used to extend the standard bag-of-words feature vector representing texts with conceptual features. The approach relies on concept hierarchies or taxonomies, adding the superconcepts of a certain term (up to a certain level) to the document representation. The generalization step in fact consists in adding more general concepts to the specific concepts found in the text, leading to some sort of 'semantic smoothing'. The basic idea is that if a term like 'arrhythmia' appears, the document should not only be represented by the concept arrhythmia, but also by the concepts heart disease and cardiovascular disease, etc., up to a certain level of generality. This in consequence increases the similarity with documents talking about some other specialization of cardiovascular disease.

In contrast to the simple term features, these conceptual features overcome a number of shortcomings of the bag-of-words feature representation by conceptually generalizing expressions along the concept hierarchy. The approach only considers noun phrases as potential concepts to be generalized.

In Hotho et al.'s approach (compare [Hotho et al., 2003]), three strategies for extending the bag-of-words model are defined: add, replace and only. In the add strategy, the concepts are simply added as additional features to the vectors. In the replace strategy, all the terms are expelled for which at least one concept has been added. When applying the only strategy, exclusively concepts are included as features. In the experiments reported in this section, the *add* strategy has been applied.

The crucial steps for such a conceptual document representation as described above are:

- assignment of words to concepts
- adding superconcepts to the document representation

The assignment of words to concepts typically requires word meaning disambiguation. The MeSH hierarchy used in the experiments described in this section only contains concepts unambiguously referred to by a single lexical entry, such that the need for disambiguation is eliminated.

In contrast to standard bag–of–word models, however, we do not assume that one token corresponds to exactly one feature, but make use of the underlying taxonomy to treat certain multi-word expressions as one feature. For this purpose, we use a candidate term detection strategy that moves a window over the input text that recognizes multi-word terms as specified by the labels of concepts in our ontology and creates corresponding features. We rely on part-of-speech annotation to only consider noun phrases in this process. As the ontology does typically not contain all inflected forms as labels for a certain concept, we use a fall-back strategy that maps words to their stems, using these as features. In these experiments, term stem extraction comprises the removal of the standard stopwords for English defined in the SMART stopword list (compare [Buckley, 1985]) and stemming using the porter stemming algorithm (consult [M.F.Porter, 1980]).

With respect to adding superconcepts of the concepts identified according to the procedure outlined above, we realize this by adding, for every concept, all superconcepts up to a maximal distance h into the concept representation. The result of this process is a *concept vector* that can be appended to the classical term vector representation. The resulting hybrid feature vectors can be fed into any standard clustering or classification algorithm.

9.1.3 Experiments

As already mentioned before, the experiments have been conducted on the OHSUMED text collection, which consists of titles and abstracts from medical journals indexed with multiple MeSH descriptors and a set of queries with associated relevance judgments.

In our experiments, we use domain ontologies automatically extracted from the text corpus as described in Section 9.1.1 on the one hand and the Medical Subject Headings (MeSH) Tree Structures ontology as a competing manually engineered ontology on the other. We performed experiments with the following configurations:

agglo-7000: automatically constructed ontology, pseudo-syntactic dependencies as features for the 7,000 most frequent terms, taxonomy creation via hierarchical agglomerative clustering;

bisec-7000: automatically constructed ontology, pseudo-syntactic dependencies as features for the 7,000 most frequent terms, taxonomy creation via Bi-Section-KMeans;

bisec-14000: automatically constructed ontology, pseudo-syntactic dependencies as features for the 14,000 most frequent terms, taxonomy creation via Bi-Section-KMeans;

mesh: manually constructed ontology compiled out of the Medical Subject Headings (MeSH)[3] containing more than 22,000 concepts enriched with synonymous and quasi-synonymous language expressions.

In all experiments, term stems were extracted as a first set of features from the documents. Conceptual features were extracted as a second set of features using the ontologies mentioned and assigning words to concepts as described above. In the following Section 9.1.3.1, we present our experimental results with respect to the classification task. In Section 9.1.3.2, we present the corresponding results on the document clustering task.

9.1.3.1 Text Classification Experiments

For the experiments in the text classification setting, we also used the 1987 portion of the OHSUMED collection. Two thirds of the entries were randomly selected as training documents, while the remainder was used as test set, resulting in a training corpus containing 36,369 documents and a test corpus containing 18,341 documents. The assigned MeSH terms were regarded as categories for the documents, and binary classification was performed on the top 50 categories that contained the highest number of positive training documents. In all cases, we used AdaBoost [Freund and Schapire, 95] with 1000 iterations as classification algorithm and binary weighting for the feature vectors. As evaluation measures for text classification we report precision, recall and F-measure[4].

Table 9.1 summarizes some of the classification results, where P is the precision of the classifier, R its recall as well as F_1 the harmonic mean between both. In particular, we distinguish between micro- and macro-averaging. In macro-averaging, the results are averaged over all the categories, while micro-averaging averages over the number of documents to be classified (compare [Cai and Hofmann, 2003]).

In all cases, the integration of conceptual features improves the results, in most cases at a significant level (compare Table 9.1). The best results for the learned ontologies could be achieved with the bisec-7000 ontology and a superconcept integration level h of 15 resulting in 44.26% macro-avg.

---

[3] The controlled vocabulary thesaurus of the United States National Library of Medicine (NLM), http://www.nlm.nih.gov/mesh/

[4] For a review of evaluation measures we refer to Sebastiani [Sebastaini, 2002] in the text classification setting and to Hotho et al. [Hotho et al., 2003] in the text clustering setting.

F_1, which is both above the bag–of–words baseline not using conceptual features (42.56%) as well as above the best version using the MeSH thesaurus (44.19%). The best results for the ontologies bisec-14000 and agglo-7000 are macro-avg. F_1 measures of 43.60% and 43.07%, respectively, thus being above the bag–of–words baseline, but not performing better than the MeSH thesaurus. Considering micro averaging, again the bisec-7000 ontology yields the best result of F_1=45.46%, outperforming the baseline (43.94%) as well as the best result using MeSH (45.43%). The versions bisec-14000 and bisec-7000 with micro-avg. F_1 of 44.67% and 44.31%, respectively, both outperform the baseline, but not the MeSH thesaurus. These results are indeed significant from a statistical point of view as shown in Table 9.1, where '*' stands for significance at a α-level of 5% and '**' for significance at a 1% α-level. In this chapter significance tests will always applied for the same purpose and assuming normally distributed data. The null hypothesis will always be that both samples are drawn from the same population and that the observed differences are due to chance. The aim will thus be to reject the null hypothesis in favor of the alternative hypothesis claiming that the differences are indeed statistically significant. The conclusion here is that the automatically learned ontologies indeed improve the baseline system, while the bisec-7000 ontology even yields better results than the MeSH thesaurus. This proves that automatically learned ontologies have indeed the potential to improve text classification approaches relying on the plain bag-of-words model.

9.1.3.2 Text Clustering Experiments

For the clustering experiments, we first compiled a corpus which contains only one label per document. We used the 106 queries provided with the OHSUMED collection and regarded every answer set of a query as a cluster. We extracted all documents for all queries which occur in only one query. This results in a dataset with 4389 documents and 106 labels (clusters). Evaluation measures for text clustering are entropy, purity, inverse purity and F_1-measure.

The purity measure is based on the well-known precision measure for information retrieval (cf. [Pantel and Lin, 2002b]). Each resulting cluster P from a partitioning $\mathbb{P}$ of the overall document set D is treated as if it were the result of a query. Each set L of documents of a partitioning $\mathbb{L}$, which is obtained by manually labeling, is treated as if it were the desired set of documents for a query. The two partitions $\mathbb{P}$ and $\mathbb{L}$ are then compared as follows.

The precision of a cluster $P \in \mathbb{P}$ for a given category $L \in \mathbb{L}$ is given by

$$\text{Precision}(P, L) := \frac{|P \cap L|}{|P|} \tag{9.1}$$

The overall value for purity is computed by taking the weighted average of maximal precision values:

$$\text{Purity}(\mathbb{P}, \mathbb{L}) := \sum_{P \in \mathbb{P}} \frac{|P|}{|D|} \max_{L \in \mathbb{L}} \text{Precision}(P, L). \tag{9.2}$$

Table 9.1. Performance Results in the Classification Setting.

Ontology	Max. Level h	macro-averaged (in %)			
		P	R	F_1	Significance
[none]	n.a.	52.60	35.74	42.56	
agglo-7000	10	52.48	36.52	43.07	no
agglo-7000	15	52.57	36.31	42.95	no
agglo-7000	20	52.49	36.44	43.02	no
bisec-7000	10	53.39	36.79	43.56	*
bisec-7000	15	54.36	37.32	**44.26**	**
bisec-7000	20	**55.12**	36.87	43.86	**
bisec-14000	10	51.92	36.12	42.60	no
bisec-14000	15	52.17	36.86	43.20	no
bisec-14000	20	53.37	36.85	43.60	*
mesh	0	53.65	37.56	44.19	**
mesh	5	52.72	**37.57**	43.87	**

Ontology	Max. Level h	micro-averaged (in %)			
		P	R	F_1	Significance
[none]	n.a.	55.77	36.25	43.94	
agglo-7000	10	55.83	36.86	44.41	no
agglo-7000	15	55.95	36.67	44.30	no
agglo-7000	20	55.76	36.79	44.33	no
bisec-7000	10	56.59	37.25	44.92	*
bisec-7000	15	**57.24**	37.71	**45.46**	**
bisec-7000	20	57.18	37.21	45.08	**
bisec-14000	10	54.88	36.52	43.85	no
bisec-14000	15	55.27	37.27	44.52	no
bisec-14000	20	56.39	37.27	44.87	*
mesh	0	56.81	37.84	45.43	**
mesh	5	55.94	**37.94**	45.21	**

We also investigate the counterpart of purity:

$$\text{InversePurity}(\mathbb{P}, \mathbb{L}) := \sum_{L \in \mathbb{L}} \frac{|L|}{|D|} \max_{P \in \mathbb{P}} \text{Precision}(L, P) \qquad (9.3)$$

and the well known

$$\text{F-Measure}(\mathbb{P}, \mathbb{L}) := \sum_{L \in \mathbb{L}} \frac{|L|}{|D|} \max_{P \in \mathbb{P}} \frac{2 \cdot \text{Recall}(P, L) \cdot \text{Precision}(P, L)}{\text{Recall}(P, L) + \text{Precision}(P, L)} \qquad (9.4)$$

where $\text{Recall}(P, L) := \text{Precision}(L, P)$.

The three measures return values in the interval $[0, 1]$, with 1 indicating optimality. The F-Measure works similarly to inverse purity, but it penalizes overly large clusters as it includes the individual precision of these clusters into the evaluation.

While (inverse) purity and F-measure only consider 'best' matches between 'queries' and manually defined categories, the *entropy* indicates how large the information content of a clustering result is.

$$E(\mathbb{P}, L) = \sum_{P \in \mathbb{P}} \text{prob}(P) \cdot E(P) \tag{9.5}$$

where

$$E(P) = - \sum_{L \in \mathbb{L}} \text{prob}(L|P) \log(\text{prob}(L|P)) \tag{9.6}$$

and

$$\text{prob}(L|P) = \text{Precision}(P, L) \tag{9.7}$$

$$\text{prob}(P) = \frac{|P|}{|D|} \tag{9.8}$$

The entropy has the range $[0,\ log(|\mathbb{L}|)]$, with 0 indicating optimality.

Table 9.2 presents the results of the text clustering task, averaged over 20 repeated clusterings with random initialization. With respect to macro-averaging, the integration of conceptual features always improves results and also does so in most cases with respect to micro-averaging.

Concerning macro-averaging, the different versions agglo-7000, bisec-7000 and bisec-14000 are over the baseline F_1-measure of 19.41% using no conceptual features with best F_1-measures of 19.93%, 20.17% and 21.11%, respectively (compare Table 9.2). However, the best result achieved with the automatically learned ontologies does not perform better compared to the version relying on the MeSH thesaurus, yielding an F-Measure of F_1=21.93%.

With respect to micro-averaging, the best results achieved with automatically learned ontologies are better compared to the baseline using no conceptual features as well as to MeSH (compare Table 9.2).

Thus, also with regard to the clustering task we can conclude that using automatically learned concept hierarchies as background knowledge improves in any case the baseline using no conceptual features. Considering macro-averaged results, we even get better results compared to using MeSH. This definitely corroborates the fact that automatically learned ontologies can also be successfully applied within a document clustering setting.

9.1.4 Summary

Summarizing, on the one hand we have presented in this section an application for automatically learned concept hierarchies within text classification or clustering approaches relying on background knowledge. The main conclusion here is that automatically learned concept hierarchies can actually compete with handcrafted concept hierarchies in terms of performance with respect to the results on these tasks. This is indeed a very promising result as it shows

Table 9.2. Performance Results in the Clustering Setting.

Ontology	Max. Level h	macro-averaged (in %)			
		Entropy	F_1	Inv. Purity	Purity
[none]	n.a.	2,6674	19,41%	17,22%	22,24%
agglo-7000	1	2,6326	19,47%	17,68%	21,65%
agglo-7000	10	2,5808	19,93%	17,55%	23,04%
agglo-7000	20	2,5828	19,88%	17,69%	22,70%
bisec-7000	1	2,5896	19,84%	17,72%	22,53%
bisec-7000	10	2,5361	20,17%	17,38%	24,02%
bisec-7000	20	2,5321	20,01%	17,38%	23,59%
bisec-14000	1	2,5706	19,96%	17,76%	22,80%
bisec-14000	10	2,4382	21,11%	17,68%	26,18%
bisec-14000	20	2,4557	20,77%	17,46%	25,67%
mesh	1	2,4135	21,63%	17,70%	27,78%
mesh	10	2,3880	**21,93%**	17,64%	28,98%

Ontology	Max. Level h	micro-averaged (in %)			
		Entropy	F_1	Inv. Purity	Purity
[none]	n.a.	3,12108	14,89%	14,12%	15,74%
agglo-7000	1	3,1102	15,34%	14,56%	16,21%
agglo-7000	10	3,1374	15,21%	14,43%	16,08%
agglo-7000	20	3,1325	15,27%	14,62%	15,97%
bisec-7000	1	3,1299	**15,48%**	14,84%	16,18%
bisec-7000	10	3,1533	15,18%	14,46%	15,98%
bisec-7000	20	3,1734	14,83%	14,23%	15,48%
bisec-14000	1	3,1479	15,19%	14,63%	15,80%
bisec-14000	10	3,1972	14,83%	14,33%	15,37%
bisec-14000	20	3,2019	14,67%	14,07%	15,36%
mesh	1	3,2123	14,92%	14,91%	14,93%
mesh	10	3,2361	14,61%	14,64%	14,59%

that, for some tasks, an automatically learned concept hierarchy can indeed replace a handcrafted one.

On the other hand, from a more general perspective we have also suggested a task-based and indirect evaluation of automatically learned concept hierarchies by integrating them as an additional parameter into a system accomplishing a certain task and the performance of which can be measured quantitatively. This goes in the direction of the suggestions of Porzel and Malaka [Porzel and Malaka, 2005]. Such an evaluation procedure indeed allows to compare the quality of different ontologies with respect to a given task. In the experiments presented in this section, the only parameter varied is the ontology itself, thus allowing to conclude that any difference in performance is due to the ontology. In fact, as discussed by Porzel and Malaka [Porzel and Malaka, 2005], an indirect evaluation of ontologies can only make sense if this requirement is fulfilled.

9.2 Information Highlighting for Supporting Search

In this section, we present an experimental study with the aim of clarifying if highlighting annotations partially produced by automatic techniques can increase user experience within a browsing framework. In particular, the aim has been to compare the performance of users relying on highlighted annotations to users which did not have such annotations with respect to a fact retrieval task. Indeed, as will be shown later, automatically generated annotations were found to add value to the browsing experience in the investigated scenario.

The user study can be seen as an indirect evaluation of the automatically populated ontologies. This sort of evaluation is thus a task-based evaluation as opposed to the quantitative evaluations with respect to a gold standard as presented in earlier chapters of this book. In this line, we present an alternative evaluation method based on analyzing the user experience of working with a system partially enriched with the help of ontology population technologies. In what follows, we briefly describe the technological settings in Section 9.2.1. In Section 9.2.2 we describe the settings of our experiments in detail before presenting the results in Section 9.2.3

9.2.1 Technological Settings

Our experiment was targeted to clarify whether the results of two information extraction tools, C-PANKOW and ESpotter [Zhu et al., 2005a], could be used to learn instances of concepts contained in the ontology, which if highlighted in the Magpie browser [Domingue and Dzbor, 2004] could increase user experience as well as performance on a fact retrieval task. The information extraction tools were used to generate lexicons from which Magpie could generate semantic annotations on the fly and highlight them to a user. Magpie, ESpotter as well as the settings with which C-PANKOW was applied to the task at hand are described below.

9.2.1.1 Magpie

Magpie [Domingue and Dzbor, 2004] is a framework developed by the *Open University*, partially responding to the challenge of the knowledge acquisition bottleneck. It allows users of web-based documents to interpret content from different conceptual perspectives by automatically generating annotations corresponding to a particular ontology as a semantic layer over the actual content of the document. This allows Magpie to provide semantic web services for documents with no semantic markup, or which are marked up according to ontologies that do not suit the user's purpose.

The end-user part of the Magpie framework consists of a browser plug-in which enables the user to choose an ontology and to toggle categories of knowledge via simple push buttons presented in a toolbar. Selecting a button highlights items in the text that are relevant to the chosen category. These dynamic annotations are generated using a lexicon which relates each concept in the ontology to the various text strings by which it is commonly represented. In early versions of Magpie, lexica were constructed by domain experts. It is this costly manual process which we have tried to automate using the two information extraction tools C-PANKOW and ESpotter. The role of C-PANKOW and ESpotter is thus to automatically enhance the lexicon which Magpie uses to generate annotations.

9.2.1.2 C-PANKOW

C-PANKOW has been applied to the task at hand downloading 100 pages and using a similarity threshold of 0.05 together with the *Hits* strategy for selecting the best concept (compare Section 8.3.2). We processed 307 KMi planet stories (compare Section 5) with C-PANKOW, yielding 1270 different instances (4.1 per document on average), which, on a scale from 0 to 3 (3 being best), were rated on average with 1.8 credits by a human evaluator. If we regard every annotation receiving at least two credits as correct, this translates into an accuracy of 58%. A total of 755 entities have been mapped to the following nine upper level categories: event, technology, place, organization, person, politician, company, project and research area and added to the Magpie lexicon.

9.2.1.3 ESpotter

ESpotter is a named entity recognition (NER) system also developed by the Open University [Zhu et al., 2005b]. It builds, on the one hand, on standard named entity recognition (NER) methods, using capitalization as an indicator for a name as well as relying on gazetteers (for example lists of common names). On the other hand, it also incorporates a domain adaptation mechanism which allows to choose the methods that are most likely to be reliable for a particular site.

Given a web page, ESpotter preprocesses it by removing markup tags and matching regular expressions with high reliability on the domain with respect to the task of recognizing entities of various types on the page. ESpotter extracted a total of 761 annotations (approx. 2.4 per document) from the KMi Planet News stories. These were 428 entities found for organization, 243 for person, 4 for research area and 86 for project. In this experiment, ESpotter's ability to recognize people's names was of particular interest.

9.2.2 Experimental Settings

The evaluation took the form of a user study conducted jointly by Victoria Uren from the Open University and the author of the present book in

November 2004. The goal of the experiment was to find out whether semantic annotations generated with the help of automatic ontology population tools improved the performance and user experience of Magpie users on information gathering tasks. The performance of three groups of participants was compared on two fact retrieval tasks, which involved searching an online database of KMi news stories. The groups were: Group A (baseline), who used standard keyword-based search techniques, Group B (Magpie/AKT), who had the news stories and a version of Magpie with a hand crafted lexicon based on internal knowledge bases from KMi and the University of Southampton (we will refer to this lexicon as AKT in what follows), and Group C (Magpie/AKT++), who had the same set up as Group B, but with the hand crafted lexicon enhanced by additions from the information extraction tools as well as of recent information from KMi's knowledge bases that had been created since the original lexicon was built. The AKT++ lexicon used by Group C represented the best lexicon we could construct exploiting all the resources at hand.

9.2.2.1 Tasks

The tasks of our user study were performed on KMi's *Planet News repository*[5]: an online newspaper featuring events at the Knowledge Media Institute. We defined two fact retrieval tasks: the *People* and the *Technology* tasks.

The *People* tasks consisted in compiling a list of important people who visited the institute. This task was defined to test the capabilities of C-PANKOW as well as of ESpotter with respect to finding new persons not included in the lexicon created from the KMi knowledge base.

In the *Technology* task, the participants were asked to compile a list of technologies, either in-house or external, used in KMi projects. This task mainly tested the C-PANKOW system, as ESpotter was not expected to find additional technologies not contained already in KMi's knowledge base (compare [Uren et al., 2005]).

The users were instructed to complete both tasks within 10 minutes. They recorded their answers by copy&pasting them into a text editor. These text files were then used as the basis for evaluating the study. Additionally, the users' interaction with the tool was recorded using Camtasia Studio[6] for further analysis.

9.2.2.2 Participants

The participants of the study were a mixture of research students (all working either in KMi or in the Open University Maths or Computer Science Department) as well as qualified researchers working at KMi. In general, they all had

---

[5] http://news.kmi.open.ac.uk/kmiplanet
[6] http://www.techsmith.com/products/studio/default.asp

sufficient web-searching skills as well as a reasonable understanding of the domain. The participants were more or less uniformly divided into the already mentioned groups A,B and C. Group A consisted of six participants, group B as well as C of seven participants each. Each of the groups used different settings for searching the KMi Planet News repository. The settings for the different groups are described in detail in the following.

9.2.2.3 Testbed

The baseline system used by Group A consisted of the *Planet News search site*, which incorporates a *Main News page* showing the most recent stories. From this site the user can access the News Archive, which lists the stories in reverse chronological order. It furthermore includes a drop-down list that allows the user to select a category of stories as well as a search option which permits simple and advanced keyword searches in which the users can search for authors, titles, stories or keywords within a certain category of stories.

Group B used the baseline system augmented with Magpie using the AKT lexicon containing the four upper level categories: person, project, research area and organization.

Group C used the baseline system augmented with Magpie but using the enhanced AKT++ lexicon. This lexicon is a superset of the original AKT lexicon containing additionally: (i) additional data from the KMi knowledge base, (ii) entities extracted with C-PANKOW and (iii) entities extracted with ES-potter. This enhanced lexicon consisted of the nine categories: person, project, research agenda, organization, place, event, politician, technology and company. The various sources were merged with the AKT lexicon consisting of 3679 items to a cumulated lexicon consisting of 6340 items. No duplicate detection was performed. A breakdown of the AKT++ lexicon of the number of entities per source is shown in the following table:

Category	AKT	KMi KB	C-PANKOW
event	0	0	74
technology	0	21	75
place	0	0	105
organization	154	474	237
person	3182	633	120
politician	0	0	23
company	0	0	53
project	192	74	70
research area	151	92	9

The above numbers already show that C-PANKOW has contributed substantially to the enrichment of the knowledge base. In particular, in the scenario considered it was, on the one hand, able to add entities for categories which were poorly or not represented in the KBs at all, such as event, technology or place. On the other hand, it is capable of a more fine-grained distinction of entities, thus specializing the category person further into politician and organization into company, respectively.

9.2.3 Results

We present the results of the user study in terms of (i) retrieval performance, (ii) an analysis of how many of the items each group retrieved were in one of the two lexica, and (iii) an analysis of interactions with the tools acquired from the Camtasia movies. For further details, the reader is referred to [Uren et al., 2005].

9.2.3.1 Retrieval Performance

The first question examined was whether having Magpie annotation available improved the participants' performance in terms of the number and quality of items retrieved within the available time span. In order to evaluate the participants' performance on the tasks, an impartial assessor neither involved in the design nor the execution of the experiments rated the items for the People task from '0' (unimportant or unrecognized), over '1' (moderately important) to '2' (important) and for the Technologies task from '0' (not a technology or unrecognized), over '1' (not an innovative technology) to '2' (innovative technology). Scores for each participant were calculated by summing up the scores for all their answers. Average scores for the three groups on both tasks are presented in Table 9.3. It is clear that both groups using Magpie achieved higher scores for both tasks than the baseline group. Group B (Magpie/AKT) did best on the People Task, whereas Group C (Magpie/AKT++) did best on the Technologies task. The differences between the scores for the People task are fairly small. None of the differences between groups are significant at the 5% α-level in two sample t-tests. Contrary to our expectation, Group C scored an average of 1.6 less than Group B. These are of course small sample groups and thus the results do not allow definite conclusions. The results for the Technology task, on the other hand, clearly show that having Magpie annotations available increased the scores of both Groups B and C compared to Group A. Group C, which used the enhanced AKT++ lexicon, obtained the highest score of all. For this task, two sample t-tests showed that the difference in performance between Group A and Group C was significant at the 5% α-level. The conclusion here is thus that automatically generated annotations have indeed the potential to improve performance on a fact retrieval task as considered in our experiments.

9.2.3.2 Answer Coverage

In addition to the objective performance on the fact retrieval task, we examined how suitable the two lexicons, i.e. AKT and AKT++, were for answering

Table 9.3. Average scores for the people and technologies tasks

Task	Group A	Group B	Group C
People	13.2	15.3	13.7
Technologies	19.2	23.4	26.7

the questions in principle. For this purpose, we determined how many of the participants' answers were in one of the two lexica. For all three groups and for both tasks, we found that the AKT++ lexicon contains more answers than the AKT lexicon. For all six cases, the differences were significant at the 2.5% level according to two-tailed t-tests. This indicates that the AKT++ lexicon was better suited to the tasks than the AKT lexicon, that means, it would have given more appropriate suggestions. To some extent, this result is obvious due to the fact that the AKT++ lexicon almost doubles the AKT lexicon in size, but it is reassuring to know that the additional entries have indeed the potential to enhance the users' browsing experience. For the People task, we are confident that the difference in the answer coverage comes from lexicon items generated either by C-PANKOW or by ESpotter, since we know that the majority of names stemming from new additions to the knowledge base are those of KMi staff. For the Technology task, a fine grained analysis determined that 19 of the answers categorized as *project* or *technology* could only have been highlighted because of additions to the lexicon by C-PANKOW. These 19 answers scored 15 using our assessor's ratings. Typical good quality additions were *XML*, *Topic Maps*, *SMS* and *Semantic Web*. They seem to represent technologies that are important to KMi but were not developed in-house and therefore do not appear in the institutional ontology. C-PANKOW is thus giving a qualitative improvement to the scope of the annotations. For a more detailed discussion of these results, the interested reader is referred to [Uren et al., 2005]. Overall, the results show that the AKT++ lexicon partially produced by automatic ontology population techniques is better suited to carry out the tested tasks than the AKT lexicon in terms of coverage and categorization of items.

9.2.3.3 Movie Analysis

The Camtasia movies recorded during the experiment were analyzed to see how often the participants selected each of the categories offered by Magpie for highlighting. Table 9.4 shows the mean usage of the different highlighting options for Group B and Group C (Group A did not use Magpie). The most used highlighting options for Group B were person and project. The most used options by Group C were person, project, politician and technology.

For the People task, Group B mainly used the person and organization options and Group C used person and politician. However, for the Technology task, whereas Group B mainly used project highlighting, Group C used primarily technology, even though the answer coverage indicates that using project would have been a better strategy. The movies were also analyzed for two additional kinds of data. We counted how often Groups B and C made a selection (typically by cut and pasting an item to their answer list) when Magpie highlighting was on, and how often, on these occasions, the item they selected had been highlighted by Magpie. The data confirms that Group C were more inclined to turn Magpie on than Group B; for both tasks the percentage of selection events that occurred with Magpie highlighting on was higher for Group C. For the People task it is very clear why. For Group B turning Magpie on gave a very low rate of return, less than one tenth of items selected with highlighting on were actually highlighted by Magpie. For Group C three quarters of people selected with highlighting turned on had been highlighted by Magpie. For the Technology task the results are very interesting because although Group C were more inclined to turn Magpie on, they were actually getting a lower rate of return than Group B (43.8% vs. 65.0%) (compare Table 9.4). It seems that the trust built up in their initial positive experience with the People task persisted into the Technology task, even though the reward rate dropped.

Table 9.4. Usage of highlighting

Task	Selections with Magpie activated (%)		Selection of highlited texts with Magpie activated (%)	
	Group B	Group C	Group B	Group C
People	11.7	51.8	7.1	74.1
Technologies	24.1	62.9	65.0	43.8

9.2.4 Summary

The results of the evaluation indeed show that for fact finding exercises of this kind, appropriate highlighting can help users in identifying more relevant items in a fixed time. Comparing the two different lexicons AKT and AKT++, the test subjects were more inclined to use the highlighting for AKT++ which had been boosted with items extracted from text. We conclude that, for a browsing system such as Magpie, semantic annotations, including the slightly noisy kind inevitably produced by automatic ontology population systems, seem to work better than small amounts of high quality, humanly generated annotation with limited domain scope. While we cannot generalize too far beyond the scenario investigated here, our results support the view that such automatic techniques have indeed the potential to alleviate the knowledge acquisition bottleneck.

The user study presented in this section is in line with the task-based evaluation principle discussed earlier in this section in the sense that a baseline system and a system relying on automatically generated annotations are compared with respect to a certain task, in this case the one of retrieving certain facts from a text repository. Once again, it is important to mention that it is this sort of task-based evaluation which will ultimately allow definite conclusions about which technologies work in the sense that they improve over a baseline and which do not.

9.3 Related Work

In this section, we discuss related work in the fields of text mining, information retrieval or natural language processing using ontology learning techniques or showing a clear potential for their application. In particular, we discuss query expansion, information retrieval, text clustering and classification as well as natural language processing tasks.

9.3.1 Query Expansion

Several researchers have analyzed the possibility of expanding a search query with additional terms derived from a thesaurus, taxonomy or ontology. The aim of expanding document retrieval queries in such a way is to overcome the problem of *vocabulary mismatch*, that is, the case in which a user queries for a document using other words than contained in it. In this case, it makes sense to expand the query with semantically related words to alleviate the problem of vocabulary mismatch. For this purpose, one needs a structured resource such as a taxonomy or thesaurus in which words are organized in a graph-like structure and connected through links corresponding to certain semantic relations. These relations are typically: synonymy, hypernymy, hyponymy, antonymy, meronymy, etc. WordNet is the standard example for such a thesaurus containing all of the above links. The hypernymy/hyponymy relation thereby makes up for around 70% of the links, thus being the most frequent relation in WordNet.

Several researchers have reported positive results concerning query expansion. Salton and Lesk [Salton and Lesk, 1971], for example, found that expansion with synonyms improved performance, while using broader or narrower terms produced too inconsistent results for being actually useful. Wang et al. [Wang et al., 1985] report that a variety of lexical-semantic relations improved retrieval performance. These experiments were, however, conducted on very small document collections. Voorhees [Voorhees, 1994] in contrast reports results on a larger collection, the TREC collection. In Voorhees' settings, WordNet synsets are added to the queries by hand, thus avoiding the problem of word sense disambiguation. The conclusions of Voorhees are twofold. On the one hand, she concludes that query expansion only helps when queries are relatively short. On the other hand, she also implements an automatic procedure to add WordNet synsets to a given query and concludes that there is a need for a lot of improvement in such a procedure before query expansion can be applied automatically. In general, it seems that using automatically derived thesauri or word associations works better than using hand-crafted resources [Fox, 1980]. The reason is that thesauri automatically derived from the document collection fit the domain in question better than general resources such as WordNet. In fact, Qiu and Fei [Qiu and Frei, 1993] used an automatically constructed thesaurus with the result of a 20% improvement in retrieval effectiveness on a small collection. Schütze and Pedersen [Schütze and Pedersen, 1997] built a co-occurrence based thesaurus and applied it within two information retrieval applications, slightly improving the retrieval performance. As already mentioned in Section 6, Grefenstette [Grefenstette, 1994] performed experiments using several small text collections, improving the retrieval performance for some of the collections with his method. In the same line, Jing and Croft [Jing and Croft, 1994] found an improvement through query expansion using an automatically constructed association thesaurus. Other successful examples of experiments in query expansion using automatically generated thesauri can be found in the work of Park and Choi [Park and Choi, 1996] as well as Crouch and Yang [Crouch and Yang, 1992].

9.3.2 Information Retrieval

Information from a thesaurus can be exploited within information retrieval essentially in two ways, either by modifying the document representation integrating conceptual descriptors or semantic features, or defining a 'semantic' similarity measure taking into account the structure of the thesaurus. Both approaches have been investigated in the context of information retrieval.

A conceptual document representation requires the disambiguation of words, which is in itself a difficult problem. Sanderson [Sanderson, 1994] has argued that word sense ambiguity in fact has only a minor effect on retrieval performance. Furthermore, he estimates that word sense disambiguation systems need to achieve an accuracy of at least 90% to be applicable for information retrieval. More recent work by Gonzalo et al. [Gonzalo et al., 1998] has however shown that this lower bound on disambiguation accuracy is far too pessimistic. In fact, in the experiments presented, indexing of texts with synsets yields up to 29% improvement with respect to a standard IR system - SMART - indexing only with words. More interestingly, the method based on conceptual indexing still performs better at a disambiguation error rate of around 30%.

Other research has focused on integrating the structure of the thesaurus into the measure assessing the similarity between the query and document vectors. Richardson and Smeaton [Richardson and Smeaton, 1995], for example, present a similarity measure based on the work of Resnik [Resnik, 1999]. However, they do not achieve an increase in retrieval performance.

9.3.3 Text Clustering and Classification

To date, the work on integrating background knowledge into text classification, text clustering or related tasks is quite heterogeneous. Green [Green, 1999] uses WordNet to construct chains of related synsets from the occurrence of terms for document representation and subsequent clustering. Green does not evaluate performance and scalability of his approach as compared to standard bag-of-words based clustering of documents. Dave et al. [Dave et al., 2003] used WordNet without word sense disambiguation and found that indexing with WordNet synsets decreased clustering performance in all their experiments. Recently, Bloehdorn and Hotho [Bloehdorn and Hotho, 2004, Hotho et al., 2003] have reported promising results when using additional conceptual features extracted from manually engineered ontologies. Other results from similar settings are reported by Scott and Matwin [Scott and Matwin, 1999] as well as Wang et al. [Wang et al., 2003]. De Buenaga Rodríguez et. al. [de Buenaga Rodríguez et al., 2000] and Ureña et. al. [Ureña et al., 2001] show a successful integration of the WordNet resource for a document categorization task, but the result is based on *manually* built synset vectors.

Alternative approaches for conceptual representations of text documents that do not require explicit manually engineered background knowledge mainly draw from dimension reduction techniques like Latent Semantic Analysis [Deerwester et al., 1990] or Probabilistic Latent Semantic Analysis [Cai and Hofmann, 2003]. These techniques compute 'concepts' statistically from term co-occurrence information. In contrast to the approach of Bloehdorn et al., the concept-like structures are, however, not easily interpretable by humans.

9.3.4 Natural Language Processing

Ontologies have important applications within natural language processing and understanding. Theoretical issues concerning the usage of ontologies for natural language processing are discussed by Bateman [Bateman, 1991], who in particular presents different types of ontologies and discusses their advantages and disadvantages from a conceptual or philosophical point of view.

From a computational point of view, they provide the necessary vocabulary and axiomatization of a certain domain, allowing for semantic construction as well as reasoning with respect to a given target language. An early example of a natural language understanding system heavily relying on axiomatized world knowledge is the JANUS system [Hinrichs, 1987]. A more recent example is the system described by McShane et al. [McShane et al., 2005]. From a processing point of view, the subtasks within natural language processing for which world knowledge in form of ontologies can be used typically are:

- ambiguity resolution

- interpretation of compounds
- interpretation of vague words
- anaphora resolution / discourse analysis

Natural language is typically highly ambiguous, whereby ambiguities occur at nearly all levels of analysis, that is, at the lexical level, at the syntactic as well as at the semantic level. At the lexical level, there are polysemous words featuring different lexical meanings, e.g. *bank*. There is also the problem of interpreting the relation between words within a compound such as *headache medicine*. Furthermore, there are prepositions such as *with, of* as well as auxiliary verbs such as *has* which are inherently vague and need to be interpreted with respect to the specific context. An ontology can help in this respect by stating which semantic relations potentially hold between different concepts, thus constraining the interpretation of vague predicates or the relations between words in a nominal compound. So called *selectional restrictions* specified with respect to a given ontology can help in the disambiguation of the meaning of polysemous words. In fact, selectional restrictions can be seen as the specification of which concepts are allowed to fill the arguments of a certain predicate represented by a verb, or can be modified by a certain adjective, etc. All the systems using an ontology as background knowledge for natural language understanding are obviously also faced with the so called *knowledge acquisition bottleneck*. For this purpose, most researchers have developed tools supporting the development of ontologies on the basis of corpus-based analysis. The JANUS system, for example, relies on two tools for knowledge acquisition from corpora: IRACQ and KNACQ [Hinrichs, 1987]. Nirenburg et al. describe their tools for knowledge acquisition in [Nirenburg et al., 1996]. Other important research on lexical acquisition has been conducted in the context of the Acquilex project[7], especially focusing on the extraction of knowledge from machine-readable dictionaries (compare Section 6.1.1).

In what follows, we further discuss some specific applications where ontologies have been used for natural language processing.

9.3.4.1 Word Sense Disambiguation

The problem of word sense disambiguation can be described as the task of assigning the correct meaning to a word in a given context. Typically, word sense disambiguation research has considered so called word sense enumerating lexica in which words are assigned a finite set of senses or meanings such as in WordNet. One of the first word sense disambiguation algorithms was the one introduced by Lesk [Lesk, 1986], in which that sense of a word is chosen, the gloss of which shows the largest overlap with the glosses for all the synsets of the words in the context of the target word. Other researchers have extended Lesk's algorithm additionally exploiting the structure of the thesaurus by not only considering the gloss

---

[7] http://www.cl.cam.ac.uk/Research/NL/acquilex/acqhome.html

of the synset of the target word, but also the glosses of synsets related to it via a lexical relation such as hypernymy, hyponymy or meronymy (see for example [Agirre and Rigau, 1996, Banerjee and Pedersen, 2003]). Other researches have adopted an information content based approach to assess the similarity of words on the basis of the WordNet hierarchy (cf. [Resnik, 1995, Jiang and Conrath, 1998]). In particular, the information content is calculated for each concept by aggregating the corpus-based frequency of all the members in the extension of a concept by calculating its information content.

9.3.4.2 Classification of unknown words

Recently, several researchers have tackled the problem of classifying unknown words with respect to an existing taxonomy (see for example [Hearst and Schütze, 1993, Alfonseca and Manandhar, 2002, Pekar and Staab, 2002, Mädche et al., 2002, Widdows, 2003b]). Pekar and Staab [Pekar and Staab, 2002] as well as Hearst and Schütze [Hearst and Schütze, 1993], among others, for example have shown how the structure of the concept hierarchy itself can be used for more accurate classification by aggregating the vectors of hyponyms to construct the vector of their hypernyms as in our approach to named entity recognition described in Section 8.2.

9.3.4.3 Named Entity Recognition (NER)

Named entity recognition typically relies to a great extent on so called gazetteers, in which named entities are assigned to their corresponding class. Named entity recognition can thus profit from ontologies automatically populated using diverse methods such as presented in [Etzioni et al., 2005], [Maynard et al., 2004] as well as the methods described in Chapter 8.

9.3.4.4 Anaphora Resolution

Some researchers have advocated 'knowledge-poor' strategies to anaphora resolution and reference resolution in general (compare [Mitkov, 1998]). However, other researchers have attempted to exploit lexical ontologies for the purpose of resolving definite descriptions (see [Poesio et al., 1997] and [Muñoz and Palomar, 2001]). Other approaches rely on richly axiomatized ontologies (compare [Cimiano et al., 2005d]). Recently, some researchers have investigated the possibility of using automatically acquired knowledge for anaphora resolution (compare [Poesio et al., 2002] and [Markert et al., 2003]). In this line, our automatically generated qualia structures could represent a valuable resource. In general, it seems quite clear that background knowledge is needed for automatic reference resolution within NLP systems.

9.3.4.5 Question Answering

Ontology learning also has important applications in question answering. To some extent, question answering also suffers from the same problem as information retrieval, i.e. the vocabulary mismatch problem. In fact, due to language's variation, in most cases people will ask for information in a different way as it is stated in a certain web page. As an example, the answer to the question *Who wrote the Lord of the Rings?* is clearly provided by the sentence *Tolkien is the author of the Lord of the Rings.* However, this correspondence can not be directly observed at the surface. Acquiring paraphrases of different ways to express the same content is thus an important issue within question answering. This issue has been for example addressed by Lin and Pantel [Lin and Pantel, 2001b].

9.3.4.6 Information Extraction

In the information extraction community, a lot of early research has addressed the induction of dictionaries from a corpus to facilitate portability to other domains. Early systems addressing the task of automatically inducing extraction rules from a corpus in an unsupervised way are the CRYSTAL [Soderland et al., 1995] as well as AUTOSLOG [Riloff, 1993] systems, for example. Recently, Faure and Poibeau [Faure and Poibeau, 2000] have shown how ontology learning techniques can be applied to the induction of automata for information extraction. They present an approach in which extraction automata can generalize over word classes automatically acquired with the ASIUM system [Faure and Nedellec, 1998] (compare Section 6.5.1), thus reducing the effort in customizing an information extraction system for a certain domain. Other corpus-based knowledge acquisition techniques have been applied, for example, to derive discourse analysis rules [Ng and Cardie, 2002, Soderland and Lehner, 1994] as well as to learn part-of-speech, word sense and concept activation knowledge for unknown words [Cardie, 1993].

9.4 Contribution and Open Issues

This chapter has discussed applications for approaches automatically learning concept hierarchies from text as well as populating them with instances. The main application of such automatically learned ontologies are definitely in the field of text mining, where noise is tolerable to some extent. We have suggested query expansion, information retrieval, natural language processing as well as clustering and classification of documents as main fields of application for such techniques. In particular, we have presented experimental evidence for the fact that automatically learned ontologies can indeed compete with handcrafted ones when used as background knowledge for clustering and classification approaches exploiting conceptual features. We have also shown that automatic population of ontologies with named entities can provide a benefit in information retrieval tasks. To our knowledge such task-based evaluations of ontologies have not been carried out before.

Further work has still to unveil the full potential of using automatically learned ontologies for query expansion or information retrieval. As discussed above, some research has shown that handcrafted ontologies can provide a measurable benefit. However, it is definitely an open issue to clarify if such an improvement can also be obtained when using automatically learned resources.

Concerning NLP, we have argued at the beginning of this book that world knowledge is crucial for certain tasks within natural language processing and understanding. Certainly, there is still a lack of empirical work conveying the usefulness of ontologies for NLP in general as well as of automatically derived world knowledge in particular.

Finally, it also seems an open issue if automatically learned ontologies can be used as a basis for reasoning. For sure, some sort of fuzzy or probabilistic reasoning will then be needed to cope with uncertain knowledge such as produced by automatic ontology learning approaches.

Part III

Conclusion

10

Contribution and Outlook

This book contributes to the state-of-the-art in ontology learning in several ways. First, we have provided a formal definition of ontology learning tasks with respect to a well-defined ontology model. The *ontology learning layer cake*, a model for representing the diverse subtasks in ontology learning has been introduced. In addition, evaluation measures for the concept hierarchy induction, relation learning as well as ontology population tasks have been defined. These evaluation measures provide a basis in order to compare different approaches performing a certain task. Most importantly, several original and novel approaches performing a certain task have been presented and compared to other state-of-the-art approaches from the literature using the defined evaluation measures.

Concerning the concept hierarchy induction task, we have presented a novel approach based on Formal Concept Analysis, an original guided agglomerative clustering method as well as a combination approach for the induction of concept hierarchies from text. All the approaches have been evaluated and have been demonstrated to actually outperform current state-of-the-art methods. We have further introduced and discussed several approaches to learning attributes and relations. In particular, we have presented approaches to learn i) attributes, ii) the appropriate domain and range for relations, as well as iii) specific relations using a pattern-based approach. Several approaches to automatically populate an ontology with instances have also been described. We have in particular examined a similarity-based approach as well as introduced the original approach of *Learning By Googling*. Corresponding evaluations have also been provided. Finally, we have have also discussed applications for ontology learning approaches and demonstrated for two concrete applications that the techniques developed in the context of this book are indeed useful. Throughout the book, we have also provided a thorough overview of related work.

Fortunately, there are a number of open issues which require further research. On the one hand, though we have undertaken a first step towards combining different ontology learning paradigms via a machine-learning approach, further research is needed in this direction to unveil the full potential of such a combination. In particular, other paradigms than our classification-based approach could be explored. One could imagine to train classifiers for each type of basic ontological relation, i.e. isa, part-of, etc. using different methods and then use a calculus as envisioned by Heyer and colleagues [Heyer et al., 2001] as well as Ogata and Collier [Ogata and Collier, 2004] to combine the results of these classifiers and reason on different types of extracted ontological relations. Such a post-extraction reasoning is in fact crucial as the different approaches can produce contradicting information and thus producing a consistent ontology needs some kind of contradiction resolution approach. In fact, one important problem is to generate the optimal ontology maximizing a certain criterion given a certain amount of - possibly contradicting - relations. Initial blueprints for such an approach can be found, for example, in the work of Haase and Völker [Haase and Völker, 2005]. A lot of further research is however needed in this direction.

Another important issue to be clarified is which similarity measures, which weighting measures and which features work best for the task of clustering words. Though we have provided some insights in the present book, much more work is needed to clarify these issues. In the same vein, further experiments are necessary to clarify the relation between syntactic and semantic similarity such as perceived by humans. These issues can only be approached from an experimental perspective. Though there has been a lot of work on this issue, much further research can be expected.

In general, from a theoretical perspective, it would be necessary to clarify what type of ontologies we can actually learn, i.e. domain ontologies, lexical ontologies, upper-level ontologies, application ontologies, etc. Work in this direction has been presented by Bateman [Bateman, 1991], for instance. In this line, it seems also necessary to ask ourselves about the limits of ontology learning techniques. Furthermore, an integration of ontology learning techniques with linguistic theories, in particular with lexicon theories such as Generative Lexicon [Pustejovsky, 1991] is definitely desirable. In addition, it seems desirable to clarify the relation between ontological and lexical semantics.

In the long term, it would definitely be interesting to acquire more complex relationships between concepts and relations in the form of rules or axioms.

Last but not least, approaches should actually have reasonable applications. We have argued that it is far from straightforward to devise applications making use of automatically learned ontologies in a reasonable way. The problem lies in the fact that there are a number of parameters to be tuned on which the success of using an ontology depends. However, the quest for applications is a necessary and crucial one. Future research should thus further examine the usefulness of automatically derived knowledge structures for certain applications.

11

Concluding Remarks

In this book, we have considered ontology learning as a reverse engineering task. Our aim has been to reconstruct the world model shared by a group of people on the basis of text documents which they produce. Our assumption here has been that the authors' world model heavily influences the creative process of writing a text. However, as we have argued several times, this knowledge is rarely discussed by the author explicitly, an exception being didactic material such as dictionaries, encyclopedias, textbooks, etc. Therefore, the reconstruction of a world model is actually highly challenging. We have presented a considerable amount of techniques to address different ontology learning subtasks, i.e. learning concept hierarchies and relations, but also populating ontologies. All the approaches rely on the assumption that meaning can indeed emerge from the way certain constructs are used (compare [Wittgenstein, 1953]). The whole work described in this book is in fact grounded on two crucial assumptions. The first one is that if we consider a heterogeneous text collection with contributions of different authors on a specific domain, we can expect a shared conceptualization implicit in the document collection which we need to unveil. The second crucial assumption is that meaning can be approximated to some extent by statistically analyzing usage. The crucial open questions thus are:

- In how far can the knowledge implicitly contained in a collection of texts from different authors be in fact regarded as shared?
- If the knowledge implicitly underlying a document collection is indeed shared, can the knowledge automatically derived from the text collection also be regarded as such ?
- What is the relation between knowledge, text and the process of writing ?
- Is the meaning of a word actually in its use as assumed by Wittgenstein [Wittgenstein, 1953]?
- To what extent can knowledge actually be extracted from text?

A lot of research in philosophy, psychology and linguistics still needs to be conducted to answer the first four questions. To answer these questions is definitely out of the scope of the present book. The fifth question is more practical in its nature, but decades of research are still to come in order to clarify the full potential of methods automatically acquiring knowledge from text. In this line, our work can be regarded as a humble contribution in this direction.

A

Appendix

A.1 Learning Accuracy

In this appendix, we formally clarify the relation between our symmetric version of the Learning Accuracy LA and Hahn et al.'s original version LA_{Hahn}. For this purpose, we introduce some mathematical notation and make some assumptions concerning the underlying mathematical structures. In particular, we assume a semi-upper lattice $(N, \leq)$ with top-element top, i.e. an order satisfying the following properties:

$$\forall x \; x \leq x \; \textit{(reflexive)} \tag{A.1}$$

$$\forall x \, \forall y \; (x \leq y \wedge y \leq x \rightarrow x = y) \; \textit{(anti-symmetric)} \tag{A.2}$$

$$\forall x \, \forall y \, \forall z \; (x \leq y \wedge y \leq z \rightarrow x \leq z) \; \textit{(transitive)} \tag{A.3}$$

$$\forall x \; x \leq top \; \textit{(top element)} \tag{A.4}$$

$$\forall x \, \forall y \, \exists z \; (z \geq x \wedge z \geq y \wedge \forall w \; (w \geq x \wedge w \geq y \rightarrow w \geq z)) \tag{A.5}$$

$$\textit{(supremum)}$$

Furthermore, we define $\prec$ as the inmediate successor relationship, i.e.

$$\forall x \, \forall y \; (x \prec y \leftrightarrow x \leq y \wedge \neg \exists z \; (x \leq z \leq y)) \tag{A.6}$$

Distance between nodes in terms of edges is now defined as follows:

$$\delta(a,b) := \begin{cases} argmin_m \; \textit{such that } a \prec a_1 \prec \ldots \prec a_{m-1} \prec b & \textit{if } a \leq b \\ argmin_m \; \textit{such that } b \prec b_1 \prec \ldots \prec b_{m-1} \prec a & \textit{if } b \leq a \\ undef. & \textit{otherwise} \end{cases} \tag{A.7}$$

And distance in terms of nodes is consequently defined as follows:

$$\delta_N(a,b) = \delta(a,b) + 1 \tag{A.8}$$

We can now define the least common subsumer of two concepts a and b as:

$$lcs(a,b) := z \ such \ that \ z \geq a \wedge z \geq b \ and \ \forall w \ (w \geq a \wedge w \geq b \rightarrow w \geq z) \tag{A.9}$$

Thus, we yield the following properties:

$$\forall a \ lcs(a,a) = a \tag{A.10}$$
$$\forall a \forall b \ lcs(a,b) = lcs(b,a) \tag{A.11}$$
$$\forall a \forall b \ lcs(a,b) = b \ if \ a \leq b \tag{A.12}$$

Our Learning Accuracy is now defined as follows:

$$LA(c,p) := \frac{\delta(top, lcs(c,p)) + 1}{\delta(top, lcs(c,p)) + \delta(c, lcs(c,p)) + \delta(p, lcs(c,p)) + 1} \tag{A.13}$$

where c stands for the *correct* and p for the *predicted* concept.
In contrast, Hahn et al.'s Learning Accuracy is defined as follows:

$$LA_{Hahn} := \begin{cases} \frac{CP}{SP} & if \ FP = 0 \\ \frac{CP}{FP+DP} & otherwise \end{cases} \tag{A.14}$$

where

- SP specifies the length of the shortest path (in terms of nodes being traversed) from the top node of the concept hierarchy to the maximally specific concept subsuming the correct node c.
- CP specifies the length of the path (in terms of nodes being traversed) from the top node to the *most specific* node which is common both to the shortest path (as defined above) and the actual path to the predicted concept p.
- FP specifies the length of the path (in terms of nodes being traversed) from the top node to the predicted concept p (FP=0 if the prediction is correct, i.e. $c \leq p$).
- DP denotes the distance (*in terms of edges*) between the predicted node and the most specific common concept.

We will make the following assumptions concerning the above definitions:

- $SP = \delta_N(top, c)$, i.e. c is the most specific concept subsuming c.

- The most specific node common both to the shortest path (as defined above) and the actual path from top to p is $lcs(c,p)$.
- Concerning the DP definition, we will assume $lcs(c,p)$ to be the most specific common concept.

Thus we get:

$$SP = \delta_N(top, c) \tag{A.15}$$

$$CP = \delta_N(top, lcs(c,p)) \tag{A.16}$$

$$FP = \begin{cases} 0 & \text{if } c \leq p \\ \delta_N(top, p) & \text{otherwise} \end{cases} \tag{A.17}$$

$$DP = \delta(lcs(c,p), p) \tag{A.18}$$

So the Learning Accuracy of Hahn et al. is in terms of our notation:

$$LA_{Hahn} := \begin{cases} \frac{\delta_N(top, lcs(c,p))}{\delta_N(top, c)} & \text{if } c \leq p \\ \frac{\delta_N(top, lcs(c,p))}{\delta_N(top, p) + \delta(p, lcs(c,p))} & \text{otherwise} \end{cases} \tag{A.19}$$

Transforming distance in terms of nodes to distance in terms of edges we yield:

$$LA_{Hahn} := \begin{cases} \frac{\delta(top, lcs(c,p)) + 1}{\delta(top, c) + 1} & \text{if } c \leq p \\ \frac{\delta(top, lcs(c,p)) + 1}{\delta(top, p) + 1 + \delta(p, lcs(c,p))} & \text{otherwise} \end{cases} \tag{A.20}$$

Furthermore, in case the concept hierarchy is a tree we get that:

$$\delta(top, a) = \delta(top, lcs(a, b)) + \delta(lcs(a, b), a) \text{ for any } b. \tag{A.21}$$

Thus, as $\delta(lcs(c,p), p) = 0$ in case $c \leq p$:

$$LA_{Hahn} := \begin{cases} \frac{\delta(top, lcs(c,p)) + 1}{\delta(top, lcs(c,p)) + \delta(lcs(c,p), c) + \delta(lcs(c,p), p) + 1} & \text{if } c \leq p \\ \frac{\delta(top, lcs(c,p)) + 1}{\delta(top, lcs(c,p)) + \delta(lcs(c,p), p) + \delta(p, lcs(c,p)) + 1} & \text{otherwise} \end{cases} \tag{A.22}$$

And this reduces to:

$$LA_{Hahn} := \begin{cases} \frac{\delta(top, lcs(c,p)) + 1}{\delta(top, lcs(c,p)) + \delta(lcs(c,p), c) + \delta(lcs(c,p), p) + 1} & \text{if } c \leq p \\ \frac{\delta(top, lcs(c,p)) + 1}{\delta(top, lcs(c,p)) + 2\, \delta(lcs(c,p), p) + 1} & \text{otherwise} \end{cases} \tag{A.23}$$

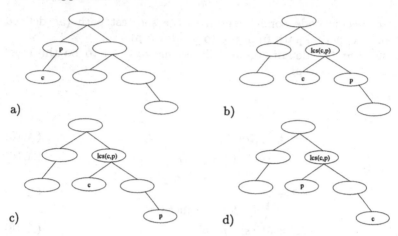

Fig. A.1. Learning Accuracy Examples

Thus, in case the concept hierarchy is a tree, our and Hahn et al.'s Learning Accuracy are equivalent for the case that $c \leq p$. The main difference is that in the other case Hahn et al.'s learning accuracy does not take into account the distance between the correct concept c and the least common subsumer of p and c, i.e. $\delta(c, lcs(c,p))$. Figure A.1 shows different configurations for the predicted concept p and the correct concept c. In example a) we have a correct but too general prediction. Thus we have $lcs(c,p) = p$. In this case both learning accuracies are the same, i.e. $LA = LA_{Hahn} = \frac{1+1}{1+1+1} = \frac{2}{3}$. In case b) we have a wrong prediction in which both p and c are at the same taxonomic level. In this case both learning accuracies are also equivalent, i.e. $LA := LA_{Hahn} := \frac{2}{4} = \frac{1}{2}$. For examples c) and d), our learning accuracy and the one of Hahn et al.'s differ. In example c) we have $LA = \frac{2}{5}$ and $LA_{Hahn} = \frac{2}{6} = \frac{1}{3}$. In example c) we have again $LA = \frac{2}{5}$ but $LA_{Hahn} = \frac{2}{4} = \frac{1}{2}$.

We hope that the discussion in this appendix has shed light on the principle differences between our and Hahn's learning accuracy. Clear advantages of our version of the learning accuracy are, however, that (i) it does not require any case distinction, (ii) it can be formulated in a clearer way, (iii) it also takes into account the distance between c and $lcs(c,p)$ in case the predicition is not correct and (iv) it is easier to implement.

A.2 Mutually Similar Words for the tourism domain

Jaccard	Cosine	L1 norm	Jensen-Shannon
(art exhibition,thing)	(agreement,contract)	(day,time)	(group,person)
(autumn,spring)	(animal,plant)	(golf course,promenade)	
(balcony,menu)	(art exhibition,washing machine)	(group,person)	
(ballroom,theatre)	(basilica,hair dryer)		
(banquet,ship)	(boat,ship)		
(bar,pub)	(cabaret,email)		
(basilica,hair dryer)	(cheque,pension)		
(beach,swimming pool)	(city,town)		
(billiard,sauna)	(conference room,volleyball field)		
(bus,car)	(golf course,promenade)		
(caravan,tree)	(group,party)		
(casino,date)	(inn,yacht)		
(cinema,fitness studio)	(journey,meal)		
(city,town)	(kiosk,tennis court)		
(conference,seminar)	(law,view)		
(conference room,volleyball field)	(library,museum)		
(cure,washing machine)	(money,thing)		
(day tour,place)	(motel,port)		
(distance,radio)	(pilgrimage,whirlpool)		
(exhibition,price list)	(sauna,swimming)		
(ferry,telephone)			
(gallery,shop)			
(golf course,promenade)			
(holiday,service)			
(journey,terrace)			
(kiosk,time interval)			
(law,presentation)			
(lounge,park)			
(motel,port)			
(nature reserve,parking lot)			
(night,tourist)			
(region,situation)			

A.3 Mutually Similar Words for the finance domain

Jaccard	Cosine	L1 norm	Jensen-Shann...
(action,average)	(access,advantage)	(archives,futures)	(cent,point)
(activity,downturn)	(acquisition,merger)	(assurance,telephone number)	(government,p...
(addition,liquidity)	(action,measure)	(balancing,countenance)	(month,year)
(afternoon,key)	(administration costs,treasury stock)	(cent,point)	
(agency,purchase)	(advice,assurance)	(creation,experience)	
(agreement,push)	(allocation,length)	(government,person)	
(alliance,project team)	(amount,total)	(loss,profit)	
(allocation,success)	(analysis,component)	(month,year)	
(analysis,negotiation)	(area,region)		
(animal,basis)	(arrangement,regime)		
(anomaly,regression)	(assembly,chamber)		
(archives,futures)	(assessment,receipt)		
(area,profitability)	(backer,gamble)		
(argument,dismantling)	(balancing,matrix)		
(arrangement,capital market)	(bank,company)		
(arranger,update)	(barometer,market price)		
(assembly,price decline)	(bid,offer)		
(assurance,telephone number)	(bond,stock)		
(automobile,oil)	(bonus share,cassette)		
(backer,trade partner)	(boom,turnaround)		
(balance sheet,person)	(bull market,tool)		
(balancing,countenance)	(business deal,graph)		
(behaviour,business partnership)	(buy,stop)		
(bike,moment)	(capital stock,profit distribution)		
(billing,grade)	(caravan,software company)		
(board,spectrum)	(cent,point)		
(board chairman,statement)	(change,increase)		
(bonus,nationality)	(commission,committee)		
(bonus share,cassette)	(company profile,intangible)		
(branch office,size)	(complaint,request)		
(broker,competition)	(controller,designer)		
(budget,regulation)	(copper,share index)		
(builder,devices)	(copy,push)		
(building,vehicle)	(credit,loan)		
(business volume,outlook)	(credit agreement,credit line)		
(business year,quota)	(currency,dollar)		
(capital,material costs)	(decision,plan)		
(capital increase,stock split)	(detail,test)		
(capital stock,profit distribution)	(diagram,support)		
(caravan,seminar)	(dimension,surcharge)		
(cent,point)	(discussion,negotiation)		
(chance,hope)	(diversification,milestone)		
(change,subsidiary)	(do,email)		
(charge,suspicion)	(document,letter)		
(chip,woman)	(effect,impact)		
(circle,direction)	(equity fund,origin)		
(clock,ratio)	(evaluation,examination)		
(code,insurance company)	(example,hint)		
(comment,foundation)	(first,meter)		
(commission,expansion)	(forecast,stock market activity)		
(communication,radio)	(function,profile)		
(community,radius)	(gesture,input)		
(company profile,intangible)	(guarantee,solution)		
(compensation,participation)	(half,quarter)		
(complaint,petition)	(increment,rearrangement)		
(computer,cooperation)	(information,trading company)		
(conference,height)	(insurance,percentage)		
(confidentiality,dollar)	(interest rate,tariff)		
(consultant,survey)	(man,woman)		
(contact,hint)	(maximum,supervision)		
(contract,copyright)	(meeting,talk)		
(control,data center)	(merchant,perspective)		
(conversation,output)	(month,week)		
(copper,replacement)	(press conference,seminar)		
(corporation,liabilities)	(price,rate)		
(cost,equity capital)	(productivity,traffic)		
(course,step)	(profit,volume)		
(court,district court)	(share price,stock market)		
(credit,disbursement)	(stock broker,theory)		
(credit agreement,overview)			
(currency,faith)			
(curve,graph)			
(decision,maximum)			
(deficit,negative)			
(diagram,support)			
(difference,elimination)			

Jaccard	Cosine	L1 norm	Jensen-Shannon
(disability insurance,pension)			
(discrimination,union)			
(diversification,request)			
(do,email)			
(effect,help)			
(employer,insurance)			
(energy,test)			
(equity fund,origin)			
(evening,purpose)			
(event,manager)			
(examination,registration)			
(example,source)			
(exchange,volume)			
(exchange risk,interest rate)			
(experience,questionnaire)			
(expertise,period)			
(faculty,sales contract)			
(fair,product)			
(flop,type)			
(forecast,stock market activity)			
(fusion,profit zone)			
(gamble,thing)			
(good,service)			
(government bond,life insurance)			
(happiness,question)			
(hold,shareholder)			
(hour,pay)			
(house,model)			
(idea,solution)			
(impact,matter)			
(improvement,situation)			
(index,wholesale)			
(information,trading company)			
(initiation,middle)			
(input,traffic)			
(institute,organization)			
(investment,productivity)			
(knowledge,tradition)			
(label,title)			
(letter,reception)			
(level,video)			
(license,reward)			
(loan,project)			
(location,process)			
(loss,profit)			
(man,trainee)			
(margin,software company)			
(market,warranty)			
(market access,name)			
(matrix,newspaper)			
(meeting,oscillation)			
(meter,share)			
(method,technology)			
(milestone,state)			
(month,year)			
(mouse,option)			
(multiplication,transfer)			
(noon,press conference)			
(occasion,talk)			
(opinion,rivalry)			
(personnel,resource)			
(picture,surcharge)			
(plane,tool)			
(police,punishment)			
(profession,writer)			
(property,qualification)			
(provision,revenue)			
(requirement,rule)			
(risk,trust)			
(sales revenue,validity)			
(savings bank,time)			
(segment,series)			
(show,team)			
(speech,winter)			
(stock broker,theory)			
(supplier,train)			
(tariff,treasury stock)			
(weekend,wisdom)			

A.4 The Penn Treebank Tag Set

1. CC Coordinating conjunction
2. CD Cardinal number
3. DT Determiner
4. EX Existential there
5. FW Foreign word
6. IN Preposition or subordinating conjunction
7. JJ Adjective
8. JJR Adjective, comparative
9. JJS Adjective, superlative
10. LS List item marker
11. MD Modal
12. NN Noun, singular or mass
13. NNS Noun, plural
14. NP Proper noun, singular
15. NPS Proper noun, plural
16. PDT Predeterminer
17. POS Possessive ending
18. PP Personal pronoun
19. PP$ Possessive pronoun
20. RB Adverb
21. RBR Adverb, comparative
22. RBS Adverb, superlative
23. RP Particle
24. SYM Symbol
25. TO to
26. UH Interjection
27. VB Verb, base form
28. VBD Verb, past tense
29. VBG Verb, gerund or present participle
30. VBN Verb, past participle
31. VBP Verb, non-3rd person singular present
32. VBZ Verb, 3rd person singular present
33. WDT Wh-determiner
34. WP Wh-pronoun
35. WP$ Possessive wh-pronoun
36. WRB Wh-adverb

References

[Abney, 1996] Abney, S. (1996). Partial parsing via finite-state cascades. In *Proceedings of the ESSLLI '96 Robust Parsing Workshop*, pages 8–15.

[Agichtein and Gravano, 2000] Agichtein, E. and Gravano, L. (2000). Snowball: Extracting relations from large plain-text collections. In *Proceedings of the 5th ACM International Conference on Digital Libraries (ACM DL)*, pages 85–94.

[Agirre et al., 2000] Agirre, E., Ansa, O., Hovy, E., and Martinez, D. (2000). Enriching very large ontologies using the WWW. In *Proceedings of the ECAI Ontology Learning Workshop*.

[Agirre and Rigau, 1996] Agirre, E. and Rigau, G. (1996). Word sense disambiguation using conceptual density. In *Proceedings of the International Conference on Computational Linguistics (COLING'96)*, pages 16–22.

[Agrawal and Srikant, 1994] Agrawal, R. and Srikant, R. (1994). Fast algorithms for mining association rules. In *Proceedings of the 20th International Conference on Very Large Databases (VLDB)*.

[Aha et al., 1991] Aha, D., Kibler, D., and Albert, M. (1991). Instance-based learning algorithms. *Machine Learning*, 6(1):37–66.

[Ahmad et al., 2003] Ahmad, K., Tariq, M., Vrusias, B., and Handy, C. (2003). Corpus-based thesaurus construction for image retrieval in specialist domains. In *Proceedings of the 25th European Conference on Advances in Information Retrieval (ECIR)*, pages 502–510.

[Alexiev et al., 2005] Alexiev, V., Breu, M., de Bruijn, J., Fensel, D., Lara, R., and Lausen, H., editors (2005). *Information Integration with Ontologies: Experiences from an Industrial Showcase*. Wiley.

[Alfonseca and Manandhar, 2002] Alfonseca, E. and Manandhar, S. (2002). Extending a lexical ontology by a combination of distributional semantics signatures. In *Proceedings of the 13th International Conference on Knowledge Engineering and Knowledge Management (EKAW)*, pages 1–7.

[Allen, 1995] Allen, J. (1995). *Natural Language Understanding*. Benjamin/Cummings Publishing Company.

[Almuhareb and Poesio, 2004] Almuhareb, A. and Poesio, M. (2004). Attribute-based and value-based clustering: an evaluation. In *Proceedings of the International Conference on Empircal Methods in Natural Language Processing (EMNLP)*, pages 158–165.

[Alshawi, 1987] Alshawi, H. (1987). Processing dictionary definitions with phrasal pattern hierarchies. *Computational Linguistics*, 13(3–4):195–202. Special Issue of the Lexicon.

[Amsler, 1981] Amsler, R. (1981). A taxonomy for english nouns and verbs. In *Proceedings of the 19th Annual Meeting of the Association for Computational Linguistics (ACL)*, pages 133–138.

[Ankolekar et al., 2004] Ankolekar, A., Paolucci, M., and Sycara, K. (2004). Spinning the OWL-S process model – towards the verification of OWL-S process models. In *Proceedings of the ISWC Workshop on Semantic Web Services: Preparing to Meet the World of Business Applications*.

[Ankolekar et al., 2002] Ankolekar et al. (2002). Daml-s: Web service description for the semantic web. In *Proceedings of the 1st International Semantic Web Conference*.

[Annas, 1981] Annas, J. (1981). *An Introduction to Plato's Republic*. Oxford: Clarendon Press.

[Artale et al., 1996] Artale, A., Franconi, E., Guarino, N., and Pazzi, L. (1996). Part-whole relations in object-centered systems: An overview. *Data Knowledge Engineering*, 20(3):347–383.

[Aussenac-Gilles et al., 2000] Aussenac-Gilles, N., Biebow, B., and Szulman, S. (2000). Revisiting ontology design: A methodology based on corpus analysis. In *Proceedings of the International Conference on Knowledge Engineering and Knowledge Management (EKAW)*, pages 172–188.

[Baeza-Yates and Ribeiro-Neto, 1999] Baeza-Yates, R. and Ribeiro-Neto, B. (1999). *Modern Information Retrieval*. Addison-Wesley.

[Banerjee and Pedersen, 2003] Banerjee, S. and Pedersen, T. (2003). Extended gloss overlaps as a measure of semantic relatedness. In *Proceedings of the 18th International Joint Conference on Artificial Intelligence (IJCAI)*, pages 805–810.

[Barendregt, 1984] Barendregt, H. (1984). *The lambda calculus, its syntax and semantics*. North-Holland.

[Baroni and Bisi, 2004] Baroni, M. and Bisi, S. (2004). Using cooccurrence statistics & the web to discover synonyms in a technical language. In *Proceedings of the 4th International Conference on Language Resources and Evaluation (LREC)*, pages 1725–1728.

[Bateman, 1991] Bateman, J. (1991). The theoretical status of ontologies in natural language processing. In *Proceedings of the Workshop on Text Representation and Domain Modeling – Ideas from Linguistics and AI*.

[Bateman, 1995] Bateman, J. (1995). On the relationship between ontology construction and natural language: a socio-semiotic view. *Journal of Human Computer Studies*, 43(5-6):929–944.

[Bechhofer et al., 2004] Bechhofer, S., van Harmelen, F., Hendler, J., Horrocks, I., McGuinees, D., Patel-Schneider, P., and Stein, L. (2004). OWL Web Ontology Language Reference. http://www.w3.org/TR/owl-ref.

[Belohlavek, 2000] Belohlavek, R. (2000). Similarity relations in concept lattices. *Journal of Logic and Computation*, 10(6):823–845.

[Bikel et al., 1999] Bikel, D., Schwartz, R., and Weischedel, R. (1999). An algorithm that learns what's in a name. *Machine Learning*, 34(1-3):211–231.

[Bisson et al., 2000] Bisson, G., Nedellec, C., and Canamero, L. (2000). Designing clustering methods for ontology building - The Mo'K workbench. In *Proceedings of the ECAI Ontology Learning Workshop*, pages 13–19.

[Bloehdorn et al., 2005] Bloehdorn, S., Cimiano, P., and Hotho, A. (2005). Learning ontologies to improve text clustering and classification. In *From Data and Information Analysis to Knowledge Engineering: Proceedings of the 29th Annual Conference of the German Classification Society (GfKl 2005)*. Springer.

[Bloehdorn and Hotho, 2004] Bloehdorn, S. and Hotho, A. (2004). Text classification by boosting weak learners based on terms and concepts. In *Proceedings of the 4th IEEE International Conference on Data Mining (ICDM)*, pages 331–334.

[Borigault et al., 2001] Borigault, D., Jacquemin, C., and L'Homme, M.-C., editors (2001). *Recent Advances in Computational Terminology*. John Benjamins Publishing Company.

[Borrigault, 1992] Borrigault, D. (1992). Surface grammatical analysis for the extraction of terminological noun phrases. In *Proceedings of the 14th International Conference on Computational Linguistics (COLING)*, pages 977–981.

[Borthwick et al., 1998] Borthwick, A., Sterling, J., Agichtein, E., and Grishman, R. (1998). Exploiting diverse knowledge sources via maximum entropy in named entity recognition. In *Proceedings of the Sixth ACL Workshop on Very Large Corpora*.

[Bos et al., 1995] Bos, J., Buitelaar, P., and Mineur, M. (1995). Bridging as coercive accomodation. In Klein, E., Manandhar, S., Nutt, W., and Siekmann, J., editors, *Working Notes of the Edinburgh Conference on Computational Logic and Natural Language Processing (CLNLP-95)*.

[Bresnan, 1994] Bresnan, J. (1994). *Lexical Functional Syntax*. Blackwell.

[Brewster et al., 2003] Brewster, C., Ciravegna, F., and Wilks, Y. (2003). Background and foreground knowledge in dynamic ontology construction. In *Proceedings of the SIGIR Semantic Web Workshop*.

[Brickley and Guha, 2002] Brickley, D. and Guha, R. (2002). RDF Vocabulary Description Language 1.0: RDF Schema. Technical report, W3C. W3C Working Draft. http://www.w3.org/TR/rdf-schema/.

[Brill, 1994] Brill, E. (1994). Some advances in transformation-based part of speech tagging. In *Proceedings of the National Conference on Artificial Intelligence (AAAI)*, pages 722–727.

[Brin, 1998] Brin, S. (1998). Extracting patterns and relations from the World Wide Web. In *Proceedings of the WebDB Workshop at EDBT '98*, pages 172–183.

[Buckley, 1985] Buckley, C. (1985). Implementation of the smart information retrieval system. Technical Report 85-686, Cornell University.

[Buitelaar, 2000] Buitelaar, P. (2000). Semantic lexicons. In Simov, K. and Kiryakov, A., editors, *Ontologies and Lexical Knowledge Bases*, pages 16–24.

[Buitelaar et al., 2006] Buitelaar, P., Declerck, T., Frank, A., Racioppa, S., Kiesel, M., Sintek, M., Engel, R., Romanelli, M., Sonntag, D., Loos, B., Micelli, V., Porzel, R., and Cimiano, P. (2006). Linginfo: Design and applications of a model for the integration of linguistic information in ontologies. In *Proceedings of the OntoLex06 Workshop at LREC*.

[Buitelaar et al., 2004] Buitelaar, P., Olejnik, D., and Sintek, M. (2004). A Protégé plug-in for ontology extraction from text based on linguistic analysis. In *Proceedings of the 1st European Semantic Web Symposium (ESWS)*, pages 31–44.

[Buitelaar and Sacaleanu, 2002] Buitelaar, P. and Sacaleanu, B. (2002). Extending synsets with medical terms. In *Proceedings of the First International WordNet Conference*.

[Burgess and Lund, 1997] Burgess, C. and Lund, K. (1997). Modeling parsing constraints with high-dimensional context space. *Language and Cognitive Processes*, 12:177–210.

[Cai and Hofmann, 2003] Cai, L. and Hofmann, T. (2003). Text categorization by boosting automatically extracted concepts. In *Proceedings of the 26th International ACM SIGIR Conference on Research and Development in Information Retrieval*, pages 182–189.

[Califf and Mooney, 2004] Califf, M. and Mooney, R. (2004). Bottom-up relational learning of pattern matching rules for information extraction. *Machine Learning Research*, 4(2):177–210.

[Calzolari, 1984] Calzolari, N. (1984). Detecting patterns in a lexical data base. In *Proceedings of the 22nd Annual Meeting of the Association for Computational Linguistics (ACL)*, pages 170–173.

[Caraballo, 1999] Caraballo, S. (1999). Automatic construction of a hypernym-labeled noun hierarchy from text. In *Proceedings of the 37th Annual Meeting of the Association for Computational Linguistics (ACL)*, pages 120–126.

[Caraballo and Charniak, 1998] Caraballo, S. and Charniak, E. (1998). New figures of merit for best-first probabilistic chart parsing. *Computational Linguistics*, 24(2):275–298.

[Cardie, 1993] Cardie, C. (1993). A case-based approach to knowledge acquisition for domain-specific sentence analysis. In *Proceedings of the 11th National Conference on Artificial Intelligence (AAAI)*, pages 798–803.

[Carletta, 1996] Carletta, J. (1996). Asessing agreement on classification tasks: The kappa statistic. *Computational Linguistics*, 22(2):249–254.

[Carpineto and Romano, 1996] Carpineto, C. and Romano, G. (1996). A lattice conceptual clustering system and its application to browsing retrieval. *Machine Learning*, 24:95–122.

[Carstensen et al., 2004] Carstensen, K.-U., Ebert, C., Endriss, C., Jekat, S., Klabunde, R., and Langer, H., editors (2004). *Computerlinguistik und Sprachtechnologie*. Spektrum-Verlag.

[Cederberg and Widdows, 2003] Cederberg, S. and Widdows, D. (2003). Using LSA and noun coordination information to improve the precision and recall of automatic hyponymy extraction. In *Conference on Natural Language Learning (CoNNL)*, pages 111–118.

[Charniak, 2000] Charniak, E. (2000). A maximum-entropy-inspired parser. In *Proceedings of the 6th Applied Natural Language Processing Conference (ANLP)*, pages 132–139.

[Charniak and Berland, 1999] Charniak, E. and Berland, M. (1999). Finding parts in very large corpora. In *Proceedings of the 37th Annual Meeting of the Association for Computational Linguistics (ACL)*, pages 57–64.

[Charniak et al., 1993] Charniak, E., Hendrickson, C., Jacobson, N., and Perkowitz, M. (1993). Equations for part-of-speech tagging. In *Proceedings of the 11th National Conference on Artificial Intelligence (AAAI)*, pages 784–789.

[Chartrand et al., 1998] Chartrand, G., Kubicki, G., and Schultz, M. (1998). Graph similarity and distance in graphs. *Aequationes Mathematicae*, 55(1-2):129–145.

[Chieu and Ng, 2003] Chieu, H. and Ng, H. (2003). Named entity recognition with a maximum entropy approach. In *Proceedings of the Seventh Conference on Natural Language Learning (CoNLL)*, pages 160–163.

[Church, 1936] Church, A. (1936). An unsolvable problem of elementary number theory. *American Journal of Mathematics*, 58:345–363.

[Church, 1988] Church, K. (1988). A stochastic parts program and noun phrase parser for unrestricted text. In *Proceedings of the Applied Natural Language Processing Conference (ANLP)*, pages 136–143.

[Ciaramita et al., 2005] Ciaramita, M., Gangemi, A., Ratsch, E., Šarić, J., and Rojas, I. (2005). Unsupervised learning of semantic relations between concepts of a molecular biology ontology. In *Proceedings of the 19th International Joint Conference on Artificial Intelligence (IJCAI)*, pages 659–664.

[Cimiano, 2003] Cimiano, P. (2003). Ontology-driven discourse analysis in GenIE. In *Proceedings of the 8th International Conference on Applications of Natural Language to Information Systems (NLDB)*, pages 77–90.

[Cimiano et al., 2004a] Cimiano, P., Handschuh, S., and Staab, S. (2004a). Towards the self-annotating web. In *Proceedings of the 13th World Wide Web Conference (WWW)*, pages 462–471.

[Cimiano et al., 2006] Cimiano, P., Hartung, M., and Ratsch, E. (2006). Finding the appropriate generalization level for binary ontological relations extracted from the Genia corpus. In *Proceedings of the International Conference on Language Resources and Evaluation (LREC)*.

[Cimiano et al., 2004b] Cimiano, P., Hotho, A., and Staab, S. (2004b). Clustering ontologies from text. In *Proceedings of the 4th International Conference on Language Resources and Evaluation (LREC)*, pages 1721–1724.

[Cimiano et al., 2004c] Cimiano, P., Hotho, A., and Staab, S. (2004c). Comparing conceptual, divisive and agglomerative clustering for learning taxonomies from text. In *Proceedings of the European Conference on Artificial Intelligence (ECAI)*, pages 435–439.

[Cimiano et al., 2005a] Cimiano, P., Hotho, A., and Staab, S. (2005a). Learning concept hierarchies from text corpora using formal concept analysis. *Journal of Artificial Intelligence Research (JAIR)*, 24:305–339.

[Cimiano et al., 2005b] Cimiano, P., Ladwig, G., and Staab, S. (2005b). Gimme' the context: Context-driven automatic semantic annotation with C-PANKOW. In *Proceedings of the 14th World Wide Web Conference (WWW)*, pages 332–341.

[Cimiano et al., 2004d] Cimiano, P., Pivk, A., Schmidt-Thieme, L., and Staab, S. (2004d). Learning taxonomic relations from heterogeneous sources. In *Proceedings of the ECAI Ontology Learning and Population Workshop*.

[Cimiano et al., 2005c] Cimiano, P., Schmidt-Thieme, L., Pivk, A., and Staab, S. (2005c). Learning taxonomic relations from heterogeneous evidence. In Buitelaar, P., Cimiano, P., and Magnini, B., editors, *Ontology Learning from Text: Methods, Applications and Evaluation*, number 123 in Frontiers in Artificial Intelligence and Applcations, pages 59–73. IOS Press.

[Cimiano et al., 2003a] Cimiano, P., S.Staab, and Tane, J. (2003a). Automatic acquisition of taxonomies from text: FCA meets NLP. In *Proceedings of the PKDD/ECML'03 International Workshop on Adaptive Text Extraction and Mining (ATEM)*, pages 10–17.

[Cimiano and Staab, 2004] Cimiano, P. and Staab, S. (2004). Learning by googling. *SIGKDD Explorations*, 6(2).

[Cimiano and Staab, 2005] Cimiano, P. and Staab, S. (2005). Learning concept hierarchies from text with a guided agglomerative clustering algorithm. In *Proceedings of the ICML Workshop on Learning and Extending Ontologies with Machine Learning Methods*.

326   References

[Cimiano et al., 2003b] Cimiano, P., Staab, S., and Tane, J. (2003b). Deriving concept hierarchies from text by Smooth Formal Concept Analysis. In *Proceedings of the GI Workshop "Lehren - Lernen - Wissen - Adaptivität" (LLWA)*, pages 72–79.

[Cimiano and Völker, 2005] Cimiano, P. and Völker, J. (2005). Towards large-scale, open-domain and ontology-based named entity classification. In *Proceedings of the International Conference on Recent Advances in Natural Language Processing RANLP*, pages 166–172.

[Cimiano et al., 2005d] Cimiano, P., Šarić, J., and Reyle, U. (2005d). Ontology-driven discourse analysis for information extraction. *Data and Knowledge Engineering*, 55(1):59–83.

[Cimiano and Wenderoth, 2005] Cimiano, P. and Wenderoth, J. (2005). Learning qualia structures from the web. In Baldwin, T., Korhonen, A., and Villavicencio, A., editors, *Proceedings of the ACL Workshop on Deep Lexical Acquisition*, pages 28–37.

[Ciravegna, 2001] Ciravegna, F. (2001). Adaptive information extraction from text by rule induction and generalization. In *Proceedings of the 17th International Joint Conference on Artificial Intelligence (IJCAI)*, pages 1251–1256.

[Ciravegna et al., 2003] Ciravegna, F., Dingli, A., Guthrie, D., and Wilks, Y. (2003). Integrating Information to Bootstrap Information Extraction from Web Sites. In *Proceedings of the IJCAI Workshop on Information Integration on the Web*, pages 9–14.

[Clark and Weir, 2002] Clark, S. and Weir, D. (2002). Class-based probability estimation using a semantic hierarchy. *Computational Linguistics*, 28(2):187–206.

[Claveau et al., 2003] Claveau, V., Sebillot, P., Fabre, C., and Bouillon, P. (2003). Learning semantic lexicons from a part-of-speech and semantically tagged corpus using inductive logic programming. *Journal of Machine Learning Research*, (4):493–525.

[Cleuziou et al., 2004] Cleuziou, G., Martin, L., and Vrain, C. (2004). Poboc: An overlapping clustering algorithm, application to rule-based classification and textual data. In *Proceedings of the European Conference on Artificial Intelligence (ECAI)*, pages 440–444.

[Cohen and Feigenbaum, 1981] Cohen, P. and Feigenbaum, E., editors (1981). *The Handbook of Artificial Intelligence*. Morgan Kaufmann. vol. 1-3.

[Collins and Singer, 1999] Collins, M. and Singer, Y. (1999). Unsupervised models for named entity classification. *Machine Learning*, 15(2):201–221.

[Copestake, 1990] Copestake, A. (1990). An approach to building the hierarchical element of a lexical knowledge base from a machine readable dictionary. In *Proceedings of the 1st International Workshop on Inheritance in Natural Language Processing*, pages 19–29.

[Craven et al., 2000] Craven, M., DiPasquo, D., Freitag, D., McCallum, A., Mitchell, T., Nigam, K., and Slattery, S. (2000). Learning to construct knowledge bases from the world wide web. *Artificial Intelligence*, 118:69–113.

[Cristianini and Shawe-Taylor, 2000] Cristianini, N. and Shawe-Taylor, J. (2000). *An Introduction to Support Vector Machines and other kernel-based learning methods*. Cambridge University Press.

[Crouch, 1988] Crouch, C. (1988). A cluster-based approach to thesaurus construction. In *Proceedings of the 11th International SIGIR Conference on Research and Development in Information Retrieval*, pages 309–320.

[Crouch and Yang, 1992] Crouch, C. and Yang, B. (1992). Experiments in automatic statistical thesaurus construction. In *Proceedings of the Annual International SIGIR Conference*, pages 77–88.

[Cui et al., 2004] Cui, H., Kan, M.-Y., and Chua, T.-S. (2004). Unsupervised learning of soft patterns for generating definitions from online news. In *Proceedings of the 13th World Wide Web Conference (WWW)*, pages 90–99.

[Curran, 2002] Curran, J. (2002). Ensemble methods for automatic thesarus construction. In *Proceedings of the Conference on Empirical Methods in Natural Language Processing (EMNLP)*.

[Curran and Moens, 2002] Curran, J. and Moens, M. (2002). Improvements in automatic thesaurus construction. In *Proceedings of the ACL Workshop on Unsupervised Lexical Acquisition*, pages 59–66.

[Daelemans et al., 1999a] Daelemans, W., Buchholz, S., and Veenstra, J. (1999a). Memory-based shallow parsing. In *Proceedings of the Conference on Computational Natural Language Learning (CoNLL)*, pages 53–60.

[Daelemans et al., 1999b] Daelemans, W., van den Bosch, A., and Zavrel, J. (1999b). Forgetting exceptions is harmful in language learning. *Machine Learning*, 34(1-3):11–41.

[Dagan and Church, 1995] Dagan, I. and Church, K. (1995). Termight: Identifying and translating technical terminology. In *Proceedings of the 7th Conference of the European Chapter of the Association for Computational Linguistics (EACL)*, pages 34–40.

[Dagan et al., 1994] Dagan, I., Pereira, F. C. N., and Lee, L. (1994). Similarity-based estimation of word cooccurrence probabilities. In *Proceedings of the Annual Meeting of the Association for Computational Linguistics (ACL)*, pages 272–278.

[Dave et al., 2003] Dave, K., Lawrence, S., and Pennock, D. (2003). Opinion extraction and semantic classification of product reviews. In *Proceedings of the 12th International World Wide Web Conference (WWW)*, pages 519–528.

[de Buenaga Rodríguez et al., 2000] de Buenaga Rodríguez, M., Hidalgo, J. M. G., and Díaz-Agudo, B. (2000). Using WordNet to complement training information in text categorization. In *Recent Advances in Natural Language Processing II*, volume 189. John Benjamins.

[Deerwester et al., 1990] Deerwester, S., Dumais, S., Landauer, T., Furnas, G., and Harshman, R. (1990). Indexing by latent semantic analysis. *Journal of the Society for Information Science*, 41:391–407.

[Defays, 1977] Defays, D. (1977). An efficient algorithm for a complete link method. *The Computer Journal*, 20(4):364–366.

[Dhillon, 2001] Dhillon, I. (2001). Co-clustering documents and words using bipartite spectral graph partitioning. In *Proceedings of the ACM SIGKDD International Conference on Knowledge Discovery and Data Mining (KDD)*, pages 269–274.

[Dill et al., 2003] Dill, S., Eiron, N., Gibson, D., Gruhl, D., Guha, R., Jhingran, A., Kanungo, T., Rajagopalan, S., Tomkins, A., Tomlin, J., and Zien, J. (2003). SemTag and Seeker: bootstrapping the semantic web via automated semantic annotation. In *Proceedings of the 12th International World Wide Web Conference (WWW)*, pages 178–186. ACM Press.

[Dimitrov, 2002] Dimitrov, M. (2002). A light-weight approach to coreference resolution for named entities in text. Master's thesis, University of Sofia.

[Dolan et al., 1993] Dolan, W., Vanderwende, L., and Richardson, S. (1993). Automatically deriving strcutured knowledge bases from online dictionaries. In *Proceed-

ings of the Pacific Association for Computational Linguistics (PACLING), pages 5–14.

[Domingue and Dzbor, 2004] Domingue, J. and Dzbor, M. (2004). Magpie: Browsing and navigating on the semantic web. In *Proceedings of the Conference on Intelligent User Interfaces (IUI)*, pages 191–197.

[Downey et al., 2004] Downey, D., Etzioni, O., Soderland, S., and Weld, W. (2004). Learning text patterns for web information extraction and assessment. In *Proceedings of the AAAI Workshop on Adaptive Text Extraction and Mining (ATEM)*.

[Duda et al., 2001] Duda, R. O., Hart, P. E., and Stork, D. G. (2001). *Pattern Classification*. John Wiley & Sons, Inc.

[Etzioni et al., 2004a] Etzioni, O., Cafarella, M., Downey, D., Kok, S., Popescu, A.-M., Shaked, T., Soderland, S., Weld, D., and Yates, A. (2004a). Web-scale information extraction in KnowItAll (preliminary results). In *Proceedings of the 13th World Wide Web Conference (WWW)*, pages 100–109.

[Etzioni et al., 2004b] Etzioni, O., Cafarella, M., Downey, D., Popescu, A.-M., Shaked, T., Soderland, S., Weld, D., and Yates, A. (2004b). Methods for domain-independent information extraction from the web: An experimental comparison. In *Proceedings of the 19th National Conference on Artificial Intelligence (AAAI)*, pages 391–398.

[Etzioni et al., 2005] Etzioni, O., Cafarella, M., Downey, D., Popescu, A.-M., Shaked, T., Soderland, S., Weld, D., and Yates, A. (2005). Unsupervised named-entity extraction from the web: An experimental study. *Artificial Intelligence*, 165(1):91–134.

[Evans, 2003] Evans, R. (2003). A framework for named entity recognition in the open domain. In *Proceedings of the International Conference on Recent Advances in Natural Language Processing (RANLP)*, pages 137–144.

[Faatz and Steinmetz, 2003] Faatz, A. and Steinmetz, R. (2003). Ontology enrichment with texts from the WWW. In *Proceedings of the 2nd ECML/PKDD Semantic Web Mining Workshop*.

[Faatz and Steinmetz, 2005] Faatz, A. and Steinmetz, R. (2005). An evaluation framework for ontology enrichment. In Buitelaar, P., Cimiano, P., and Magnini, B., editors, *Ontology Learning from Text: Methods, Applications and Evaluation*, number 123 in Frontiers in Artificial Intelligence and Applications, pages 77–91. IOS Press.

[Faure and Nedellec, 1998] Faure, D. and Nedellec, C. (1998). A corpus-based conceptual clustering method for verb frames and ontology. In Velardi, P., editor, *Proceedings of the LREC Workshop on Adapting lexical and corpus resources to sublanguages and applications*, pages 5–12.

[Faure and Poibeau, 2000] Faure, D. and Poibeau, T. (2000). First experiments of using semantic knowledge learned by ASIUM for information extraction task using INTEX. In *Proceedings of the ECAI Workshop on Ontology Learning*, pages 7–12.

[Fellbaum, 1998] Fellbaum, C. (1998). *WordNet, an electronic lexical database*. MIT Press.

[Fernandez et al., 1997] Fernandez, M., Gomez-Perez, A., and Juristo, N. (1997). METHONTOLOGY: From ontological art towards ontological engineering. In *Proceedings of the AAAI Workshop on Ontological Engineering*, pages 33–40.

[Fikes et al., 1972] Fikes, R., Hart, P., and Nilsson, N. (1972). Learning and executing generalized robot plans. *Artificial Intelligence*, 3:251–288.

[Finin et al., 1994] Finin, T., Fritzson, R., McKay, D., and McEntire, R. (1994). KQML as an Agent Communication Language. In *Proceedings of the 3rd International Conference on Information and Knowledge Management (CIKM'94)*, pages 456–463.

[Finkelstein-Landau and Morin, 1999] Finkelstein-Landau, M. and Morin, E. (1999). Extracting semantic relationships between terms: Supervised vs. unsupervised methods. In *Proceedings of the International Workshop on Ontological Engineering on the Global Information Infrastructure*, pages 71–80.

[Firth, 1957] Firth, J. (1957). *A synopsis of linguistic theory 1930-1955*. Studies in Linguistic Analysis, Philological Society, Oxford. Longman.

[Fisher, 1987] Fisher, D. (1987). Knowledge acquisition via incremental conceptual clustering. *Machine Learning*, (2):139–172.

[Fleischman and Hovy, 2002] Fleischman, M. and Hovy, E. (2002). Fine grained classification of named entities. In *Proceedings of the 19th International Conference on Computational Linguistics (COLING)*, pages 1–7.

[Fodor, 1998] Fodor, J. A. (1998). *Concepts: Where Cognitive Science Went Wrong*. Oxford University Press.

[Fotzo and Gallinari, 2004] Fotzo, H. N. and Gallinari, P. (2004). Learning generalization/specialization relations between concepts - application for automatically building thematic document hierarchies. In *Proceedings of the 7th Conference on Computer Assisted Information Retrieval (RIAO)*.

[Fox, 1980] Fox, E. (1980). Lexical relations: Enhancing effectiveness of information retrieval systems. *SIGIR Forum*, 15(3):5–36.

[France, 1994] France, R. (1994). Weights and measures: an axiomatic model for similarity computations. Technical report, Virginia Tech.

[Frantzi and Ananiadou, 1999] Frantzi, K. and Ananiadou, S. (1999). The C-value / NC-value domain independent method for multi-word term extraction. *Journal of Natural Language Processing*, 6(3):145–179.

[Frege, 1892] Frege, G. (1892). Über Sinn und Bedeutung. *Zeitschrift für Philosophie und philosophische Kritik*, 100:25–50.

[Freitag and Kushmerick, 2000] Freitag, F. and Kushmerick, N. (2000). Boosted Wrapper Induction. In *Proceedings of the 17th National Conference on Artificial Intelligence (AAAI)*, pages 577–583.

[Freund and Schapire, 95] Freund, Y. and Schapire, R. (95). A decision theoretic generalization of on-line learning and an application to boosting. In *Proceedings of the Second European Conference on Computational Learning Theory (EuroCOLT-95)*, pages 23–27.

[Gamallo et al., 2005] Gamallo, P., Agustini, A., and Lopes, G. (2005). Clustering syntactic positions with similar semantic requirements. *Computational Linguistics*, 21(1):107 – 145.

[Gamallo et al., 2002] Gamallo, P., Gonzalez, M., Agustini, A., Lopes, G., and de Lima, V. S. (2002). Mapping syntactic dependencies onto semantic relations. In *Proceedings of the ECAI Workshop on Machine Learning and Natural Language Processing for Ontology Engineering*, pages 15–22.

[Ganter, 1984] Ganter, B. (1984). Two basic algorithms in concept analysis. Technical Report 831, TH Darmstadt.

[Ganter and Reuter, 1991] Ganter, B. and Reuter, K. (1991). Finding all closed sets: A general approach. *Order*, 8:283–290.

[Ganter and Wille, 1999] Ganter, B. and Wille, R. (1999). *Formal Concept Analysis - Mathematical Foundations*. Springer Verlag.

[Gasperin et al., 2001] Gasperin, C., Gamallo, P., Agustini, A., Lopes, G., and de Lima, V. (2001). Using syntactic contexts for measuring word similarity. In *Proceedings of the ESSLLI Workshop on Semantic Knowledge Acquisition and Categorization*.

[Girju and Moldovan, 2002] Girju, R. and Moldovan, M. (2002). Text mining for causal relations. In *Proceedings of the FLAIRS Conference*, pages 360–364.

[Goddard and Swart, 1996] Goddard, W. and Swart, H. (1996). Distance between graphs under edge operations. *Discrete Mathematics*, 161:121–132.

[Godin et al., 1995] Godin, R., Missaoui, R., and Alaoui, H. (1995). Incremental concept formation algorithms based on galois (concept) lattices. *Computational Intelligence*, 11(2):246–267.

[Gonzalo et al., 1998] Gonzalo, J., Verdejo, F., Chugur, I., and Cigarran, J. (1998). Indexing with WordNet synsets can improve text retrieval. In *Proceedings of the COLING/ACL '98 Workshop on Usage of WordNet for NLP*, pages 38–44.

[Graham et al., 1980] Graham, S., Harrison, M., and Ruzzo, W. (1980). An improved context-free recognizer. *ACM Transactions on Programming Languages and Systems*, 2(3):415–462.

[Green, 1999] Green, S. (1999). Building hypertext links by computing semantic similarity. *IEEE Transactions on Knowledge and Data Engineering*, 11:713–730.

[Grefenstette, 1994] Grefenstette, G. (1994). *Explorations in Automatic Thesaurus Construction*. Kluwer.

[Grefenstette, 1995] Grefenstette, G. (1995). Evaluation techniques for automatic semantic extraction: Comparing syntactic and window based approaches. In Boguraev, B. and Pustejovsky, J., editors, *Corpus Processing and Lexical Aquisition*, pages 205–216. The MIT Press.

[Grefenstette, 1999] Grefenstette, G. (1999). The WWW as a resource for example-based MT tasks. In *Proceedings of ASLIB'99 Translating and the Computer 21*.

[Grobelnik and Mladenic, 2006] Grobelnik, M. and Mladenic, D. (2006). *Text Mining Recipes*. Springer-Verlag. to appear.

[Gruber, 1993] Gruber, T. (1993). Toward principles for the design of ontologies used for knowledge sharing. In *Formal Analysis in Conceptual Analysis and Knowledge Representation*. Kluwer.

[Guarino et al., 1999] Guarino, N., Masolo, C., and Vetere, G. (1999). Ontoseek: Content-based access to the web. *IEEE Intelligent Systems*, 14(3):70–80.

[Guarino and Welty, 2000] Guarino, N. and Welty, C. A. (2000). A formal ontology of properties. In *Proceedings of the 12th European Workshop on Knowledge Acquisition, Modeling and Management*, pages 97–112.

[Haase and Völker, 2005] Haase, P. and Völker, J. (2005). Ontology learning and reasoning – dealing with uncertainty and inconsistency. In *Proceedings of the Workshop on Uncertainty Reasoning for the Semantic Web (URSW)*, pages 45–55.

[Haav, 2003] Haav, H.-M. (2003). An application of inductive concept analysis to construction of domain-specific ontologies. In *Proceedings of the VLDB Preconference Workshop on Emerging Database Research in East Europe*.

[Hahn and Schnattinger, 1998a] Hahn, U. and Schnattinger, K. (1998a). Ontology engineering via text understanding. In *Proceedings of the 15th IFIP World Computer Congress*, pages 429–442.

[Hahn and Schnattinger, 1998b] Hahn, U. and Schnattinger, K. (1998b). Towards text knowledge engineering. In *Proceedings of the 15th National Conference on*

Artificial Intelligence and the 10th Conference on Innovative Applications of Artificial Intelligence (AAAI'98/IAAI'98), pages 524–531.

[Handschuh, 2005] Handschuh, S. (2005). *Creating Ontology-based Metadata by Annotation for the Semantic Web.* PhD thesis, University of Karlsruhe.

[Handschuh and Staab, 2002] Handschuh, S. and Staab, S. (2002). Authoring and annotation of web pages in CREAM. In *Proceedings of the 11th International World Wide Web Conference (WWW)*, pages 462–473. ACM Press.

[Handschuh et al., 2001] Handschuh, S., Staab, S., and Mädche, A. (2001). CREAM — Creating relational metadata with a component-based, ontology-driven annotation framework. In *Proceedings of the 1st Conference on Knowledge Capture, (K-CAP)*, pages 76–83. ACM Press.

[Harris, 1968] Harris, Z. (1968). *Mathematical Structures of Language.* Wiley.

[Hearst, 1992] Hearst, M. (1992). Automatic acquisition of hyponyms from large text corpora. In *Proceedings of the 14th International Conference on Computational Linguistics (COLING)*, pages 539–545.

[Hearst and Schütze, 1993] Hearst, M. and Schütze, H. (1993). Customizing a lexicon to better suit a computational task. In *Proceedings of the ACL SIGLEX Workshop on Acquisition of Lexical Knowledge from Text.*

[Hendrickx and van den Bosch, 2003] Hendrickx, I. and van den Bosch, A. (2003). Memory-based one-step named-entity recognition: Effects of seed list features, classifier stacking, and unannotated data. In *Proceedings of the Conference on Computational Natural Language Learning (CoNLL)*, pages 176–179.

[Hersh et al., 1994] Hersh, W., Buckley, C., Leone, T., and Hickam, D. (1994). Ohsumed: An interactive retrieval evaluation and new large text collection for research. In *Proceedings of the 17th ACM SIGIR Conference on Research and Development in Information Retrieval*, pages 192–201.

[Heyer et al., 2001] Heyer, G., Läuter, M., Quasthoff, U., Wittig, T., and Wolff, C. (2001). Learning relations using collocations. In *Proceedings of the IJCAI Workshop on Ontology Learning.*

[Hindle, 1990] Hindle, D. (1990). Noun classification from predicate-argument structures. In *Proceedings of the Annual Meeting of the Association for Computational Linguistics (ACL)*, pages 268–275.

[Hinrichs, 1987] Hinrichs, E. (1987). The syntax and semantic of the JANUS semantic interpretation language. Technical Report 6652, BBN Laboratories.

[Hirschman and Chinchor, 1997] Hirschman, L. and Chinchor, N. (1997). Muc-7 named entity task definition. In *Proceedings of the 7th Message Understanding Conference (MUC-7).*

[Hofmann, 1999] Hofmann, T. (1999). Probabilistic latent semantic indexing. In *Proceedings of the 22nd ACM SIGIR International Conference on Research and Development in Information Retrieval*, pages 50–57.

[Holsapple and Joshi, 2002] Holsapple, C. and Joshi, K. (2002). A collaborative approach to ontology design. *Communications of the ACM*, 45(2):42–47.

[Horrocks et al., 2000] Horrocks, I., Fensel, D., Broekstra, J., Decker, S., Erdmann, M., Goble, C., van Harmelen, F., Klein, M., Staab, S., Studer, R., and Motta, E. (2000). Oil: The ontology inference layer. Technical report, Vrije Universiteit Amsterdam, Faculty of Sciences.

[Hotho et al., 2003] Hotho, A., Staab, S., and Stumme, G. (2003). Ontologies improve text document clustering. In *Proceedings of the IEEE International Conference on Data Mining (ICDM)*, pages 541–544.

[Ide and Veronis, 1998] Ide, N. and Veronis, J. (1998). Word sense disambiguation: The state of the art. *Computational Linguistics*, 24(1):1–40.

[Iria, 2005] Iria, J. (2005). T-Rex: A flexible relation extraction framework. In *Proceedings of the 8th Annual Colloquium for the UK Special Interest Group for Computational Linguistics (CLUK'05)*.

[Isozaki and Kazawa, 2002] Isozaki, H. and Kazawa, H. (2002). Efficient support vector classifiers for named entity recognition. In *Proceedings of the 17th International Conference on Computational Linguistics (COLING)*, pages 1–7.

[Iwanska et al., 2000] Iwanska, L., Mata, N., and Kruger, K. (2000). Fully automatic acquisition of taxonomic knowledge from large corpora of texts. In Iwanksa, L. and Shapiro, S., editors, *Natural Language Processing and Knowledge Processing*, pages 335–345. MIT/AAAI Press.

[Jelinek, 1985] Jelinek, F. (1985). Markov source modeling of text generation. In Skwirzynski, J., editor, *The Impact of Processing Techniques on Communications*, volume E91 of *NATO ASI*, pages 569–598. Dordrecht.

[Jiang and Conrath, 1998] Jiang, J. and Conrath, D. (1998). Semantic similarity based on corpus statistics and lexical taxonomy. In *Proceedings of the International Conference on Research in Computational Linguistics (ROCLING)*.

[Jing and Croft, 1994] Jing, Y. and Croft, W. (1994). An association thesaurus for information retrieval. In *Proceedings of the 4th International Conference on Computer Assisted Information Retrieval (RIAO)*, pages 146–160.

[John and Langley, 1995] John, G. and Langley, P. (1995). Estimating continuous distributions in Bayesian classifiers. In *Proceedings of the 11th Conference on Uncertainty in Artificial Intelligence*, pages 338–345.

[Johnston and Busa, 1996] Johnston, M. and Busa, F. (1996). Qualia structure and the compositional interpretation of compounds. In *Proceedings of the ACL SIGLEX workshop on breadth and depth of semantic lexicons*.

[Joshi and Schabes, 1997] Joshi, A. and Schabes, Y. (1997). Tree-adjoining grammars. In *Handbook of Formal Languages*, volume 3, pages 69–124. Springer.

[Jurafsky and Martin, 2000] Jurafsky, D. and Martin, J. (2000). *Speech and Language Processing: An Introduction to Natural Language Processing, Computational Linguistics and Speech Recognition*. Prentice-Hall.

[Kamp and Reyle, 1993] Kamp, H. and Reyle, U. (1993). *From Discourse to Logic*. Kluwer.

[Karkaletsis et al., 2000] Karkaletsis, V., Paliouras, G., and Spyropoulos, C. (2000). Learning decision trees for named-entity recognition and classification. In *Proceedings of the ECAI Workshop on Machine Learning for Information Extraction*.

[Kaufman and Rousseeuw, 1990] Kaufman, L. and Rousseeuw, P. (1990). *Finding groups in data: an introduction to cluster analysis*. Wiley.

[Kavalec and Svátek, 2005] Kavalec, M. and Svátek, V. (2005). A study on automated relation labelling in ontology learning. In Buitelaar, P., Cimiano, P., and Magnini, B., editors, *Ontology Learning from Text: Methods, Evaluation and Applications*, number 123 in Frontiers in Artificial Intelligence and Applications, pages 44–58. IOS Press.

[Kazama et al., 2002] Kazama, J., Makino, T., Ohta, Y., and Tsujii, J. (2002). Tuning support vector machines for biomedical named entity recognition. In *Proceedings of the ACL Workshop on Natural Language Processing in the Biomedical Domain*.

[Keller et al., 2002] Keller, F., Lapata, M., and Ourioupina, O. (2002). Using the web to overcome data sparseness. In *Proceedings of the Conference on Empirical Methods in Natural Language Processing (EMNLP)*, pages 230–237.

[Kohonen, 1995] Kohonen, T. (1995). *Self-Organizing Maps*. Springer.

[Kronlid, 2003] Kronlid, F. (2003). Modes of explanation - aristotelian philosophy and pustejovskyan linguistics. Ms. University of Göteborg.

[Kubat and Matwin, 1997] Kubat, M. and Matwin, S. (1997). Addressing the curse of imbalanced training sets: one-sided selection. In *Proceedings of the 14th International Conference on Machine Learning (ICML)*, pages 179–186. Morgan Kaufmann.

[Landauer and Dumais, 1997] Landauer, T. and Dumais, S. (1997). A solution to plato's problem: The latent semantic analysis theory of acquisition, induction and representation of knowledge. *Psychological Review*, 104:211–240.

[Lappin and Leass, 1994] Lappin, S. and Leass, H. (1994). An algorithm for pronominal anaphora resolution. *Computational Linguistics*, 20(4):535–561.

[Lavrac and Dzeroski, 1994] Lavrac, N. and Dzeroski, S. (1994). *Inductive Logic Programming: Techniques and Applications*. Ellis Horwood.

[Lee, 1999] Lee, L. (1999). Measures of distributional similarity. In *Proceedings of the 37th Annual Meeting of the Association for Computational Linguistics (ACL)*, pages 25–32.

[Lesk, 1969] Lesk, M. (1969). Word-word associations in document retrieval systems. *American Documentation*, 20(1):27–38.

[Lesk, 1986] Lesk, M. (1986). Automatic sense disambiguation using machine readable dictionaries: how to tell a pine cone from an ice cream cone. In *Proceedings of the 5th Annual International Conference on Systems Documentation*, pages 24–26.

[Levin, 1993] Levin, B. (1993). *English Verb Classes and Alternations: A Preliminary Investigation*. University of Chicago Press.

[Lin and Hovy, 2000] Lin, C. and Hovy, E. (2000). The automated acquisition of topic signatures for text summarization. In *Proceedings of the 18th Conference on Computational Linguistics (COLING)*, pages 495–501.

[Lin, 1993] Lin, D. (1993). Principle-based parsing without overgeneration. In *Proceedings of the Annual Meeting of the Association for Computational Linguistics (ACL)*, pages 112–120.

[Lin, 1998a] Lin, D. (1998a). Automatic retrieval and clustering of similar words. In *Proceedings of the 36th Annual Meeting of the Association for Computational Linguistics and 17th International Conference on Computational Linguistics (COLING-ACL)*, pages 768–774.

[Lin, 1998b] Lin, D. (1998b). An information-theoretic definition of similarity. In *Proceedings of the International Conference on Machine Learning (ICML)*, pages 296–304.

[Lin, 1998c] Lin, D. (1998c). Using collocation statistics in information extraction. In *Proceedings of the Seventh Message Understanding Conference (MUC-7)*.

[Lin and Pantel, 2001a] Lin, D. and Pantel, P. (2001a). DIRT - discovery of inference rules from text. In *Proceedings of the ACM SIGKDD Conference on Knowledge Discovery and Data Mining*, pages 323–328.

[Lin and Pantel, 2001b] Lin, D. and Pantel, P. (2001b). Discovery of inference rules for question answering. *Natural Language Engineering*, 7(4):343–360.

[Lin and Pantel, 2001c] Lin, D. and Pantel, P. (2001c). Induction of semantic classes from natural language text. In *Proceedings of the ACM SIGKDD Conference on Knowledge Discovery and Data Mining*, pages 317–322.

[Lin and Pantel, 2002] Lin, D. and Pantel, P. (2002).   Concept discovery from text. In *Proceedings of the International Conference on Computational Linguistics (COLING)*, pages 577–583.

[Lindig, 2000] Lindig, C. (2000). Fast concept analysis. In Stumme, G., editor, *Proceedings of the International Conference on Conceptual Structures (ICCS)*. Shaker Verlag, Aachen, Germany.

[Mädche, 2002] Mädche, A. (2002).   *Ontology Learning for the Semantic Web*. Kluwer Academic Publishers.

[Mädche et al., 2002] Mädche, A., Pekar, V., and Staab, S. (2002). Ontology learning part one - on discovering taxonomic relations from the web. In *Web Intelligence*, pages 301–322. Springer Verlag.

[Mädche and Staab, 2000] Mädche, A. and Staab, S. (2000). Discovering conceptual relations from text. In *Proceedings of the 14th European Conference on Artificial Intelligence (ECAI)*, pages 321–325.

[Mädche and Staab, 2001] Mädche, A. and Staab, S. (2001). Ontology learning for the semantic web. *IEEE Intelligent Systems*, 16(2):72–79.

[Mädche and Staab, 2002] Mädche, A. and Staab, S. (2002). Measuring similarity between ontologies. In *Proceedings of the European Conference on Knowledge Acquisition and Management (EKAW)*, pages 251–263.

[Maher, 1993] Maher, P. (1993). A similarity measure for conceptual graphs. *Intelligent Systems*, 8:819–837.

[Manning and Schütze, 1999] Manning, C. and Schütze, H. (1999). *Foundations of Statistical Language Processing*. MIT Press.

[Markert et al., 2003] Markert, K., Modjeska, N., and Nissim, M. (2003). Using the web for nominal anaphora resolution. In *Proceedings of the EACL Workshop on the Computational Treatment of Anaphora*.

[Maynard et al., 2003] Maynard, D., Bontcheva, K., and Cunningham, H. (2003). Towards a semantic extraction of named entities. In *Proceedings of Recent Advances in Natural Language Processing (RANLP)*.

[Maynard et al., 2004] Maynard, D., Bontcheva, K., and Cunningham, H. (2004). Automatic language-independent induction of gazetteer lists. In *Proceedings of the 4th International Conference on Language Resources and Evaluation (LREC)*.

[McShane et al., 2005] McShane, M., Nirenburg, S., and Beale, S. (2005). An implemented, integrative approach to ontology-based NLP and interlingua. Technical report, Institute for Language and Information Technologies, University of Maryland, Baltimore County.

[Meersman, 2001] Meersman, R. (2001). Ontologies and databases: More than a fleeting resemblance. In *OES/SEO Workshop*.

[M.F.Porter, 1980] M.F.Porter (1980). An algorithm for suffix stripping. *Program*, 14(3):130–137.

[Miller and Charles, 1991] Miller, G. and Charles, W. (1991). Contextual correlates of semantic similarity. *Language and Cognitive Processes*, 6:1–28.

[Minsky and Papert, 1969] Minsky, M. and Papert, S. (1969). *Perceptrons: An Introduction to Computational Geometry*. The MIT Press.

[Missikoff et al., 2002] Missikoff, M., Navigli, R., and Velardi, P. (2002). The usable ontology: An environment for building and assessing a domain ontology. In *Proceedings of the International Semantic Web Conference (ISWC)*, pages 39–53.

[Mitchell, 1997] Mitchell, T. (1997). *Machine Learning*. McGraw-Hill, New York.

[Mitkov, 1998] Mitkov, R. (1998). Robust pronoun resolution with limited knowledge. In *Proceedings of the Joint Meeting of the International Conference on Computational Linguistics and the Association for Computational Linguistics (COLING-ACL)*, pages 869–875.

[Monard and Batista, 2002] Monard, M. C. and Batista, G. E. A. P. A. (2002). Learning with skewed class distributions. In *Advances in Logic, Artificial Intelligence and Robotics (LAPTEC'02)*, pages 173–180. IOS Press.

[Montemagni and Vanderwende, 1992] Montemagni, S. and Vanderwende, L. (1992). Structural patterns vs. string patterns for extracting semantic information from dictionaries. In *Proceedings of the International Conference on Computational Linguistics (COLING)*, pages 546–552.

[Morin and Jacquemin, 1999] Morin, E. and Jacquemin, C. (1999). Projecting corpus-based semantic links on a thesaurus. In *Proceedings of the 37th Annual Meeting of the Association for Computational Linguistics (ACL)*, pages 389–396.

[Muñoz and Palomar, 2001] Muñoz, R. and Palomar, M. (2001). Semantic-driven algorithm for definite description resolution. In *Proceedings of Recent Advances in Natural Language Processing (RANLP)*, pages 180–186.

[Murtagh, 1984] Murtagh, F. (1984). Complexities of hierarchic clustering algorithms: state of the art. *Computational Statistics Quarterly*, 1:101–113.

[Muslea et al., 2001] Muslea, I., Minton, S., and Knoblock, C. (2001). Hierarchical wrapper induction for semistructured information sources. *Journal of Autonomous Agents and Multi-Agent Systems*, 4:93–114.

[Myaeng and Lopez-Lopez, 1992] Myaeng, S. and Lopez-Lopez, A. (1992). Conceptual graph matching: A flexible algorithm and experiments. *Experimental and Theoretical Artificial Intelligence*, 4:107–126.

[Navigli and Velardi, 2004] Navigli, R. and Velardi, P. (2004). Learning domain ontologies from document warehouses and dedicated websites. *Computational Linguistics*, 30(2):151–179.

[Ng and Cardie, 2002] Ng, V. and Cardie, C. (2002). Combining sample selection and error-driven pruning for machine learning of coreference rules. In *Proceedings of the Conference on Empirical Methods in Natural Language Processing (EMNLP'02)*, pages 55–62.

[Nirenburg et al., 1996] Nirenburg, S., Mahesh, K., Viegas, E., Beale, S., Raskin, V., and Onyshkevych, B. (1996). Technological and conceptual tools for lexical knowledge acquisition. Technical report, Computing Research Laboratory, New Mexico State University.

[Nirenburg and Raskin, 2004] Nirenburg, S. and Raskin, V. (2004). *Ontological Semantics*. MIT Press.

[Niu et al., 2003] Niu, C., Lei, W., Ding, J., and Srihari, R. (2003). A bootstrapping approach to named entity classification using successive learners. In *Proceedings of the 41st Annual Meeting of the Association for Computational Linguistics (ACL)*, pages 335–342.

[Ogata and Collier, 2004] Ogata, N. and Collier, N. (2004). Ontology express: Statistical and non-monotonic learning of domain ontologies from text. In *Proceedings of the ECAI Workshop on Ontology Learning and Population*.

[Ohta et al., 2002] Ohta, T., Tateisi, Y., and Kim, J. (2002). The GENIA corpus: an annotated research abstract corpus in molecular biology domain. In *Proceedings of the 10th Internationl Conference on Human Language Technology (HLT)*, pages 73–77.

[Pantel and Lin, 2001] Pantel, P. and Lin, D. (2001). A statistical corpus-based term extractor. In *Proceedings of the 14th Biennial Conference of the Canadian Society on Computational Studies of Intelligence: Advances in Artificial Intelligence*, pages 36–46.

[Pantel and Lin, 2002a] Pantel, P. and Lin, D. (2002a). Discovering word senses from text. In *Proceedings of the ACM Conference on Knowledge Discovery and Data Mining (KDD-02)*, pages 613–619.

[Pantel and Lin, 2002b] Pantel, P. and Lin, D. (2002b). Document clustering with committees. In *Proceedings of the 25th Annual International ACM SIGIR Conference on Research and Development in Information Retrieval*, pages 199–206.

[Pantel and Ravichandran, 2004] Pantel, P. and Ravichandran, D. (2004). Automatically labeling semantic classes. In *Proceedings of the Human Language Technology Conference of the North American Chapter of the Association for Computational Linguistics (HLT/NAACL)*, pages 321–328.

[Pantel et al., 2004] Pantel, P., Ravichandran, D., and Hovy, E. (2004). Towards terascale knowledge acquisition. In *Proceedings of the International Conference on Computational Linguistics (COLING)*, pages 771–777.

[Paolucci et al., 2002] Paolucci, M., Kawmura, T., Payne, T., and Sycara, K. (2002). Semantic matching of web services capabilities. In *Proceedings of the 1st International. Semantic Web Conference (ISWC)*.

[Park, 2004] Park, Y. (2004). Glossont: A concept-focused ontology building tool. In *Proceedings of the 9th International Conference on the Principles of Knowledge Representation and Reasoning (KR)*, pages 498–506.

[Park and Choi, 1996] Park, Y. and Choi, K.-S. (1996). Automatic thesaurus construction using bayesian networks. *Information Processing Management*, 32(5):543–553.

[Pasca, 2004] Pasca, M. (2004). Acquisition of categorized named entities for web search. In *Proceedings of the Conference on Information and Knowledge Management (CIKM)*, pages 137–145.

[Pekar and Staab, 2002] Pekar, V. and Staab, S. (2002). Taxonomy learning: factoring the structure of a taxonomy into a semantic classification decision. *Proceedings of the 19th Conference on Computational Linguistics (COLING)*, 2:786–792.

[Pennacchiotti and Pantel, 2006] Pennacchiotti, M. and Pantel, P. (2006). A bootstrapping algorithm for automatically harvesting semantic relations. In *Proceedings of the International Workshop on Inference in Computational Semantics (ICoS-06)*, pages 87–96.

[Pereira et al., 1993] Pereira, F., Tishby, N., and Lee, L. (1993). Distributional clustering of english words. In *Proceedings of the 31st Annual Meeting of the Association for Computational Linguistics (ACL)*, pages 183–190.

[Peters, 2002] Peters, W. (2002). Extraction of implicit knowledge from WordNet. In *Proceedings of the Workshop on Ontologies and Lexical Knowledge Bases (OntoLex)*.

[Petersen, 2002] Petersen, W. (2002). A set-theoretical approach for the induction of inheritance hierarchies. *Electronic Notes in Theoretical Computer Science*, 51.

[Pinto and Martins, 2004] Pinto, H. and Martins, J. (2004). Ontologies: How can they be built? *Knowledge and Information Systems*, 6(4):441–464.

[Pinto et al., 2004] Pinto, H., Staab, S., and Tempich, C. (2004). DILIGENT: Towards a fine-grained methodology for distributed, loosely-controlled and evolving engineering of ontologies. In *Proceedings of the European Conference on Artificial Intelligence (ECAI)*, pages 393–397.

[Pivk et al., 2005] Pivk, A., Cimiano, P., and Sure, Y. (2005). From tables to frames. *Journal of Web Semantics: Science, Services and Agents on the World Wide Web*, 3(2-3):132–146.

[Poesio and Almuhareb, 2004] Poesio, M. and Almuhareb, A. (2004). Feature-based vs. property-based KR: An emprical perspective. In Varzi, A. and Vieu, L., editors, *Proceedings of the International Conference on Formal Ontology in Information Systems (FOIS)*, Forntiers in Artificial Intelligence and Applications, pages 177–184. IOS Press.

[Poesio and Almuhareb, 2005] Poesio, M. and Almuhareb, A. (2005). Identifying concept attributes using a classifier. In Baldwin, T., Korhonen, A., and Villavicencio, A., editors, *Proceedings of the ACL Workshop on Deep Lexical Acquisition*, pages 18–27.

[Poesio et al., 2002] Poesio, M., Ishikawa, T., im Walde, S. S., and Viera, R. (2002). Acquiring lexical knowledge for anaphora resolution. In *Proceedings of the 3rd Conference on Language Resources and Evaluation (LREC)*.

[Poesio and Vieira, 1998] Poesio, M. and Vieira, R. (1998). A corpus-based investigation of definite description use. *Computational Linguistics*, 24(2):183–216.

[Poesio et al., 1997] Poesio, M., Vieira, R., and Teufel, S. (1997). Resolving bridging references in unrestricted text. In *Proceedings of the Workshop on Operational Factors in Practical, Robust Anaphora Resolution for Unrestricted Texts*.

[Pollard and Sag, 1994] Pollard, C. and Sag, I. (1994). *Head-Driven Phrase Structure Grammar*. University of Chicago Press.

[Porzel and Malaka, 2005] Porzel, R. and Malaka, R. (2005). A task-based framework for ontology learning, population and evaluation. In Buitelaar, P., Cimiano, P., and Magnini, B., editors, *Ontology Learning from Text: Methods, Applications and Evaluation*, number 123 in Frontiers in Artificial Intelligence and Applications, pages 107–121. IOS Press.

[Provost, 2000] Provost, F. (2000). Machine learning from imbalanced data sets 101. In *Proceedings of the AAAI Workshop on Imbalanced Data Sets*.

[Pustejovsky, 1991] Pustejovsky, J. (1991). The generative lexicon. *Computational Linguistics*, 17(4):209–441.

[Pustejovsky et al., 1993] Pustejovsky, J., Anick, P., and Bergler, S. (1993). Lexical semantic techniques for corpus analysis. *Computational Lingustics, Special Issue on Using Large Corpora II*, 19(2):331–358.

[Qiu and Frei, 1993] Qiu, Y. and Frei, H.-P. (1993). Concept-based query expansion. In *Proceedings of the 16th ACM SIGIR International Conference on Research and Development in Information Retrieval*, pages 160–169.

[Quinlan, 1986] Quinlan, J. (1986). Induction of decision trees. *Machine Learning*, 1(1):81–106.

[Quinlan, 1990] Quinlan, J. (1990). Learning logical definitions from relations. *Machine Learning*, 5:239–266.

[Raskin and Nirenburg, 1996] Raskin, V. and Nirenburg, S. (1996). Adjectival modification in text meaning representation. In *Proceedings of the International Conference on Computational Linguistics (COLING)*, pages 842–847.

[Ratsch et al., 2003] Ratsch, E., Schultz, J., Šarić, J., Cimiano, P., Wittig, U., Reyle, U., and Rojas, I. (2003). Developing a protein interactions ontology. *Comparative and Functional Genomics*, 4(1):85–89.

[Ravichandran and Hovy, 2002] Ravichandran, D. and Hovy, E. (2002). Learning surface text patterns for a question answering system. In *Proceedings of the 40th*

Annual Meeting of the Association for Computational Linguistics (ACL), pages 41–47.

[Ravichandran et al., 2005] Ravichandran, D., Pantel, P., and Hovy, E. (2005). Randomized algorithms and NLP: Using locality sensitive hash functions for high speed noun clustering. In *Proceedings of the 43rd Annual Meeting of the Association for Computational Linguistics (ACL)*, pages 622–629.

[Reinberger and Daelemans, 2003] Reinberger, M.-L. and Daelemans, W. (2003). Is shallow parsing useful for the unsupervised learning of semantic clusters? In *Proceedings of the 4th Conference on Intelligent Text Processing and Computational Linguistics (CICLing)*, pages 304–313. Springer Verlag.

[Reinberger and Daelemans, 2004] Reinberger, M.-L. and Daelemans, W. (2004). Unsupervised text mining for ontology extraction: an evaluation of statistical measures. In *Proceedings of the 4th International Conference on Language Resources and Evaluation (LREC)*, pages 491–494.

[Reinberger and Spyns, 2004] Reinberger, M.-L. and Spyns, P. (2004). Discovering knowledge in texts for the learning of dogma-inspired ontologies. In Buitelaar, P., Handschuh, S., and Magnini, B., editors, *Proceedings of the ECAI Workshop on Ontology Learning and Population*, pages 19–24.

[Reinberger and Spyns, 2005] Reinberger, M.-L. and Spyns, P. (2005). Unsupervised text mining for the learning of dogma-inspired ontologies. In Buitelaar, P., Cimiano, P., and Magnini, B., editors, *Ontology Learning from Text: Methods, Applications and Evaluation*, number 123 in Frontiers in Artificial Intelligence and Applications, pages 29–43. IOS Press.

[Reinberger et al., 2003] Reinberger, M.-L., Spyns, P., Daelemans, W., and Meersman, R. (2003). Mining for lexons: applying unsupervised learning methods to create ontology bases. In *Proceedings of the International Conference on Ontologies, Databases and Applications of Semantics (ODBASE)*, Lecture Notes in Computer Science, pages 803–819. Springer.

[Reinberger et al., 2004] Reinberger, M.-L., Spyns, P., Pretorius, J., and Daelemans, W. (2004). Automatic initiation of an ontology. In *Proceedings of the Conference on Ontologies, Databases and Applications of Semantics (ODBASE)*, Lecture Notes in Computer Science, pages 600–617. Springer Verlag.

[Resnik, 1993] Resnik, P. (1993). *Selection and Information: A Class-Based Approach to Lexical Relationships*. PhD thesis, University of Pennsylvania.

[Resnik, 1995] Resnik, P. (1995). Using information content to evaluate semantic similarity in a taxonomy. In *Proceedings of the 14th International Joint Conference on Artificial Intelligence (IJCAI)*, pages 448–453.

[Resnik, 1997] Resnik, P. (1997). Selectional preference and sense disambiguation. In *Proceedings of the ACL SIGLEX Workshop on Tagging Text with Lexical Semantics: Why, What, and How?*

[Resnik, 1999] Resnik, P. (1999). Semantic similarity in a taxonomy: An information-based measure and its application to problems of ambiguity in natural language. *Journal of Artificial Intelligence Research (JAIR)*, 11:95–130.

[Resnik and Elkiss, 2003] Resnik, P. and Elkiss, A. (2003). The linguist's search engine: Getting started guide. Technical Report LAMP-TR-108/CS-TR-4541/UMIACS-TR-2003-109, University of Maryland, College Park.

[Resnik and Smith, 2003] Resnik, P. and Smith, N. (2003). The web as a parallel corpus. *Computational Lingusitics*, 29(3):349–380.

[Ribas, 1995] Ribas, F. (1995). On learning more appropriate selectional restrictions. In *Proceedings of the 7th Conference of the European chapter of the Association for Computational Linguistics (EACL)*, pages 112–118.

[Richardson and Smeaton, 1995] Richardson, R. and Smeaton, A. (1995). Using WordNet in a knowledge-based approach to information retrieval. In *Proceedings of the BCS-IRSG-Colloquium*.

[Riloff, 1993] Riloff, E. (1993). Automatically constructing a dictionary for information extraction tasks. In *Proceedings of the 11th National Conference on Artificial Intelligence (AAAI)*, pages 811–816.

[Rosenblatt, 1959] Rosenblatt, F. (1959). *Principles of Neurodynamics*. Spartan Books.

[Rumelhart et al., 1986] Rumelhart, D., Hinton, G., and Williams, R. (1986). Learning representations by back-propagating errors. *Nature*, 323:533–536.

[Russel and Norvig, 2003] Russel, S. and Norvig, P. (2003). *Artifical Intelligence: A Modern Approach*. Prentice Hall. 2nd edition.

[Ryu and Choi, 2005] Ryu, P.-M. and Choi, K.-S. (2005). An information-theoretic approach to taxonomy extraction for ontology learning. In Buitelaar, P., Cimiano, P., and Magnini, B., editors, *Ontology Learning from Text: Methods, Applications and Evaluation*, Frontiers in Artificial Intelligence and Applications, pages 15–28. IOS Press.

[Sabou, 2005] Sabou, M. (2005). Learning web service ontologies: an automatic extraction method and its evaluation. In Buitelaar, P., Cimiano, P., and Magnini, B., editors, *Ontology Learning from Text: Methods, Applications and Evaluation*, Frontiers in Artificial Intelligence and Applications, pages 125–139. IOS Press.

[Salton, 1971] Salton, G. (1971). Experiments in automatic thesaurus construction for information retrieval. In *Proceedings of the IFIP Congress*, volume TA-2, pages 43–49.

[Salton and Buckley, 1988] Salton, G. and Buckley, C. (1988). Term-weighting approaches in automatic text retrieval. *Information Processing and Management*, 24(5):515–523.

[Salton and Lesk, 1971] Salton, G. and Lesk, M. (1971). Computer evaluation of indexing and text processing. In Salton, G., editor, *The SMART Retrieval System: Experiments in Automatic Document Processing*, pages 143–180. Prentice-Hall.

[Salton and McGill, 1983] Salton, G. and McGill, M. J. (1983). *Introduction to Modern Information Retrieval*. McGraw-Hill, New York, NY ,USA.

[Sanchez and Moreno, 2004a] Sanchez, D. and Moreno, A. (2004a). Automatic generation of taxonomies from the WWW. In *Proceedings of the Conference on Practical Aspects of Knowledge Management (PAKM)*.

[Sanchez and Moreno, 2004b] Sanchez, D. and Moreno, A. (2004b). Creating ontologies from web documents. In *Proceedings of the 7th Catalan Conference on Artificial Intelligence (CCIA)*.

[Sanchez and Moreno, 2005] Sanchez, D. and Moreno, A. (2005). Web-scale taxonomy learning. In Biemann, C. and Pass, G., editors, *Proceedings of the Workshop on Extending and Learning Lexical Ontologies using Machine Learning Methods*.

[Sanchez-Graillet and Poesio, 2004] Sanchez-Graillet, O. and Poesio, M. (2004). Acquiring bayesian networks from text. In *Proceedings of the 4th International Conference on Language Resources and Evaluation (LREC)*, pages 955–958.

[Sanderson, 1994] Sanderson, M. (1994). Word sense disambiguation and information retrieval. In *Proceedings of the 17th SIGIR ACM International Conference on Research and Development in Information Retrieval*, pages 49–57.

340   References

[Sanderson and Croft, 1999] Sanderson, M. and Croft, B. (1999). Deriving concept hierarchies from text. In *Proceedings of the SIGIR Conference on Research and Development in Information Retrieval*, pages 206–213.

[Schmid, 1994] Schmid, H. (1994). Probabilistic part-of-speech tagging using decision trees. In *Proceedings of the International Conference on New Methods in Language Processing*.

[Schmid, 2000] Schmid, H. (2000). Lopar: Design and implementation. In *Arbeitspapiere des Sonderforschungsbereiches 340*, number 149.

[Schulte im Walde, 2000] Schulte im Walde, S. (2000). Clustering verbs semantically according to their alternation behaviour. In *Proceedings of the 18th International Conference on Computational Linguistics (COLING)*, pages 747–753.

[Schutz and Buitelaar, 2005] Schutz, A. and Buitelaar, P. (2005). RelExt: A tool for relation extraction from text in ontology extension. In *Proceedings of the International Semantic Web Conference*, pages 593–606.

[Schütze, 1992] Schütze, H. (1992). Context space. In *Working Notes of the AAAI Fall Symposium on Probabilistic Approaches to Natural Language*, pages 56–60.

[Schütze, 1993] Schütze, H. (1993). Word space. In *Advances in Neural Information Processing Systems 5*, pages 895–902.

[Schütze, 1998] Schütze, H. (1998). Automatic word sense discrimination. *Computational Linguistics*, 24(1):97–123.

[Schütze and Pedersen, 1997] Schütze, H. and Pedersen, J. (1997). A cooccurrence-based thesaurus and two applications to information retrieval. *Information Processing and Management*, 33(3):307–318.

[Scott and Matwin, 1999] Scott, S. and Matwin, S. (1999). Feature engineering for text classification. In *Proceedings of the International Conference on Machine Learning (ICML)*, pages 379–388.

[Sebastaini, 2002] Sebastaini, F. (2002). Machine learning in automated text categorization. *ACM Computing Surveys*, 34:1–47.

[Sedgewick, 1984] Sedgewick, R. (1984). *Algorithms*. Addison-Wesley.

[Sekine et al., 1998] Sekine, S., Grishman, R., and Shinnou, H. (1998). A decision tree method for finding and classifying names in japanese texts. In *Proceedings of the 6th ACL Workshop on Very Large Corpora*.

[Shamsfard and Barforoush, 2004] Shamsfard, M. and Barforoush, A. (2004). Learning ontologies from natural language texts. *Human-Computer Studies*, 60(1):17–63.

[Shieber, 2004] Shieber, S., editor (2004). *The Turing Test*. MIT Press.

[Shortliffe, 1976] Shortliffe, E. (1976). *Computer-based Medical Consultations: MYCIN*. Elsevier.

[Sigletos et al., 2003] Sigletos, G., Paliouras, G., Spyropoulos, C., and Hatzopoulos, M. (2003). Mining web sites using wrapper induction, named entities and post-processing. In *Proceedings of the 1st European Web Mining Forum*, pages 97–112.

[Sirin et al., 2002] Sirin, E., Hendler, J., and Parsia, B. (2002). Semi-automatic composition of web services using semantic descriptions. In *Proceedings of the ICEIS Workshop on Web Services: Modeling, Architecture and Infrastructure*.

[Snow et al., 2004] Snow, R., Jurafsky, D., and Ng, A. (2004). Learning syntactic patterns for automatic hypernym discovery. In *Proceedings of Advances in Neural Information Processing Systems 17*.

[Soderland, 1999] Soderland, S. (1999). Learning information extraction rules for semi-structured and free text. *Machine Learning*, 34(1-3):233–272.

[Soderland et al., 1995] Soderland, S., Fisher, D., Aseltine, J., and Lehnert, W. (1995). Crystal: Inducing a conceptual dictionary. In *Proceedings of the International Joint Conference on Artificial Intelligence (IJCAI)*, pages 1314–1321.

[Soderland and Lehner, 1994] Soderland, S. and Lehner, W. (1994). Corpus-driven knowledge acquisition for discourse analysis. In *Proceedings of the 12th National Conference on Artificial Intelligence (AAAI)*, pages 827–832.

[Sowa, 2000a] Sowa, J. (2000a). *Knowledge Representation: Logical, Philosophical and Computational Foundations*. Brooks/Cole.

[Sowa, 2000b] Sowa, J. (2000b). Ontology, metadata and semiotics. In Ganter, B. and Mineau, G., editors, *Conceptual Structures: Logic, Linguistic and Computational Issues*, Lecture Notes in Artificial Intelligence, pages 55–81. Springer.

[Sporleder, 2002] Sporleder, C. (2002). A galois lattice based approach to lexical inheritance hierarchy learning. In *Proceedings of the ECAI Workshop on Machine Learning and Natural Language Processing for Ontology Engineering (OLT)*.

[Srikant and Agrawal, 1997] Srikant, R. and Agrawal, R. (1997). Mining generalized association rules. *Future Generation Computer Systems*, 13(2–3):161–180.

[Staab et al., 1999] Staab, S., Braun, C., Bruder, I., Düsterhöft, A., Heuer, A., Klettke, M., Neumann, G., Prager, B., Pretzel, J., Schnurr, H.-P., Studer, R., Uszkoreit, H., and Wrenger, B. (1999). Getess - searching the web exploiting german texts. In *Proceedings of the 3rd Workshop on Cooperative Information Agents*, pages 113–124. Springer Verlag.

[Staab et al., 2001] Staab, S., Erdmann, E., and Mädche, A. (2001). Engineering ontologies using semantic patterns. In *Proceedings of the IJCAI Workshop on E-Business and Intelligent Web*.

[Staab and Studer, 2004] Staab, S. and Studer, R., editors (2004). *Handbook on Ontologies*. International Handbooks on Information Systems. Springer.

[Steinbach et al., 2000] Steinbach, M., Karypis, G., and Kumar, V. (2000). A comparison of document clustering techniques. In *KDD Workshop on Text Mining*.

[Stolfo et al., 1997] Stolfo, S., Fan, W., Lee, W., Prodromidis, A., and Chan, P. (1997). Credit card fraud detection using meta-learning: Issues and initial results. In *Working Notes of the AAAI Workshop on AI Approaches to Fraud Detection and Risk Management*.

[Stumme et al., 2003] Stumme, G., Ehrig, M., Handschuh, S., Hotho, A., Mädche, A., Motik, B., Oberle, D., Schmitz, C., Staab, S., Stojanovic, L., Stojanovic, N., Studer, R., Sure, Y., Volz, R., and Zacharias, V. (2003). The karlsruhe view on ontologies. Technical report, University of Karlsruhe, Institute AIFB.

[Sure, 2003] Sure, Y. (2003). *Methodology, Tools and Case Studies for Ontology based Knowledge Management*. PhD thesis, University of Karlsruhe.

[Surowiecki, 2004] Surowiecki, J. (2004). *The Wisdom of Crowds: Why the Many Are Smarter Than the Few and How Collective Wisdom Shapes Business, Economies, Societies and Nations*. Doubleday Books.

[Tanev and Magnini, 2006] Tanev, H. and Magnini, B. (2006). Weakly supervised approaches for ontology population. In *Proceedings of the 11th Conference of the European Chapter of the Association for Computational Linguistics (EACL)*, pages 17–24.

[Tufis and Mason, 1998] Tufis, D. and Mason, O. (1998). Tagging Romanian Texts: a Case Study for QTAG, a Language Independent Probabilistic Tagger. In *Proceedings of the First International Conference on Language Resources and Evaluation (LREC)*, pages 589–96.

342   References

[Turcato et al., 2000] Turcato, D., Popowich, F., Toole, J., Fass, D., Nicholson, D., and Tisher, G. (2000). Adapting a synonym database to specific domains. In *Proceedings of the ACL Workshop on Recent Advances in Natural Language Processing and Information Retrieval*.

[Turing, 1950] Turing, A. (1950). Computing machinery and intelligence. *Mind*, 49(236).

[Turney, 2001] Turney, P. (2001). Mining the web for synonyms: PMI-IR versus LSA on TOEFL. In *Proceedings of the 12th European Conference on Machine Learning (ECML)*, pages 491 – 502.

[Ureña et al., 2001] Ureña, L. A., de Buenaga, M., and Gómez, J. M. (2001). Integrating linguistic resources in TC through WSD. *Computers and the Humanities*, 35(2):215–230.

[Uren et al., 2005] Uren, V., Cimiano, P., Motta, E., and Dzbor, M. (2005). Browsing for information by highlighting automatically generated annotations. In *Proceedings of the 3rd International Conference on Knowledge Capture (K-CAP)*, pages 75–82.

[Uschold, 1996] Uschold, M. (1996). Building ontologies: Towards a unified methodology. In *Proceedings of the 16th Annual Conference of the British Computer Society Specialist Group on Expert Systems*.

[Velardi et al., 2001] Velardi, P., Fabriani, P., and Missikoff, M. (2001). Using text processing techniques to automatically enrich a domain ontology. In *Proceedings of the ACM International Conference on Formal Ontology in Information Systems (FOIS)*, pages 270–284.

[Velardi et al., 2005] Velardi, P., Navigli, R., Cuchiarelli, A., and Neri, F. (2005). Evaluation of OntoLearn, a methodology for automatic population of domain ontologies. In Buitelaar, P., Cimiano, P., and Magnini, B., editors, *Ontology Learning from Text: Methods, Applications and Evaluation*, number 123 in Frontiers in Artificial Intelligence and Applications, pages 92–106. IOS Press.

[Volz et al., 2003] Volz, R., Oberle, D., Staab, S., and Studer, R. (2003). OntoLiFT prototype. Technical report, Institute AIFB, University of Karlsruhe. WonderWeb Deliverable D11.

[Voorhees, 1994] Voorhees, E. (1994). Query expansion using lexical-semantic relations. In *Proceedings of the 17th annual international ACM SIGIR conference on Research and development in information retrieval*, pages 61–69.

[Wang et al., 2003] Wang, B., McKay, R., Abbass, H., and Barlow, M. (2003). A comparative study for domain ontology guided feature extraction. In *Proceedings of the Australian Computer Society (ACSC)*, pages 69–78.

[Wang et al., 1985] Wang, Y.-C., Vandendorpe, J., and Evens, M. (1985). Relational thesauri in information retrieval. *Journal of the American Society for Information Science*, 36(1):15–27.

[Weischedel, 1989] Weischedel, R. (1989). A hybrid approach to representation in the JANUS natural language processor. In *Proceedings of the 27th Annual Meeting of the Association of Computational Linguistics (ACL)*, pages 193–202.

[Welty and Ide, 1999] Welty, C. and Ide, N. (1999). Using the right tools: enhancing retrieval from marked-up documents. *Computers and Humanities*, 33(10):59–84.

[Widdows, 2003a] Widdows, D. (2003a). A mathematical model for context and word-meaning. In *Fourth International and Interdisciplinary Conference on Modeling and Using Context*, pages 369–382.

[Widdows, 2003b] Widdows, D. (2003b). Unsupervised methods for developing taxonomies by combining syntactic and statistical information. In *Proceedings of the*

Human Language Technology Conference/ North American Chapter of the Association for Computational Lignuistics (HLT/NAACL), pages 276–283.

[Widdows, 2004] Widdows, D. (2004). *Geometry and Meaning*. Number 172 in Lecture Notes. CSLI Publications.

[Wiederhold, 1994] Wiederhold, G. (1994). Interoperation, mediation and ontologies. In *Proceedings of the International Symposium on 5th Generation Computer Systems; Workshop on Heterogeneous Cooperative Knowledge-Bases*, pages 33–48.

[Wille, 1982] Wille, R. (1982). Restructuring lattice theory: an approach based on hierarchies of concepts. *Ordered Sets*, pages 445–470.

[Witten and Frank, 1999] Witten, I. and Frank, E. (1999). *Data Mining: Practical Machine Learning Tools and Techniques with Java Implementations*. Morgan Kaufmann.

[Wittgenstein, 1953] Wittgenstein, L. (1953). *Philosophical Investigations*. Blackwell Publishing.

[Yamada and Baldwin, 2004] Yamada, I. and Baldwin, T. (2004). Automatic discovery of telic and agentive roles from corpus data. In *Proceedings of the the 18th Pacific Asia Conference on Language, Information and Computation (PACLIC)*.

[Yamaguchi, 2001] Yamaguchi, T. (2001). Acquring conceptual relationships from domain-specific texts. In *Proceedings of the IJCAI Workshop on Ontology Learning*.

[Yarowsky, 1995] Yarowsky, D. (1995). Unsupervised word sense disambiguation rivaling supervised methods. In *Proceedings of the Annual Meeting of the Association for Computational Linguistics (ACL)*, pages 189–196.

[Zadeh, 1975] Zadeh, L. (1975). The concept of a linguistic variable and its application to approximate reasoning. *Information Sciences*, 8-9.

[Zhang et al., 1992] Zhang, K., Statman, R., and Shasha, D. (1992). On the editing distance between unordered labeled trees. *Information Processing Letters*, 42(3):133–139.

[Zhang et al., 1996] Zhang, K., Wang, J., and Shasha, D. (1996). On the editing distance between undirected acyclic graphs. *International Journal of Foundations of Computer Science*, 7(1):43–57.

[Zhou and Su, 2002] Zhou, G. and Su, J. (2002). Named entity recognition using an HMM-based chunk tagger. In *Proceedings of the 40th Annual Meeting of the Association for Computational Linguistics (ACL)*, pages 473–480.

[Zhu et al., 2005a] Zhu, J., Uren, V., and Motta, E. (2005a). Espotter: Adaptive named entity recognition for web browsing. In *Proceedings of the Conference on Professional Knowledge Management (KM)*.

[Zhu et al., 2005b] Zhu, J., Uren, V., and Motta, E. (2005b). ESpotter: Adaptive named entity recognition for web browsing. In *Proceedings of the WM2005 Workshop on IT Tools for Knowledge Management Systems*.

[Zipf, 1932] Zipf, G. (1932). *Selective Studies and the Principle of Relative Frequency in Language*. Cambridge.

Index